Crime, Gender and Social Order in Earl

This is the first extended study of gender and crime in early modern England. It considers the ways in which criminal behaviour and perceptions of criminality were informed by ideas about gender and order, and explores their practical consequences for the men and women who were brought before the criminal courts.

Dr Walker's innovative approach demonstrates that, contrary to received opinion, the law was often structured so as to make the treatment of women and men before the courts incommensurable. For the first time, early modern criminality is explored in terms of masculinity as well as femininity. The household is shown to have a direct relation to the nature and reception of all sorts of criminal behaviour for men and for women.

Illuminating the interactions between gender and other categories such as class and civil war have implications not merely for the historiography of crime but for the social history of early modern England as a whole. This study therefore goes beyond conventional studies of crime, and challenges hitherto accepted views of social interaction in the period.

GARTHINE WALKER is Lecturer in History, School of History and Archaeology, Cardiff University.

Cambridge Studies in Early Modern British History

Series editors

ANTHONY FLETCHER
Victoria County History, Institute of Historical Research, University of London

JOHN GUY
Visiting Research Fellow, Clare College, Cambridge

JOHN MORRILL
*Professor of British and Irish History, University of Cambridge,
and Vice-Master of Selwyn College*

This is a series of monographs and studies covering many aspects of the history of the British Isles between the late fifteenth century and the early eighteenth century. It includes the work of established scholars and pioneering work by a new generation of scholars. It includes both reviews and revisions of major topics and books, which open up new historical terrain or which reveal startling new perspectives on familiar subjects. All the volumes set detailed research into our broader perspectives and the books are intended for the use of students as well as of their teachers.

For a list of titles in the series, see end of book.

CRIME, GENDER AND SOCIAL ORDER IN EARLY MODERN ENGLAND

GARTHINE WALKER

CAMBRIDGE UNIVERSITY PRESS

CAMBRIDGE UNIVERSITY PRESS
Cambridge, New York, Melbourne, Madrid, Cape Town, Singapore, São Paulo, Delhi

Cambridge University Press
The Edinburgh Building, Cambridge CB2 8RU, UK

Published in the United States of America by Cambridge University Press, New York

www.cambridge.org
Information on this title: www.cambridge.org/9780521573566

© Garthine Walker 2003

This publication is in copyright. Subject to statutory exception
and to the provisions of relevant collective licensing agreements,
no reproduction of any part may take place without the written
permission of Cambridge University Press.

First published 2003
Third printing 2006
This digitally printed version 2008

A catalogue record for this publication is available from the British Library

ISBN 978-0-521-57356-6 hardback
ISBN 978-0-521-09117-6 paperback

For Kevin

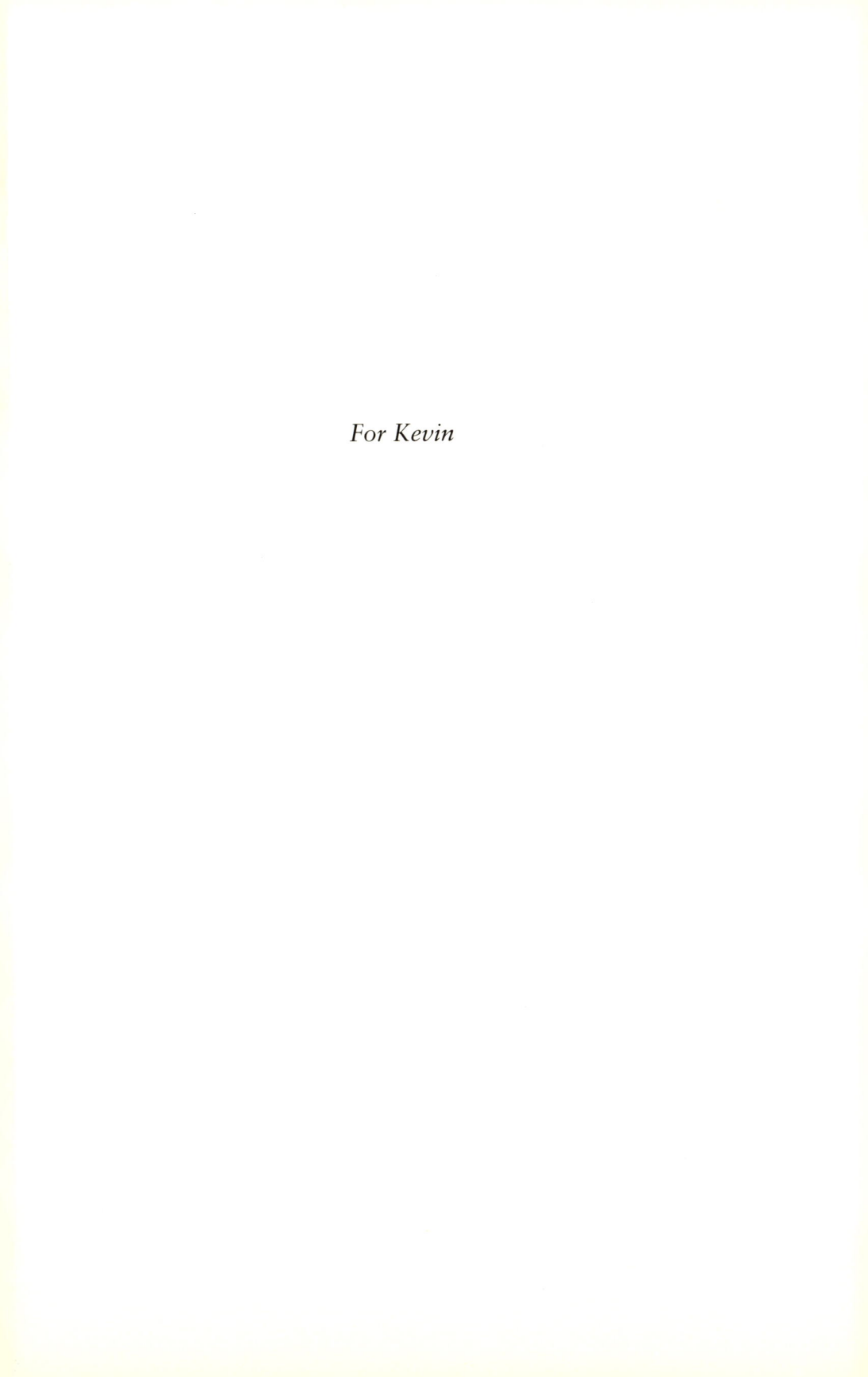

CONTENTS

List of figures and tables	page xi
Preface	xiii
Note on quotations and dates	xv
List of abbreviations	xvi

1	Introduction	1
	Histories of crime and gender	1
	Household	9
	The setting	13
	The scope of this book	22
2	Men's non-lethal violence	23
	Measuring violence	24
	Violence and manhood	33
	Men's violence against women	49
3	Voices of feminine violence	75
	Modes of women's violence	75
	Women's violence, men's silence	81
	Assertions of female force	86
	Women beware women	96
	Scolding	99
4	Homicide, gender and justice	113
	Categories of culpability	114
	Order, honour and the nature of man	116
	Women, disorder and deeds against nature	135
5	Theft and related offences	159
	Patterns of criminality	160
	Before the courts	176

6	Authority, agency and law	210
	An elite mechanism	213
	Plebeian use of the law	221
	Resistance: forcible rescues	249
	Popular resistance	262
7	Conclusion	270

Bibliography 280
Index 306

FIGURES AND TABLES

FIGURES

3.1	Allegedly armed assailants	*page* 79
3.2	Alleged victims of female assailants	80
4.1	Outcomes for defendants in homicide cases	135
4.2	Verdicts/sentences for homicide including infanticide	136
4.3	Punishments for homicide including infanticide	137
4.4	Verdicts/sentences for homicide excluding infanticide	137
4.5	Punishments for homicide excluding infanticide	137
4.6	Women's methods of suicide	145
4.7	Men's methods of suicide	145
4.8	Homicide weapons/methods	146
4.9	Outcomes for female defendants in infanticide cases	151
5.1	Women's and men's participation in property offences	160
5.2	Items stolen by women and men	162
5.3	Categories of prosecuted property offences	187

TABLES

2.1	Defendants in cases of non-lethal violence	25
5.1	Value of goods stolen by male and female defendants	161

PREFACE

This book concerns the interactions of criminal behaviour, gender and social order in early modern England – both the conceptual interactions of these categories and their practical implications for early modern women and men. The scope of such a project is potentially immense. One might incorporate a history of the incidence and character of criminal acts, a history of criminal justice, a history of jurisprudence. Traditionally defined social and cultural history rubs shoulders with well-established legal history and political histories of local and central governance and polity, as well as with newer historiographies of gender. It is impossible to write a 'total' history, although my approach does not exclude new questions being asked by others. Even with all the materials we have to work with, so much will necessarily remain unsaid in any one account. I have tried, however, to weave disparate strands of various bodies of work into tableaux that reveal some of the textures of early modern life. This study is in part a history of social meanings. It is also a study of the dynamics of social interaction and the role of gender as a dynamic force. It therefore offers more, I hope, than a conventional study of crime *per se*. It is nonetheless primarily written in dialogue with the historiography of the social history of early modern crime.

This project has had a lengthy gestation. Like many first monographs, its origins lie in a Ph.D. thesis. But what you will read here is substantially different from my doctoral work on crime, gender and social order in early modern Cheshire. After being awarded my doctorate in 1994, I undertook a considerable amount of additional research, and almost the entire book has been written anew. Unhappily, my progress was hampered by the affliction of an illness that lasted for a period of years. There were moments when I despaired of ever being well enough to finish the book. However, in the autumn of 2000, I was able to recommence work in earnest on the project.

During the chequered course of the book's production, I have, inevitably, accrued many debts. First of all, thanks are due to my Ph.D. supervisors, Jenny Kermode and Brian Quintrell, from whose enthusiasm for my project and generosity with their time and expertise I benefited enormously. It was their inspired undergraduate teaching, along with Mike Power's, that originally turned me into an early modernist. My doctoral work was funded by a postgraduate research grant from the University of Liverpool, and was assisted towards completion by the award of a Scouloudi Research Fellowship at the Institute of Historical Research, where I was thrilled to be accepted into a lively community of historians. My working life has been all the more gratifying as a result of the camaraderie of past and current colleagues in History Departments at the Universities of Liverpool, Warwick, and latterly Cardiff, which I joined in 1995. I am grateful to Caitlin Buck, Bernard Capp, Kate Chedgzoy, Andy Croll, Liz Foyster, Emma Francis, Laura Gowing, Tom Green, Pat Hudson, Bill Jones, Gwynfor Jones, Cheryl Koos, Tim Meldrum, Sara Mendelson, Frances Nerthercott, Diane Purkiss and Andy Wood for their ideas and enthusiasms in conversation and in their work. I owe a special debt to Anthony Fletcher, who has read the entire manuscript, for his personal and intellectual generosity. William Davies has been a patient editor. I should also like to thank the staff at the various repositories and libraries where I undertook research for their efficiency and good cheer. Thanks, too, to my family – Milly Walker, Colin Scott, Tom Walker, Colleen Walker, Matt Walker, Veronica Murphy, Noel Rubie, Lena Angelides, Nigel and Yasmin Gray, Gloria Passmore, and John and Jean Passmore – for their support over the years, which I appreciate more than they can know. During the writing of this book, my own household has expanded to include Joe and Emily Passmore, who have greatly enriched my life. But my greatest gratitude is reserved for Kevin Passmore, my husband, colleague, companion and best friend. He has been a pillar of strength during my illness, a perceptive critic of my work, a constant provider of intellectual stimulus, and much, much more besides. Without him, neither this book nor this author would be in their current shape, and that is why I am dedicating this book to him.

GARTHINE WALKER
Cardiff

NOTE ON QUOTATIONS AND DATES

Quotations from original sources are given modern English spelling and punctuation, capitalisation has been standardised, and the abbreviations and contractions used by court clerks have been expanded. Occasional clerical errors (such as repeated words) have been silently corrected, and legal formulae removed without ellipses. Examinations, depositions and petitions are rendered in the first rather than the clerical third person. Dates follow Old Style, but the year is taken to begin on 1 January.

ABBREVIATIONS

CCRO, MF	City of Chester Record Office, Mayors' Files
CCRO, QSF	City of Chester Record Office, Quarter Sessions and Crownmote Files
Coke, *Third Part of the Institutes*	Edward Coke, *The Third Part of the Institutes of the Laws of England: concerning High Treason and other Pleas of the Crown* (London, 1644)
CRO, QJB	Cheshire Record Office, Quarter Sessions Records, Quarter Sessions Books
CRO, QJF	Cheshire Record Office, Quarter Sessions Records, Quarter Sessions Files
Dalton, *Countrey Justice*	Michael Dalton, *The Countrey Justice: Containing the Practice of the Justices of the Peace out of their Sessions* (London, 1619)
P&P	*Past and Present*
PRO, CHES 21	Public Record Office, Palatinate of Chester Great Sessions Records, Crown Books
PRO, CHES 24	Public Record Office, Palatinate of Chester Great Sessions Records, Gaol Files
PRO, CHES 38	Public Record Office, Palatinate of Chester Great Sessions Records, Miscellanea
Pulton, *De Pace Regis*	Ferdinando Pulton, *De Pace Regis et Regni viz., A Treatise Declaring which be the Great and Generall Offences of the Realme, and the Chiefe Impediments of the Peace of the King and Kingdome* (London, 1609)
Sharpe, *County Study*	J.A. Sharpe, *Crime in Seventeenth-Century England: A County Study* (Cambridge, 1983)
Sharpe, *Crime*	J.A. Sharpe, *Crime in Early Modern England*, 2nd edn (London, 1999)
TRHS	*Transactions of the Royal Historical Society*

1

Introduction

HISTORIES OF CRIME AND GENDER

In an important review essay of 1986, Joanna Innes and John Styles described the social history of crime and the criminal law as 'one of the most exciting and influential areas of research in eighteenth-century history'.[1] It would be somewhat optimistic to make such a statement today about the field as a whole. In some respects, the history of crime appears to be a history that has been standing still. One may observe that the field is not so much reflective of new approaches and interpretations as it is the honing of older ones. Much recent work remains characterised by aspects of what in the 1970s and 1980s was known as the 'new' social history approach. Books are still produced in the mould of 'history from below' or which draw on the methods of positivist social science in order to identify patterns in social behaviour by, for example, counting numbers of indictments and analysing statistically verdicts and sentences over time.[2] It is noticeable that the approach, assumptions and scope of some recent contributions, while being fine pieces of scholarship in their own terms, are similar to those of older works.[3] In this present work, I wish not to dismiss these traditions, but to develop their strengths.

The 'new' social history approach remains fruitful. In line with the latter stance, one historiographical strand has emphasised the amount of

---

[1] Joanna Innes and John Styles, 'The crime wave: recent writing on crime and criminal justice in eighteenth-century England', *Journal of British Studies* 25 (1986), 380.
[2] Malcolm Gaskill, *Crime and Mentalities in Early Modern England* (Cambridge, 2000); Gwenda Morgan and Peter Rushton, *Rogues, Thieves and the Rule of Law: The Problem of Law Enforcement in North-East England, 1718–1800* (London, 1998).
[3] For example, Morgan and Rushton, *Rogues, Thieves and the Rule of Law* published a decade and a half after J.A. Sharpe, *Crime in Seventeenth-Century England: A County Study* (Cambridge, 1983). The only real concession in the former to advances in the field is a separate chapter on women's crime. Incidentally, on the issue of gender, Sharpe himself did not so much revise the second edition of his textbook on early modern crime as insert the odd paragraph that sat somewhat at odds with his otherwise undisturbed original narrative: J.A. Sharpe, *Crime in Early Modern England*, 2nd edn (London, 1999).

1

communal participation in enforcing the law and the degree of discretion involved at every stage of the criminal process.[4] The most recent developments here have been in the work of John Beattie and Peter King. The late Roy Porter situated Beattie's work on London crime in the tradition of E.P. Thompson's social history wherein law is seen as 'the creature of the ruling class', but one that 'because it needed legitimacy,... had to possess a power not primarily coercive but consensual'.[5] Porter's error is born of certain similarities between Marxist and non-Marxist accounts of the law. For Beattie's approach has more in common with that of non-Marxist social science, which focuses on law as a system in its own right, a system within a system that was not always aligned with the wishes of the elite.[6] We may place King's contribution in the older social science tradition, too, partly because of its explicit engagement with and critique of the well-known arguments of Thompson, Douglas Hay and Peter Linebaugh, which were articulated in the 1970s.[7] The result is an extremely sophisticated argument about how procedures and practices changed over time, which problematises the extent to which the law was a tool of the ruling class.

The Thompsonian tradition remains fruitful too. The idea that the law was 'a multiple use-right available to most Englishmen [sic]' has been reinforced and modified.[8] For instance, Andy Wood has shown how free miners were able to use customary law as a resource in their struggles for autonomy.[9] Such studies suggest not so much that the common people shared with their rulers a consensual view of the legitimacy of the system, but rather that law provided a resource to which many sorts of people might turn to bolster their own claims of legitimacy for their own ends. This takes us beyond the view of earlier histories that merely identified aspects of 'class antagonism' and even 'class hatred' in early modern society,[10] a view that has been generally

---

[4] Cynthia B. Herrup, *The Common Peace: Participation and the Criminal Law in Seventeenth-Century England* (Cambridge, 1987).
[5] Roy Porter, 'F for felon', *The London Review of Books* 24, 7 (2002), 23.
[6] J.M. Beattie, *Policing and Punishment in London, 1660–1750: Urban Crime and the Limits of Terror* (Oxford, 2001).
[7] Peter King, *Crime, Justice and Discretion in England, 1740–1820* (Oxford, 2000). See also Douglas Hay, Peter Linebaugh, John G. Rule, E.P. Thompson and Cal Winslow, *Albion's Fatal Tree: Crime and Society in Eighteenth-Century England* (London, 1975) and Peter Linebaugh, *The London Hanged: Crime and Civil Society in the Eighteenth Century* (London, 1991).
[8] John Brewer and John Styles, 'Introduction' to John Brewer and John Styles eds., *An Ungovernable People: The English and their Law in the Seventeenth and Eighteenth Centuries* (London, 1980), 20.
[9] Andy Wood, 'Custom, identity and resistance: English free miners and their law, c. 1500–1800', in Paul Griffiths, Steve Hindle and Adam Fox eds., *The Experience of Authority in Early Modern England* (London, 1996), 249–85.
[10] Buchanan Sharp, *In Contempt of All Authority: Rural Artisans and Riot in the West of England, 1586–1660* (Berkeley, 1980), 7–8, 33; Joel Samaha, 'Gleanings from local criminal court records: sedition among the "inarticulate" in Elizabethan Essex', *Journal of Social History* 8 (1975), 61–79.

rejected on the grounds that few of those who resisted the law or exhibited disorderly behaviour seem to have had a developed sense of (modern) class consciousness or any idea of an alternative social order.[11] Debates over class and status have thus continued to inform the field as a whole.[12]

There has been less integration of a study of gender into that of crime *per se*, and there is some truth in the contention of poststructuralists that social history has tended to universalise the male experience.[13] First, although some work on women's criminality has been undertaken, the experience of ordinary women who came before the courts as defendants, plaintiffs and witnesses in other than supposedly 'female' crimes has remained largely obscure.[14] This poses something of a puzzle for two reasons. Court records are among the most potentially illuminating of all early modern historical sources, offering vivid insights into the nature of social interaction and diverse aspects of early modern life. It is no accident that both the currently standard textbooks on the social history of the period are written by historians whose own research interests originally lay in the history of crime and the law.[15] Indeed, for historians of women (as opposed to historians of crime), court records have 'probably afforded us a greater understanding of women in the past, as individuals, within the family and the community than any other type of material yet examined'.[16] Moreover, given that historians have emphasised the broad participatory base of the legal system, the absence of any real consideration of what this meant for women is conspicuous.[17] Secondly, assumptions (largely unacknowledged) about gender often appear

---

[11] Sharpe, *Crime*, 198; Wrightson, *English Society*, 65. See also Roger B. Manning, *Village Revolts: Social Protest and Popular Disturbance in England, 1509–1640* (Oxford, 1988); Keith Lindley, *Fenland Riots and the English Revolution* (London, 1982).

[12] An excellent discussion of the concept of class in early modern historiography is found in Wood, *Politics of Social Conflict*, ch. 1.

[13] For a lengthier critique, see Garthine Walker, 'Crime, gender and social order in early modern Cheshire', unpublished Ph.D. thesis, University of Liverpool (1994), 2–16.

[14] Examples of recent studies that focus on women rather than gender include Mark Jackson, *New-Born Child Murder: Women, Illegitimacy and the Courts in Eighteenth-Century England* (Manchester and New York, 1996); Jenny Kermode and Garthine Walker eds., *Women, Crime and the Courts in Early Modern England* (London, 1994); Ulinka Rublack, *The Crimes of Women in Early Modern Germany* (Oxford, 1999). For a pioneering work, see J.M. Beattie, 'The criminality of women in eighteenth-century England', *Journal of Social History* 8 (1974–5), 80–116.

[15] Keith Wrightson, *English Society, 1580–1680* (London, 1982); J.A. Sharpe, *Early Modern England: A Social History, 1550–1760* (London, 1987).

[16] Olwen Hufton, 'Women and violence in early modern Europe', in Fia Dieteren and Els Kloek eds., *Writing Women into History* (Amsterdam, 1991), 75.

[17] For example, Anthony Fletcher and John Stevenson, 'Introduction' to Anthony Fletcher and John Stevenson eds., *Order and Disorder in Early Modern England* (Cambridge, 1985), 1–40; Herrup, *Common Peace*; James Sharpe, 'The people and the law', in Barry Reay ed., *Popular Culture in Seventeenth-Century England* (London, 1985), 244–70; Keith Wrightson, 'Two concepts of order: justices, constables and jurymen in seventeenth-century England', in John Brewer and John Styles eds., *An Ungovernable People: The English and their Law in the Seventeenth and Eighteenth Centuries* (London, 1980), 21–46.

to be based on little other than our own culture's stereotypes, which may or may not be pertinent to the early modern period.[18] These assumptions have informed the selection, organisation and interpretation of historical evidence in such a manner as to produce results that reproduce those very assumptions contained in the premise. A few behaviours for which women were disproportionately prosecuted relative to men are labelled as peculiarly 'feminine', such as witchcraft, infanticide and scolding. By definition, all other offences must implicitly be 'masculine'. Yet, thirdly, the extent to which criminality was related to masculinity has scarcely been addressed. Historians tend to accept criminality in general to be a masculine category without conceptualising or contextualising it in terms of gender. Male criminality is thus normalised, while female criminality is seen in terms of dysfunction, an aberration of the norms of feminine behaviour.[19]

In fact, as we shall see, neither women nor men committed acts solely in line with the prescriptions either of their own society or of ours. The supposedly 'feminine' crimes are typical neither of female behaviour nor of prosecutions of women. Women participated in most categories of crime. Indeed, they were far more likely to participate in the non-'feminine' offences than they were in those labelled as women's crimes. For every one woman who was suspected of infanticide or indicted as a scold (and even fewer were prosecuted for witchcraft) at quarter sessions and assizes in Cheshire, for instance, eight were prosecuted for some kind of theft, ten were prosecuted for assault, and twenty-five were bound to the peace or to be of good behaviour. Women seem to have committed more 'male' crimes than they did 'female' ones! Discussion of the peculiarly 'female' crimes would seem therefore not to take us very far in assessing the nature of female criminality. Part of the explanation for the unsatisfactory account of gender within histories of crime, then, is conceptual.

This state of affairs is also related to the crime historian's method of choice: quantification of formal judicial records to establish patterns of indictment, jury verdicts and sentences. Quantification shows us time and again that women constituted a minority of those prosecuted for most categories of crime. What tends to happen is that women are counted, and being a minority of offenders, are subsequently *dis*counted as unimportant. However, the conventional sources chosen for quantification themselves may underestimate the degree of women's participation in the legal process. Prosecuting by recognisance, for instance, provided an alternative to formal indictment

---

[18] For example, Carol Z. Wiener, 'Sex-roles and crime in late Elizabethan Hertfordshire', *Journal of Social History* 8 (1974–5), 38–60; Frank McLynn, *Crime and Punishment in Eighteenth-Century England* (Oxford, 1991), chs. 6 and 7.

[19] See also Garthine Walker and Jenny Kermode, 'Introduction' to Kermode and Walker eds., *Women, Crime and the Courts*, 1–7.

and one in which greater numbers of women featured as both complainants and offenders.[20] But even when we include recognisances in our study, an interpretation based on aggregates of individuals alone is bound to mislead. We have to analyse figures in *context* if we are to make sense of them. Attending to context begins within quantification itself. At various points in subsequent chapters, I therefore analyse criminal acts in terms of the groups that carried them out, thereby demonstrating that women's participation had a higher profile than simple aggregates of 'men' and 'women' suggest. These groups frequently coalesced around the household. Indeed, we shall see that the household is implicated repeatedly in criminal activity, which is why a short section is devoted to it below. Context is also provided by a systematic qualitative analysis of court records such as depositions and examinations, petitions, JPs' memoranda books, letters and so forth, and of other types of narrative source, such as pamphlets of various kinds, ballads and moral commentaries. In the chapters that follow, I have contextualised quantitative data within early modern discursive frameworks. With regard to property crimes, to give but one example, this allows for 'different forms of illegal appropriation [to] be systematically investigated as economic activities with their own histories'.[21] By analysing narrative sources, historians are able to do more than reveal information about crime, criminality and the legal process. They may open windows through which we may view aspects of the wider culture and ways of thinking and doing in early modern society. Hence, the history of crime becomes a broader cultural history of the period.

Systematic qualitative analyses need not be restricted to studies of gender.[22] Nor is a qualitative study necessarily superior to a quantitative one. Method has to be determined by the questions that one wishes to ask. Ideally, in asking questions about gender and crime, one's interpretation would arise from a dialogue between qualitative and quantitative analyses. The major shortcoming of a recent study of women's crime in early modern Germany, for example, is that it neglects to place an otherwise brilliant analysis within any quantitative framework, which makes it difficult to ascertain the relative significance of the material or of the author's conclusions.[23]

The analysis of discursive frameworks potentially provides a bridge between the older 'new' social history approach to crime and the newer approaches of the 1990s. In line with broader historiographical advances, it is

---

[20] Robert B. Shoemaker, *Prosecution and Punishment: Petty Crime and the Law in London and Rural Middlesex, c. 1660–1725* (Cambridge, 1991), 207–16.
[21] Innes and Styles, 'The crime wave', 401.
[22] See, for instance, the excellent use of qualitative material in King, *Crime, Justice and Discretion*, and Gaskill, *Crime and Mentalities*.
[23] Rublack, *Crimes of Women*.

possible to embark on a linguistic analysis of texts, to read them for their semantic content or the way in which they are discursively constructed in particular material circumstances.[24] Despite this, the method of reading narrative sources in histories of crime remains largely in the social history tradition, in which narratives are read for the conventional information that they contain. The reason for a certain ambivalence towards discourse analysis is, I believe, rooted in general concerns among social historians about the threat posed to the integrity of the discipline by postmodernism. Close textual analysis is associated, for good reason, with poststructuralist linguistic theory, the premises of which deny the validity of a 'real' past that is accessible to historians. Poststructuralism stresses that we are dealing only with representations of the past, not the past itself. The implication of this is that none of these representations is more valid than any other. This is anathema to social historians, who conventionally wish to recover evidence of the experience of early modern people, and whose methods involve the evaluation and re-evaluation of competing historical analyses in the light of which is the more convincing.[25] At the same time, early modern social historians of crime have tended to shy away from explicit engagement with the theoretical issues raised by a poststructuralist approach. This is evident in responses to the writing of the French poststructuralist historian/philosopher Michel Foucault, which invariably emphasise the empirical shortcomings of his thesis. For example, Pieter Spierenburg sought to refute Foucault's account of the prison as a modern form of punishment by charting the sixteenth-century origins of the institution.[26] However, Spierenburg's insistence that the origins of the prison shaped the institution as it evolved does not take us far in refuting Foucault's account. For Foucault had not written a conventional history of the prison, nor did he argue that incarceration sprang up as a new type of punishment in the nineteenth century. Rather, Foucault argued that the discourse of imprisonment typified a style by which the modern state ruled, in the same way that the discourse of punishing and eradicating the body of a traitor exemplified the style of power held by sixteenth-century monarchical rule. Foucault was concerned with these styles of punishment as expressions

---

[24] For example, Natalie Zemon Davis, *Fiction in the Archives: Pardon Tales and their Tellers in Sixteenth-Century France* (Oxford, 1988); Garthine Walker, 'Just stories: telling tales of infant death in early modern England', in Margaret Mikesell and Adele Seefe eds., *Attending to Early Modern Women: Culture and Change* (London, 2003), forthcoming; Garthine Walker, ' "Strange kind of stealing": abduction in early modern Wales', in Michael Roberts and Simone Clarke eds., *Women and Gender in Early Modern Wales* (Cardiff, 2000), 50–74; Garthine Walker, 'Rereading rape and sexual violence in early modern England', *Gender and History* 10, 1 (1998), 1–25.

[25] See the debates in Keith Jenkins ed., *The Postmodern History Reader* (London, 1997).

[26] Pieter Spierenburg, *The Prison Experience: Disciplinary Institutions and their Inmates in Early Modern Europe* (New Brunswick, 1991).

of power, not as empirical descriptions of penal regimes.[27] Shifting the date of the prison's origin does not necessarily invalidate Foucault's point about the nature of punishment.

Poststructuralism, however, is neither the only nor necessarily the most useful theoretical approach to the narrative sources available to historians of crime. My own method is informed by the linguistic theory of M.M. Bakhtin. While Bakhtin is best known to early modernists for his work on carnival and the grotesque, his potential contribution is far wider. Whereas Derrida followed Saussure in his concern with the deep structures of language (*langue*), Bakhtin theorised about *everyday* language *use* (*parole*). I do not intend here to elaborate upon Bakhtin's work, but to point to two of his central concepts – heteroglossia and multivocality.[28] In a crude simplification, any utterance is dialogic in a dual sense. First, it is produced in a dialogue with sources that draw on certain other discourses according to context. In speaking or writing, we draw on all sorts of explicit and unacknowledged ideas. Secondly, it is produced in dialogue with the listener or reader, in that we assume the responses of those we address. Therefore, there are three categories of 'voice' in any given discourse: those of source, author and listener. For example, law is not a pure product of reason or natural justice, but is the product of academic discourses, religious ideas and unacknowledged prejudices, which might well not differ too much from those of the common people. We will see this, for instance, in chapter four, when we discuss homicide law, which was constructed in part according to elite and popular ideas about masculine behaviour. Law also contains the voice of the people, the ruled, in the sense that people's behaviour and the problem of enforceability are taken into account in framing law. Law itself is then a negotiation, not something pre-existent and fixed which is then negotiated. Narratives such as pre-trial statements produced by the legal process provide a further example of multivocality. They contain within them the speaker's agenda, popular ideas, plus the anticipation of how the law will act and needs to be accommodated. Descriptions of violence, and the meanings intended and inferred from them, like other forms of expression, varied according to the particular circumstances in which they were uttered and heard. In a legal setting, they might be differently constructed from those uttered among fellowship in the alehouse. Speech about violence drew upon a range of concepts, images, metaphors and vocabulary that themselves were part of or variously conditioned by ideas about gender, class, law, religion and more. In this sense, an account of a violent exchange (or anything else, for that matter) involves a number of 'voices'.

[27] Michel Foucault, *Discipline and Punish: The Birth of the Prison*, trans. Alan Sheridan (London, 1977).
[28] See Simon Dentith ed., *Bakhtinian Thought: An Introductory Reader* (London, 1995).

As we shall see in the following chapters, attending to the multivocality of discourse reveals the pervasiveness and shortcomings of a superficial mapping of terms such as violent/non-violent, aggressive/passive onto those of male/female. Paying attention to the richness of lay social theories, schemas and scenarios concerning violence also allows us to challenge views of an early modern 'crisis' in gender relations. Such accounts tend to privilege rather rigid notions of class or gender as a primary determinant, or 'core', of gender identity. But there was in fact a multiplicity of gendered discourses, and thus 'voices', with which early modern people spoke and through which they constituted and positioned themselves, and were positioned by others, as subjects. The images and concepts used to depict behaviour and disposition cohered within narratives to provide an explanatory framework within which culpability could be evaluated. The images and concepts themselves, however, could be incongruent, incompatible and even contradictory. An account of infanticide, for instance, may contain within it and be structured by multiple 'voices': those of law and motherhood, say, as well as violence and burial. To acknowledge this does not privilege structure over agency. For, as I have suggested, when we read qualitative materials for the various languages or voices within them we may glimpse the way in which early modern people positioned themselves in their narratives and learn something of their subject position.[29] By interpreting narrative sources, legal or otherwise, not as monovocal texts but for the multiple voices that are contained within them, and by marrying qualitative with quantitative material, I hope to offer a more sensitive interpretation of crime and subjectivities in early modern England than is usually presented in the historical literature.

The concept of gender with which I work is close to that of Joan Scott's theorisation. In employing gender as an analytic concept,

> we need to deal with the individual subject as well as social organization and to articulate the nature of their interrelationships, for both are crucial to understanding how gender works, how change occurs. Finally, we need to replace the notion that social power is unified, coherent, and centralized with something like Foucault's concept of power as dispersed constellations of unequal relationships, discursively constituted in social 'fields of force'. Within these processes and structures, there is room for a concept of human agency as the attempt (at least partially rational) to construct an identity, a life, a set of relationships, a society with certain limits and with language – conceptual language that at once sets boundaries and contains the possibility for negation, resistance, reinterpretation, the play of metaphoric invention and imagination.[30]

---

[29] See, for example, John H. Arnold, 'The historian as inquisitor: the ethics of interrogating subaltern voices', *Rethinking History* 2, 3 (1998), 379–86; Walker, 'Just stories: telling tales of infant death'.

[30] Joan W. Scott, 'Gender: a useful category of historical analysis', *American Historical Review* 91 (1986), 1067.

Introduction

This does not mean that gender is *the* primary category. It has a privileged place in my work because of the particular questions I am asking. But one could just as easily use this method to investigate class, religion or any other category of difference. Indeed, while gender remains my primary concern, class and, to a much lesser extent, religion, are discussed at various points in the pages that follow.

HOUSEHOLD

One of the most important ways in which we can question the universalisation of the autonomous male subject is through consideration of the role of the household in early modern crime. The ubiquity of the analogy between household and state in early modern rhetoric, theology and law is routinely remarked upon by historians. The presentation of the household as little commonwealth conflated personal and public authority in a patriarchal and Christian vision in which the rule of husbands, fathers, magistrates, ecclesiastics and monarchs each legitimated that of the others. The ideology of the household thus resided at every level of the various institutions of governance: central and local, secular and ecclesiastical, formal and informal.[31] In many practical respects as well as in theory, the household was the relevant social, economic and political unit. When population was calculated, whether in official censuses or by Gregory King, households were counted, not people. Taxation, too, was effectively based on household, not individual, wealth. Certain forms of taxation, such as the hearth and window taxes, were imposed upon the physical manifestation of the household – the dwelling-house – itself. The franchise was similarly based on the property of the household unit. When the Levellers demanded in 1646 the abolition of the property qualification and the extension of the franchise, their conception of universal (i.e., 'manhood') suffrage was restricted to all (male) heads of households. These few examples suggest some of the interconnected meanings of the household as a cultural form.

The term 'household' was used to describe the collective body of persons who lived together in a family unit. In most households, this included with the nuclear family maidservants and servants in husbandry or apprentices. In this sense, household and family were virtually synonymous. Relatives by blood or marriage who lived elsewhere were perhaps more appropriately

---

[31] Important overviews include Susan Dwyer Amussen, *An Ordered Society: Gender and Class in Early Modern England* (Oxford, 1988); Anthony Fletcher, *Gender, Sex and Subordination in England 1500–1800* (London and New Haven, 1995); G.J. Schochet, *Patriarchalism in Political Thought: The Authoritarian Family and Political Speculation and Attitudes Especially in Seventeenth-Century England* (Oxford, 1975); Rachel Weil, *Political Passions: Gender, the Family and Political Argument in England, 1680–1714* (Manchester, 1999).

termed kin. Many households, chiefly among the poorer sorts of people, conformed not to this pattern but took various forms as was expedient. They functioned as households, nonetheless, even when quite unrelated people lived together.[32] With the exception perhaps of the vagrant poor, everyone was part of some sort of household, no matter how far it deviated from the ideal. Household also referred to the way in which the household was 'held' or maintained by its members, the economy that formed its basic unit of production and consumption. It is no coincidence that the word 'economic' originated in the Greek term for 'housekeeping' or 'household management'. Household denoted, too, the physical structure in which a family resided, whether mansion, farmhouse or single room sublet from another tenant. A further meaning of household was the material contents of the domestic unit, such as household goods and furniture. The family (broadly defined), the manner in which they got their living, their physical dwelling and their collective goods and chattels: 'household' encompassed all these things.

These interconnected meanings of household pervaded understandings of social, political and economic interaction. Craig Muldrew has emphasised that the circulating capital in the early modern economy was household credit in social terms. In other words, the currency of most earning, spending, lending and borrowing was not cash but a household's reputation for honesty, fair dealing and reliability. Establishing, communicating and negotiating credit-worthiness and trust was therefore an exercise in moral, as well as economic, competition. Yet competing households were, at the same time, mutually dependent. Everyone was involved in multiple chains of credit. If debtors did not promptly discharge their debts, creditors might be unable to pay theirs. Self-interest and practicality thus fostered a moral imperative that obligations to pay debts, deliver goods and perform services were met.[33] In modern western society, too, social and economic standing is related to family and household, and is informed by various cultural meanings. But whereas in modern society, credit ratings affect the individual, the early modern household played a *direct* role in the regulation of credit. This has important repercussions for any study of inter-household disputes, and indeed for diverse other matters of order and disorder.

The 'dominant' ideology professed from pulpit, parliament and courts of law established that the household was the foundation upon which good

---

[32] Margaret Pelling, 'Old age, poverty and disability in early modern Norwich', in Margaret Pelling and Richard M. Smith eds., *Life, Death and the Elderly: Historical Perspectives* (London, 1991), 74–101.

[33] Craig Muldrew, *The Economy of Obligation: The Culture of Credit and Social Relations in Early Modern England* (Basingstoke, 1998).

governance rested.[34] Household order was a microcosm of that desired elsewhere, in parish, county, kingdom and even the cosmos. Good household governance was therefore deemed essential and, like the household itself, was defined variously. A properly governed household was characterised by orderly and appropriate conduct within it, with due authority and deference being displayed as precise relationships demanded, and the absence of illicit alliances of all kinds. Thus the household's inhabitants 'are so squared and framed by the word of God, as they may serve in their several places, for useful pieces in God's building'.[35] Good household governance also encompassed good husbandry or enterprise, which ensured the proper use of household resources and could be taken as an index of the morality of household members. Moreover, just as the household embodied those who peopled it, inhabitants represented their households within and outside its walls. Interpersonal relations were understood in the light of, among other things, both the relative household positions of individuals and the relative positions of their households. In all these ways, household obligations were fundamental to common definitions of order and disorder.

A great many disputes between individuals that resulted in indictments being filed for a range of misdemeanours, including assault, or in the issuing of recognisances to keep the peace or for good behaviour, are revealed on closer inspection to be ongoing intra-household disputes. A majority of the quarrels that came before quarter sessions were apparently between heads of households.[36] This is a practical consequence not of married men's greater propensity for quarrelling and fighting, but of their legal accountability for the conduct of their household members and their own responsibility for maintaining good order. Many complaints about violent behaviour collapsed the different meanings of household into each other. In relating before a Justice of the peace how Ambrose Wettenhall had fallen upon him before beating at his doors and windows with a staff and tearing a crossbar and part of the latch off one of his doors, Robert Bruen explicitly depicted Wettenhall as endangering his entire household – the physical edifice and the whole family who lived there. The JP's warrant also made explicit reference to house and family, stating that Wettenhall might well inflict some bodily harm on Bruen's wife and the rest of the household. The recognisance collapsed the meanings still further: only Robert Bruen – who as head

---

[34] On 'household governance' see Amussen, *Ordered Society*; Julie Hardwick, *The Practice of Patriarchy: Gender and the Politics of Household Authority in Early Modern France* (University Park, Pennsylvania, 1998); Mary Elizabeth Perry, *Gender and Disorder in Early Modern Seville* (Princeton, 1990); Lyndal Roper, *The Holy Household: Women and Morals in Reformation Augsburg* (Oxford, 1989).

[35] Matthew Griffith, *Bethel: Or, a Forme for Families* (London, 1633), frontispiece.

[36] In Hertfordshire, too, the named protagonists in at least two-thirds of cases involving interpersonal violence were married men: Wiener, 'Sex roles and crime', 45.

of the household stood for the rest of the domestic establishment – was mentioned as a person towards whom Wettenhall had to be of particularly good behaviour.[37] This has obvious implications for the quantification of female offenders. Frequently, depositional evidence and even Justices' warrants allege the involvement of women, but only husbands or fathers, as the household's public face, were held formally accountable in that they alone were bound over by recognisance or indicted.[38] This has nothing to do with the concept of male heads of households 'possessing' their wives, children or other household dependants. The patriarchal extremism of fictional characters, who declared, for example, 'I will be master of what is mine own, She is my goods, my chattels, she is my house', was actually the speech of male ignorance, as other married, male characters pointed out.[39] Anyone could crave the peace against a *feme covert* (or an infant under the age of fourteen), although such persons had to be bound by sureties rather than by their own pledge.[40] It must often have seemed more sensible to prosecute only the head of the household. It was not only cheaper, but his bond stood for other members of his household as he was responsible for household order. It is telling that so many disputes that came in various forms before magistrates concerned competition between households over material and cultural resources. In this sense, much litigation and the precipitating quarrels were not strictly inter*personal* at all. While the existence of the 'dark figure' of unrecorded crime means that we will never know what proportion of women relative to men committed offences without being formally held to account, we can surmise that women's place in the household meant that they were especially likely to be excluded from the official court record.

The early modern household, with its broad spectrum of meaning, provides a crucial context for understanding the dynamics of disorder in early modern England. Household is thus a useful category of analysis *apropos* disorderly and violent behaviour. This is not to reify the household, or to deny the importance of other analytic categories. Acknowledging that the household, like gender, was everywhere does not imply that the household (any more than gender) is *the* primary category. The household served as one category of differentiation and inclusion alongside others. The manner in which the household informed such behaviours is in turn related to gender, class, and so forth. At the level of both ideology and praxis, tensions between ideology and praxis created conceptual spaces in which people could

---

[37] CRO, QJF 97/2/150, /90, /91 (1669). See also QJF 81/2/301 (1653), QJF 55/3/83 (1626).
[38] For example, CRO, QJF 25/3/33, /34, QJB 1/3 fos. 25v–29r (1593); QJF 29/2/64, QJB 1/3 fo. 64r (1599); QJF 49/2/151 (1620); QJF 53/2/163, QJB 1/5 fos. 113v–114v (1624); QJF 53/3/64, /53, /54 (1624); QJF 57/2/94, /95 (1628); QJF 89/2/156 (1661); QJF 89/2/167 (1661); QJF 89/2/56, /126 (1661); QJF 89/2/76, /79 (1661); QJF 89/2/188 (1661).
[39] William Shakespeare, *The Taming of the Shrew* (1596), III, ii, 232.
[40] Dalton, *Countrey Justice*, 147.

construct meanings other than dominant ones while remaining within the terms of 'dominant' household ideology.

THE SETTING

Cheshire has been selected as the geographical location for this study for its unrivalled, rich and extensive criminal court records.[41] Although I deploy the sources of a county administration, this is not a conventional county study. To create a manageable amount of data, the quantitative aspect of the study is confined to Cheshire material in alternate years during the 1590s, 1620s, 1650s, 1660s and all years for which sessions were held during the 1640s. But the story I tell here is not one about Cheshire *per se*. The conceptual questions asked of the material and the interpretations that follow are applicable to early modern England as a whole. I do not here consider in depth the relationship between local society and the types and incidence of crime. This does not preclude a further study in which alternative questions could be asked that would illuminate such a county perspective. I have, however, tried to weave a broader thread through the narrower web of social, economic, political and topographical peculiarities of the region in order to give a textured account of early modern life. This means that an understanding of the county setting is desirable as background.

Early modern Cheshire has conventionally been seen as a 'dark corner of the land', politically, socially and economically underdeveloped due to its institutional idiosyncrasies as a Palatinate, its isolation as a north western border county, and its character as an upland pastoral region.[42] This view of

---

[41] The main primary sources are those of the county quarter sessions and Palatinate great sessions. Quarter Sessions Books (CRO, QJB), which survive from 1559, contain a record of indictments, presentments, certified recognisances and orders. Quarter Sessions Files (CRO, QJF), which start from 1571, contain examinations, depositions, informations, warrants, letters, indictments that were returned *ignoramus*, and recognisances that were discharged before the sessions, as well as the original documents of items entered in the court books. The Great Sessions Crown Books (PRO, CHES 21) calendar the business of each session, while the Gaol Files (PRO, CHES 24) contain indictments, presentments, coroners' inquisitions, calendars of gaol deliveries, mainprizes and supporting documents. Unfortunately, a full set of depositions has not survived for the great sessions. The quarter and great sessions material has been supplemented by that of other courts. The City of Chester enjoyed a separate jurisdiction from 1507, and therefore held its own quarter sessions. The Sessions Files (CCRO, QSF) are incomplete, and subsequently have not been used in the quantitative study to the same extent as those of the aforementioned courts. Their contents, however, are similar to those of the county quarter sessions. I have also examined the Diocese of Chester Consistory Court Papers (CDRO, EDC 5), and various other classes of document as indicated in the bibliography.

[42] For example, J. Beck, *Tudor Cheshire* (Chester, 1969), 1–3; G. Barraclough, 'The Earldom and County Palatine of Chester', *Transactions of the Historic Society of Lancashire and Cheshire*, 103 (1951), 24; Dorothy J. Clayton, *The Administration of the County Palatine of Chester 1442–1485* (Manchester, 1990), 215–16; B.E. Harris ed., *Victoria History of the Counties of England. Cheshire* (hereafter, *VCH Cheshire*) Vol. II, 31–2.

Cheshire is mistaken. Granted, as a Palatinate, some aspects of central and local government relations did remain particular. The terms of military service for Cheshire knights were slightly different from those elsewhere; taxation was calculated by a traditional unit of assessment, the 'mize'; Cheshire had its own Exchequer Court that dealt with (among other things) the business which elsewhere would have gone before the Westminster Chancery; assizes took the form of the Palatinate Court of Great Sessions, which had a civil as well as criminal jurisdiction. Despite this, Cheshire was no more and no less peculiar than any other county.[43]

Palatinate status gave Cheshire only nominal independence. The county's judicial and administrative business came under the supervision of Justices of the peace appointed by the Crown in 1536. Following the Diocese of Chester's creation in 1541, Cheshire was subject to routine ecclesiastical administration. The city of Chester and the County both returned Members of Parliament from 1543. The Port of Chester was absorbed into the national customs system in 1559. A royal Lord Lieutenant was in office by the later sixteenth century.[44] Links with central government and the rest of the political nation were hardly obscure. Sir Thomas Egerton became Master of the Rolls in 1594, Lord Keeper in 1596 and Lord Chancellor in 1603. His son, John Egerton, Earl of Bridgewater was a member of the Privy Council from 1626, President of the Council of Wales and Lord Lieutenant of North and South Wales from 1631. Sir Thomas Savage became the Queen's Chancellor in the 1620s, and although his duties often kept him away from Cheshire, his son John remained active in county affairs. Sir Ranulphe Crewe, the Cheshire knight, became Lord Chief Justice of King's Bench in January 1625. Sir Urian Legh, an active Cheshire Justice of the peace in the early seventeenth century, was knighted for his bravery at the siege of Cadiz. The Cheshire lawyer John Bradshaw, who later was Chief Justice of Cheshire, was a Commissioner of the Great Seal in 1646, and President of the short-lived Court of Justice which was created on the last day of the Long Parliament. Another Cheshire man, who became Lord Mayor of London in 1641, had retained links with his home town of Nantwich, where, in 1638, he established

---

[43] For an expanded discussion see Walker, 'Crime, gender and social order', 16–38.
[44] Barry Coward, 'The Lieutenancy of Lancashire and Cheshire in the sixteenth and seventeenth centuries', *Transactions of the Historic Society of Lancashire and Cheshire* 119 (1969), 39–64; R.N. Dore, *Cheshire* (London, 1977), 12–13; G.P. Higgins, 'The government of early Stuart Cheshire', *Northern History* 12 (1976), 32–52; G.P. Higgins, 'County government and society in Cheshire, c. 1590–1640', M.A. thesis, University of Liverpool (1973), 12; Alfred Ingham, *Cheshire: Its Traditions and History* (Edinburgh, 1920), 78; Annette Kennett, *Archives and Records of the City of Chester* (Chester, 1985), 34; J.S. Morrill, *Cheshire, 1630–1660: County Government and Society during the English Revolution* (Oxford, 1974); Dorothy Sylvester, *A History of Cheshire*, 2nd edn (London 1980), 60.

almshouses.[45] The anti-episcopal petition of 1641 was sponsored by Sir William Brereton, and many of the signatures were those of Cheshire men; Brereton, of course, became an important parliamentary commander in the civil wars. Sir George Booth was likewise a prominent Parliamentarian, who later led the rising of 1659. Nor was Cheshire isolated from the affairs of the nation in wider terms. Chester's port gave the county an important strategic position as a main embarkation point for troops, travellers, mail and supplies to and from Ireland. Trade to and from the Continent and America also came through Chester. (It was only at the end of the seventeenth century that Liverpool overtook Chester as a port, due to the silting up of the River Dee.) Cheshire was privileged by more than one royal visit: James I visited in 1617, Charles I in 1642 and reputedly again in 1645. During the wars, in addition to three important battles at Nantwich, Middlewich and Rowton Moor near Chester, the county suffered many smaller battles and military engagements. The ordinary men and women of Cheshire played a significant role in the civil wars.[46] The assumption that Cheshire was not integrated into the affairs of the nation seems spurious.

Cheshire's criminal justice system operated in much the same way as elsewhere. The court of great sessions was equivalent in criminal matters to the assizes. Indeed, many contemporaries used the terms 'assizes' and 'great sessions' interchangeably, which convention I have followed here. The great sessions were presided over by a Chief Justice and his deputy who usually remained in office for several years rather than perambulating circuits as assize judges did. Sir Henry Townshend, for instance, held his post for over forty years.[47] Nevertheless, Chief Justices were royal appointees, who certainly were neither socially nor professionally isolated from Westminster. They were very much part of the legal elite that congregated in Sergeant's Inn.[48] Indeed, the Lord Chancellor's speech on James Whitelocke's appointment as Chief Justice instructed that one of his duties was to 'keep good quarter with Westminster Hall'.[49] Great sessions were biannual, and lasted between two

---

[45] Higgins, 'County government', 20, 18–19, 28; Ingham, *Cheshire*, 238–9, 240, 241–2, 276; James Hall, *A History of the Town and Parish of Nantwich* (Manchester, 1972), 126–7, 365–71. Sir Urian Legh was the hero of a Cheshire ballad entitled 'How a Spanish Lady Woo'd a Cheshire Man'.

[46] Simon Harrison, Annette M. Kennet, Elizabeth J. Shepherd and Eileen M. Willshaw, *Tudor Chester: A Study of Chester in the Reigns of the Tudor Monarchs, 1485–1603* (Chester, 1986), 31; Hall, *Nantwich*, 121; *Royal Commission on Historical Manuscripts. Sixth Report* (London, 1877), 64, 85, 135, 435, 438, 470.

[47] *VCH Cheshire*, Vol. I, 37. Chester's Chief Justice additionally presided over sessions in three Welsh counties (Flint, Denbigh and Montgomery) in the Chester Circuit.

[48] For example, both Thomas Chamberleyne and James Whitelocke were transferred to the King's Bench in the 1620s.

[49] James Whitelocke, *Liber Famelicus of Sir James Whitelocke*, ed. John Bruce (Manchester, 1858), 80.

and six days. Virtually all felonies prosecuted in the county were brought before this tribunal. Sufficient regional variations in the character and operation of assize courts elsewhere make Cheshire's great sessions not especially unusual. The second inquest that was sworn in at the great sessions, for example, existed also in Staffordshire and Lincolnshire. In fact, every county had 'a distinctive pattern of local government'.[50] Cheshire quarter sessions were held at four of five towns each year: the Epiphany sessions at Chester, the Easter sessions at Knutsford, the Trinity sessions at Nantwich and the Michaelmas sessions alternately at Northwich and Middlewich. Here, as elsewhere, Justices usually dealt with most sorts of criminal complaints other than the more serious felonies.[51]

The county had seven large administrative units, or hundreds: Bucklow, Macclesfield, Northwich and Nantwich on the eastern side, and Wirral, Broxton and Eddisbury in the west. Cheshire's lack of hundredal juries was not unique. By the 1590s, local justices held regular meetings in their hundreds, and strong hundredal organisation provided the basis for the implementation of much of the county's financial and social policy.[52] Including those in the City of Chester, Cheshire had eighty-four parishes and a few extra-parochial liberties. As in other northern counties, parishes were generally large: eight contained over fifteen townships – Great Budworth and Prestbury each had over thirty – a further four contained more than ten townships. Excluding the nine city parishes, only eleven had a solitary township within their boundaries.[53] Seventeenth-century Cheshire also had between 250 and 300 manors, many of whose manorial courts were still in regular biannual business.[54] As incorporated boroughs, both Congleton and Macclesfield had their own administrative and judicial mechanisms, but inhabitants nonetheless brought suits before county quarter sessions. The same applied to eleven seigniorial boroughs, whose borough courts were still functioning.[55]

---

[50] J.S. Morrill, *The Cheshire Grand Jury, 1625–1659* (Leicester, 1976), 6; *VCH Cheshire*, Vol. I, 38. Sarah Mercer, 'Crime in late-seventeenth-century Yorkshire: an exception to a national pattern?', *Northern History* 27 (1991), 106–19. For assize courts see, for example, Beattie, *Crime and the Courts*, 5; Herrup, *Common Peace*, 43–51, 62–5.

[51] For example, Beattie, *Crime and the Courts*, 283–8; Herrup, *Common Peace*, 42–5; Shoemaker, *Prosecution and Punishment*.

[52] F.I. Dunn, *The Ancient Parishes, Townships and Chapelries of Cheshire* (Chester, 1987), 7; Morrill, *Grand Jury*, 41–2, 9, 30–1.

[53] Dunn, *Parishes, Townships and Chapelries*; Higgins, 'County government', 196–8; Dorothy Sylvester, 'Parish and township in Cheshire and north-east Wales', *Journal of the Chester Archaeological Society* 54 (1967), 23–35.

[54] For example, at Nantwich, Stockport, Macclesfield, Bromborough and Kinderton. Dorothy Sylvester, 'The manor and the Cheshire landscape', *Transactions of the Historic Society of Lancashire and Cheshire*, 70 (1960).

[55] Morrill, *Cheshire*, 6; C.B. Phillips and J.H. Smith, *Lancashire and Cheshire from AD 1540* (London, 1994), 30–5.

The City of Chester was a county in its own right, and thus held its own quarter sessions independently of the county, and capital felonies were tried at the crownmote court, both of which were presided over by the mayor – documentation pertaining to the quarter sessions and the crownmote continued to be filed together throughout the early modern period. The current mayor and aldermen who were former mayors were empowered to act as JPs within the city. The mayor and sheriffs were also responsible for other administrative duties that would otherwise have come under the direction of the county bench. These included the publication and enforcement of central government directives, such as those concerning trade and taxation, poor law and the regulation of the assizes of ale and bread. In addition, the mayor headed the city Assembly, which consisted of two sheriffs, a recorder, twenty-four aldermen and forty common councilmen.[56] Chester was also the home of the ecclesiastical courts for the Diocese of Chester. The seventeenth-century consistory courtroom in Chester Cathedral has survived intact to this day. Criminals or dangerous suspects in the city were incarcerated not in the county's gaol in Chester Castle, but in the city's Northgate, which was flanked by towers with a prison over it and dungeons cut out of the rock below. The city sheriff, however, arranged the execution of felons condemned at the city courts and at the Palatinate great sessions.

The number of different courts in operation in Cheshire indicates the unhelpfulness of the concept of the 'county study' for the social history of crime and the courts in early modern England. Any 'county study' of crime or the legal process should ideally take account of the various jurisdictions within which a variety of suits could be brought. In addition to those courts mentioned above, Cheshire people prosecuted suits at a range of central courts at Westminster, such as those of star chamber and queen's or king's Bench. These would also have to be considered.[57] The same is true for other counties. Only if we could analyse *all* prosecutions in all operative legal arenas would

---

[56] The mayor was also chief officer in the portmote court, while the city sheriff presided over the passage and pentice courts. Kennett, *Archives and Records*, 17, 19, 22–31, 88–9; Harrison et al., *Tudor Chester*, 24; Simon Harrison, Annette M. Kennet, Elizabeth J. Shepherd and Eileen M. Willshaw, *Loyal Chester: A Brief History of Chester in the Civil War Period* (Chester, 1984), 14.

[57] The Public Record Office (PRO), London, holds most of the documentation generated by these courts. Social historians of crime have largely shown a disinterest in or ignorance of central Westminster courts. Nor have they paid much attention to the multiplicity of local courts: courts baron, urban borough courts of requests or their equivalents, local small claims courts, along with the quasi-legal institutions set up to regulate trade or industry. Consequently, there has as yet been no attempt to write a comprehensive social history of law; rather what has been achieved is a limited social history of crime. Given the way that interpersonal disputes could be played out in a multiplicity of ways in any number of jurisdictions, 'county studies' are unreliable gauges of behaviour and litigation within counties.

a county-based study of prosecution for various types of social conflict be comprehensive. L.A. Knafla has demonstrated that, for instance, while property offences prosecuted at the Kent assizes in the early seventeenth century constituted seventy-four per cent of the total number of prosecutions, the figure was reduced to a mere ten per cent if prosecutions at quarter sessions and other local courts were taken into account. More recently, Sarah Mercer has pointed to the discrepancies which occur between 'crime rates' calculated not only from different courts but also in different regions. Simply comparing prosecutions of one jurisdiction, such as that of the assizes, may be fundamentally flawed as not all assize courts in England necessarily dealt with a similar cross-section of unlawful behaviour.[58]

We might wish to know something of Cheshire's economic profile. In very general terms, Cheshire may be described as 'pastoral vale country'. Cheshire was renowned for its cheeses and for the rearing and fattening of cattle. Cheese production was most common in the south and west of the county, and although much cheese was marketed in London and the Home Counties, the greatest part of Cheshire's cheese was sold locally. Large-scale beef production was also important to the county's economy, with thousands of cattle being sold on the Midland and Home Counties markets after being reared and/or fattened in north Cheshire. Only in the Wirral, the peninsula in the north west of the county, did arable land form a major determinant of the local economy. Around the county borders in the east, there were areas of moorland, hence the preponderance of marl pits in that area. Small areas of wood-pasture land were dotted throughout the county, in addition to the important forests of Delamere and Macclesfield and large heaths such as those at Knutsford and Rudheath. In the north east of the county and Macclesfield forest, sheep, horses and pigs were additionally important.[59]

Chester was the only city in the county. It had 4,000 or 5,000 inhabitants in the mid-sixteenth century and almost 10,000 by 1664, by which time the population of Nantwich was just under 3,000 and that of Macclesfield over 2,500. Congleton and Stockport had between 1,500 and 2,000 inhabitants. The remaining Cheshire towns were smaller, with fewer than 1,000 inhabitants each.[60] There were thirteen market towns in the county for which Chester acted as the distributive centre: Nantwich, Macclesfield, Congleton, Knutsford, Middlewich, Northwich, Altrincham, Stockport and Sandbach

---

[58] L.A. Knafla, ' "Sin of all sorts swarmeth": criminal litigation in an English county in the early seventeenth century', in E.W. Ives and A.H. Manchester eds., *Law, Litigants and the Legal Profession* (London, 1983), 50–67. Mercer, 'Crime in late-seventeenth-century Yorkshire'.

[59] Dore, *Cheshire*, 13; Higgins, 'County government', 3–4; Howard Hodson, *Cheshire 1660–1780: Restoration to Industrial Revolution* (Chester, 1978), 93; Ingham, *Cheshire*, 263–5; Phillips and Smith, *Lancashire and Cheshire*, 28–9; Joan Thirsk, *England's Agricultural Regions and Agrarian History, 1500–1750* (London, 1987), 38–9, 41–4.

[60] Hodson, *Cheshire*, 93.

in the south and east of the county, and Frodsham, Malpas, Halton and Tarvin in the west. Each of these towns was important to the local market economy, holding busy markets each week and at least one annual fair that lasted between one and three days. Chester held markets on Wednesdays and Saturdays, and enjoyed two annual fairs. In addition to the towns, a number of populous townships were scattered throughout eastern Cheshire. For example, Rainow near Bollington, Sutton near Macclesfield, and Bollin and Pownall Fees in Wilmslow parish were not large enough to form towns as such, yet all were integrated and industrialising communities in the seventeenth century.[61]

By the early seventeenth century, there were about sixty different crafts or occupations in Chester although these were predominantly related to the provision of food, clothes and domestic equipment for local markets. Chester was the largest centre for the Cheshire leather trades. Leather craftsmen formed the largest male occupational group in the city – roughly twenty per cent of all freemen were engaged in branches of the trade. The leather trades also thrived in Congleton, where the main leather market was held, and Macclesfield. Even in Nantwich and Sandbach, where there were fewer tanneries, a large number of the local inhabitants got their livings in the various trades associated with the leather industries. Tanners, shoemakers, cordwainers and cobblers were all prominent in Nantwich, along with glovers, who constituted a smaller specialist group of artisans. Tanning could be a lucrative trade: Hugh Worthington, a Wilmslow tanner whose inventory was proved in 1669, was worth £1,200 when he died. His goods and chattels included twenty cattle, £189 in ready gold and silver, and £275 in leather. In Congleton, too, tanners and skinners figured prominently amongst the more substantial taxpayers.[62]

Another industry for which the county was renowned was salt. Nantwich was the centre of the salt industry up until the later seventeenth century. In the late sixteenth century, there were over 200 salt houses in Nantwich alone, with about 100 in both Northwich and Middlewich. Only after 1670, when the discovery of rock-salt in Northwich led to the development of a more commercially viable method of creating salt than the boiling and evaporation of sea water, did Nantwich lose its central importance in the trade. Women rarely 'occupied' the wich-houses, in which brine was evaporated for making salt: in the early seventeenth century, only two of seventy-one occupiers in Nantwich were female, and only four of thirty-two in Middlewich. Women were, however, employed alongside men as wallers, an occupation that

---

[61] Hall, *Nantwich*, 81; Harrison et al., 18; Higgins, 'County government', 11–12; Hodson, *Cheshire*, 93–4.
[62] Hall, *Nantwich*, 270–1; Harrison et al., *Loyal Chester*, 10–11; Higgins, 'County government', 4–5; Hodson, *Cheshire*, 75, 140; Phillips and Smith, *Lancashire and Cheshire*, 46–7.

entailed heavy and dangerous work: they gathered salt from the bottom of large barrels of boiling sea water with wooden rakes, and then deposited it into wicker baskets from which the surplus water could drain leaving a residue of salt at the bottom. The inflated number of single women living in the salt towns suggests that the industry did provide major female employment.[63]

The weaving and stocking trades were common in the south and east of the county, although in the City of Chester those craftsmen involved in textiles and weaving were amongst the most substantial freemen, along with merchants and ironmongers, often holding the office of mayor in the early seventeenth century. The linen industry was especially associated with Stockport (a town also renowned for its hat manufacture) and Wilmslow. The cloth trades in general were well represented in Cheshire by the early seventeenth century, although it never developed into a major textile centre. It has been estimated that in the late sixteenth and early seventeenth centuries, nearly a third of the Cheshire population were employed in domestic industry and piece-work, spinning and weaving flax and hemp. Since the sixteenth century, silk and mohair buttons were manufactured in Macclesfield. While 'skilled' male workers produced the button moulds and metal backs in small workshops, most of the work was undertaken by women and children under the putting-out system.[64] There was also some small-scale coal mining in the north and east of Cheshire, into which part of the north west coalfield extended, such as at Worth in Poynton and Stockport. In addition, the Neston area in the north east constituted one end of the north Wales coalfield. While Cheshire's coal production did not approximate anything like that of Lancashire and north Wales, its existence was important locally.[65]

Like other northern counties, such as Lancashire and Yorkshire, Cheshire was relatively poor. It consistently had one of the lowest taxation rates in England: in the Poll Tax of 1641, only seven English counties had a lower assessment rate, and for Ship Money, only six. With two-thirds of the gentry being worth less than £500 *per annum* in the early seventeenth century, the average Cheshire gentleman was worth half as much as many of his counterparts in the south east. Cheshire gentlemen were nonetheless major landowners. For example, Sir Henry Delves in 1663 was the sole landowner in seventeen of the eighteen townships of Wybunbury parish. In the first half of the seventeenth century, the lower gentry and wealthier yeomen of Cheshire do seem to have improved their lot, prospering through cattle

[63] Hall, *Nantwich*, 254–5; Higgins, 'County government', 9; Phillips and Smith, *Lancashire and Cheshire*, 50–2.
[64] Hodson, *Cheshire*, 145–50, 138; Gail Malmgreen, *Silk Town: Industry and Culture in Macclesfield, 1750–1835* (Hull, 1985), 10.
[65] Phillips and Smith, *Lancashire and Cheshire*, 47–8.

farming as the prices of milk, cheese, meat and hides rose, along with the rental value of land.[66] During a period in which some members of the gentry were becoming more affluent, other middling people and the lower orders suffered from the economic climate. One study of the parish of Mottram-in-Longdendale in the north eastern tip of the county has shown that between 1570 and 1680 cattle herd sizes became increasingly smaller. Rising inflation and a decline in real wages caused especial difficulties in the industrialising pastoral areas of eastern and north eastern Cheshire. In 1673, when between three and five hearths were necessary for a household to be considered comfortably off, ninety-four per cent of Congleton households had two hearths or less, and forty-five per cent were exempt from the hearth tax altogether. In Chester, forty-one per cent of households were too poor to be taxed. Of those that were not exempt, forty-six per cent had only one hearth, and a further twenty-one per cent had two.[67] A great part of the population lived only marginally above the basic level of subsistence. Given that there was very little arable land in the county, it is not surprising that Cheshire appears to have suffered from the dearths of the 1590s, 1621–3 and 1647–9.[68] For instance, wheat cost from between 43 shillings and 4 marks (£2 13s. 4d.) per bushel in the dearth year of 1597, but a mere 3s. 8d. in the 'plentiful' year of 1625. There were similar differentials in the prices of equal measures of other commodities in the respective years. Rye cost between 42s. and 44s. in 1597 and 2s. 8d. in 1625. Peas and beans cost up to 32s. in 1597 but only 2s. 8d. in 1625. Malt cost as much as 40s. and 4s. respectively, barley 30s. and 2s. 6d., oats 20s. and 2s., and ale a groat (4d.) and 2d. a quart. A Cheshire labourer might earn something in the region of 6d. daily with food and drink, or 10d. daily without. A woman in service, even 'of the best sort', probably earned less than 40s. *per annum*, while the City of Chester wage assessment stated that a female servant of 'the third sort' should earn only 20s. annually. Even the daily wages of an artisan have been estimated at a mere 7d. ob. In Chester, in 1597, the highest annual wage, for master craftsmen, was £5. No wonder the prices of that year were described as 'very fearful'.[69] For most early modern Cestrians, life was undoubtedly hard. Relative poverty is potentially relevant to the nature of crimes committed and prosecuted, and to crime's gendered nature. This

---

[66] Higgins, 'County government', 45, 37–9, 49–50, 235; Hodson, *Cheshire*, 73–4.
[67] Hodson, *Cheshire*, 95–7; Roger Wilbraham, cited in Hall, *Nantwich*, 207.
[68] Parish Register of Nantwich, cited in Hall, *Nantwich*, 111–12; Richard Wilbraham's Journal, cited in Hall, *Nantwich*, 111–12; Harrison et al., *Tudor Chester*, 18; Joyce Powell, 'The parish of Mottram-in-Longdendale, 1570–1680', Local History Certificate dissertation, University of Manchester (1976), cited in Hodson, *Cheshire*, 76. For other commentators on the hardness of the times, Hodson, *Cheshire*, 111–13; Higgins, 'County government', 56.
[69] Hall, *Nantwich*, 111–13, 122; Harrison et al., *Tudor Chester*, 18, 24; Higgins, 'County government', 56–7.

study, however, places poverty as a backdrop to criminal activity rather than seeking to establish causal connections.

THE SCOPE OF THIS BOOK

Throughout the analyses in this book, I have tried to illuminate the marriage of discourse and practice. What follows is thus not about abstract ideas of gender and crime, but about how those ideas impacted on prosecutions, verdicts and sentences. A major theme is the relative leniency or harshness with which women were treated compared to men within the legal process. Throughout the book, I challenge the ways in which historians have conventionally depicted male and female offenders without attending to the contexts of particular crimes and misdemeanours. The book raises issues about the centrality of the early modern household to understandings and practices of criminal behaviour. It also considers some of the wider implications of civil war for perceptions of criminal behaviour.

In chapters two and three, I deal respectively with male and female non-lethal violence. I ask questions about the 'styles' of violence attributed to men and women and about how violence was understood in terms of gendered concepts. I am particularly interested in how certain discourses hindered and facilitated complaints and justifications of violent acts, how these discourses operated differently for women and for men, with practical repercussions, and how they changed over time. Chapter four considers homicide, investigating the ways in which the categories of culpability inscribed in law were not equally applicable to women and to men, and what this meant in practice for suspects. In chapter five, I turn to theft and related offences such as receiving stolen goods. Again, gendered assumptions made by contemporaries and historians are interrogated in the light of evidence of what women and men actually did. Different sorts of theft are considered in the light of their own histories, the extent to which they had gendered associations, and the practical implications of such associations. The sixth chapter investigates issues of authority, agency and law. Here, I focus on several aspects of plebeian use of the law, in particular concerning bastard-bearing, requesting permission to build cottages on common land, and involvement in forcible rescue, to ask broader questions about the agency of early modern people who operated within a hierarchical social order.

2

Men's non-lethal violence

'Menacing layeth together fire and coals in the house of peace, assault bloweth it and maketh it burn. And battery doth endeavour to consume the whole building to the ground.'[1] Early modern legal classifications of non-lethal violence perceived bodily harm and aggressive words and gestures not as separate categories, but to lie upon a continuum of violence.[2] Threatening words, attempted harm by force and violence, and battery involving actual loss or injury were 'things of several natures'. Yet their purpose was the same: 'to hurt him against whom they are bent'. 'Bitter' or 'disgrace[ful]' speeches were not merely like 'smoke, a breath, or blast of wind' that would 'vanish and be dispersed in the air like dust'. Verbal abuses constituted 'the chief impediment' to the peace of the realm. They were 'firebrands' to 'grudges, quarrels, conspiracies', to 'assaults, batteries, riots, routs, unlawful assemblies, forces, and forcible entries...forgeries, perjuries, and oppressions', and to 'most other tragical and turbulent stratagems', including 'mayhems, manslaughters and murders'.[3]

To some extent, modern opinion also places violent deeds and words on a continuum. Historians have nonetheless tended not to conceptualise physical and non-physical violence like this, approaching them instead as distinct and separate activities. Further dichotomies are frequently mapped onto those of deeds and words: violent/non-violent, active/passive, serious/trivial, masculine/feminine. Explicitly or by implication, men's aggressive behaviour is characterised as physical, active and potentially serious; women's as verbal, non-'active' and trivial. Men's behaviours have thus become the benchmark of violence while women's violence is effaced. These categorisations are typical of assumptions about violence and gender that masquerade as 'common sense', seeming thereby to require no justification. In this and the following chapter, I scrutinise common assumptions in order to distinguish between

---

[1] Pulton, *De Pace Regis*, fo. 1v.
[2] Pulton, *De Pace Regis*, fo. 1v; Dalton, *Countrey Justice*, 160.
[3] Pulton, *De Pace Regis*, fos. 1–2v; William Lambarde, *Eirenarcha, or the Office of Justices of Peace* (London, 1581), 134–6.

the valid, less valid, and erroneous conclusions to which historians have come.

A further aim is to explore the meanings that early modern people attached to violence. Here, practices and discourses are not easily separated. Ideas about violence were not homogenous. Nor were they determined solely by categories such as gender or class. Verbal, physical and symbolic acts of violence, speech about those acts, and any ensuing litigation all involved negotiation. Violence was rewarded and deprecated, legalised and outlawed according to individual, social and historical context. I deploy the term 'violence' in the wide sense appropriate to early modern legal and social usage, which included the perpetrator's intention (to control, intimidate, punish or harm) and accompanying emotion as well as any damage inflicted. In this chapter, I consider first how we might 'measure' non-lethal violence in the past, whether perpetrated by men or by women, by using the records of early modern criminal courts. I then discuss men's violence towards men and towards women respectively. Women's violence is discussed in chapter three.

MEASURING VIOLENCE

Historiographically, early modern violence has primarily been 'measured' quantitatively. Simple aggregates invariably show that men were the great majority, typically eighty to ninety per cent, of violent offenders.[4] Cheshire prosecutions for non-lethal violence against the person were no exception (see Table 2.1). Such figures are usually presented as unproblematic evidence of men's greater propensity for violence across the ages, and are not contextualised historically. Thus, assault (like homicide and other 'serious' offences) was 'overwhelmingly' and self-explanatorily male.[5]

Table 2.1 shows the numbers of men and women prosecuted at the Cheshire quarter and great sessions for simple or aggravated assault and those bound over by recognisance to keep the peace or to be of good behaviour towards other people. Indictments for assault and bindings over were the principal means whereby 'menacings [threats]... affrays, assaults,

---

[4] J.M. Beattie, 'The criminality of women in eighteenth-century England', *Journal of Social History* 8 (1974–75), 81–2; J.M. Beattie, *Crime and the Courts in England* (Oxford, 1986); Olwen Hufton, 'Women and violence in early modern Europe' in Fia Dieteren and Els Kloek eds., *Writing Women into History* (Amsterdam, 1991), 77; J.A. Sharpe, *Crime in Early Modern England*, 2nd edn (London, 1999), 154–5, 159–60; Robert B. Shoemaker, 'Reforming male manners: public insult and the decline of violence in London, 1660–1740' in Tim Hitchcock and Michèle Cohen eds., *English Masculinities, 1660–1800* (London, 1999), 133; Pieter Spierenburg, 'How violent were women? Court cases in Amsterdam, 1650–1810', *Crime, Histoire et Sociétés/Crime, History and Societies* 1, 1 (1997), 13.
[5] Sharpe, *Crime*, 154–5; David T. Courtwright, *Violent Land: Single Men and Social Disorder from the Frontier to the Inner City* (London, 1996), 9.

Table 2.1 *Defendants in cases of non-lethal violence*

Process	Female	Male	Total
Indictments for assault/assault & battery	231 (19.2%)	970 (80.8%)	1,201
Recognisances for the peace/good behaviour	784 (20.6%)	3,025 (79.4%)	3,809
Total	1,015 (20.3%)	3,995 (79.7%)	5,010

injurious and violent handlings, and misentreatings of the person, batteries, malicious strikings, *et cetera*' came before the courts.[6] Quarter sessions and assizes were, however, just two among numerous tribunals authorised to hear such cases. In Kent, for example, certain local courts (hundred, borough, town, market and marsh) dealt with three times as many offences against the person as did quarter sessions and assizes combined. If figures for manor courts and the central courts of star chamber and king's bench were included, the proportion of total cases of this kind heard at quarter and assizes would be smaller still.[7] Furthermore, numerous other offences, such as frequently prosecuted misdemeanours concerning damage to property, involved interpersonal violence too. Measuring the incidence of prosecutions for violence against the person (let alone violent behaviour *per se*) is not a simple exercise.

Evaluating the extent and nature of violence used against the person in individual cases is even less straightforward. The content and form of bills of indictment were determined by legal conventions, categories and procedures. The descriptive value of indictments could pertain more to law than to the incident referred to. An indictment 'ought to be framed so near the truth as may be'. But this was no general or absolute version of truth, but 'all the truth *that by law is requisite*', for 'every part of the indictment material ought to be found [*billa vera*] by the oath of the jurors'. This impinged upon what was included and excluded. An indictment founded upon statute law, for instance, had to include the material words of the relevant statute. But an erroneous phrase or mis-spelt word – in the medieval Latin of legal documents, unlike the vernacular, spelling was standardised – could render the indictment void. The greater the detail, the greater the potential for error.

---

[6] Lambarde, *Eirenarcha*, 135.
[7] Louis A. Knafla, ' "Sin of all sorts swarmeth": criminal litigation in an English county in the early seventeenth century', in E.W. Ives and A.H. Manchester eds., *Law, Litigants and the Legal Profession* (London, 1983). *Kent at Law, 1602. Vol. I, The County Jurisdiction: Assizes and Sessions of the Peace*, ed. Louis A. Knafla (London, 1994).

Manuals for Justices of the peace and lawyers provided document templates and advised brevity.[8] Indictments for assault rarely deviated from minimal formulaic phrasing even to allege that injuries were 'perilous' or 'grievous'; fewer than ten per cent of indictments indicated that blood had been drawn.[9]

Nor can the perceived gravity of violent acts routinely be read from the categories under which defendants were prosecuted. Technically, law differentiated between 'assault' (threatened or attempted harm), 'affray' (putting people in fear by demeanour or actions, but not words alone), and 'battery' (actual bodily harm). In practice, distinctions between and within these categories were unclear.[10] Clerks habitually recorded 'assault and affray' in formal Books of Indictments, for instance, when prosecutions were actually for battery.[11] Battery itself might refer to an affront such as tweaking someone's nose, a slap on the face, bludgeoning someone senseless with a cudgel or even attempted rape or murder.[12]

The cheapest, most convenient, and most commonly used legal sanction against violence towards the person was binding over by recognisance. Recognisances for the peace or good behaviour were ostensibly granted to provide security against present or future danger, not to punish past wrongdoing.[13] Yet past abuses often constituted reasonable fear of further harm. The range of conduct leading to requests for bindings over was incredibly wide.[14] The drafting of recognisances and the warrants that precipitated them were subject to fewer legal strictures than indictments.[15] They are potentially more informative, but are not systematically so, for the amount of detail included varied regionally, temporally and according to the habit and inclination of individual JPs and their clerks.

Narrative accounts of interpersonal violence in examinations, depositions, petitions, letters, and so forth, provide the richest evidence of the nature and

---

[8] Dalton, *Countrey Justice*, 365; my italic. Lambarde, *Eirenarcha*, 383–402.
[9] For exceptions see CRO, QJF 51/1/28 (1622); QJF 55/3/3 (1626); QJF 81/2/39 (1653); QJF 89/4/121 (1662).
[10] Coke, *Third Part of the Institutes*, 158; Dalton, *Countrey Justice*, 177, 33, 34; Matthew Hale, *Pleas of the Crown* (London, 1678), 113; Pulton, *De Pace Regis*, fos. 2v–3r, 5r; Lambarde, *Eirenarcha*, 134–6; Robert B. Shoemaker, *Prosecution and Punishment*.
[11] For example, CRO, QJB 2/4, fo. 52r; see also CRO, QJF 29/3/8 (1599); QJB 2/6, fos. 128r, 129v; see also CRO, QJF 83/2/29–/31, /45 (1653); PRO, CHES 21/4, fo. 164r; see also CHES 24/127/1/175 (1648).
[12] For example, PRO, CHES 24/127/1/293 (1648); CHES 24/116/4 (1622), indictment of Thomas Barber; CRO, QJF 25/4/20 (1596); QJF 51/2/95 (1622); QJF 81/4/12, 26 (1651).
[13] Dalton, *Countrey Justice*, 144.
[14] The remit for binding over to good behaviour was broader than that for the peace. Dalton, *Countrey Justice*, 169–75; Pulton, *De Pace Regis*, fos. 18, 22.
[15] Pulton, *De Pace Regis*, fo. 18; Dalton, *Countrey Justice*, 335–9; Lambarde, *Eirenarcha*, 80–132.

degree of violence inflicted and the meanings ascribed to it. Yet here, too, the terminology of violence was often opaque. Terms like 'violence' and 'strike' were imprecise. 'Violence' denoted aggressive or intimidating speech or gestures as well as varying degrees of physical force. It could, however, imply the perceived illegitimacy of the action.[16] 'Striking' incorporated a multitude of ways of hitting someone with or without a weapon. If the latter, we are rarely able to distinguish between, say, a half-hearted slap with the back of the hand and a full-blown punch. A 'blow' similarly denoted violent application of either fist or weapon. Other terms were more specific and sometimes connoted the emotion accompanying the deed. To 'spurn' was to kick hard with contempt. To 'tread on' someone was to trample or crush them underfoot with contemptuous cruelty. To 'pull' or 'pluck' was to drag (a person, their clothing, or whatever) with considerable force. To pull someone by the ear, nose, or hair of the head was an act of chastisement or insult depending on context. The expression 'to box [slap about] the ears' was another gesture of reprehension used to '*rebuke* or *correct* another for some saucy speech or action'.[17] None of these terms was ascribed particularly to men although, by the later seventeenth century, men are occasionally said to have thrown 'punches'. Even biting and scratching were not gender-specific. Biting was acknowledged as a form of male defence in battle. Knocking out a man's front teeth was therefore classified as mayhem, an aggravated injury that hindered his ability to serve in wartime.[18] In general, though, fighting with teeth and, especially, nails was considered 'unmanly'. John Bulwer asserted that 'Fury hath furnished all men with weapons', but left the nail (and the tongue) to 'the impotent part of humanity': namely, 'children and vixens'.[19] Nonetheless, although the meanings ascribed to scratching and biting were gendered, the acts themselves were attributed to both sexes. On its own, the language of assault fails to reveal much about what was peculiarly masculine about violence.

Allegations of armed assault do not take us much further. The stock phrase '*vi et armis*, viz. *cum gladiis baculis*' ('by force and arms, namely with swords, staves') or other suchlike weapons, had, by the fifteenth century, evolved into a legal fiction which insinuated or strengthened allegations of force and violence. After 1545, however, when it ceased to be an essential component of indictments for trespass, the literal meaning of the phrase was somewhat revived. Hence, it was 'not amiss to use those words, so long

---

[16] Susan Dwyer Amussen, 'Punishment, discipline and power: the social meanings of violence in early modern England', *Journal of British Studies* 34, 1 (1995), 2–4.
[17] John Bulwer, *Chirologia: or the Natural Language of the Hand* (London, 1644), 64; original italic.
[18] Pulton, *De Pace Regis*, fo. 15v.
[19] Bulwer, *Chirologia*, 65, 138. CRO, QJF 81/4/102 (1654).

as the circumstances of the fact do require them'.[20] About forty per cent of seventeenth-century bills of indictment alleged the use of weapons. In Cheshire, as elsewhere, women constituted a minority of defendants: four and a half times as many men as women were prosecuted for armed assault.[21] Yet comparing male and female violence in absolute terms obscures important similarities. Women and men's relative participation in armed assaults was almost identical: four out of ten women and four out of ten men.[22] Evidence concerning incidents involving weapons leading to bindings over by recognisance suggests a similar parity. Where groups of alleged assailants were involved, indictments for assault are generally silent about their relative roles. Distinctions were made between principals and accomplices only in special circumstances such as mayhem.[23]

References in indictments to specific weapons cannot be taken at face value, of course. Specificity is lost in the translation of vernacular terms into Latin for the legal record and then back into the vernacular by the historian. Daggers and knives of all types, for instance, were rendered as *cultellis*, irrespective of whether the blade in question was 'a great arming dagger', a butcher's knife or a lady's pocket-knife. The terms *bacillum*, *baculum* and *fustis* translate respectively as a staff or stick, a staff or cudgel, and a staff, cudgel or club.[24] Many seventeenth-century indictments purport that 'swords and staves', 'swords and daggers' or 'staves and daggers' were used, usually with an additional weapon. This was not always formulaic: Raphe Leycester, esquire, for example, allegedly pierced his opponent's belly inflicting a six-inch-deep sword wound.[25] For the most part, though, the use of 'swords', at least, was probably a residue from the pre-1545 legal fiction. Most men and all women were legally prohibited from carrying a sword or rapier. Even if people wished to flout the law, swords were expensive. Moreover, given that three or more weapons were usually listed on indictments, even manually dextrous individuals were unlikely to wield simultaneously a sword, a staff and, say, a pitchfork. In contrast, a variety of staves and knives designed for non-violent purposes were inexpensive and readily available. Indeed, everybody – male and female – carried a knife.[26] The additional third or

---

[20] Statute 37 Hen.VIII, c.8 (1545); Phillipa C. Maddern, *Violence and the Social Order: East Anglia, 1422–1442* (Oxford, 1992), 29; Dalton, *Countrey Justice*, 364; Lambarde, *Eirenarcha*, 401; Pulton, *De Pace Regis*, fo. 174v.

[21] See also Beattie, 'Criminality of women', 82–9; Shoemaker, *Prosecution and Punishment*, 213; Wiener, 'Sex roles and crime', 39, 47–9.

[22] 41.6 per cent of female and 43.5 per cent of male defendants were accused of armed assault. See also Finch, 'Women and violence in the later Middle Ages', 29.

[23] For example, PRO, CHES 24/102/3, indictment of Richard and Simon Harecourt (1591); CHES 24/104/1, indictment of Richard Starkey et al. (1595). For mayhem, see Pulton, *De Pace Regis*, fos. 15–17.

[24] *Thomae Thomasii Dictionarium* (London, 1587).   [25] CRO, QJF 55/3/3 (1626).

[26] Knives could be worth as little as 1*d*. or as much as several shillings. PRO, CHES 24/133/1, coroners' inquisitions re. Booth and Bradford (1661).

alternative weapons cited on indictments suggest the same. Only occasionally were these military weapons, such as canons or halberds (a spear-cum-battle-axe mounted on a handle five to seven feet long).[27] Several incidents involved 'long staves', or 'staves fortified with iron tips', which probably referred to the traditional weapon of the peasantry, the quarterstaff (a stout pole, six to eight feet in length, and tipped with iron).[28] Frequently weapons took the form of cudgels (clubs), billhooks (heavy, hooked, choppers for pruning and cutting brushwood; Cheshire billhooks had a back as well as a front edge) or pitchforks ('pikels' in local parlance). But any common tool would do: a spade, a whip, 'a hoe or mattock with iron teeth', 'a broach or spit', even 'a stirrup-leather'.[29] All these items came within the legal definition of offensive and defensive weapons, which included tools and implements of all kinds, the 'casting of stones or blocks, pouring of hot coals, scalding water or lead', and indeed 'any thing that a man wears for his defence, or takes into his hands, or useth in his wrath to cast at, or strike another'.[30] Evidence from recognisances, examinations and depositions confirms the basic pattern while expanding the variety of implements. A labourer who was bound over 'dares not carry his ordinary tools and implements wherewith he useth to labour and get his living...lest he should incur the danger of the forfeiture' of the recognisance.[31] In sum, people used as weapons whatever came to hand. While this might suggest a certain spontaneity in the use of arms, it lends no weight to the view that early modern people were prone to spontaneous outbursts of violence. Given that nearly everybody had recourse to 'weapons', we might wonder that so few people employed them to injure, maim or kill.[32]

Narrative conventions

Legal narratives in the form of examinations, depositions, petitions and letters provide the richest evidence of the meanings of violence. Each of these classes of document constituted a genre in its own right. Moreover, descriptions of violence, and the meanings intended and inferred from them, varied according to the context in which they were uttered and heard. Certain characteristics can nevertheless be identified as common to all these forms.

---

[27] CRO, QJF 23/1/27 (1593), PRO, CHES 24/132/3, presentment of Edward Crymes (1659).
[28] For example, CRO, QJF 23/1/27 (1593); QJF 49/1/48 (1620); QJF 49/2/117 (1620); QJF 53/2/33 (1624); QJF 55/2/13 (1626); QJF 76/4/2 (1649).
[29] CRO, QJF 77/4/3 (1650); PRO, CHES 24/118/3, indictment of Edward and John Broadhurst (1626); CHES 24/118/3, indictment of Thomas and William Dod (1626); CRO, QJF 75/1/165 (1647); QJF 77/2/15 (1649).
[30] Pulton, *De Pace Regis*, fos. 4v, 40v; Thomas Blount, *Nomo-lexikon: A Law Dictionary* (London, 1670).
[31] CRO, QJF 51/1/135 (1622).   [32] Maddern, *Violence and the Social Order*, 20.

Accounts generated by legal processes adhered to general conventions that were embedded in popular legal discourse. These were intended to throw a favourable light on one party and to undermine the other, as the following case demonstrates. Prosecuted at Over Court on May Day 1620 for arrears of rent, Raphe Nixon *alias* Buckley compounded with Adam Cragg, his landlord's bailiff. If Nixon pleaded guilty he could have three further weeks in which to find the money to pay. Nixon duly confessed. But Cragg afterwards went 'secretly' to the steward and procured a warrant of distraint, and went with his fellow, Robert Buckley, to execute the warrant on Nixon's cattle. Nixon described what happened. His wife Margaret took hold of Cragg's horse's bridle,

and desired him with pitiful requests to turn again and not to serve [the warrant]. But her requests were nothing regarded but very rudely [Cragg] rode over her and all to tore her clothes and hurt her body with his horse's foot; and she being conceived with child, with this rude and ill useration and offer when she would [merely] have saved her cattle from serving, Adam Cragg drew his sword and did wound her and strive her ill, and cut off one of her fingers on her right hand to her great hindrance, and caused the conceived seed to swerve in her womb, and she stood in great danger of her life the same night.

Cragg also 'wounded and struck' Nixon, who had nothing to defend himself with but 'a little walking-staff about a yard long'. Robert Buckley threatened that Raphe and Margaret Nixon 'should be worse dealt with yet, and worse used'. Cragg declared that Margaret 'had a stout heart but... we will have her broken'.

First, Raphe Nixon implied that Cragg had assaulted without any 'just cause' or provocation. What amounted to 'just cause' was, of course, a matter of opinion. The phrase usually meant that no provocative words or deeds had been offered at the time of the incident; any history of conflict was conveniently disregarded. Margaret Nixon merely 'would have saved her cattle'. From a bailiff's perspective, this attempted rescue was a disorderly and criminal act. But Nixon evoked an alternative discourse of rescue in which her actions were constructed as reasonable and positive means of conserving and protecting household resources.[33] Margaret held on to Cragg's horse's bridle, sure enough, but she entreated Cragg with 'pitiful requests', suggesting thereby that she was both appealing for Cragg's pity and compassion and a fitting object of it. Instead, Cragg drew his sword and brutally assaulted her. We shall see later that women were frequently portrayed as passive and suffering victims of male violence. This positioning of the protagonists relates to another common narrative strategy, that of claiming the moral high ground. Nixon portrayed Cragg drawing his sword

---

[33] On rescue see below, pp. 249–62.

Men's non-lethal violence   31

on a defenceless woman and an (almost) unarmed man. Furthermore, Nixon honoured an agreement that Cragg broke. Breaking a promise implied untrustworthiness and unreliability, which undermined a person's social and economic credit. A further general convention was to discredit one's adversary by labelling them as any manner of 'common' disturber of the peace: barrator, scold, drunkard, brawler, night-walker, idle-body, keeper of a disorderly or unlicensed alehouse, or other such disruptive, dissolute person. Several witnesses deposed that Raphe and Margaret Nixon were 'not of good fame, nor honest conversation, but evil doers, rioters and perturbers of the peace'.

The efficacy of legal stories of violence depended as much, and sometimes more, on the relative social credit of the parties than on the nature or extent of the actual force used. It would have been difficult to discern whether Cragg's abuse had caused Margaret Nixon to miscarry, for her pregnancy was no further developed than a 'conceived seed'.[34] The claim that her finger had been amputated was more verifiable, and directly adversely affected her ability to fulfil her duties as a husbandman's wife.[35] Yet when Margaret craved the protection of the peace against Cragg and Buckley at the quarter sessions she was turned down. Instead, she and her husband were bound over to be of their good behaviour towards Cragg. This was not necessarily because Margaret's injuries had been exaggerated, for three months later she successfully indicted Cragg for the assault. Explanations perhaps lie elsewhere. Cragg and Buckley, remember, were servants of Nixon's landlord, Sir Randle Mainwaring, a notable Justice. The debt for which Cragg sued Nixon at Over Court was for rent owed to Mainwaring. Moreover, Buckley had an interest in the land that Nixon currently held. Mainwaring conveniently was sitting on the quarter sessions bench that denied Margaret the protection of the peace.[36] The fact of the violence was one consideration among many and, from certain perspectives, probably not the most important.

Legal stories were also spun around the particulars of legal provision. Certain forms of aggravated assault were inscribed in law. For instance, legislation of 1553 stipulated that the penalty for armed assault and battery in a church or churchyard was the cutting off of the offender's ear.[37] Although by the later sixteenth century the courts tended to fine rather than mutilate offenders, bills of indictment continued to include details of such acts as a

---

[34] See below, pp. 60–3.   [35] See also CRO, QJF 76/2/34 (1648).
[36] CRO, QJF 49/1/152, /92, /93, /24, QJF 49/2/171 (1620); PRO, CHES 21/3, fos. 42r, 46r; PRO, CHES 24/115/3, CHES 24/115/4. See also CRO, QJF 55/1/97 (1626); QJF 49/3/80 (1620), QJF 89/3/31 (1661).
[37] Statute 5 & 6 Edward VI, c.4. Pulton, *De Pace Regis*, fo. 8v. Conviction before the church courts carried the penalty of excommunication; CDRO, EDC 5/1669/11.

means of exacerbating the sense that good order had been violated.[38] Being beaten in one's own house or on one's land magnified the damage done to one's dignity and reputation.[39] But law did not provide the whole context. Neither the use of weapons, nor the extent of wounds, nor other aggravating circumstances had a straightforward relation to the perceived gravity of an offence.[40]

There were many dimensions to the ascription of 'seriousness'. Social, economic and political relationships, local or national politics, individual enmities or attachments, and categories of difference such as class and gender, all intersected with law to produce particular stories and outcomes. Individual opinions played their part too. William and Jane Bennett agreed that Mary Jeynson had been 'very violent' towards Jane Cornell in July 1667. However, whereas William deposed that Jeynson took Cornell by the arms and shook her so that she fell down, Jane deposed that Jeynson shook Cornell and then 'threw' her down, which is not quite the same thing.[41] Jane Bennett ascribed greater force to Jeynson's act than her husband did. Perhaps this was related to gender – men, as we shall see, were often ambivalent in depicting feminine violence.

Speech about violence drew upon a wide range of concepts, images, metaphors, vocabulary and schema that were part of, and conditioned by, various sets of ideas about gender, class, law, religion and more. Discourses of 'righteous' as well as 'wrongful' violence existed. Violence on the part of the state, manifested in formal punishments, for example, or in military combat, was conceptualised as 'righteous', as was the correction of wayward subordinates within the household or workshop. Violence in the name of religion was similarly acceptable: 'The Lord', after all, 'is a man of war' (Exodus 15:3). One fable instructed that reciting the gospel alone would not prevent a vicious dog from attacking, it 'being incapable of religion'. However, the combination of the gospel and a well-aimed stone 'did the deed. The curs of the Antichrist are not afraid of our gospel, but of our stones: let us fight, and they will fly.'[42]

If we attend to the multiple discourses with which early modern people spoke, we may discern how they constituted and positioned themselves as subjects. Women and men were not simply defined by gendered language and concepts; they utilised words and ideas in attempts to define themselves and others according to the context in which they acted and spoke, and

---

[38] For example, CRO, QJF 23/3/8 (1593); QJF 23/4/10 (1594); PRO, CHES 24/134/2, presentment of Peter Haslewell (1663); CHES 24/136/3, presentment of Thomas Breech (1669).
[39] For example, CRO, QJF 23/4/14 (1594); QJF 29/2/24 (1599).
[40] Fines are also unhelpful as they tended to be adjusted according to paying capacity.
[41] CRO, QJF 95/2/98, /93 (1667).
[42] Thomas Adams, *The Soldiers Honour* (London, 1617), sig. B1v.

their intentions. Not everyone spoke or acted from equivalent positions of advantage, however. The availability or otherwise of languages of violence also affected the likelihood of complaints being made. Having dealt with these general issues, we shall now turn to their inscription in particular contexts: male-on-male violence and male violence against women.

VIOLENCE AND MANHOOD

Here, I consider the relationships between violence and manhood, particularly the discourses that hindered and permitted complaints and justifications of particular forms of male aggression. Men comprised four-fifths of those prosecuted for assault; in eighty per cent of these cases, their victims were male too.[43] Even allowing for the under-representation of women and the predominance of household groups among defendants, violence and masculinity seem connected. Certain historians have taken apparent connections at face value, and endorsed what sounds suspiciously like a transhistorical notion of machismo.[44] Others have identified violence as a means of attaining manhood and affirming it publicly, but have seldom interrogated 'violence' itself as a category.[45] Either way, conceptions of masculine honour tend to be underpinned by an assumption of the self-knowing, autonomous individual. In some circumstances honour pertained to the individual, although differently perhaps from modern notions of individual identity.

In the following pages, I discuss the articulation and conceptualisation of male-on-male violence within four discursive fields. These are the relation between manhood and household; the construction of the 'man of honour' that was formalised in homicide law; the implications of hierarchy and status; and models of manhood that privileged self-control, restraint and litigation over physical aggression. These fields overlapped. Concepts of manhood were multiple, complex and interconnected.

Household honour

In the early modern period, individual and household honourability were tightly entwined. Indeed, men's (and women's) household responsibilities

---

[43] See Table 2.1; men were named as victims in 79.3 per cent of 970 male-perpetrated assaults.
[44] Sharpe, *Crime*, 154–5, 159–60; Courtwright, *Violent Land*, 9.
[45] Susan Dwyer Amussen, ' "The part of a Christian man": the cultural politics of manhood in early modern England' in Susan D. Amussen and Mark A. Kishlansky eds., *Political Culture and Cultural Politics in Early Modern England* (Manchester, 1995), 213–33; Elizabeth A. Foyster, *Manhood in Early Modern England: Honour, Sex and Marriage* (London, 1999), 178–89; Paul Griffiths, *Youth and Authority: Formative Experiences in England, 1560–1640* (Oxford, 1996), 136, 171, 207–8; Lyndal Roper, *Oedipus and the Devil: Witchcraft, Sexuality and Religion in Early Modern Europe* (London, 1994), 107–24; Shoemaker, 'Reforming male manners'.

were an important means whereby honour was attained.[46] Household honour was at once collective and personal. Family members, including servants, experienced this honour differently, according to their particular obligations and relationships. Household honour was commonly refracted through an individual's area of competence and place within the household hierarchy. This was especially so for the master and mistress. A married man formally and publicly represented his household; in a sense, he *was* his household.[47] The metaphor was commonplace. Man's body and his household were 'very fitly and aptly' comparable; 'the stomach [being] as it were a kitchen', and so forth.[48] One writer undertook 'to describe in every part, the body of a man, both inwardly and outwardly, from top to toe: and then, compareth it unto an house... well governed by one of worth'. Household and biological bodies alike

> have blemishes and blots,
> Impediments and crookedness,
> deformities and spots:
> And many imperfections more,
> which often times are done
> By violence or mischance,
> yea, often times they come,
> Through lack of care of looking to...[49]

The 'body' of the male subject was delimited not just by his physiological skin but by the physical and symbolic boundaries of his house.

Complainants about male violence frequently conflated household and personal honour. Being beaten in one's own house or grounds was especially shameful.[50] An adversary's unwanted presence within one's house was an affront. Robert Irish came, drunk, to John Read's house late one evening 'in an insulting manner to pick quarrels with me'. Read explained why he had thrown Irish out: Irish's brother had seduced and run off with Read's daughter, 'who now live together in a lewd and sinful manner, he being married to another woman and she to another man, I being much incensed thereby and not enduring to see any so near a confederate as the said Robert to intrude into my house... [I] required Irish to return and depart my house,

---

[46] Fletcher, *Gender, Sex and Subordination*, 126. For women's honourability being imagined in their capacities as housewives, see Garthine Walker, 'Expanding the boundaries of female honour in early modern England', *TRHS* 6th ser., 6 (1996), 235–45.

[47] Cynthia B. Herrup, *A House in Gross Disorder: Sex, Law and the Second Earl of Castlehaven* (Oxford, 1999), 17.

[48] Robert Underwood, *A New Anatomy: Wherein the Body is Very Fitly and Aptly Compared to a Household* (London, 1605); Edward Jewel, *A Brief Discourse of the Stomach and Parts Subservient Unto It* (London, 1678), 2.

[49] Underwood, *A New Anatomy*, 16.   [50] CRO, QJF 74/4/10 (1647).

which he refusing I put him forth of my doors'.[51] The dwelling-house was culturally and legally sanctioned as 'a place of protection and defence' against 'injury and violence'.[52] Infracting household boundaries was a violatory act.

If the body was conceptualised as a house, the household was conceptualised as a 'body', whose boundaries encompassed its inhabitants and resources.[53] This household 'body' and men's own flesh each symbolised the other as the objects of violence.[54] The threatened injury afflicted the master's honour, person, property, family and the family's ability to operate in the future as an economically and socially reliable unit. Complainants made much of this, asserting that the law's protection was necessary not only to safeguard themselves but also their wives and families who were all prevented from following their 'necessary occasions' or 'their ordinary calling without great danger of life'.[55] Joseph Sefton, nursing a black eye, 'durst not go home that night for that Barker had struck him and threatened him further'.[56] Thomas Starkey esquire extended his household further, requesting that a violent son be remanded in custody for the 'preservation' of the 'lives, tenants and houses' of himself, his wife and their other children; 'I, my wife, our servants and tenants were in much danger.'[57] The organic household unit had allegedly been injured, not just the honour or the corporal bodies of individual males.

The household provides an important context for manhood and violence in a further sense. As I pointed out in the previous chapter, a great many violent disputes arose from conflict between households, and group assaults frequently reflected household organisation and obligations. The vast majority of male defendants were prosecuted for their participation in group assaults.[58] In a typical case, the Knights – husband, wife and son – 'violently' assaulted a fellow 'by pulling his hair...and otherwise abusing him' so that had not someone 'come in to his aid he had been spoiled or badly wounded by and amongst them'. All three Knights were bound to their good behaviour.[59] Similarly, a husband, wife and two sons threw Richard Maddock to the ground and gave him 'many great strokes and...threatening speeches against him, whereupon he is in dread and fear of bodily harm from the said persons'.[60] Historians long ago recognised that assaults commonly

---

[51] CRO, QJF 79/4/83 (1652).
[52] Pulton, *De Pace Regis*, fo. 42; Dalton, *Countrey Justice*, 187.
[53] Thomas Pickering, *Christian Oeconomie: Or, A Short Survey of the Right Manner of Erecting and Ordering a Familie* (London, 1609).
[54] For example, CRO, QJF 73/3/57 (1645); QJF 74/2/87 (1646); QJF 75/1/43 (1647).
[55] For example, CRO, QJF 74/2/85, /56 (1646); QJF 75/1/43, /82 (1647); QJF 81/2/301 (1653); QJF 95/2/115 (1667).
[56] CRO, QJF 81/4/48 (1653). [57] CRO, QJF 49/1/151 (1622).
[58] The figure is 72.7 per cent. [59] CRO, QJF 87/1/84, /79, /80 (1659).
[60] CRO, QJF 53/1/42 (1624).

occurred in the context of quarrels about other things – land boundaries, diverted watercourses, contested tithes, borrowed goods, broken fences, grazing rights and so on – but they failed to acknowledge explicitly that these were *household* issues.[61] Patterns of crime have been explained in terms of the interests of individuals or of broad categories such as class.[62] Studies of crime that seek to establish a crude 'sexual division of criminality', and which focus on 'the people' have similarly overlooked the significance of the household.[63] In contrast, recent discussions of certain offences associated with women – defamation, infanticide, witchcraft – have illuminated connections between prosecution and household roles and ideology.[64] Crucially, the household's significance extends beyond forms of disorder conventionally classified as 'feminine' and beyond female offenders. Early modern people did not act only according to perceived individual or class interests, they also had other interests and identities, including those of the household in which they lived. It was frequently in their capacity as masters of households that men entered into disputes.

It is impossible to deduce for certain the proportion of assaults by relatives or household members. Most included participants who definitely, or apparently, lived under the same roof or were otherwise related. Frequently these were spouses, or parents and children.[65] Co-defendants with the same surname were likely to be related or co-inhabitants. If we add these to those where husbands and wives were prosecuted together, a full three-quarters of group assaults involved people from the same household or family. It is worth noting that seemingly unrelated defendants could likewise be bound in ties of household, kinship and mutual support: stepchildren, household servants, servants in husbandry, apprentices, various other relatives (whether inhabiting the household or not). Bonds between parents and grown-up children, and between adult siblings, 'were routinely recognised between households' and 'could involve a powerful sense of obligation'.[66] Sometimes connections

---

[61] T.C. Curtis, 'Quarter sessions appearances and their background: a seventeenth-century regional study' in J.S. Cockburn ed., *Crime in England, 1500–1800* (London, 1977), 135–54.
[62] For example, J.S. Cockburn, 'Patterns of violence in English society', *P&P* 130 (1991), 70–106; J.A. Sharpe, 'The history of violence in England: some observations', *P&P* 103 (1985), 206–24; Lawrence Stone, 'Interpersonal violence in English society, 1300–1980', *P&P* 101 (1983), 22–33.
[63] Sharpe, *Crime*, 154; Sharpe, 'The people and the law'.
[64] Amussen, *Ordered Society*, ch. 5; Laura Gowing, *Domestic Dangers: Women, Words and Sex in Early Modern London* (Oxford, 1996); Laura Gowing, 'Secret births and infanticide in seventeenth-century England', *P&P* 156 (1997), 87–115; Diane Purkiss, *The Witch in History: Early Modern and Twentieth-century Representations* (London, 1996); Walker, 'Expanding the boundaries'.
[65] For example, CRO, QJF 51/1/99 (1622); QJF 51/1/4 (1622); QJF 53/1/72 (1624); QJF 53/3/15 (1624).
[66] Keith Wrightson and David Levine, *Poverty and Piety in an English Village: Terling, 1525–1700*, 2nd edn (1979; Oxford, 1995), 188–97, quotation at 194; Anne Laurence, *Women in England, 1500–1760: A Social History* (London, 1994), 88–9.

can be corroborated. John Higginbotham and Katherine Day, for instance, turn out to be son- and mother-in-law.[67] Additional information reveals that individuals with different names were often servants or apprentices in the household concerned. For instance, Lawrence, Thomas, Edward, Ann and Elizabeth Wright were indicted for several assaults in 1626, along with William Hartley and Roland Garlic; we learn from a related recognisance that Hartley was indeed a servant of Lawrence Wright's, and the chances are that Garlic was, too.[68] Moreover, further disagreements between households, or which involved several household members, appear in the record as isolated incidents, only some of which may be reconstructed.[69]

Non-lethal violence and many other offences that are usually considered as individual acts by men might better be understood in relation to the household. The importance of the household is evident in several of the cases discussed in the next section, where servants were involved in their masters' disputes and *vice versa*; and wives or other family members were implicated.

A code of honour and a language of law

The depiction and evaluation of male-on-male violence drew upon an honour code in which physical retaliation was an appropriate masculine response to affronts. As one writer explained, an 'injury in words is taken away by the injury of deed,... a lie is falsified with a box on the ear, or any blow with what else thing soever'. Such responses were essential 'lest he remained dishonoured'.[70] The ritual of the duel constituted one well-known form of this.[71] But neither violent retaliation to perceived affronts nor formal challenges to fight were the preserve of aristocrats and gentlemen. This construction of manliness was ubiquitous in legal testimony. It was manifest in verbal or written 'challenges' by men of all sorts. A common soldier 'said he would fight with the best man under [Lieutenant William Nightingale's] command and laid down his wager'. A husbandman 'challenged me to duel with him without any just provocation to him given... and hath offered me money to fight with him'.[72] It informed the labelling of adversaries as 'cowards',

---

[67] CRO, QJF 57/1/5, /20 (1628). [68] CRO, QJF 55/2/13–/16 (1626).
[69] For example, CRO, QJF 49/2/19, /21 (1620); QJF 53/2/189 (1624); QJF 53/4/13 (1625), 53/3/74 (1624); QJF 55/1/26, /29, /24, /27; QJF 55/2/8, /18, /83, /95, /161 (1626).
[70] [H]annibale Romei, *The Courtier's Academie* (London, 1597), 151; John Davies, *The Scourge of Folly* (London, 1611), 23.
[71] On duelling see V.G. Kiernan, *The Duel in European History: Honour and the Reign of Aristocracy* (Oxford, 1986); Donna Andrew, 'The code of honour and its critics: the opposition to duelling in England, 1700–1850', *Social History* 5 (1980), 409–34.
[72] CCRO, MF69/2/101 (1646–1647); PRO, CHES 24/125/4, articles re. Evered Sherman (1641). See also CRO, QJF 49/2/147 (1620); QJF 51/3/105 (1622); QJF 53/4/96 (1625); QJF 75/1/36 (1647); QJF 79/2/68 (1651); QJF 81/2/226 (1653); QJF 83/2/79, /80 (1655); QJF 97/1/62 (1669); CCRO, MF69/2/101 (1647).

especially for refusing challenges. A constable complained that yeoman Richard Shaw 'did challenge me to fight him in a field and would have had me to put my hand to a note which he then showed me that thereby I might engage myself to have met [him] in the field, which I refused and afterwards Shaw called me "coward" with divers other base speeches'.[73] George Mainwaring, gentleman, asserted that he called out for help because he was 'unable to resist being then out of breath and fearing [his opponent] might have some knife or such like weapon'; his opponent 'loosed' him but called him '"cowardly rogue" and "rascal", saying sarcastically again and again, "What a man! And call 'Help! Help! Help!' cowardly dastard!"'.[74] Men's claims that they would either kill or be killed also invoked the conception of the 'man of honour'.[75]

These concepts were sanctioned in homicide law, which provided a particularly appropriate schema of righteous and wrongful violence given that lethal and non-lethal violence might be indistinguishable in all except the victim's fate. The legal category of manslaughter required that both parties enter voluntarily into a fight in which each was equally at risk. Full culpability for killing was therefore mitigated and the death penalty was seldom applied. Conversely, killings in which the assailant had taken unfair advantage of his victim were legally constructed as cowardly, dishonourable acts meriting capital punishment. Tales of non-lethal violence appropriated these ideas. Assaults were presented as unequal, unprovoked, unexpected. One villain crept up behind a man as he went 'to make water' in his backyard at night-time, and attacked him while 'my face [was] towards the wall'.[76] Weapons were allegedly used against unarmed complainants. Some weapons carried particular nuances. The use of swords or daggers evoked the aggravated homicide of the 1604 Stabbing Statute.[77] Deponents emphasised this: 'Tilston Bruen, gentleman, did in rude and barbarous manner without any provocation at all, assault John Kinsey, gentleman (an attorney of this court), and did draw out his rapier and in a violent and resolute manner thrust therewith at Kinsey'; 'had not another person interposed, Bruen would have slain Master Kinsey' who was 'unarmed with not even a rod in his hands to defend himself'.[78] Another complainant asserted that as a consequence of a frenzied stabbing, 'I lost so much of my blood that I was scarce able to stand and [was] thereby

---

[73] CRO, QJF 75/1/36 (1647). See also QJF 53/3/103, /104 (1624); QJF 83/2/63 (1655); QJF 83/2/79 (1655); QJF 83/4/66 (1656); QJF 87/1/115 (1659); QJF 97/1/62 (1669).
[74] PRO, CHES 24/127/2, articles against Thomas Clemence (1648).
[75] For example, CRO, QJF 53/1/46 (1624); QJF 81/3/61 (1653); QJF 83/4/103 (1656).
[76] PRO, CHES 24/127/2, articles against Thomas Clemence (1648); CHES 24/127/2, petition of Robert Cudworth (1648).
[77] See below, pp. 115, 122–3.
[78] PRO, CHES 24/135/2, depositions against Tilston Bruen (1665).

in great danger of the loss of my life.'[79] Even encounters which produced less dangerous wounds were fashioned as 'great and outrageous misdemeanour[s]' in the light of the Stabbing Statute if an appropriate weapon – a 'little dagger made of a rapier blade', say, or a 'rapier in a staff' – and other circumstances – being 'stabbed...into the back with a thwittle' (a large knife) – invited it.[80]

The very adoption of a conceptual framework that fused codes of male honour and capital liability evoked homicide. Concepts shared with homicide law could nevertheless have subtly different meanings when applied to non-lethal violence. Mitigating notions in homicide cases might even exacerbate a defendant's culpability when no one died. Whereas manslaughter was categorised as a lesser evil than murder, it was obviously more serious than a fight in which both parties lived. Stressing that someone was 'barbarous wounded and dry-beaten...to the hazard of his life, whereof he languishes' positioned assault and homicide upon a continuum whereby the former conceptually merged into the latter.[81] Assailants were regularly portrayed as potential killers to magnify their crimes. William Turner (who had only a walking stick with which to defend himself) was so badly injured by Richard Whittingham with a back-sword that he lay under the surgeon's hands for nineteen weeks. When Turner's father attempted 'to have his remedy by law', Whittingham fled and allegedly 'at London slew a kinsman of his own'. An allegation that he was a mercenary added to the dishonour of the assault. Hiring assassins was associated with avarice and covetousness, especially concerning property and sex.[82]

Constructing a savage yet cowardly male assailant fashioned the victim positively in contrast. There was nothing inherently dishonourable about 'running away' if neither reconciliation nor an equal fight seemed possible.[83] However, if the disadvantaged victim won, the assailant would be ridiculed. Humiliating one's opponent bestowed honour upon the victor. It was also tremendously funny. Witnesses deposed that they saw Master Tuchett striking two men on horseback with his cane 'insomuch as...[passers-by] laughed at the two men on horseback', saying '"Look! Look! One little man beats two!"' and 'bade them light for shame'.[84]

---

[79] CCRO, MF71/1/11 (1649).
[80] CRO, QJF 53/4/38, /30 (1624); QJF 87/1/101 (1659); QJF 77/4/97, /94 (1650).
[81] CRO, QJF 74/2/92 (1646).
[82] CRO, QJF 55/2/111 (1626). See also QJF 29/1/35 (1599); QJF 29/2/28, /30, /31 (1599). *Sundrye Strange and Inhumaine Murthers Lately Committed* (London, 1591); Gilbert Dugdale, *A True Discourse of the Practices of Elizabeth Caldwell* (London, 1604); Martin Wiggins, *Journeymen in Murder: The Assassin in English Renaissance Drama* (Oxford, 1991).
[83] CRO, QJF 89/2/56 (1661); QJF 93/1/110 (1665).   [84] CRO, QJF 81/4/69 (1654).

Hierarchy and status

In a society acutely aware of hierarchy and degree, the rights and wrongs of violence were measured accordingly. Birth, office, age, peer group, occupation, gender, marital status and other forms of identity all conferred status of different sorts. Status was signified in manifold ways: in gesture and speech, visually, as in dress codes, and spatially, as in church seating arrangements and superiors' claims to 'inviolable personal space'. Inferiors, for example, were expected to stop and press themselves into the sides of narrow ways to allow their 'betters' to pass.[85] To wield violence was to assert authority and superiority. Master Robert Bromfield, having from horseback struck a husbandman with his sword, exclaimed afterwards that he was sorry not to have killed him 'to teach all knaves to let men pass quietly'.[86] Robert Lord Cholmondley expressed no remorse when in 1673 he mortally wounded one of two carters who refused to pull over to allow his coach to pass by. Instead, he justified his act by constructing it as violence under provocation: he had retaliated to frightful 'affronts', 'very great provocations' and 'insolence'. 'I had the unhappiness to be affronted by some rustics, whose words and blows provoked returns of both sorts from me and my company', Cholmondley explained. The King pardoned him.[87] Bromfield and Cholmondley behaved according to the maxim that the 'natural' civility of their class freed them from the social and legal constraints that bound inferior men. Law frequently upheld such attitudes even though they were contested.[88]

Concerns with precedence existed at all social levels. William Walker, husbandman, was affronted when two eighteen-year-old husbandmen requested that he make room for them to pass him on a causeway next to a deep ditch of water. It was, Walker retorted, up to him 'whether he would or no, and turned his horse across the causeway and struck' them, and rode after them up the lane, striking at them 'very, very often' with his staff.[89] The dynamic here was generational: inferiors were expected to give adults preference in narrow ways. The insubordination of youth was a common early

---

[85] Anna Bryson, *From Courtesy to Civility: Changing Codes of Conduct in Early Modern England* (Oxford, 1998), 88–9.
[86] CRO, QJF 74/1/56, /81 (1646).
[87] PRO, CHES 38/41, 'Examinations concerning the death of James Woodall'. CRO, DDX X/7, Cholmondley of Cholmondley Collection: Private Correspondence, 'King's Pardon, lawyers' opinions and other papers relating to a murder committed by Robert Lord Cholmondley and others at Bunbury', Lord Cholmondley to John Snell, 27 August 1673; Cholmondley to Sir Orlando Bridgeman, 29 August 1673; Cholmondley to John Snell, 8 September 1673; Cholmondley to Snell, 22 September 1673.
[88] Keith M. Brown, 'Gentlemen and thugs in seventeenth-century Britain', *History Today* 40 (October, 1990), 30.
[89] CRO, QJF 81/3/99 (1653).

modern theme: age-relations were frequently portrayed in terms of contest and friction.[90]

Some legal stories mirror the terms of contemporary civility literature. In 1665, for example, Ann Latchfield described Jack Hunt's abuse of a gentleman in her tavern. As Richard Haughton passed through the chamber where Hunt and others were drinking, he courteously 'pulled off his hat, and said "by your leave, gentlemen"'. Someone inquiring who he was, Hunt announced that 'it was one Haughton that had married Nan Lidderland', whom he knew 'well enough' for Haughton had stolen a horse of his. Hunt thus defined Haughton not through lineage and polite form (Richard Haughton of Haughton, gentleman), but through criminal behaviour and marriage to a woman whom he described familiarly and hence, in this context, disrespectfully. Therewith Hunt railed against Haughton, calling him 'false thief' and declaring that 'my flesh riseth for to see him'. After Haughton requested that the ale-wife take his rapier and 'lay it up, for these were urging words', Hunt exclaimed that he could not suffer to remain in Haughton's presence and went outside to call for a quart of beer from the common. Haughton followed and attempted to reason with him, saying 'Jack Hunt, thou art mistaken...' but Hunt assaulted him, threatened to 'make his neck stretch' (invoking the capital penalty for horse-theft), and had to be restrained by the company, including his own wife and the ale-wife.[91]

Throughout Ann Latchfield's tale, Haughton was civility personified. He doffed his hat in salutation. He expressly resisted the temptation to respond with 'heat and violence' to Hunt's 'urging words'. He demonstrated his possession of inner civil qualities that Hunt lacked. He reinforced his own superiority by addressing Hunt by his Christian name, by using the familiar and patronising 'thou', and by interrupting and contradicting him. In contrast, within the conventional discourse of class hierarchy, Hunt marked himself as inferior and uncivil by demonstrating an insensitivity to Haughton's status in the company of others, in contradicting a man of higher social status, by assaulting Haughton when the latter attempted reconciliation, and by setting himself 'as it were, in a place of judgement'.[92] Hunt was also defined negatively by his rage. Rage was frequently presented as the negative image of the positive characteristic of reason displayed by the civil man.

The extent to which discourses of social differentiation informed magistrates' reception of such complaints varied. In the early 1650s, for example, the Cheshire magistracy was primarily constituted of lesser Puritan gentry whose families were not traditional county governors, and a few young men

---

[90] Ilana Ben-Amos, *Adolescence and Youth in Early Modern England* (London, 1994), 16–19; Griffiths, *Youth and Authority*, 123–31, 60.
[91] CRO, QJF 93/2/160 (1665).
[92] Bryson, *From Courtesy to Civility*, 88–9, 159–60, 164–7.

from more established families without experience of civil or military service. Not one JP sitting on the county bench in January 1651 was of higher status than 'esquire'. The bench at this time displayed a heightened sensitivity to distinctions between gentlemen and non-gentlemen, and used the discourse of civility to reinforce social differentiation. In the context of the early republic, these distinctions were highly politicised. William Raven, gentleman, complained in January 1651 that one Shaw (humble enough to have served as petty constable) 'reviled me with base and unseemly language', such as 'base, dishonest man' and other 'opprobrious' terms 'unfit here to be expressed'. Shaw then threatened to strike Raven's servants with a pole, to which Raven 'bade him strike at his peril'. Shaw's ill behaviour positioned him as one of 'the meanest and vilest sort of people' in comparison to, in the bench's terms, Master Raven's 'good words to persuade him to be quiet'. The magistrates issued a warrant of good behaviour against Shaw 'forasmuch as such behaviour of a mean man towards a gentleman is against good manners'.[93]

At the same sessions, the code of manners served contrarily as a language of exclusion to deny 'status' to John Bretland, a gentleman, because he 'hath of late uttered foul speeches and behaved himself uncivilly' towards Sir George Booth and Thomas Marbury, esquire.[94] Here, the 'civil' discourse of manners served as a tool of political differentiation. Bretland and Raven had very different relationships with the magistracy. Raven, although of modest estate, had during the first civil war acted as assistant to the 'deputy lieutenants' (Cheshire's equivalent of a County Committee), one of whom, Henry Brooke, was present on the bench.[95] In contrast, Bretland was a reputed Royalist whose estate had been sequestered in 1647, since when he had been at variance with Booth and other Parliamentarians over the validity of the charges against him.[96] The 'civil' discourse of manners was a resource for bolstering and undermining particular versions of manhood in different contexts and for various ends.

The concept of spatial deference was connected to concerns about bodily boundaries. Grabbing an opponent's hair and 'yanking him around' insulted and dishonoured him. Hair pulling was associated with chastisement, and was prohibited by the 'rules' of duelling.[97] William Brown held William Barlow by the hair, saying that 'he would teach him to know that he was a Brown, better than any of the Barlows'.[98] Tearing an opponent's clothes carried similar connotations, as did forcibly taking or knocking his hat from his

[93] CRO, QJB 1/6, fo. 244, CRO, QJF 77/4/70 (1651).   [94] CRO, QJB 1/6, fo. 244 (1650).
[95] Morrill, *Cheshire*, 82.   [96] Morrill, *Cheshire*, 112, 209, 216–22.
[97] Robert C. Davis, *The War of the Fists: Popular Culture and Public Violence in Late Renaissance Venice* (Oxford, 1994), 70.
[98] CRO, QJF 89/3/72 (1661).

head.[99] Vestiary affronts were greatly significant. Clothing, including headgear, was an idiom that communicated identities, status and values. The male body displayed its strength and authority through hats and other garments. In many respects, clothing stood for the body itself. Hence, tailors of fashionable attire were termed 'body-makers'.[100] The modern perception of dress as supplementary and superficial to a 'real' or 'deep' body underneath is clearly inappropriate here. In the ritual doffing of one's hat, the inferior uncovered first and waited for the superior's permission to cover his head again. Men of equal status proceeded simultaneously.[101] Uncovering one's head was a 'sign of honour'; having one's head forcibly uncovered therefore connoted dishonour.[102] Thus, Parliamentarian propaganda held that after the battle at Tarporley, Royalist troops who had fled to Chester claimed 'they had got Sir William [Brereton's] hat and feather, a great trophy, though upon examination it was found to be one of their own soldier's'.[103] Witnesses deposed that John Evans, husbandman, had struck Master Arnold Hill with his whip, rendering 'Master Hill's face all bloody', and had forcibly taken Master Hill's hat from his head and kept it from him.[104] A seventy-year-old man assaulted by a group of 'young' men associated having his hat knocked into the dirt, and being thrown into the fire so that his clothes were burned, with being 'jeered' at.[105] Both 'hat and hair' (of whatever length) were symbols of manhood.[106] Pulling men's hair and taking their hats connoted emasculation. They were especially subversive acts when perpetrated by men of inferior status or indeed by females.

Complainants sometimes made more of acts such as hair pulling, hat-knocking, clothes-tearing and being spat at, than they did of verbal insults or flesh wounds. John Shrigley, gentleman, complained that some malcontents had 'so violently wronged and abused [his servant] by pulling his hair of his head, and otherwise abusing him' that 'to save himself [he] overwent his hat'. The implications of hierarchy and status become clearer with the

---

[99] PRO, CHES 24/129/2, indictment of Clement, CHES 21/4, fo. 256v (1651). CRO, QJF 87/1/41 (1659).
[100] John Bulwer, *Anthropometamorphosis: Man Transform'd, or, the Artificiall Changling Historically Presented* (London, 1653), sig. A4v. F.E. Baldwin, *Sumptuary Legislation and Personal Regulation in England* (Baltimore, 1926); N.B. Harte, 'State control of dress and social change in pre-industrial England', in D.C. Coleman and A.H. John eds., *Trade, Government and Economy in Pre-Industrial England. Essays presented to F.J. Fisher* (London, 1976).
[101] Bryson, *From Courtesy to Civility*, 89–90.
[102] Nathaniel Walker, *The Refin'd Courtier* (London, 1663), 161.
[103] *Cheshire's Success Since their Pious and Truly Valient Colonel Sir William Brereton Came to their Rescue* (London, 1643), 3.
[104] CRO, QJF 95/4/51, /50 (1668).   [105] CRO, QJF 79/4/31 (1652).
[106] Ann Rosalind Jones and Peter Stallybrass, *Renaissance Clothing and the Materials of Memory* (Cambridge, 2000), 79.

knowledge that the servant, Raphe Shrigley, had recently been appointed in place of a stone-getter's son who had been dismissed. The latter and his parents had carried out the assault.[107] But this case also suggests the way that household and bodily boundaries could merge in perceptions of honour and injury. The role of menservants in violent encounters that concerned the household they inhabited suggests a further connection of masculinity with violent honourability. In 'faithfully and diligently' demeaning 'himself in the affairs of his master', a servant could stand in for the master as the object of abuse.[108]

Restraint versus fisticuffs

Susan Amussen has argued that the late sixteenth and seventeenth centuries saw the replacement of the 'traditional' model of manhood by a 'reformed' model that rejected violence in favour of restraint and recourse to law. Although Amussen notes that appropriate manly behaviour was context-specific and involved the negotiation of discourses of Christian morality, class and gender, she privileges an oppositional model of manhood. The reformed model was available only to those with sufficient means to pay for lawsuits. The lower orders 'necessarily' continued to use violence 'to assert their manhood and defend their reputations'. The (dominant) 'reformed', godly masculinity of property-holders was thus at variance with the (subordinate) 'traditional', violent version of the lower orders.[109]

Cultural polarisation is indeed one context in which differing and changing meanings of violence might be understood. The human mind was presented by contemporary commentators 'in its twofold state', namely, 'man in his unconverted wrathful nature; armed' and 'man in his converted innocent nature; naked and unarmed'.[110] But alternative masculinities were not mutually exclusive. The discourse of restraint was not the preserve of a godly or social elite, just as the idea of the 'man of honour' did not belong exclusively to the gentry. Discourses of manhood constituted a cultural resource that all sorts of men appropriated and modified.[111] Husbandman Edward Johnson advised his neighbour 'to be patient and quiet' when the latter wished to retaliate for an 'express and base wrong' inflicted upon him by a man he

[107] CRO, QJF 87/1/84, /19, /20, /79–/81 (1659). See also CRO, QJF 29/4/15 (1600); QJF 87/1/41, /101 (1659); QJF 89/4/32 (1662); QJF 93/4/36 (1666). PRO, CHES 24/136/4, indictment of Meredith Lloyd (1669).
[108] Pickering, *Christian Oeconomie*, 156.
[109] Amussen, 'Part of a Christian man', 227, 214–16.
[110] J. Mason, *The History of the Young Converted Gallant* (London, 1675).
[111] See also Foyster, *Manhood*, 32–9; Mervyn James, *English Politics and the Concept of Honour, 1485–1642* (Cambridge, 1978).

'could not endure to look upon'. (Johnson's advice went unheeded: 'George was impatient, and did strike Francis with a stick.')[112]

Alternative versions of manhood were juxtaposed in legal narratives. Several times during 4 and 5 December 1624, Hugh Kinsey and two others armed with a pitchfork, a drawn sword and a long rapier, beat on the doors, walls and windows of mercer Matthew Smallwood's house, 'daring him to come forth with many opprobrious terms'. When Smallwood refused, they scoffed that Smallwood, his brother and friends 'durst not show their faces', invoking 'common opinion [that] holdeth base and cowardly men [to be] more infamous than unjust [men]'.[113] Smallwood spoke in a different discourse. He told them first that it was too late at night and 'not fit time for me to come forth'. The following morning, 'it was the Sabbath day and therefore unfit for such matters'. Later, after sermon and communion, 'it had been fitter for them to have been at church than to have sitten in the Alehouse and then to come to disturb me'. Smallwood's discursive framework was one of godly manhood similar to that which Amussen delineated. But Smallwood and two husbandmen had allegedly undertaken a related assault with staves and short daggers upon one Robert Kinsey on 3 December.[114] A discourse of reformed manhood did not necessarily signify the renunciation of violence.

Complaints that countered fisticuffs with legal proceedings were not all overtly godly. Formal challenges were often presented simply as an unlawful alternative to lawful means of dispute-settlement. The extent to which seeking redress through violence was condemned officially varied from time to time. In the 1650s, for instance, the Cheshire bench was particularly concerned to stamp out such behaviour, thereby facilitating prosecutions such as that of a husbandman for 'scandalous and provoking words' after he tried to provoke a shoemaker by saying 'I will fight with thee.'[115] If assertive acts of violence were not always viewed positively, running away was consistent with some constructions of manly behaviour. Asserting that one had fled to avoid having one's brains knocked out was construed as sensible rather than unmanly.[116] The legal definition of killing in self-defence, after all, stipulated that a man was to flee as far as he could in order to save his life.

The discourse of restraint accommodated notions of positive violence in self-defence or upon provocation. Recourse to law and the exercise of self-control were entirely compatible with the admission that 'I was fain to shrink

---

[112] CRO, QJF 85/4/109 (1658).   [113] Romei, *Courtier's Academie*, 106.
[114] CRO, QJF 53/4/96, /16, /17; CRO, QJB 1/5, fo. 132r (1625).
[115] CRO, QJF 87/2/2/95, CRO, QJB 2/7 (unfoliated) (Trinity Sessions, 1659).
[116] CRO, QJF 93/1/110 (1665).

from' another's unreasonable violence.[117] When Philip Ashton deliberately 'jostled' George Powdrey in a doorway and accused him of purposely blocking his way, Powdrey retorted that although he was 'as good a man' as Ashton, he would not quarrel because Ashton stood bound to his good behaviour. Ashton thereupon called Powdrey 'base fellow and coward', saying 'if I [Powdrey] were not a coward I would then strike and loose him from his good behaviour'. Powdrey 'was constrained to go my way, and leave him, lest I be enforced to have stricken him'. Powdrey's restraint existed only within certain limits.[118] Raphe Wickstead, labourer, 'desirous to be at peace' with Hamlet Currier 'did patiently undergo all his threatenings', but when Currier attacked him physically with a quarterstaff Wickstead was 'constrained to close with him, in which closing Currier did bite me' so 'that if I had not been very careful, I had lost a finger'. This had implications for his household, of course: such injuries were commonly said to prevent men from earning their living and to ruin whole families. Wickstead 'willingly put up with all these wrongs because I would not take advantages of my neighbour'. Currier, in contrast, maliciously had Wickstead imprisoned.[119] Portraying oneself as a man of sobriety and restraint did not rely upon the wholly successful display of those characteristics.

Anna Bryson has noted that the developing discourse of civility of the later sixteenth and seventeenth centuries constituted 'an effort, sometimes strained, to articulate social languages and imperatives which were often contradictory'.[120] 'Traditional' and 'reformed' attitudes coexisted, at times in single narratives. Courtesy writers lamented the popularity of duelling and the 'exaggerated bravado and aggression with which gallants expressed "honour"', yet continued to identify courage and physical prowess as the marks of a gentleman. Puritan commentators condemned duelling while happily describing in detail 'fashionable means of self-defence'.[121] Young people were warned not to confuse negative 'desires of revenge' and 'rage' with positive 'courage and an uncontrollable magnanimity'. Fraudulent parasites and users were condemned as cowards who, having encouraged young fellows to take revenge on their foes with their assistance, 'if there be any evident danger in the enterprise, then they shrink from him, leaving him in the brawl; which sometimes costs him his life, or at least much trouble'.[122] Concerns were expressed about men of all social classes. Elite male youth, for instance, were a source of particular worry for moralists, who condemned their dissolute lifestyles which involved drinking, gambling, wenching, blaspheming,

---

[117] CRO, QJF 83/2/122 (1655).   [118] CRO, QJF 55/1/40 (1626).
[119] CRO, QJF 81/4/102 (1654).   [120] Bryson, *From Courtesy to Civility*, 165, 240–1.
[121] Bryson, *From Courtesy to Civility*, 236; William Higson, *Institutions, Or Advice to his Grandson* (London, 1658).
[122] J.W., *Youths Safety: Or, Advice to the Younger Sort of Either Sex* (London, 1698), 5–6.

violence and cowardice long before Restoration rakes appeared on the scene. Eighteenth-century objections about elite men's loutish behaviour echoed mid-sixteenth and seventeenth-century complaints that it was fashionable for a gentleman 'to be a roister, which word I do not well understand unless it signify a ruffian'.[123]

Violence remained a component of many masculine leisure activities throughout the period. Ballads exalted aggression and combative skill as desirable attributes for male youth throughout the sixteenth and seventeenth centuries. In one ballad, the eponymous London apprentice originally hailed from Cheshire.[124] Chivalric tales about young men who brilliantly fought and killed for 'a desire for glory and the lady's hand' were extremely popular. Their appeal was grounded in 'male fantasies of toughness' and those other symptoms of budding masculinity, 'adventure and fame'.[125] Elite male sports like wrestling and fencing involved violent competition, as did the cudgel-play and street fights between groups of young men from a wide social spectrum. All of these had their own rituals and rules. On Shrove Tuesday, Chester apprentices (like those elsewhere) engaged in cudgel-play, football and cockfighting, all of which worried the authorities.[126] 'Hunting resembles a battle in field' because of the regularity with which men were killed.[127] This too was condemned by some and exalted by others. The duel itself was a spectator sport. In an advertisement of the challenge given and accepted between Richard Gravener, gentleman, soldier and scholar, and Thomas Blunne, shoemaker and scholar, spectators were asked to give the men 'stage-room' in the Red Bull where they were to fight with eight conventional weapons, including rapier and dagger, back-sword and halberd.[128] Tavern culture has been implicated in fostering male violence. The 'entertaining of bearwards', who exhibited their performing bears in alehouses, for instance, 'getteth fighting and bloodshed'.[129] Certainly, drinking and playing

---

[123] *The Institucion of a Gentleman* (1555; London, 1568), sig. A5; Giovanni Della Casa, *A Short Discourse of the Life of Servingmen* (London, 1578), sig. A3v; Henry Peacham, *The Compleat Gentleman* (London, 1622), 9–10; Francis Lenton, *The Young Gallants Whirligigg: Or Youths Reakes* (London, 1629), 5, 9–10. See also John Evelyn, *A Character of England*, reprinted in T. Park ed., *Harleian Miscellany*, 10 (1808–13), 189–98; *The Character of a Town-Gallant* (1675; London, 1680).
[124] *The Honour of an Apprentice of London, Wherein is Declared his Matchless Manhood*... (London, 1664).
[125] Bernard Capp, 'Popular literature' in Barry Reay ed., *Popular Culture in Seventeenth-Century England* (London, 1985), 206–7; Sarah Annice Todd, 'The representation of aggression in the seventeenth-century English broadside ballad', Ph.D. thesis, University of Wales, Aberystwyth (1998), 129–58.
[126] Griffiths, *Youth and Authority*, 137–49; Roper, *Oedipus and the Devil*, 113–16.
[127] W.D., 'A dittie of hunting', in Della Casa, *Short Discourse*, sig. F4.
[128] *A Challenge from Richard Gravener, Gentleman and Soldier, Scholar*... (London, 1629).
[129] PRO, CHES 21/3 fo. 75r, presentment of John Wainwright (1622).

at various games in alehouses provided a context for many fights.[130] Being questioned by JPs whether he had broken Randle Hollinshead's ribs, yeoman Robert Burges replied that he had not, but 'that at some such times as [they] had been playing at tables together in Wilmslow there had passed some buffets betwixt them'.[131]

There was no essential tension between godliness and defending honour with violence. 'Righteous' violence was used to justify armed conflict, and the British civil wars were no exception.[132] Military treatises and sermons delivered to the troops linked 'effeminacy and cowardice', and urged soldiers to 'be of good courage, and let us play the man'. Those 'with any spark of manhood in them' would wish to fight to honour God and defend their country.[133] Godly rhetoric of defending peace and order, of resistance, and of 'Godly rule' constituted means by which people sought 'to understand... [and] to control and regulate the impact of the Civil War'. Royalists portrayed themselves as fighting in defence of order, law and peace, while many Parliamentarians adapted the Calvinist theory of resistance to stress that 'the community had a *duty* to take action against a King who broke the laws of God by favouring false religion'. Radical writers and orators developed further a rhetoric of godly rule that stressed the practical role of the people as representatives and agents of God's work. Glenn Burgess considers that for political purposes, these discourses constituted 'weapons rather than ideas'.[134] As sets of ideas circulating during the 1640s, however, they were appropriated with regard to less momentous affairs. Elite codes of manners, whether emphasising due retaliation or godly restraint, constituted resources that enabled ordinary people to define and redefine their relationships with others. Ideas about manhood were intricately linked to ideas about violence in early modern England. The conceptual interrelations of these categories provide the backdrop to evaluations of other sorts of non-lethal violence: male violence against women, including rape and

---

[130] Amussen, 'Punishment, discipline and power', 24–7; Thomas Brennan, *Public Drinking and Popular Culture in Eighteenth-Century Paris* (Princeton, 1988), 32–60.

[131] PRO, CHES 38/41, 'Examinations concerning Ann Hollinshead *v.* Robert Burges', examination of Burges, 11 October 1625.

[132] Anthony Fletcher, *The Outbreak of the English Civil War* (London, 1981), 405–18; John Morrill, 'The religious context of the English civil war', *TRHS*, 5th ser., 34 (1984), 155–78; Charles Carlton, *Going to the Wars: The Experience of the British Civil Wars, 1638–1651* (London, 1992), 48–50.

[133] Donald Lupton, *A Warrelike Treatise on the Pike* (London, 1642), W. Bridge, *A Sermon Preached unto the Volunteers of the City of Norwich and Yarmouth* (London, 1643), both cited in Carlton, *Going to the Wars*, 47–8. Della Casa, *Short Discourse*, sigs. B1, B3v.

[134] Glenn Burgess, 'The impact on political thought: rhetorics for troubled times' in John Morrill ed., *The Impact of the English Civil War* (London, 1991), 74–5, 78–82. See also Judy Sproxton, *Violence and Religion: Attitudes towards Militancy in the French Civil Wars and the English Revolution* (London and New York, 1995); Euan Cameron, *The European Reformation* (Oxford, 1991), 353–6, 375.

sexual assault; violence inflicted by women upon men; and violence between women.

MEN'S VIOLENCE AGAINST WOMEN

In late twentieth-century Britain, women's experiences of men's violence were articulated more strongly than hitherto, with the development of new and modified discourses such as 'domestic violence', 'sexual harassment' and 'date rape'. These languages and concepts were not equally available to all women in every circumstance.[135] In early modern society, fewer specific models of masculine violence existed to legitimate women's complaints. Patriarchal ideas imbued early modern culture with multiple ways of justifying or excusing men's violence against women. Moreover, the 'normal' terms of reference for violent incidents were largely inappropriate, for they were informed by codes of masculine honour that required both parties to be male. Some women nonetheless found ways of speaking about the harm they suffered at men's hands.

Early modern patriarchalism endorsed violence as a means of maintaining gender and social hierarchy. Righteous violence therefore included 'reasonable correction' of wives by husbands, children by parents, and servants and apprentices by masters and mistresses. Beyond the household, categorising violence between women and men was less clear-cut. Certain discourses emphasised the heinousness or dishonour of men's unauthorised and unjust assaults, including those upon women. It was 'unmanly' for 'a man to beat a woman'. Any 'point of manhood' or 'valour, demands equality of combatants' whereas 'nature hath disarmed [women] of corporal strength'.[136] However, when violence was constructed as upholding patriarchy – whether in a domestic context, when the men concerned acted in official capacities such as that of constable, or otherwise – women's violence towards men even if in self-defence connoted the subversion of gender and social order. For example, a 'poor woman' assisted an ale-wife who had come to blows with John Spark over his unpaid dues, by hitting Spark over the head with his own rule-staff. For this indignity, Spark spun round, took the rule-staff from her, 'and stroke her half-a-dozen blows with it at the least' before anyone was able to stop him. Spark beat the woman not in self-defence but in retaliation for injuring his pride. The apparent futility of female violence (he easily disarmed her) and the practice of male force reaffirmed masculine

---

[135] For example, Aileen McColgan, *The Case for Taking the Date Out of Rape* (London, 1996); Marianne Hester, Liz Kelly and Jill Radford, *Women, Violence and Male Power* (Buckingham, 1996).

[136] William Heale, *An Apologie for Women: Or an Opposition to Mr Dr G. His Assertion that Men Should Beat their Wives* (London, 1608), 2, 13.

power and superiority.[137] Legal narratives that alleged male violence against women demonstrate the negotiation of these various discourses.

The denial of female defences

A woman's self-defence was easily configured as her disorderly behaviour rather than her assailant's in discourses that stressed, on the one hand, the desirability of women's corporal weakness and frailty and, on the other, the 'unnatural' disorderliness of feminine violence. The spectre of women's physical self-defence undermined the portrayal both of a weak, feeble and vulnerable female victim and of a dangerously violent male aggressor. It served to emasculate the male assailant and made the woman concerned seem dangerously powerful. Female strength was rarely asserted. Instead, deponents and examinants stressed female passivity and non-engagement on the one hand and male brutality on the other. Female vulnerability tends to be discussed by historians in terms of its negative consequences for women.[138] But it could operate as an empowering discourse, too. Christianity communicated the message that suffering was redemptive and valuable, and constructed the qualities of idealised femininity – the passive acceptance of suffering, humility and meekness – as victimhood.[139] Vulnerability and passive suffering implied feminine virtue and evoked a certain pathos.

Women's agency was frequently effaced in narratives of male violence. On Friday 13 June 1628 Richard Poole allegedly stabbed Bridget Wood's dog, having 'in friendly manner called and enticed [it] unto him'. 'Not so contented', Poole subsequently stabbed Bridget herself, inflicting several injuries including a 'very dangerous and desperate' head wound. The informants (her husband, six other men and a woman) declared:

We do verily think, if company had not come in and rescued her, he would have murdered her. And after he was kept from striking her, she being then all blood and, it was thought, wounded to death and lying upon the ground in a trance as though she had been dead...

Without the intervention of others, Bridget Wood was no match for Poole. The informants depicted an entirely passive Bridget. All the action was

---
[137] CRO, QJF 53/4/39–/43 (1624).
[138] For example, Ross Balzaretti, '"These are things that men do, not women": the social regulation of female violence in Langobard Italy' in Guy Halsall ed., *Violence and Society in the Early Medieval West* (Woodbridge, 1998), 182.
[139] Joanne Carlson Brown and Rebecca Parker, 'For God so loved the world?' in Carol J. Adams and Marie M. Fortune eds., *Violence Against Women and Children: A Christian Theological Sourcebook* (New York, 1995), 36–7; Helen Hackett, *Virgin Mother, Maiden Queen: Elizabeth I and the Cult of the Virgin Mary* (Basingstoke, 1995), 178; Joy Wiltenburg, *Disorderly Women and Female Power in the Street Literature of Early Modern England and Germany* (London, 1992), 196.

either Poole's or theirs. Bridget neither spoke nor acted in self-defence, her silence being reinforced by her death-like trance. She existed merely as the object of violence.[140] Eliding female action was one way of negotiating the semantic difficulties presented by female retaliation. A story in which the woman's response was absent necessarily directed attention and responsibility towards the male adversary. Such a strategy was convenient when the woman concerned might be implicated in the action. Bridget Wood's informants omitted to remind the magistrate that she at that time stood bound to keep the peace towards Poole. Moreover, Poole successfully indicted her, her husband, her daughter and another fellow (probably their manservant), for assaulting him on the same day.[141] Portraying women in terms of vulnerability and defencelessness accentuated the unacceptability of male aggression and simultaneously deflected attention from women's roles in altercations.[142]

Women's self-representation had different nuances. Few described themselves in entirely passive terms, but nonetheless discursively removed themselves from the fray by emphasising passive resistance rather than active responses. Elinor Gorst claimed that Thomas Hewitt violently ejected her from her dwelling-house with such force that an iron staple to which she clung was wrenched from the door-post. A witness deposed that Elinor told her that Hewitt's violence 'had forced her to take up an iron staple'. These versions are subtly different, though in both the staple represented Elinor and Hewitt's relative strength. In the witness's account, Elinor claimed that she responded actively to Hewitt's violence. In her official story, however, Elinor resisted by clinging to the house rather than directing her strength towards the body of her assailant. She asserted active defence only once: she pushed Hewitt away when he tried to strangle her. Ultimately her actions were futile. Unlike the remarkably passive Bridget Wood, it was only after a struggle that Elinor Gorst's helplessness was embodied in the image of her lying senseless outside.[143]

Other than crying out and waiting to be rescued, the only appropriate response within the terms of the dominant gender code was to run away. Fleeing was neither passive nor feminine. Descriptions of women's flights follow masculine conventions: women and men claimed to have run away only from excessive (usually life-threatening) violence. One woman said that a man struck her so hard with a pickel that 'I can scarce lift up my arm to my head'; when he threatened to 'give me more... I was forced to run into

---

[140] CRO, QJF 49/3/68 (1620).
[141] CRO, QJF 57/2/78, /73–/77, /44, /32, /33, QJB 1/5, fo. 214v (1628).
[142] See also CRO, QJF 49/3/68 (1620); QJF 53/3/73, /48, /92, /100 (1624); QJF 53/2/170, /163 (1624); QJF 71/2/49 (1642); QJF 81/2/222 (1653).
[143] CRO, QJF 93/3/71 (1665). See also CRO, QJF 81/2/310 (1653).

the house lest he should have killed me'.[144] Christopher Proctor described how a man knocked his mother-in-law to the ground, held her by the throat and beat her about the head. Proctor pulled him off, enabling her to run towards the house. But a second man intercepted her, 'threw her down upon the stones', stamped his foot three times upon her heart, and kicked her.[145] It was, alas, another story of feminine failure in the face of brutal male force.

Breaking women's boundaries

In early modern rhetoric, household and other personal and social boundaries were interchangeable. This pertained to men as well as women, but notions of feminine vulnerability intensified in particular ways the sense that moral and physical boundaries had been breached. Legal practice informed and reinforced these ideas. Formal indictments and legal testimony asserted that men had assailed and broken doors, locks and hinges of women's houses, and stressed the terror experienced by women and girls inside. Thomas Coughin informed magistrates about William Weston, 'a man of desperate disposition' who had already been indicted for assaulting him. Knowing that Coughin was absent, Weston 'came to my house and pushed at the door to have broken down the door upon my wife and a servant maid. And when he could not get in to them, he gave forth railing speeches against them in such manner as they were sore affrighted.'[146] The inadequacy of female defences against unsolicited and unruly male intrusion was constructed as a problem that only the re-establishment of orderly and powerful manhood would resolve.

The conflation of household and bodily boundaries was common in allegations of violence against wives and widows.[147] Household discourses and practices provided a repertoire of particularly appropriate images and metaphors for depicting violence against women. Housewives, after all, exercised *de facto* control of domestic space. The doors and windows of the household were sites of female work and sociability and bounded the conceptual limits of feminine control. The maintenance of household boundaries provided the means whereby women attained status and authority.[148]

---

[144] CRO, QJF 79/4/57 (1652). See also QJF 49/3/111 (1620); QJF 81/2/222 (1653); QJF 93/1/110 (1665).
[145] CRO, QJF 93/1/110 (1665).
[146] CRO, QJF 49/4/65 (1620). See also QJF 79/4/7 (1651); QJF 91/2/87 (1663); QJF 91/4/65 (1663); PRO, CHES 24/127/1/52 (1648); PRO (Star Chamber, James I) STAC 8/157/21 (1604); STAC 8/87/14 (1611).
[147] For example, CRO, QJF 49/2/64 (1620); QJF 51/3/102 (1622); QJF 53/3/101 (1624); QJF 79/3/16 (1651); QJF 85/2/5 (1657).
[148] Mendelson and Crawford, *Women in Early Modern England*, 205–8; Lena Cowen Orlin, 'Women on the threshold', *Shakespeare Studies* 25 (1997), 50–8; Purkiss, *Witch in History*, 97–8; Walker, 'Expanding the boundaries'.

Mistresses of middling households drew on this authority to articulate the broader damage inflicted when they and their households were subject to violent assaults. Coverture did not come into it. Ann Blackshaw emphasised how past violence by three men struck at the future health of her household. As a consequence of a head wound, 'I believe [my son] is never likely to be so well as formerly.' Her husband received a blow with a pitchfork 'of which he is likely to be lame as long as he lives'. Another son and a grandchild had been beaten and were consequently afraid to go to school on their own. As for herself: 'they also beat and maimed me in the arm and the left hip, [so] that I am afraid and verily believe I shall never again be perfectly well thereof as formerly I have been'. Nor could she put her cow in her own backyard, for they threatened ('with a great club') that 'if I did, I should never milk her more'.[149] Women presented physical violence in terms of its disastrous implications for previously orderly households. In doing so, men's violence was portrayed as striking at the heart of social order.

Images of men's violation of women's interior, private space frequently connected breaking the boundaries of their houses with sexual insult and physical violence on the bodies of wives and widows. Five members of the Holland family beat on the dwelling-house walls of Margaret and Thomas Lawrenson who had locked themselves inside, 'burst the window', and called Margaret 'pocky whore'.[150] Two men 'entered [a widow's house] by violence' at daybreak. They grabbed her 'by my throat and thrust me up against the wall and there did abuse me and hurt my back upon a door', called her 'cheating baggage and cheating naught', before breaking her window by throwing stones.[151] Broken or open doors and windows symbolised women's exposure to personal, proprietorial and sexual dangers and their bodies' receptivity to sexual occupation. Breaking a woman's glass windows, a popular ritual of protest against whoredom, was at once an invasive masculine act and one that suggested woman's sexual availability and desire for occupation. These forms of boundary violation undermined female household authority; complaints of such actions asserted it.

The precarious position of widows as householders was highlighted in allusions to the fragility of widows' household boundaries, which in their case literally defined and delimited female-headed space. Widows presented themselves as helpless victims who lacked male protection. But what women constructed as feminine virtue, men rewrote as the physical and social inadequacy of female householders in a society where households were supposed

---

[149] CRO, QJF 79/3/16 (1651).
[150] CRO, QJF 53/3/104 (1624). The Holland and Lawrenson households were at variance over household boundaries being crossed and not put right: the Lawrensons had accused the Hollands of not returning borrowed goods.
[151] CRO, QJF 87/2/2 (1659).

to be governed by men. A widowed ale-wife complained that her house, her self and her household (these are her distinctions) had been greatly endangered by her son leaving her door off its hinges and the candles burning all night. A male customer immediately assailed her: 'thou liest', he spat, 'for thou left it open for knaves and rogues to lie with thee'.[152] Note the disrespect in his usage of the familiar second personal singular. The concomitant of female autonomy was a lack of male protection that could easily be interpreted as a lack of male control and the problem defined as one of feminine disorder.

Sexual transgression underwrote these stories. Nantwich widow, Jane Minshull, reported that, around midnight, Thomas Cawdell broke through two doors into her house, 'putting me and my family into great fear, in so much as I, for fear of my life, fled from out of my bed and having no other clothes upon save only my smock, was forced to run out of the back door... and through a hedge' to a neighbour's house 'to save myself' from him. A night-time assault upon a dwelling-house, due to the combination of darkness and increased personal vulnerability, evoked burglary, a heinous non-clergiable felony. Minshull's virtual nakedness as she lay in bed in darkness with an intruder present and then ran outside for help, signified her bodily and sexual vulnerability. Minshull's smock denoted a state of undress, not one of attire. The smock, or shift, was an undergarment worn next to the skin, day and night, and infrequently changed or laundered. An intermediate layer between outer clothing and flesh, the shift was 'a sort of second skin'. As a common metaphor for women's licit and illicit sexual activity, it had a carnal value.[153] Further testimony reinforced the sexual-social implications of Cawdell's behaviour. Earlier he had broken one of Minshull's glass windows, called her 'a whore', and threatened to 'ruinate' her house. One witness heard him say, ambiguously, just that he would 'ruin' her.[154] Violence against widows imperilled their property, household and family, as well as their bodies and reputations.

In tales like these, where actual or attempted sexual assaults were not explicitly claimed, the dangers posed by violent males were underscored by sexual metaphors. Some women had greater access than others did to discourses of sexual violation. Jane Minshull, with her glass windows, was one of Nantwich's wealthier inhabitants.[155] She felt able to draw on sexualised language perhaps because her class position and economic status were strong

---

[152] CRO, QJF 49/3/111 (1620). See also QJF 87/2/2 (1659).
[153] For example, 'A wench with her smock-dowry, no portion but her lips and arms', Thomas Middleton and Thomas Dekker, *The Roaring Girl* (1611), V, ii; Philip Massinger and John Fletcher, *The Elder Brother: A Comedy* (1637), III, iii.
[154] CRO, QJF/89/3/176, /177 (1661).
[155] She was possibly one of the wealthy merchant Minshulls.

enough to deflect the ignominy so easily associated with besieged chastity. Telling tales of *a priori* sexual violence was more problematic.

Sex

Rape – a non-clergiable capital felony – was notoriously difficult to prosecute. It constituted a mere one per cent of indicted felonies and had an extremely low conviction rate. Once convicted, however, few men escaped the gallows.[156] No other form of sexual violence had explicit legal status. If a woman successfully fought off the rapist, screamed loudly enough to attract neighbours, or otherwise prevented or dissuaded him, the act was merely assault/affray/battery. This construction of sexual violence as all or nothing was reflected in juridical discourse that devalued women's accusations. Although 'true rape' was 'a most detestable' capital crime, judges, justices and jurors were explicitly warned to distrust women's allegations. Hale opined that 'it is an accusation easy to make and hard to be proved, and harder to be defended by the party accused though "never so innocent" '.[157]

It is grimly ironic that in juridical discourse women's accusations of rape epitomised the lightness and wantonness of female speech. For of all forms of violence against women, rape and attempted rape were the most difficult for women to articulate. As an act of sexual and social destruction, rape worked both a literal and figurative silencing of women.[158] The high premium placed culturally on female chastity, and the power of gossip and reputation to damage women's positions within households and communities undoubtedly discouraged accusations of rape. Women who spoke out were subject to censure.[159] Even people who expressly believed Margaret Knowsley's claim that a local preacher had attempted to rape her nonetheless condemned her for publicising the fact.[160] Men's threats of further violence also silenced women. As 'soon as John Wolfe had done abusing' Margaret Hesketh, he 'threatened me that he would thrash me that I should not be able neither to go nor stand if ever he catched me by myself if ever I declared what he had

---

[156] Nazife Bashar, 'Rape in England between 1550 and 1700' in London Feminist History Group ed., *The Sexual Dynamics of History* (London, 1983), 34–5, 38; Beattie, *Crime and the Courts*, 124–5; Walker, 'Rereading rape and sexual violence', 1.

[157] Matthew Hale, *Historia Placitorum Coronae: The History of the Pleas of the Crown* (London, 1800), 2 vols., Vol. I, 634.

[158] See also Jocelyn Catty, *Writing Rape, Writing Women in Early Modern England* (Basingstoke, 1999), 4.

[159] For example, CRO, QJF 89/4/109, /110 (1662); QJF 73/3107 (1645).

[160] Steve Hindle, 'The shaming of Margaret Knowsley: gossip, gender and the experience of authority in early modern England', *Continuity and Change* 9, 3 (1994), 391–419; Lynda E. Boose, 'The priest, the slanderer, the historian and the feminist', *English Literary Renaissance* 25, 3 (1995), 320–40.

done to me'.[161] Ellen Howley was told that 'I should either be his whore or he would kill me.' She replied, 'I had but a life to lose and I would rather die than do so.'[162]

Assertions of rape were stifled also by the fact that rape ceased to count as a crime when it looked like sex.[163] Legally rape required non-consensual penile penetration (unless the victim was nine years old or under, whereupon the act was felonious regardless of the child's consent).[164] But descriptions of sexual intercourse unravelled allegations of rape. The language of sexual practice evoked discourses of sin and culpability in which women were responsible for illicit heterosexual activity. More particularly, penetrative sex was constructed as an engagement of male will and female submission. Talking about rape as sex (a legal imperative) therefore implied the very submission, or consent, that was necessarily absent in rape. Sex compromised accusations of rape in other ways too. Accused men were advised to say that they had had prior consensual sexual relations with the raped woman.[165] It is no coincidence that the vast majority of both formal charges and guilty verdicts pertained to cases where female consent was immaterial because the victim was under ten years old. Unsurprisingly, overt sexual language was conspicuously absent from the majority of accounts of rape given by older females. But without it their cases were extremely weak.[166]

Women side-stepped the issue of female complicity by relating their own unconsciousness or thwarted attempts to escape. Elizabeth Heath said two men spiked her drink and carried her home 'as senseless or dead'. While she was unconscious, they 'cut or pulled off' her pubic hair and inflicted other, unspecified, abuses that bruised her genitals and thighs. She would have remained ignorant, but the men's subsequent bragging caused gossip, which she 'after[wards] perceived to be true for that I found my [pubic] hair to be wanting, and for that my thighs and secret parts were black and sore'.[167] Another woman was said to have been rendered 'insensible through fright [and] overmuch struggling', before others intervened to save her.[168]

---

[161] PRO, CHES 38/41, 'Examinations against John Wolfe and Joseph Lowe', depositions of Margaret Hesketh and Elizabeth Hesketh (1682).
[162] CRO, QJF 91/4/54 (1664).
[163] Walker, 'Rereading rape and sexual violence', 5–7.
[164] Statute 18 Elizabeth I, c.6 (1575) created an ambiguity regarding the consent of girls aged between ten and twelve years old. Antony E. Simpson, 'Vulnerability and the age of female consent: legal innovation and its effect on prosecutions for rape in eighteenth-century London' in G.S. Rousseau and Roy Porter eds., *Sexual Underworlds of the Enlightenment* (Manchester, 1987), 181–205.
[165] Dalton, *Countrey Justice*, 257; T.E., *Lawes Resolutions*, 395.
[166] Walker, 'Rereading rape and sexual violence'.
[167] PRO, CHES 24/135/6 (1667), examination of Elizabeth Heath.
[168] CRO, QJF 91/4/54 (1663); CCRO, MF86/125 (1668); CCRO, QSE/5/25 (1592); CRO, QJF 91/4/54 (1664).

Similarly, Ann Taylor, a twenty-six-year-old husbandman's wife, demanded from Edward Sproston three shillings owed to her husband for ditching. But 'he took me in his arms, and carried me into a parlour and would have forced me upon the top of the bed in the room, but I with much struggling got from him and almost out of the house, but he overtook me and used the same endeavour until a child of his came into the room, and so he desisted in his violence to me but swore twice if he could but meet with me in a convenient place it should not be the last time'.[169] Ann tried hard to escape but was thwarted. It was not her struggling that saved her. Exhibiting sufficient strength to escape the rapist was problematic for similar reasons to those discussed above in the context of men's general violence against women. Being rescued, on the other hand, was part of an established genre of the romance narrative and was coded as a positive means by which women might escape rape.[170]

Women and girls who were not rescued spoke similarly about how much they had done to escape before they were overcome by brutal male force. More than anything else, rape was portrayed as violence.[171] Thirteen-year-old Margaret Hesketh said that:

John Wolfe came to me (together with Joseph Lowe, son of Roger Lowe of Merton) and said he would fuck me and I said he should not and I forthwith run away as fast I could and got over two hedges and John Wolfe and Joseph Lowe run after me and overtook me in the next field but one, and John Wolfe laid fast hold on me and threw me down upon the ground and pulled up my coats and smock to my bare belly and I cried mainly out and struggled with him as long as my breath would serve and then he pulled out his privy member and put it into my body and would not let me go till he had had his full will and pleasure on me although I endeavoured to hinder him as much as I could, all the while crying and struggling with him according to my strength, no person passing by to interrupt him, Joseph Lowe standing by and encouraging John Wolfe in the action.[172]

Explicit stories of struggling and self-defence were not compromising if the man had won. Moreover, despite the implications of female complicity in carnal knowledge, at least some lawyers conceded that 'if she which is ravished assent for fear of death at the time of the ravishment, it is a rape against her will, notwithstanding such consent; for assent must be voluntary'.[173]

The concomitant of female weakness being imperative to a convincing rape narrative was that women's overt claims to physical strength were usually

---

[169] CRO, QJF 91/3/81 (1663). See also CDRO, EDC 5/1639/120; CCRO, QSE/5/25 (1592).
[170] Catty, *Writing Rape*, 25.
[171] Walker, 'Rereading rape and sexual violence'. See also Patricia Frances Cholakian, *Rape and Writing in the* Heptaméron *of Marguerite de Navarre* (Carbondale, 1991), 218–19.
[172] PRO, CHES 38/41, 'Examinations against John Wolfe and Joseph Lowe', examination of Margaret Hesketh (1682). See also PRO, STAC 8/154/22 (1611).
[173] T.E., *Lawes Resolutions*, 395.

ineffective. Mary Janson told a triumphant story: 'I overcame him', 'with my main strength I prevailed that he did not lie with me', 'I was strong enough for him'. The accused man redefined her behaviour as disorderly femininity – she was physically violent, and also malicious, greedy and kept an unlicensed alehouse. Her claim that he posed a sexual threat was simply dismissed: 'she hath very much frequented my house since [the alleged attempt], whereby it is apparent she conceived no danger by me'.[174] Female strength was turned around and used against the woman concerned. Similarly, a witness deposed that he had asked Ann Swinnerton,

...how Sir Edward [Mosely] being but a little man and she such a lusty woman should be ravished by him! 'Why', said she, 'should you wonder at that?' Then she put her leg between my legs, and put other leg setting her foot against the wall, saying 'Now, in this posture as you see me here, I myself could ravish any woman whatsoever.'

Physical prowess and debauchery were both negative manifestations of female 'lustiness'. Ann Swinnerton's robust physique and her claim that she possessed the wherewithal to rape a woman together undermined her accusation of rape, and simultaneously gave credence to other deponents' claims of her unchaste, deceitful character. Mosely was acquitted.[175]

The sexual nature of rape was signified obliquely in women's narratives in, for instance, the rapist's arrangement of the woman's body and clothing.[176] Thirty-year-old Elizabeth Darlington accused Raphe Lathom of making 'an uncivil attempt on me, and pulled up my clothes, and I believe if I had not cried out he would have ravished me'.[177] An eye-witness saw Richard Kelsall 'fling' Joan Amson (who was under the age of consent) on a bed; Kelsall 'had up her clothes' so that 'I saw her bare and him betwixt her legs'.[178] But such descriptions could easily backfire. The arrangement of clothing was part of a discourse of sexual responsibility. The sight of a woman 'with her clothes pulled up past the middle of her thighs and a man betwixt her legs' indicated sex, consensual or otherwise.[179] Margaret Jarott and John Nickell were seen pressed together against a wall, Nickell 'having his arms about her neck and belly to belly...her clothes were down but I could not discern that she at all struggled or endeavoured to get from him'. Although Jarott's clothes were down, the apparent lack of effort to free herself during the fifteen minutes that this pose was held and her telling Nickell 'that he had the best "things" in Cheshire' implied that she would have consented to her clothes being

---

[174] CRO, QJF 89/1/43 (1661).
[175] *The Arraignment and Acquittal of Sir Edward Mosely* (London, 1648), 11.
[176] For example, CDRO, EDC 5/1640/82; EDC 5/1597/88; CCRO, QSE/5/25 (1592); CRO, QJF 79/4/56 (1652); QJF 91/1/117 (1663).
[177] CRO, QJF 89/4/109 (1662). [178] CDRO, EDC 5/1640/82.
[179] CDRO, EDC 5/1626/32.

'up'.[180] Accused men frequently asserted that women had not objected to them arranging their clothing. One claimed, 'I took her unto me, and pulled her legs about my thighs, sitting in a chair, and took up her clothes and did offer to have had the use of her body but [I] would not enter.'[181] Another said, 'I pulled up her clothes and asked her whether she was as willing as me, and she said she was.'[182]

Torn garments connoted sexual struggle, and had long been associated with rape.[183] 'Pulling at [women's] clothes' was 'very abusive and uncivil'.[184] A yeoman claimed to have sent his daughter away from home after his other children informed him that Master John Aldersey had 'rudely handled their sister by pulling and tearing her clothes and sometimes following her into the loft and chambers above stairs'.[185] A trial pamphlet related a husband's account of finding his raped wife 'thrown upon the ground; with all her clothes torn, the bedclothes torn and hanging half way upon the ground, my wife crying and wringing her hands, with her clothes all torn off her head, her wrist sprained'.[186] But dishevelled, even torn, clothing could signify disorderly, consensual sex. An accused rapist, being asked how the woman 'came to be so with her clothes torn and ruffled in this manner (none but he and she being in the room)... answered, "She always went very ill favouredly in her apparel"'. It was apparently a successful defence.[187] Only regarding the rape of little girls whose virginal status was less debatable did sexual injuries tend to be described more explicitly. When a fourteen-year-old 'virgin', 'a girl of little stature', was raped, it was 'her secret part', not her clothing, that was said to be 'very ill rent and torn'.[188]

In narratives of sexual abuse, doors and walls could serve as barriers between women and either rapist or escape.[189] Fifteen-year-old Margaret Baker told her mother that William Hill took her into his house 'and shut his doors upon her and in his bedchamber did rear her up to a chest' and raped her, 'hurt[ing] her very sore'.[190] Thomas Croakes allegedly 'shut and locked [his] shop door' before attempting to rape Margaret Baxter; witnesses saw her 'endeavouring and striving to escape and fly from [him] forth at the shop window', but Croakes dragged her back 'and she fell down'.[191] The violation of extra-bodily boundaries was also emphasised in allegations that other violent offences, such as robbery, had accompanied rape. A yeoman's wife accused John Boulton of raping her and taking her money by the

---

[180] CRO, QJF 79/1/51, /52 (1651).   [181] CCRO, QSF/73/64 (1629).
[182] PRO, CHES 38/41, 'Examinations against John Wolfe and Joseph Lowe' (1682).
[183] T.E., *Lawes Resolutions*, 393.   [184] CCRO, MF86/125 (1668).
[185] CRO, QJF 79/1/61 (1651).   [186] *Arraignment and Acquittal of Sir Edward Mosely*, 3.
[187] *Arraignment and Acquittal of Sir Edward Mosely*, 5.
[188] CCRO, QSF/79I/45, /39 (1667).
[189] For example, CCRO, QSF/79I/39 (1667); CRO, QJF 89/3/198 (1661).
[190] CRO, QJF 79/1/76 (1651).   [191] CDRO, EDC 5/1639/120.

roadside at night. Both her information and the indictment clearly presented the theft as robbery, which, like rape, lay beyond the remit of benefit of clergy. The trial jury recast robbery as grand larceny, perhaps because only 20*d*. had been stolen. Although the robbery and the rape were prosecuted separately, the elision of the violence of robbery was paralleled in the erasure of the violence of rape. Boulton was acquitted.[192]

Sexual discourses, with their negative connotations of female responsibility, obstructed the articulation of rape and sexual assault.[193] Allegations of rape were unravelled and invalidated by portrayals of rape as sex. The consequence of sex – pregnancy – further undermined rape allegations. For conception was legally accepted as proof of consent, according to the widely held theory that generation occurred from the mixing in the womb of a male and a female seed emitted at orgasm.[194] In the context of illicit or forced sex, pregnancy imprinted guilt upon women's bodies. But this was not the sole meaning derived from the pregnant body under siege.

The pregnant body

When pregnancy prefigured assault, it provided a discursive framework for discussing male violence. Assaults on pregnant women were seen as particularly heinous. In medical, legal and popular discourses, miscarriage ensued from being 'beaten, pushed hard, hit, and thrown', from the mother experiencing extreme emotions such as 'great anger and fear from shock and fright', and from her physical over-exertion such as was necessary in self-defence.[195] Indictments explicitly drew attention to the assaulted woman's pregnant state. One assailant 'did tread on her belly with his feet', inducing a premature labour that lasted for nine days and the baby girl's death one week later. Another sat on 'the body and belly' of a 'heavily pregnant' woman for an hour and, in a crude parody of both rape and giving birth, 'with all his weight... cruelly pressed down on and crushed her'.[196]

Women's narratives stressed connections between emotional and physical damage. Agnes Cappur's baby died in her womb as a direct consequence

---

[192] PRO, CHES 24/127/1/16, CHES 24/127/1/15 (1648), indictments, recognisance, and jury return regarding John Boulton, CHES 21/4, fo. 146v.

[193] Walker, 'Rereading rape and sexual violence' elaborates upon these themes.

[194] T.E., *Lawes Resolution*, 395; Matthew Hale, *History of the Pleas of the Crown* (London, 1736), 631; Fletcher, *Gender, Sex and Subordination*, 47; Angus McLaren, *Reproductive Rituals* (London, 1984), 16–22.

[195] Eucharius Rösslin, *The Rose Garden for Pregnant Women and Midwives, Newly Englished*, trans. Wendy Arons (London, 1994), 84; *Whipping Tom Brought to Light and Exposed to View* (London, 1681); McLaren, *Reproductive Rituals*, 101.

[196] PRO, CHES 24/129/1 (1651), indictment of Richard Davies; CHES 24/116/4 (1622), indictment of Richard Smallwood; CHES 24/125/4 (1640), order re. John Fletcher. See also PRO, CHES 24/131/4 (1656), indictment of Edward Minshull et al.

of the terror she felt when John Read attacked her and drew blood with a bill-hook.[197] Mary Martin miscarried 'by reason of the hurt I received by the blow with his elbow upon my stomach and with the affright which I took upon the same'.[198] Elizabeth Sutton experienced 'terror and fear' when robbed by a gang of four who threatened to beat her if she resisted. In line with medical opinion that 'a woman miscarries if she vomits or becomes sick a great deal', Elizabeth was afterwards so sick 'by reason of the sudden fear I then took' that her unborn child 'is fallen into great extremity and sickness' and in danger of miscarrying.[199]

Responsibility for avoiding such experiences did not rest solely with the mother.[200] For anyone to engage wilfully in behaviour that promoted dangerous emotional or physical states in a pregnant woman was understood to be tantamount to attempting abortion. At the same time, pregnancy was thought to render women 'not like or able to do any violence or wrong'.[201] This was not because either aggression or physical strength was believed naturally to be lacking. Illness and incapacity had not yet been naturalised as routine conditions of pregnancy. Sickness in fact connoted *un*natural corruption of some kind. Rather, the non-aggression of expectant mothers was partly a social phenomenon. In order to protect their unborn infants, women were understood not to engage in violence. The wilful avoidance of anger and physical exertion could thus be constructed as an assertion of maternal responsibility.

Targeting a married woman's belly was understood to be a symbolic act of denigration and destruction. The parts of the body connected with pregnancy and childbirth – belly, breasts, thighs – bore, in the popular idiom of insult, the visible consequences of sexual misconduct. Elizabeth Gandy claimed that three men and a woman 'all...laid violent hands on me, [I] being great with child and at my count's end, and threw me down under them and trod upon me with their feet in a most barbarous and uncivil manner'. One man in particular 'spurned me upon my belly, thighs, and legs, and did much hurt unto me, and put me in great fear and in danger of my life'.[202] The derision implied in spurning struck at and defiled not only the woman and her unborn child but also her husband and household. A Chester baker thus drew particular attention to the fact that his wife had been kicked in the belly and he struck on the head (a site of male honour)

---

[197] PRO, CHES 24/102/4 (1591), indictment of John Read.
[198] CRO, QJF 49/2/168 (1620).
[199] Rösslin, *Rose Garden*, 82. CRO, QJF 51/3/103 (1622).
[200] See also Ulinka Rublack, 'Pregnancy, childbirth and the female body in early modern Germany', *P&P* 150 (1996), 84–110.
[201] CRO, QJF 55/2/121 (1626); QJF 51/3/103 (1622); QJF 89/2/262 (1661).
[202] CRO, QJF 53/3/98 (1624).

when he reported an assault made upon them.[203] The repercussions of such defilement could be devastating. Ellen Dodd informed magistrates that her neighbours, Thomas and Joan, 'fell upon' her, and 'knowing my husband to behave himself harshly and sternly to me', Joan 'struck me sore, [I] being great bellied' and Thomas called her 'Robert Smith's whore'. This combined physical, symbolic and verbal abuse had repercussions: Ellen's husband beat her so hard with a cudgel that it broke, and 'cast me out of doors to my no little sorrow and shame being most basely and wrongfully both used and accused' by Thomas and Joan, 'as the marks they have given me in my body will testify'.[204] Ellen's bruises on her body thus communicated the wider damage inflicted upon her reputation, marriage and household.

In these stories, violence was imaged as corrupting hitherto healthy bodies and productive household economies. Mary Martin was diligently carrying 'a pail of water upon her head' when Richard Woodcock inflicted the blow to her stomach that 'destroyed' the 'fruit of my body'; he injured the Martin household also by setting his pigs in their fields to 'devour and spoil' their corn.[205] Households were similarly imperilled by the life-threatening condition of the assaulted wife who lay 'in danger of death', 'in extremity of sickness', 'sick in such a manner that I had been very likely to have lost my life'.[206] Violence infected the household and, with the death of a spouse and heir, could effectively dissolve it. Elizabeth Sutton's reproductive body 'putrefied', signalling the 'evil smelly fluids' associated materially with foetal death and figuratively with moral and social corruption.[207] In the worst-case scenario, the pollution of a pregnant body infected the entire social and political order.

The discursive potency of pregnancy did not arise merely from the social significance of maternity and housewifery, though these did provide a range of positive subject positions from which married women spoke.[208] The authority to declare oneself pregnant was inscribed in the body itself by the tactile experience of 'quickening', the moment around the fifth month when life and soul entered previously inert matter in the womb. The veracity of pregnancy had largely to be taken on trust.[209] Unlike spinsters or widows, for whom the negative implications of illegitimacy generally outweighed positive gains, married women's declarations that they were quick with child when assaulted were taken seriously.[210] Only in exceptional circumstances, such as in pleading benefit of belly, in prosecutions for rape, or in pregnancies

---

[203] CCRO, MF86/134 (1668).   [204] CRO, QJF 89/2/232 (1661).
[205] CRO, QJF 49/2/168 (1620).   [206] CRO, QJF/51/3/103 (1622); QJF 49/2/168 (1620).
[207] CRO, QJF/51/3/103 (1622).   [208] Walker, 'Expanding the boundaries'.
[209] Barbara Duden, *Disembodying Women: Perspectives on Pregnancy and the Unborn*, trans. Lee Hoinacki (Cambridge, Mass., 1993), 83, 94.
[210] For an exception of a single woman, see CRO, QJF 89/1/87 (1661).

that never ended, were wives divested of this authority and other 'expert' testimony deemed more reliable. Married women often drew on this discourse even before quickening occurred: I was 'gone with child about twelve weeks to my best knowledge', or even 'conceived with conceived seed'.[211] The epistemology of pregnancy provided some women with a discourse that could be used against those who had allegedly inflicted violence upon them.

Domestic abuse

The conventions described above – especially the emphasis upon female suffering, passivity and vulnerability, and the rescuing role of neighbours and kin – were drawn on when women were assaulted in their own homes by husbands, fathers or masters. The special nature of household and familial obligations not only intensified these discourses but also made available others in which male violence could be legitimated or challenged.

Historical research has established that family violence was a 'regular and sometimes brutal manifestation of patriarchal power' in the early modern period.[212] Although this power was limited, violence inflicted in the course of exercising household authority was easier to justify than to condemn. In patriarchal rhetoric, wrongful violence by superiors struck against social order, yet corporal punishment in the household was seldom construed as 'wrongful'. Even conduct books that advised that wives be reproved only with words of 'meekness' and patience, nevertheless conceded that husbands were legally entitled to correct their wives with condign and moderate physical punishment.[213] Only 'if he threatens to *kill* or *outrageously* beat her, or if the wife has notorious cause to fear that he will do so' could a wife crave security of the peace against her husband. The point at which 'reasonable correction' merged into outrageous violence was unclear.[214] Furthermore, in complaining about their husbands, wives were notionally overstepping the boundaries of orderly behaviour. John Wing described any rebellious or

---

[211] CRO, QJF 49/2/168 (1620); QJF 49/2/171 (1620).
[212] Susan Dwyer Amussen, 'Gender, family and the social order 1560–1725' in Anthony Fletcher and John Stevenson eds., *Order and Disorder in Early Modern England* (Cambridge, 1985), 196–218; Susan Dwyer Amussen, '"Being stirred to much unquietness": violence and domestic violence in early modern England', *Journal of Women's History* 6, 2 (1994), 70–89; Fletcher, *Gender, Sex and Subordination*, 192–3; Linda A. Pollock, 'Rethinking patriarchy and the family in seventeenth-century England', *Journal of Family History* 23, 1 (1998), 4, 20–2.
[213] Daniel Cawdrey, *Family Reformation Promoted* (London, 1656), 116; *The Great Advocate and Oratour for Women, Or, the Arraignement, Tryall and Conviction of all Such Wicked Husbands (or Monsters) who Hold it Lawfull to Beat their Wives, or to Demeane Themselves Severely and Tyrannically towards them* (n.s., 1682).
[214] Dalton, *Countrey Justice*, 163; T.E., *Lawes Resolutions*, 128; Pickering, *Christian Oeconomie*, 133.

undutiful wife, and not only a murderous one, as 'a home-rebel, a house-traitor'.[215] There was even a sense in which, by intervening in marital disputes, secular authorities undermined the very values of social order they wished to uphold. Although real household and marital relations rarely reflected the patriarchal ideal, the sheer weight of patriarchal ideology weakened the position of wives, and other household members, who officially complained about the adult male head.[216]

The message that spousal discord was ultimately the fault of the wife was communicated in many forms, including tracts that stressed that people 'marry equally in all respects'. A 'loving, kind and honest' wife was man's 'sweetest comfort', but 'there is no greater plague nor torment...than to be matched with an untoward, wicked, and dishonest woman'.[217] Whereas the contrasting attributes of kindness and honesty are wickedness and dishonesty, the opposite of 'loving' here is not 'unloving' or 'hating', but 'untoward', plainly intimating that a wife who was difficult to control was perverse. The husband's duty to control and correct his disobedient wife was understood as a requisite of maintaining his household authority and honourability.[218] Men stood in for their households as we have seen. But where internal household relations were concerned, the commonest metaphor was that of the man being the 'head' that must 'oversee and guide the body, that little domestical body'. If he stands 'lower than the shoulders...doubtless it makes a great deformity in the family', William Whately opined. 'That house is a misshapen house, and...a crump-shouldered, or hunch-backed house, where the husband hath made himself an underling to his wife.' To disfigure one's house in this manner was 'a sin,...not humility, but baseness'.[219]

Before magistrates and in court, accused men rarely denied that they had beaten wives, children or servants. Men framed their violence as a means of upholding order – an acceptable response to wifely disorder or negligence. 'Backwardness in the religious service of God', carelessness in managing household affairs, ill-behaviour towards neighbours and friends, and misdemeanour in regard of themselves and their husbands were all said to

---

[215] John Wing, *The Crowne Conjugall, or the Spouse Royal: A Discoverie of the True Honour and Happiness of Christian Matrimoniel* (London, 1632), 297; he used similar metaphors on 198.
[216] Margaret Hunt, 'Wife-beating, domesticity and women's independence in eighteenth-century London', *Gender and History* 4, 1 (1992), 14. For wives' relatively few options in dealing with violent husbands see Mendelson and Crawford, *Women in Early Modern England*, 133–45.
[217] *The Court of Good Counsell. Wherein is Set Down the True Rules How a Man Should Choose a Good Wife from a Bad* (London, 1607), sig. B1.
[218] *Court of Good Counsell*, sig. B4v.
[219] Cawdrey, *Family Reformation*, 19; William Whately, *A Bride-bush. Or, A Direction for Married Persons* (London, 1623), 98.

legitimate wife-beating.[220] Critics pointed out that husbands were thereby permitted to punish wives for 'some small and trivial faults' that in other contexts were 'virtues'. The 'nimbleness of women's tongues', for example, was 'sometimes... employed to their husbands' disturbance, yet for the most part are busied in their good'.[221] Certainly, ballads and jest-books depicted wives being beaten, tied, chained and humiliated (one had her head shaved) as means of 'curing' shrewishness.[222]

Some abused wives nonetheless did find voices in which to speak of male violence. In particular, they portrayed the husband's behaviour as the wilful destruction of the household's economic, social and moral integrity, in spite of their own noble efforts to maintain it. This was a powerful discourse. It was proclaimed from the pulpit that 'if any provide not for his own, and specially those of his own house, he hath denied the faith, and is worse than an infidel (1 Timothy 5:8)'.[223] The failure of husbands to provide for their families was stressed in stories told in secular and ecclesiastical courts that conflated physical and other forms of cruelty.[224] Wife-beaters were depicted as wastrels, who drank away household means, 'embezzled' their wives' personal goods, and redirected to mistresses material and emotional resources that properly belonged to their wives.[225] Katherine Stokes, for example, requested protection from magistrates by repeatedly connecting the physical and economic implications of her husband's behaviour. He attacked her with 'his drawn knife' because she refused to give him money to go drinking. His continual 'cruel and inhuman dealing' of her compelled her to seek redress of 'her miserable estate'. She wished to 'live in safeguard of my life, my husband having consumed and made away his living'. In order to maintain herself and her children, Katherine asked the bench to permit her to continue selling ale. Even her rescue by strangers 'who came travelling their way' had economic undertones, for it implied that her house was conveniently situated for ale-selling. Her husband's violation of her physical and economic security was reinforced by her vulnerability as a woman: 'for the safeguard of my life I was enforced to come out of my house as naked as ever I was born or else the truth is I had been murdered'. A husband's violence made the household no longer a place of succour but one of mortal danger.[226]

---

[220] Heale, *Apologie*, 34–5.   [221] Heale, *Apologie*, 36–7.
[222] Archie Armstrong, *A Banquet of Jests* (London, 1640), 227–8, 307–8; Todd, 'Representation of aggression', 167–8.
[223] Cawdrey, *Family Reformation*, sig. A1.
[224] Amussen, *Ordered Society*, 128–9; Gowing, *Domestic Dangers*, 210; Joanne M. Ferraro, 'The power to decide: battered wives in early modern Venice', *Renaissance Quarterly* 48, 3 (1995), 496–502; Foyster, *Manhood*, 181–95.
[225] For example, PRO, CHES 21/3, fo. 173v (1628); CHES 24/127/1/534, petition of Katherine Newton (1648).
[226] CRO, QJF 49/2/146 (1620).

Beaten wives also evoked the husband's destruction of the sexual union that theoretically lay at the heart of the healthy Protestant household. Mary Jones detailed her husband George's adulterous relationship with his mistress, Dorothy, whom he had brought into the house. Dorothy brought George a posset and fed it to him while he lay in bed. A posset, depending on the recipe, was conventionally a delicacy or a cold remedy. Either way, a man's wife should have administered it to him. Afterwards, Dorothy undressed and joined George in the bed where Mary rightfully should have slept. Mary forced home the point: George 'has never put off his clothes to lie with me since Dorothy Walklate [sic] came to live in the house'. When Mary threatened to tell neighbours, George beat her and threw her out of the house. Household order had been usurped.[227]

Anti-wife-beating discourse constructed the violent husband as one who undermined not only his wife's authority as mistress of the household, and thereby the household's economic and social credit, but also his own manhood. Marriage bestowed manhood; the destruction of marital relations was associated with its loss. Manhood was displayed through men's mastery over their households, their social inferiors, and over themselves. Inflicting physical correction unreasonably by definition betrayed a man's lack of mastery over both the person he beat and himself.[228] Men's unreasonable violence towards their wives was associated with 'unmanly' cowardice. Balladeers wrote that a man whose wife 'seldom shall go without her face black' was one who 'from a man he'll perhaps turn his back'; wife-beaters were 'dastardly knaves' who 'dare not with swords and staves/ meet men in the field for their lives'. If 'you desire to be men complete', advised another, no matter how skilled in other masculine pursuits, 'whatever you do your wives do not beat'.[229] Some conduct books relayed the same message.[230] Men who abused women were condemned as 'unmanlike men, and stain of your sex'.[231] Unnecessary cruelty – physical, emotional or economic – was a corollary of unmanliness and dishonour.

The mixed message of wifely submission and equality that pertained to the spousal relationship did not extend to that of parents and children. Patriarchy insisted that children owed their parents 'natural' obedience. Children's use of violence against their parents was accordingly constructed as an act against nature. A man's violence towards his mother was 'strange and unnatural'.[232] Another had 'unnaturally beated his own mother and stricken forth four of

---

[227] CRO, QJF 93/4/83, /111 (1665). A posset was a hot milky drink curdled with alcohol and flavoured with sugar and spices.
[228] Foyster, *Manhood*, 186–93.
[229] *The Married-Woman's Case*; *Well Met Neighbour*, both cited in Todd, 'Representation of aggression', 164; M.P., *Hold Your Hands, Honest Men* (London, 1634).
[230] *Court of Good Counsell*, sig. C2.   [231] Heale, *Apologie*, 2.
[232] CRO, QJF 51/1/119 (1622).

her teeth'.[233] A mother spoke of her son's abuse 'both by unseemly words and by striking me and drawing blood on me very uncivilly and unnaturally'.[234] The involvement of law in regulating the behaviour of one's children was itself presented as proof that 'natural' authority and duty had been subverted. As one father said, 'my son hath been so unnaturally abusive unto me that I have been enforced to procure a warrant of good behaviour against him'.[235] Early modern authorities persistently expressed concerns that ill-governed households would breed up disorderly subjects and workers and result in disruptions in social order more widely. One writer stressed that the lack of '*family* Reformation' and '*discipline* in families' was the cause of all the *miscarriages* abroad' and 'all those *disorders* in towns and nations, *drunkenness, uncleanness, profaneness*', and so forth that 'fills the *gaols*, and furnishes the *gallows*'. Another spoke of wife-beaters as 'contrivers how to dissolve this *economical harmony* between man and wife and thereby to crack the axle-trees of our *microcosm* asunder, with whose ponderous weight the burdened Earth begins to sink into the gulf of dark confusion'.[236]

The meanings attributed to family violence and the discourses in which it was framed were not static. Change has been considered primarily in terms of the *longue durée*. Margaret Hunt has argued that in the final decades of the seventeenth century a discursive shift occurred. The rejection of wife-beating on the grounds that it was unchristian, uncivilised and counterproductive began to be replaced by the demonisation of family violence. The effect was the gradual production of the culture of 'secrecy and stigma' that characterises modern domestic violence.[237] But the meanings and language of domestic violence were subject also to short-term fluctuations. During the tumultuous years of the mid-seventeenth century, which experienced civil wars, regicide, the moral order of republican rule and restoration of the monarchy, the legitimate extent of responses to the abuse of authority were central issues in political rhetorics of all persuasions.[238] The ubiquitous analogy between domestic and political power relations, and the dynamics of national and local political interest, meant that the political environment had profound implications for real women and men in both opening up and closing down ways in which domestic disputes could be framed.

Before and during the early civil war years, royal authority was legitimated by theories of divine right, patriarchalism, and sometimes 'social contract'. Royalists argued that God would hardly give men 'power or providence

---

[233] CRO, QJF 55/2/135 (1626).   [234] CRO, QJF 51/1/119, QJF 51/2/117 (1622).
[235] CRO, QJF 74/4/55, /56 (1647); QJB 1/6, fo. 117v (1646).
[236] Cawdrey, *Family Reformation*, 45; *Great Advocate*, 46. Original italics.
[237] Hunt, 'Wife-beating, domesticity and women's independence', 24–8.
[238] Carole Pateman, *The Disorder of Women* (Oxford, 1989), 36–53. See also Susan Kingsley Kent, *Gender and Power in Britain, 1660–1990* (London, 1999), 19–29; Schochet, *Patriarchalism in Political Thought*.

which is natural and ordinary in a father over his children...more than the King can challenge over his people'. It was 'no more possible in right for...a people to choose their rulers than to choose their fathers'.[239] The commonwealth was a household, a multitude being merely 'a heap of stones, before they were cemented and knit together into one building' and became 'a people' subject to the authority of the King who, like a husband and father, was the household's head. Just as wife and husband entered into a binding marriage contract instituted by God, the people and the King were bound by a similar contract. Resisting the monarch was analogous to a wife violating her marriage vows: both were sins even if the monarch/husband had abused his power.[240] From this perspective, it was the King's duty to use violence to imprint his authority over Parliamentary 'rebels' in the same way that a husband should use force if necessary to bring to order an insubordinate wife.

Parliamentarian discourses responded by reconceptualising this relationship. A few, John Milton among them, proposed that divorce should be freely available to both individuals and 'a whole people' who were subjected to 'unworthy bondage'. The misinterpretation of scripture had 'changed the blessing of matrimony not seldom into a familiar and co-inhabiting mischief; at least into a drooping and disconsolate household captivity'. To compel the continuation of such a bond was 'a violent and cruel thing'. 'No effect of tyranny can sit more heavy on the commonwealth than this household unhappiness on the family. And farewell all hope of true reformation in the State, while such an evil as this lies undiscerned or unregarded in the house.'[241] Most early Parliamentarian discourse was typically less extreme. By abusing his power, the King/husband/father weakened (but did not necessarily destroy) his right to govern his realm/household. While the people/wife/child had the right to resist tyrannical rule, the King's/husband's authority was nevertheless 'natural'. During the first civil war, remember, most opponents of Charles I envisaged resistance, not overthrow.

In 1646, the Parliament's forces were victorious both locally (with the surrender of Chester) and nationally (Charles I fled to Scotland). County administration resumed something like normal business. It is, I would argue, no coincidence that complaints about family violence shifted in perspective. Pre-war condemnations of excessive violence by husbands had been condemned mainly in terms of unnecessary cruelty. In contrast, stories told to magistrates

---

[239] Dudley Digges, *An Answer to a Printed Book Intituled Observations upon some of His Majesties Late Answers and Expresses* (Oxford, 1642), 2, 3; Dudley Digges, *The Unlawfulnesse of Subjects Taking Up Arms Against their Soveraigne in What Case Soever* (Oxford, 1643), 77.
[240] Digges, *Unlawfulnesse of Subjects*, 15.
[241] John Milton, *The Doctrine and Discipline of Divorce* (London, 1643), 2, 8.

between 1646 and 1648 were informed by an intensified discourse of abused power. Supplicants stressed that wife-beating was not sanctioned by 'natural' social hierarchy. Isabel Carter complained that her husband 'hath dealt so cruelly and unnaturally with me' that she had been forced to run away from home, fearing for her life. He swore that 'he should do God good service' by killing her, making 'his bloody intent' obvious both when he was excessively drunk and 'when he was sober'. He undermined familial authority also by 'caus[ing] his children to promise him on their knees' that they should neither hinder him nor protect her when he used violence against her. Isabel begged the bench to take such course with him 'that she may be freed from this continual fear and danger'. The violent husband was now presented to the Parliamentarian bench as 'unnatural'. The bench confirmed that this was indeed 'cruel and unnatural' dealing, and issued a warrant of behaviour against him.[242]

In effect, narratives of family violence reflect the broadening of the category of 'unnatural' abuse. Before the civil war, it was primarily violence against parents that was considered to be unnatural. A man's assault on his brother and mother in 1626, for instance, described as 'unnatural' only the act against the mother.[243] But by 1648, a yeoman told the Cheshire bench of his brother's 'most unnatural' threats to kill him. (The brother, incidentally, drew on another language that had gained currency during the war years: each time he was bound over he broke the bond, saying that 'no laws are now observed'.)[244] The experience of civil war and the accompanying political rhetoric challenged notions that the use of violence was divinely ordained and that resistance to authority was 'unnatural'.[245]

This did not mean, however, that conventional hierarchies were disregarded. The combination of Presbyterian beliefs held by many JPs (the Cheshire bench was dominated by moderates in the years 1646–8), the outbreak of the second civil war in late 1647, and mutinies in the New Model Army, meant that magistrates in 1648 were extremely sensitive to rebuttals of authority. Again, this impacted upon the stories told of familial abuses and their legal outcomes. The county bench declared that in refusing to allow his stepmother 'a competent maintenance', Stephen Rathbone 'acted very unnaturally and contrary to his father's order'. He was entreated to maintain his stepmother 'which by Law and in all good conscience he ought' to do. The implications of this failure to honour his parents extended beyond the domestic context. The court 'doth wonder' that Stephen Rathbone and his father, 'who have been willing to be observed for piety in religion, should

---

[242] CRO, QJF 74/2/81, QJB 1/6, fo. 115v (1646).   [243] CRO, QJF 55/2/135, /138 (1626).
[244] CRO, QJF 76/3/56 (1648).
[245] Carole Pateman, *The Sexual Contract* (Stanford, 1988), 39–40.

now so forget themselves as to swallow up the woman's estate and live in plenty and to expose her to want and misery, who before her intermarriage was known to live in good esteem and plenty'.[246] In the fragile political environment of the summer of 1648, the breakdown of authority at gentry level, and especially among those who were supposedly exemplars of godly living, was a cause of great concern for Cheshire's magistrates.

The trial and execution of Charles I in January 1649 further problematised ideas about 'unnatural' abuses of power. Until then, Parliamentarian rhetoric had presented the King's behaviour as an abuse of power.[247] During the trial, John Bradshaw (who shortly afterwards became Chief Justice of Chester) echoed conventional complaints against wife-beaters in arguing that Charles I had been 'a destroyer' of the nation instead of protecting it as he was bound to do. As one republican tract put it, 'When my *wife* turneth *adulteress*, my *covenant* with her is broken. And when my *King* turneth tyrant, and continueth so, my *covenant* with him also is broken.' But the notion that 'a people' had the 'power both to question and to punish tyrannous princes' was radical indeed.[248] Regicide made possible Royalist appropriation of the discourse of tyranny that previously had been the preserve of the Parliament. In monarchical rhetoric, the execution of a king was a tyrannical act and the Parliamentarian regime based on violence, such as 'the unchristian usage of old and sick people, women and children, beaten, wounded or killed upon no provocation; women and maids ravished...others tortured'.[249] The accusation of tyranny, then, became a mainstay of Royalist propaganda.[250] Furthermore, the analogous terms of national and domestic governance invited an uncomfortable image that would not serve women's interests in court: the corollary of the people assuming the right to execute a tyrannous monarch was that wives might kill abusive husbands. This, of course, was petty treason, and no one across the political spectrum countenanced such an action when it applied to wives rather than subjects. Moreover, it evoked Royalist rhetoric in which regicide was definitively treason. As a consequence of all this, almost immediately following the King's death, the term 'unnatural' seems to have been excised from complaints about abusive husbands. Wives instead focused on their present economic circumstances and elided issues of domestic tyranny. In 1649 and the early 1650s petitions to quarter sessions

---

[246] CRO, QJF 76/2/32, /33, QJB 1/6, fo. 181v (1648).
[247] Elizabeth Skerpan, *The Rhetoric of Politics in the English Revolution, 1642–1660* (London, 1992), 95–125.
[248] N.T., *The Resolver Continued, or Satisfaction to Some Scruples about Putting the Late King to Death* (London, 1649), 6, 1, 22.
[249] Fabian Philipps, *King Charles the First, No Man of Blood: But a Martyr for his People* (London, 1649), 33.
[250] Skerpan, *Rhetoric of Politics*, 134–6, 146–7.

made only oblique references to, or glossed over, husbands' cruelty.[251] Margaret Bosson, for example, said merely that her husband lived 'very unquietly with me' upon discovering after their marriage that 'my means was sorry small and my debts great and many'; she did not detail how this 'unquiet' living was manifested.[252]

During the 1650s, however, the Cheshire bench once again invoked law and 'natural' justice to underpin claims that they upheld social order. Both locally and nationally, government distanced itself from the more radical elements of republicanism and placed great emphasis on promoting conventional familial and civil hierarchies and godly living. It is telling, for instance, that twice as many works were published in the 1650s than in any of the decades before or after that explicitly focused on the godly discipline of children.[253] The analogy of family and state evidently retained its potency: the 'many late disasters' in the nation were 'sad effects of children's disobedience'. Such disobedience and lack of 'natural affection' was 'a ring-leading sin, a very root or spring of manifold wickednesses, ... the very way to fall, ... It hath exposed some men to punishment of death by the civil Magistrate.' The 'father and mother' to be honoured in the fifth commandment were 'all persons whatsoever that are in authority over others', namely magistrates, ministers and masters, as well as mothers and fathers, even in treatises concerned primarily with the parent–child relationship.[254]

In the same way that parents were bound by 'Nature itself' and scripture to discipline their children, men were 'exhorted to love, nourish, and cherish their wives'.[255] By mid-decade, narratives of marital discord adopted similar language of natural and Christian obligation. Katherine Bratt, a shoemaker's wife, complained to the Cheshire bench that her husband 'very hardly and unnaturally used' her. What was presented as 'unnatural' here was his wilful determination to break the bond of marital unity by secret means. First, he had for some time 'used me harshly upon purpose to drive me from him (though he hath had by me thirteen children)'. And 'now of late about a month since', he had cast her out with their two youngest children, 'one sucking on my breasts and both naked of clothes... not allowing a penny towards' their subsistence. Moreover, 'for justifying of this unjust doings he

---

[251] CRO, QJF 77/3/16, /41 (1649); QJF 79/2/170 (1651).
[252] CRO, QJF 79/2/164 (1651).
[253] For example, Thomas Cobbet, *A Fruitful and Useful Discourse Touching the Honour Due from Children* (London, 1656); W.C., *A Schoole of Nurture for Children, or the Duty of Children in Honouring their Parents* (London, 1656); Michael Jermin, *The Fathers Institution of his Childe* (London, 1658); Henry Jessey, *A Catechism for Babes or Little Ones* (London, 1652).
[254] W.C., *Schoole of Nurture*, sig. A2, 33, 35, 45–9, 2–4. See also Cobbet, *Fruitful and Useful Discourse*, sig. A3–A4, 2–3.
[255] W.C., *Schoole of Nurture*, 50–1; Cobbet, *Fruitful and Useful Discourse*, 7, 247.

casts forth in speeches that I am a whore and that the child sucking on my breast is none of his and refuseth to own it or baptise it'. While Katherine's husband acted to dissolve their marriage, she evoked legal discourse to establish that she was the preserver of order within and beyond the household. If his accusations were true, Katherine declared, 'I desire no favour but that the rigour of the law may be executed upon me' and that 'I may receive condign punishment'. But of that fault, 'I call God to witness, I am clear.' She asked the bench to order that she and her husband should 'live peaceably together, I giving him no offence'. But if his 'malice against me be such that we may not live together' – which was plainly the case she was making – Katherine wanted maintenance for herself, the two infants, and 'also for those [children] he hath at home with him, because I know they cannot be but much neglected by reason he is by night and day at shop or abroad and none that can tend them as children ought to be used'. This construction of the 'unnatural' husband and father who sought to destroy household unity was effective. But, crucially, it was not protection from violence that wives sought from the bench, but economic assistance. In these stories, husbands failed to fulfil their obligations despite their wives meeting their part of the contract. The court ordered that he was to pay her 12*d.* weekly 'rather because he had £14 portion with her, and hath been twenty years her husband'.[256] The emphasis on the household head's duty to protect those creatures in his care was particularly effective in Cheshire at this time. But in the later seventeenth century and the eighteenth century, with a renewed stress on the frailty of women, it replaced the good housewife as the dominant discourse in complaints about abusive husbands.[257]

Following the Restoration of the monarchy in 1660 stories of familial violence shifted in form once again. When sons were accused of abusing their mothers the 'unnaturalness' of the act was no longer a central issue. It was rarely mentioned. Both here and with regard to wife-beating, the focus was now on violence *per se* rather than on its conflation with other categories of abuse.[258] The importance of household obligations remained. When Mary Stretch was beaten by George Deakin, with whom she may or may not have lived, it was her twenty-three-year-old daughter, Mary, who had him bound over. Mary junior displaced Deakin as husband/father, thereby removing the legitimacy of any 'correction' he might have administered. She introduced him into her narrative as the man 'who says my mother is his wife' and ended by reporting that her mother said that 'she durst not go live with him for

---

[256] CRO, QJF 83/2/171 (1655).
[257] See the unsuccessful petition of Ann Venables, CRO, QJF 102/4/146 (1675). Hunt, 'Wife-beating, domesticity and women's independence', 15.
[258] For sons' abuses of mothers that were not said to be 'unnatural', see CRO, QJF 89/3/199, /180 (1661); QJF 89/3/232, /34–/35 (1661); QJF 89/4/43 (1662); QJF 95/4/37 (1667).

she was afraid that he would kill her'. Thus framed, his violence to Mary junior was presented outside any household context. Mary described a physical struggle for a place in the household. Deakin turned her out of her mother's house; she came in again; he threw her out once more, saying 'I should not be there where he was' for she intended to testify against him. Her two younger siblings had 'run out for fear' and called to neighbours that Deakin was killing their mother. The story ended with all three children being locked out of the house, and their mother lying on the floor inside where Deakin had thrown her.[259] Deakin was bound over by recognisance.

Mary Stretch effectively told a story of a false tyrant – the Restoration of the monarchy had restored tyranny as a discourse of domestic violence. A comparison of two editions of William Heale's *Apologie for Women* demonstrates the shift in focus. In 1609, with a subtitle that stated his 'opposition' to the view that 'it was lawful for husbands to beat their wives', Heale argued that wife-beating was against natural, civil and moral law and was, in any case, counterproductive. In 1682, an (unattributed) expanded edition was published as *The Great Advocate and Oratour for Women, Or, the Arraignement, Tryall and Conviction of all Such Wicked Husbands (or Monsters) who Hold it Lawfull to Beate their Wives, or to Demeane themselves Severely and Tyrannically towards them*. The language of the title was reflected in the contents. Wife-beaters were 'irrational', 'overgrown monsters of tyranny', 'monsters who will be apprentices to the Devil', 'who seem to have banished all humanity' and were 'cankered with vice'. Such husbands acted upon 'the violent whirlwind of unbridled passion', 'an excess of rage and madness'. Moreover, the abusive husband struck at the heart of social order. He was 'a professed enemy to true religion'. Wife-beating was 'a hateful impiety' that 'violates the holy rites of marriage'. It was 'detestable to God, and to all his sacred laws', and 'opposite to the Law of Nature'. To suggest that wife-beaters acted lawfully was 'diabolical'. It was necessary to 'lop off such gangrened members of an unhappy state or kingdom, lest they infect the whole body with such a fatal distemper, as will prove mortal and destructive to all human societies, with whom they shall converse'.[260]

This demonisation of abusive husbands was matched by wives being portrayed as even more passive, patiently enduring their husbands' abuse just as 'tender reeds (whose nature yields to every gentle gale) lie prostrate, crowd together and whisper in trembling fear' in the face of 'the black terrifying hurricane'. They endeavoured 'to wipe off their crystal tears (as pure and clear as is their innocency) without the discovery of their grief'.[261] A similar phenomenon has been traced with respect to pamphlet and ballad depictions

---

[259] CRO, QJF 97/3/82–/84 (1669).   [260] *Great Advocate*, sigs. A2r–A2v, 72, 46, 149–50.
[261] *Great Advocate*, sig. A3v, 29–30.

of spousal murder: accounts of murderous husbands were far more common in the later decades of the seventeenth century than they had been before 1642.[262] In legal stories of domestic violence, these cultural shifts were reflected in men's violence being portrayed simply as violence, with far less legitimisation of the wife's role. Randle Furnifall's treatment of his wife and maidservant in 1669 was presented as unacceptable for no other reason than it was drunken violence. When his wife, seeing that he was drunk, tried to take his flagon from him, he 'struggled with her and threw her down, and when she got up again' he struck her 'upon the head with the flaggon'.[263] Ellen Furnifall, like Mary Stretch senior, remained relatively passive in these stories. The women themselves appear not to have deposed against their husbands. Being asked about her marital status, Mary Stretch said that she married Deakin by the laws of God but not by 'the Bishop's laws'. She appears in the narratives of three other deponents only in her silent prostrate state. Ellen Furnifall was described as offering some resistance, but by the end of the story she too was categorically lying on the floor.[264] These post-Restoration accounts are similar to those of unrelated male aggressors and female victims. A model of feminine passivity was increasingly adopted in witness testimony of spousal abuse. Whereas there had previously been positive discursive means available in which wives could tell their own stories of domestic violence, the success of complaints about abusive husbands became dependent on the woman's silence; these tales could only be told by a third party. At the same time, witnesses inferred that violence within the home was unacceptable. This, I suggest, was indicative of a broader change in attitudes towards violence, gender and social order.

We have seen that in various ways cultural phenomena tended to undermine women's complaints about male violence or even to silence women altogether. Inhibiting discourses, however, did not pertain only to women. Male speech, while being freer than women's, was also subject to certain restraints. This was especially so when men wished to complain about women's violence. It is to women's violence that we now turn.

---

[262] Frances E. Dolan, *Dangerous Familiars: Representations of Domestic Crime in England, 1550–1700* (London, 1994), 89–91, n. 1; Wiltenburg, *Disorderly Women*, 214, 221.
[263] CRO, QJF 97/2/121 (1669).
[264] CRO, QJF 97/3/82–/84 (1669); QJF 97/2/121 (1669).

3

Voices of feminine violence

Existing historiography presents women as victims rather than perpetrators of violence. It is true that typically a minority of violent offenders, between ten and twenty per cent, were female.[1] Yet privileging victimhood over agency is an interpretative matter. The low incidence of women's violence relative to men's has been considered a consequence of biology, of prescriptive social roles, of the internalisation (by either or both sexes) of patriarchal ideology. Whatever the case, the upshot is the same: female violence was typically perceived as 'same-sex violence', 'rather trivial' and inconsequential.[2] Feminine violence that by conventional standards was 'serious' – when women killed, for instance – is sensationalised as an aberration from 'normal' gendered behaviour. 'Unnaturally' violent women are either (like infanticidal mothers) casualties of oppressive gender codes or (like those who impersonated male highway robbers) rejecters of them. This interpretative model of men's violence as 'normal' and women's as numerically and thus culturally insignificant is inadequate. I am not contesting the fact that women were a minority of those prosecuted for violent crimes. I am suggesting, however, that exploring women's violence in its own terms may prove more fruitful for the historian than simply dismissing it as an anomaly.

MODES OF WOMEN'S VIOLENCE

Household concerns

One well-rehearsed explanation for the low incidence of women as sole assailants cites women's 'more dependent and passive' nature, and their reliance upon men, especially their husbands, to settle their quarrels for them.[3]

---

[1] See above, pp. 24–5, and Table 2.1, p. 25.
[2] Spierenburg, 'How violent were women?', 19, 26–7, 11. See also Amussen, 'Part of a Christian man'; Beattie, 'Criminality of women'; Finch, 'Women and violence', 38; Kloek, 'Criminality and gender', 15–17; Sharpe, *Crime*, 154–5; Wiener, 'Sex roles and crime'.
[3] Wiener, 'Sex roles and crime', 49; Kloek, 'Criminality and gender', 15, 22; Mendelson and Crawford, *Women in Early Modern England*, 44.

Such a view reflects a somewhat literal, and inappropriate, interpretation of the doctrine of coverture. Even in theory, the unity of person enshrined in coverture pertained only to certain things, notably married women's property. In 'nature and in some other cases by the law of God and man', husband and wife 'remain diverse', and 'in criminal and other special causes our law argues them several persons'.[4] Evidence of practice, too, fails to confirm wifely passivity. Far from being kept from the fray by protective husbands, married women constituted the greatest single category – over half – of all female defendants in assault cases.[5] Indeed, over seventy per cent of all assaults involving one or more female assailant involved wives.[6] While many married women were prosecuted alongside their husbands, the majority of female assailants who acted alone were likewise married.[7] Given that at any one time less than a third of the adult female population were married (though most married at some point),[8] wives were hugely over-represented as defendants for assault. We might further note that almost three-quarters of male defendants were similarly prosecuted with co-defendants, yet no one has argued that the great majority of early modern men were therefore dependent and passive.[9] Explaining the comparatively low incidence of assault by women relative to assault by men primarily in terms of dependence and passivity is unconvincing.

The predominance of wives as assailants indicates the extent to which household structure and obligations informed patterns of female violence, just as they did male.[10] It was as mistresses of households that women most often entered disputes that Justices heard about at quarter sessions and assizes, and which came before other courts.[11] The same is true of other cases where household concerns were at stake. In rescues of goods and chattels out of legal custody, eight out of ten included participants who definitely or apparently either lived under the same roof or were otherwise related, especially spouses or parents and children.[12] Over three-quarters of these involved female participants, although they were outnumbered by men by

---

[4] T.E., *Lawes Resolutions*, 4. J.H. Baker, *An Introduction to English Legal History*, 3rd edn (London, 1990), 550–7.
[5] Wives constituted 54.2 per cent, spinsters 35.6 per cent, and widows 10.2 per cent of female defendants.
[6] 70.7 per cent of such groups.   [7] 60.7 per cent of sole-female-perpetrated assaults.
[8] Peter Laslett, 'Mean household size in England since the sixteenth century', in Peter Laslett and Richard Wall eds., *Household and Family in Past Times* (Cambridge, 1972), 145.
[9] The figure is 72.7 per cent.   [10] See above, pp. 33–7.
[11] For the Court of Requests, see Tim Stretton, *Women Waging War in Elizabethan England* (Cambridge, 1998), 103, 137–43; for consistory courts, see Foyster, *Manhood*, 148–9.
[12] Eighty per cent of groups prosecuted for rescue of goods and chattels included household/family members. For example, CRO, QJF 55/2/34 (1626) mother, son; QJF 57/3/8 (1628) husband, wife, son; QJF 95/2/122, /123 (1667) husband, wife, two sons, daughter.

a ratio of two to one.[13] And seventy per cent of such women were wives, usually the mistresses of the households in question, such as Jane Lessonby, a husbandman's wife, who in 1668 grabbed a pair of iron tongs and vigorously tussled with the sheriff's bailiffs to prevent them from taking her goods.[14] While married couples regularly rescued goods together, a full third of wives committed rescues in their husbands' absence, often with household servants assisting. Wives had a similarly high profile in disputes over land and buildings that led to suits for forcible disseisin and forcible entry and detainer. These latter offences involved the use of physical or threatened violence to keep out (hence to detain) or to eject and dispossess (disseise) whomever lawfully possessed or held the property in question, usually after making an entry by force. Married women made up half of the total number of women accused, and were allegedly involved in the majority of cases involving two or more defendants. In comparison, spinsters and widows featured in only one in seven such cases.

The high profile of wives' non-lethal violence here is unlikely merely to reflect wifely obedience to violently disposed husbands. Both household ideology and practical circumstances required wives to maintain the integrity of their households with and without their husbands' participation. During the civil wars, this well-established tradition was extended even to women's defence of their homes against a military enemy.[15] Contextualising women's non-lethal violence in terms of household authority and obligations challenges the historiographical insistence upon women's negligible participation in all but archetypal 'feminine' offences and the supposed trivial nature of their actions.

Tooth and nail

Evidence for how women fought does not support a view that women's behaviour was characterised by weakness and passivity. The language in which precise acts of violence were described made little concession to the sex of the accused. Women, like men, spurned, trod, kicked, pulled and pushed, struck on the face and body, pulled head-hair, and threw opponents to the ground and objects at opponents. The stereotypical modern 'cat fight' imagined by some historians, which involved 'a few scratches, a slap in the face, or pulling hair', is somewhat anachronistic.[16] If the terminology of

---

[13] Of 113 individuals prosecuted for rescuing household goods and livestock, thirty-eight (33.6 per cent) were female and seventy-five (66.4 per cent) were male.
[14] CRO, QJF 95/4/58 (1668).
[15] Carlton, *Going to the Wars*; Alison Plowden, *Women All on Fire: The Women of the English Civil War* (Stroud, 1998).
[16] Quoting Spierenburg, 'How violent were women?', 10.

violence was applied to assailants of both sexes, gender nonetheless impacted upon the reception of such deeds. Scratching, for instance, was disparaged in theory as a feminine act to which women resorted in the absence of weapons and skill.[17] Yet in legal records, its feminine associations were evoked to undermine men who scratched rather than to describe women's actions. Later in this chapter, we shall explore the particular meanings connoted by specific acts of female violence.

Given that weapons were associated with masculine combat, one might expect to discover a greater gender differential in armed assaults.[18] Certainly a comparison of simple aggregates of female and male defenders would seem to confirm male predominance in this area: four-and-a-half times as many men as women were prosecuted for armed assaults.[19] However, comparing aggregates obscures some important similarities. As proportions of the total number of defendants of their own sex, women and men were equally likely to be prosecuted for armed assault; just over forty per cent of each were so accused.[20] Granted, the nature of the evidence means that our conclusions must be tentative. We cannot be certain that weapons were deployed even where indictments contained the phrase *vi et armis*, viz. *cum gladiis baculis* (by force and arms, namely with swords, staves) or other weapons. Moreover, every co-defendant did not necessarily wield the weapons cited.[21] This was equally applicable to male co-defendants, and not merely to women as some historians have implied.[22] If women really did leave weapon-use to male partners, it follows that solitary female and all-female groups of defendants would rarely have been armed. Yet, as Figure 3.1 shows, it was actually in all-female groups of assailants that women were allegedly most often armed. Significantly, too, women prosecuted for single-handed assaults were almost as likely as lone males to be accused of using weapons.[23] Men, furthermore, were most likely to be accused of armed assault when they had acted in mixed-sex groups. Although women in general were far less likely to use weapons than men, the association of weaponry with masculine violence is not as clear-cut as has been assumed.

The picture of female weapon-use is broadened by including the evidence of examinations, depositions, recognisances, warrants and so forth. Interestingly, the gender discrepancy remains modest. Women were co-defendants

---

[17] Bulwer, *Chirologia*, 65, 138.
[18] Beattie, *Crime and the Courts*, 97. Bulwer, *Chirologia*, 138.
[19] See also Beattie, 'Criminality of women', 82–9; Shoemaker, *Prosecution and Punishment*, 213; Wiener, 'Sex roles and crime', 39, 47–9.
[20] 41.6 per cent of female and 43.5 per cent of male defendants were accused of armed assault. See also Finch, 'Women and violence', 29.
[21] On quantifying weapon-use from the evidence of indictments, see ch. 2 above, pp. 27–9.
[22] Wiener, 'Sex roles and crime', 45.
[23] 13.7 per cent of females and 27.4 per cent of men were prosecuted for sole-perpetrated assaults; respectively 23.3 per cent and 29.7 per cent were allegedly armed.

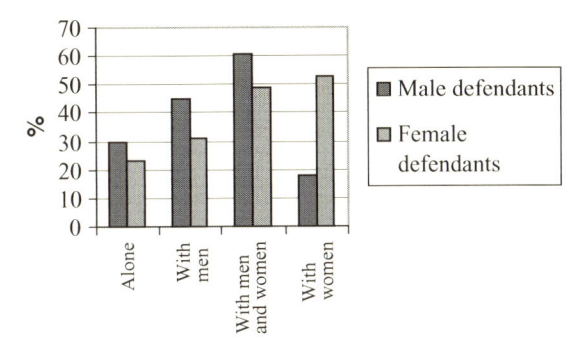

Figure 3.1 Allegedly armed assailants

in assaults involving all categories of arms, including those suggestive of premeditation because they were unlikely to be borne in the course of one's daily occasions, such as 'firearms, canons, swords, shields, short daggers and quarterstaves' or 'swords, pitchforks, canons, and quarterstaves'.[24] Hence, in a dispute over the lease of Ridley Field in Nantwich in 1572, Mistress Ann Hassall, armed with a quarterstaff, led a daylong patrol of the field to prevent the Crockett household from taking possession. Crockett's servants confessed to being 'greatly afraid lest Ann Hassall and her company would fight with their master'.[25] Even without formal training, armed women might pose a considerable threat. The most significant gender difference in weapon-use is that in some sole-perpetrated assaults men used swords/rapiers or firearms, whereas no women did so. Men were also a little more inclined to use agricultural or workshop tools than women, who in turn had a slightly greater propensity to fight with knives.[26] In general, women, like men, armed themselves with whatever was to hand: any household or agricultural tool, stones; one woman even threw boiling water in the face of a man who came to collect a debt.[27] It would seem short-sighted to accept at face value the contemporary anti-female view that 'a woman ordinarily [has] only that one weapon of the tongue to offend with'.[28]

Hammer and tongs

The idea that women's violence was 'same-sex' violence requires review also. Women's targets were not invariably female. In fact, in nearly three-quarters

[24] CRO, QJF 55/2/14 (1626); QJF 76/4/2 (1649).
[25] PRO, DDX 196, 'Examinations touching the death of Roger Crocket', fo. 3v.
[26] Other studies confirm women's propensity to fight with knives: Beattie, *Crime and the Courts*, 101; Spierenburg, 'How violent were women?', 15–19, 24–6.
[27] CRO, QJF 53/3/2 (1624).
[28] Richard Allestree, *The Whole Duty of Man, Laid Down in a Plain and Familiar Way for the Use of All, But Especially the Meanest Reader* (1659; London, 1678 edn), 257.

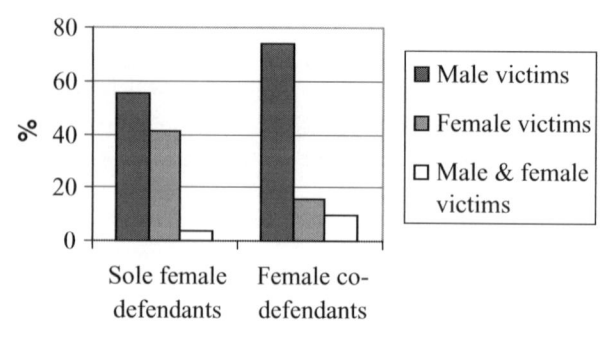

Figure 3.2 Alleged victims of female assailants

of female-perpetrated assaults, the victims were male (see Figure 3.2). This cannot be explained away as women's peripheral involvement in assaults where the chief assailant was male, for the majority of women's victims were men regardless of whether women acted alone or with others in any combination. The predominance of male victims may in part reflect gendered styles of prosecution – men generally possessed greater means to prosecute by indictment than did women, who favoured the cheaper binding over by recognisance. But this alone is unlikely to account for the almost identical gender breakdown of women and men's victims.[29] Men additionally comprised nearly half of those who craved security of the peace or behaviour against women.[30] Apparently, many men did consider some women to be sufficiently dangerous or disorderly to prosecute them.

Any female–male antagonism that might be inferred from these figures is implausible unless situated within the context of clashing household interests. Women's violence was typically undertaken in defence of their households, and men were numerically more likely than women to be the aggressors in such situations, especially as bailiffs, constables and assessors were male. Nevertheless, the prevalence of male victims remains perplexing in the light of the associations of violence with the performance of manhood that were considered in chapter two. If being beaten by another man was a mark of emasculation, assaults by women were potentially yet more humiliating. Moreover, the cultural scripts whereby men positioned themselves relative to other men were inappropriate when their opponents were female. The conventional view of men's physiological, hence 'natural',

---

[29] Victims in female-perpetrated assaults/batteries were 71.4 per cent male, 19.5 per cent female, and 9.1 per cent both male and female, and in male-perpetrated assaults/batteries 70.8 per cent male, 20.6 per cent female, and 8.5 per cent both male and female.
[30] Of named individuals towards whom women were bound over by recognisance, 48.7 per cent were male and 51.3 per cent were female.

greater strength and courage over weaker, more fearful women simply would not do.[31] Female-on-male altercations raised tricky questions: 'Is this any commendation to men, that they have been and are over-reached by women? Can you glory... in their strength, whom women overcome?... [Is] strength so slightly seated in your masculine gender, as to be stained, blemished, and subdued by women?'[32] But many men did complain that they had been assaulted by women or feared future harm at women's hands. How, then, did they articulate feminine violence against them without bringing 'shame upon themselves'?[33]

WOMEN'S VIOLENCE, MEN'S SILENCE

Unsurprisingly, perhaps, male victims tended to downplay women's physical prowess and to highlight alternative forms of feminine disorder, such as women's abusive words.[34] This was easy to do given the range of negative stereotypes embodying the vociferous woman: scold, shrew, gossip, defamer, slanderer, formal curser, fishwife, religious dissenter, female preacher and more, each richly furnished with further derogatory associations. The conflation of verbal, physical and sexual disorder that was contained in these categories flattened out more three-dimensional depictions of women's physical violence. Chester's Mayor and Recorder imprisoned Elizabeth Morris (until she found sureties) after seeing her 'give, or offer to give, a stroke or blow' to a man in the Pentice Court, but her fault was described in terms of her *general* lewdness and ill behaviour rather than in those of a specific act of violence.[35] Similarly, an ale-wife who twice hit with a pair of tongs a customer who refused to pay his due was not bound by recognisance to keep the peace against him. Instead, she had to answer for keeping disorder in her house.[36] Additionally, women's violent acts were frequently undifferentiated from those of others. Men who admitted that they were 'violently used and stricken' were often silent about which of multiple assailants had delivered the blows.[37] Richard Dunn craved security of the peace against Cicely Calister, her husband and daughter following an argument at which

---

[31] For these ideas about gender difference, see Fletcher, *Gender, Sex and Subordination*, ch. 4.
[32] Ester Sowernam, *Ester Hath Hang'd Haman: or, an Answer to a Lewd Pamphlet entituled The Arraignment of Women* (London, 1617), 36.
[33] Sowernam, *Ester Hath Hang'd Haman*, 37.
[34] For example, CRO, QJF 51/1/133 (1622); QJF 51/2/123 (1622); QJF 53/2/163 (1624); QJF 74/1/107 (1646); QJF 83/2/121 (1655).
[35] CDRO, EDC 5/1640/57, *William Edwards c. Elizabeth Morris wife of Roger*, responses of William Edwards.
[36] CRO, QJF 53/4/39–/43 (1624).
[37] For example, CRO, QJF 53/1/60, /42, /72 (1624); QJF 53/2/163 (1624); QJF 73/3/88 (1645); QJF 74/1/107 (1646); QJF 83/2/121 (1655).

the latter two were not even present and when the most he could say about Cicely was that she had taken up 'a stone, but did not cast it but kept it in her hand'.[38]

It was conventional also to stress alternative objects of female violence. Regardless of actual bodily harm, men situated injuries inflicted by women not on their biological bodies but on their households (family members, livestock, goods, land, dwelling-house), clothing or other symbols of status and honour. While these things all stood for the male body, the vulnerability and unmanliness associated with actual bodily harm was absent. Women's disorderliness, but not the fragility of the victim's manhood, was thereby emphasised.[39] William Beckett reminded magistrates that Mary Wright had previously been convicted for scolding and 'is in no ways reformed for the same', before explaining how she 'wickedly' practised to pull his house down on his head 'by endeavouring to strike out certain great pins and stays which hold up my left floor'. Her intention, unrealised of course, was 'to murder me and my children'. Petitioning again several months later, Beckett as before focused on Wright's damage to his property and her verbal abuse.[40] Likewise, Robert Cleaton described at length his neighbour Margaret Thorniley's habitual violence towards his cattle. He added almost incidentally that Thorniley had entered his house, 'assaulted me and pulled me by the hair of the head', thrown stones at him, run at him with a spit, and threatened 'to be my death'. These behaviours constituted evidence of Thorniley's disorderliness rather than Cleaton's fear for his personal safety. His explicit concern was that 'she will do...some bodily harm to my children, or mischief to my cattle, and I dare not send my children (being but young) about my occasions as formerly I have done lest she...should meet with them'. Thorniley posed no physical threat to *him*, and even his children's fear was mitigated by their tender age.[41] Women's physical violence towards adult males was frequently presented as a nuisance, nothing more.

The genre of comic violence provided alternative voices in which to articulate and deny the seriousness of feminine force.[42] 'Unmanly' male victims were, however, as vulnerable to ridicule for transgressing gender norms as were the 'unwomanly' female assailants. A ballad related how a 'valiant cook-maid' staged a robbery to steal back the wages that her master had just paid his journeymen-tailors, in order to 'make [her master] some sport'. In

---

[38] CRO, QJF 79/1/73–/75, /70 (1651); CCRO, MF 86/44 (February 1668).
[39] For example, CRO, QJF 51/1/123 (1622); QJF 74/1/107 (1646); QJF 83/2/121 (1655); QJF 87/1/84 (1659); QJF 91/1/89, /127 (1663); QJF 93/1/128, /73, /5 (1665); QJF 95/4/88 (1668); QJF 97/1/84, /85, /45, /43 (1669).
[40] CRO, QJF 51/1/123 (1622), QJF 51/4/159, /172, /173.
[41] CRO, QJF 97/2/140, /141 (1669).
[42] Davis, *Fiction in the Archives*, 98; Wiltenburg, *Disorderly Women*, 184, 190

male attire and with 'nothing in her hand but a black pudding', the cook-maid accosted the men on the highway. The 'faint-hearted tailors delivered her their money very quietly, for fear they should have been shot through with a black pudding'![43] This 'weapon' connoted the cook-maid's conventional, non-threatening, feminine status (she presumably made the pudding herself in the kitchen). The pudding also signified the illusionary nature of her performance of masculine power, in its shape (phallic), contents (blood) and name ('puddings' was slang for testicles). The cook-maid emasculated her victims because she lacked physical prowess, not because she possessed it. Similar ideas informed testimonial discourse. A soldier garrisoned in Chester in 1646 seemingly enjoyed the spectacle of a woman and a swineherd fighting, bidding them 'fight on and welcome!' The woman took the swineherd's ten pigs by threatening to knock out his brains, though in the event she merely hit him on the hand. Her menaces and his fear were equally risible.[44] Laughter could drown out the more discordant implications of women's violence.

When merriment was inappropriate, comic conventions could still inject derision into accounts of female aggression. Robert Cleaton and other male deponents reduced Margaret Thorniley's behaviour to farce. They described her over and again running to and fro and up and down and round in circles, swearing and cursing, chasing and striking with her pitchfork at cattle that trespassed in her field, and throwing it at cattle who moved too far away from her to stab them. On one such occasion, her 'pikel [did] stick in the cow, whereupon the cow came roaring down the hill' with Thorniley in hot pursuit, roaring likewise that she wanted her pikel back. Later that day, her pitchfork unrecovered, she was 'still running after the cow and swearing that she would not lose her pikel so, and she bid the Devil go with [the cow] for she would have her pikel again'. She twice asked one of the deponents to retrieve it for her (he declined). This was a woman outsmarted by dumb beasts. Despite inflicting harm on her neighbour's livestock, Thorniley's violence was ludicrously inadequate for its purpose.[45]

If feminine violence was depicted as inconsequential and/or funny, its potential for disruption was nevertheless understood to be deadly serious. Deponents further discredited Margaret Thorniley by alleging that she had previously attempted to murder her husband; she tried to cut his throat while he slept, and to run him through with a spit. She failed, but the husband 'durst not live with her', and had fled. Thorniley epitomised the most dangerous sort of woman who subverted household, social and moral order.

---

[43] *A Leicestershire Frolick; Or, the Valiant Cook-Maid. Being a Merry Composed Jest* (London, 1680), sig. A1r.
[44] CCRO, MF 69/1/52, /53 (1646).   [45] CRO, QJF 97/2/140, /141 (1669).

Interestingly, this disorderliness was not translated into a bodily threat to her male detractors.[46] In another case, JPs heard that Alice Fallowes, harbouring a 'deadly grudge' towards William Burges, plotted an ambush, intending 'to have killed him upon the sudden before he should be aware to make defence'. Burges himself stressed that his vulnerability came not from her physical threat but from his being outnumbered, from the surprise element of ambush, and from the skill of assassins hired to kill him for twenty nobles.[47] Others deposed that Fallowes was determined to kill him herself. She waited all day and evening in a cow-house, pitchfork in hand, ready to jump Burges as he passed homewards from Macclesfield market. After a considerable time, her two menservants, whom Fallowes had instructed 'to come to her aid if need required', decided to 'go in to our supper and stay here no longer, since he cometh not'. Alice Fallowes 'stayed a while' longer before admitting defeat. What an anticlimax! As it happened, Burges had long since arrived home by a different route. Yet allegedly, three years later, Alice still claimed that had Burges come by, she would have attempted to 'have sticked [her pikel in]to him till his death'.[48] In such accounts, women were simultaneously disorderly and incompetent. The inconsequence of their actions was wedded to their deadly intent.

Men's stories were not wholly successful in silencing voices of feminine force. Speech about women's violence, like other antithetical discourses about women, indicated ambiguities surrounding women's roles, agency and power. The prescriptive view of women's physical as well as moral frailty was at odds with the plain observation that 'diverse women [were] of a diverse stature, strength, complexion, and disposition'.[49] Redefinitions of feminine strength as weakness were not entirely convincing, as in the argument that while man's greater strength and courage resulted from the male's superior heat, woman's 'proneness to anger argue[s] imbecility of mind and strength of imagination not heat'.[50] Such ambiguities are suggested by legal narratives also, which reveal alternative visions of female violence. Hamnet Partington, for example, stressed his female neighbour's verbal abuse, and conflated her and her children's actions, yet his narrative hints at emasculation nonetheless. First, Mistress Warburton, 'calling me "Rogue" and "Rascal", offered to come over a hedge to fight with me'. Challenging someone to fight was effectively an assertion of the challenger's equality or superior status to the person challenged. Secondly, Partington complained that Warburton and her children had 'not ceased vehemently to provoke and stir me up to

---

[46] CRO, QJF 97/2/140, /141 (1669).
[47] The sum of £6 13s. 4d.; one noble was a gold coin worth 6s. 8d.
[48] CRO, QJF 27/2/1–/5, /45 (1597).   [49] *Great Advocate*, 40.
[50] A. Ross, *Arcana Microcosmi, or The Hidden Secrets of Man's Body Disclosed* (London, 1651), 86, cited in Fletcher, *Gender, Sex and Subordination*, 61.

anger and passion'. Anger was commonly understood to result from blood boiling because of 'apprehension of some injury offered to a man's self'.[51] Partington's confession therefore invested Warburton with the power to injure him. Moreover, he implied that she might further strip him of his manhood by forcing him to forgo his self-restraint.[52] Another man reported but gave no details of the beating he received from a woman and her children, instead emphasising her violence towards his livestock – she stabbed his horse's face with a pitchfork – and verbal abuse. But his claim that she frequently 'scandalised me' hints perhaps at the ignominy attached to her physical abuse of him (which he glossed over) as well as what she said.[53]

Men denied the validity of women's violence as long as they had the strength of body and mind to quash it. This was 'natural'. Only when women turned to *un*natural or *super*natural violence – poison, witchcraft, other 'secret' methods – was the inadequacy of male defences acknowledged. Underhand, invisible means enabled women to traverse men's boundaries, and to manipulate, doctor or destroy male bodies as if they were mere wax or dough in their hands. Regaining the power of speech after 'his tongue was taken from him for about half an hour' during the night, a schoolmaster told his wife that Mary Baguley was witching him to death. Baguley had 'twitched him by the back and sat upon his legs', and 'crushed his heart in pieces'. He lived for ten further nights and days, spitting blood, suffering 'trembling fits', gnashing and grinding his teeth, constantly bathed in sweat. His wife sat with him and could do nothing except witness his 'great pain and torment'. Meanwhile, the physically absent witch, who in the symmetry of witch-beliefs was his wife's anti-figure, 'hath done her work'. She 'did sit upon his heart' and squeezed the life out of him drop by drop.[54]

In less exceptional circumstances men were silent, or at least taciturn, about women's physical violence against them, emphasising instead feminine physical incapacity and other manifestations of female disorderliness. We saw earlier that sympathetic accounts of female victims of men's assaults evoked notions of positive feminine vulnerability and passivity. Here we have seen the same ideas being utilised in portrayals of female-on-male assaults to stave off the ignominy of compromised manhood. These concepts rested upon a shared foundation. It was a cornerstone of patriarchal ideology that female violence breached social order. As such, it informed widely held views about 'natural' capacities and the consequences of 'unnatural' behaviour. The ability to assault and fight one's enemies, for example, was thought to

---

[51] John Downame, *Spiritual Physicke to Cure the Diseases of the Soule* (London, 1616), sigs. F2v, F3v.
[52] CRO, QJF 53/2/163 (1624).   [53] CRO, QJF 74/1/107 (1646).
[54] PRO, CHES 38/41, 'A particular of the felons in Chester Castle, April 1675', examinations concerning Mary Baguley, 1674.

arise from the emotion of 'boldness' fortifying the soul. Boldness in man was a noble passion, 'bereaving him of weakness and fear'. The associations of strength and courage did not extend to a bold woman, however. Rather, when 'boldness passeth the bounds she ought to keep, none causeth greater disorders, nor is more an enemy to man, and to civil society'.[55] Such views would seem to offer little scope for female violence to be constructed in anything other than negative terms.

ASSERTIONS OF FEMALE FORCE

Do not be fooled by the prevalence of certain patriarchal discourses. Positive models of feminine force did exist in early modern England. Granted, virtuous female violence was easily recast negatively. Conventional depictions of Amazons as a noble warrior-tribe, for instance, were from the mid-sixteenth century matched by sneering portrayals of lustful, incompetent 'man-killers'. Detractors made much of a supposed Amazonian law that prohibited a woman from sexual intercourse or marriage until she slew a man with her own hands and displayed his head as a trophy; so that 'many of them have died old wrinkled beldames', still virgins.[56] By the later seventeenth century, 'Amazon' had become a derogatory term applicable to any non-submissive woman. Contemporaneous to the Amazon's depreciation, however, a virtuous virago figure based on scriptural, classical or historical tradition was reinforced in popular song, poetry, dramatic works and prose of all kinds.[57]

This virtuous warrior-woman fought an individual battle against oppressive and unjust violence. As men normally occupied the positions that enabled oppression or unjust treatment of others, her targets were invariably male. Yet far from subverting order, the warrior-woman upheld and reinforced it. Writers who denounced Amazons as man-hating husband-killers praised Biblical and apocryphal heroines such as Deborah and Judith, whom God 'raised up' to be 'mother and deliverer to His oppressed people', but

---

[55] *A Physical Discourse Touching the Nature and Effects of the Courageous Passions* (London, 1658), 4–6, 30–1.
[56] John Knox, *The First Blast of the Trumpet Against the Monstruous Regiment of Women* (Geneva, 1558), fo. 11r; Thomas Heywood, *Gynaikeion: Or, Nine Books of Various History Concerning Women* (London, 1624), 223; Bulwer, *Anthropometamorphosis: Man Transform'd*, 321–5, 517.
[57] For example, Anthony Gibson, *A Woman's Worth Defended Against All Men in the World* (London, 1599); Heywood, *Gynaikeion*; Thomas Heywood, *The Exemplary Lives and Memorable Acts of Nine of the Most Worthy Women in the World* (London, 1640); Sowernam, *Ester Hath Hang'd Haman*, 11–13. Carol Barash, *English Women's Poetry, 1649–1714: Politics, Community and Linguistic Authority* (Oxford, 1996), 32–7, 85–6; Simon Shepherd, *Amazons and Warrior Women: Varieties of Feminism in Seventeenth-Century English Drama* (Brighton, 1981), 1–15.

who acted 'without usurpation of any civil authority'.[58] The warrior-woman was an emblem of social and political order, as demonstrated by her incorporation into Elizabeth I's iconography.[59] Didactic literature presented as 'fair and wise' a wife who cropped her hair, 'framed herself to ride, and wears armour like a man, and so accompanied [her husband] valiantly, faithfully, and patiently in all his troubles and perils'. Feminine courage was defined by its objective, which in this instance was to give 'her husband great comfort in his adversity'.[60] The earthier heroines of street literature similarly embraced patriarchal values in courageously saving husbands, or lovers whom they subsequently married or saved from death or imprisonment, after following them into battle or across the sea, usually dressed in male attire.[61] One such ballad extolled the virtues of a Commander's wife who in male clothing fought bravely beside her husband, and saved his life, during the siege of Chester.[62] In the extremely popular Long Meg of Westminster stories, the butts of the jokes were decidedly the braggarts, corrupt legal officials, cowardly gentlemen and other dastardly fellows whom Meg resisted or 'corrected' with her combative skills and wit. Sleazy manhood deserved its comeuppance. Like other virtuous viragos, Meg championed 'good' patriarchal order, as was (somewhat ambiguously) manifested in her downright refusal of her new husband's request that they fight together in play. 'Never let it be said, though I can cudgel a knave that wrongs me, that Long Meg shall be her husband's master, and therefore use me as you please.'[63] Exemplary narratives of virtuous female force plainly effected a patriarchal rhetoric to encourage women's loyalty and service.

There was, however, more than one way to engage with these stories. The virtuous warrior-woman was a cultural resource for ordinary women. This applied even to queenly virtue, supposedly far beyond Everywoman's reach, for the state–household analogy enabled a slippage between queen and commoner. A monarch's defence of her realm from foreign invasion, say, might

[58] Knox, *The First Blast of the Trumpet*, fos. 41v–46v.
[59] Heywood, *Exemplary Lives*, 185, 199, 211ff.; Lady Diana Primrose, *A Chaine of Pearle. Or, A Memoriall of the Peerles Graces, and Heroick Vertues of Queene Elizabeth, of Glorious Memory* (London, 1630), 9–10, 12. Hackett, *Virgin Mother, Maiden Queen*, 39–50; Carole Levin, *The Heart and Stomach of a King: Elizabeth I and the Politics of Sex and Power* (Philadelphia, 1994), 140–8; Winfried Schleiner, ' "*Divina virago*": Queen Elizabeth as an Amazon', *Studies in Philology* 75 (1978), 163–80; Shepherd, *Amazons and Warrior Women*, 22, 29.
[60] *Court of Good Counsell*, sig. E3r; D.T., *Asylum Veneris, or A Sanctuary for Ladies* (London, 1616), 123–6.
[61] Wiltenburg, *Disorderly Women*, 63–9.
[62] Cited in Plowden, *Women All on Fire*, xiii; *The Valiant Commander with his Resolute Lady* (s.n., 1685).
[63] *The Life and Pranks of Long Meg* (London, 1582), sig. B3r. Shepherd, *Amazons and Warrior Women*, 70–4; Diane Dugaw, *Warrior Women and Popular Balladry 1650–1850* (Cambridge, 1989), 31–45.

resonate with women who defended their households from more mundane foes. Moreover, the virago's characteristics were those to which women were taught to aspire. Her violence was defensive, never offensive. She selflessly defended her monarch, husband, children, nation or religion. Self-sacrifice imbued her acts. She was compelled to act with force and violence only by exceptional circumstances. Law sanctioned this model of female force. Technically, it constituted no breach of the peace for a wife to beat her husband's assailant, for daughters to fight in defence of their parents, or for maidservants of their masters or mistresses. Mothers could legitimately use violence to protect a child 'being then within age, and not able to defend him or her self'.[64] The same message was communicated elsewhere. The Chester mystery play *The Slaughter of the Innocents*, which was performed as late as 1600, valorised precisely this maternal duty to protect one's children even with violence.[65] The notion that women had a duty to defend, protect and save connected also with those discourses of self-sacrifice and martyrdom that evoked such pathos when women were victims, and, of course, with household ideology. These cultural models together afforded a positive construction of female force that was particularly appropriate in the household context of so much interpersonal violence. Women could in practice draw upon this construct to define their circumstances as exceptional and their violence as legitimate.

Legal stories that attempted to justify women's violence often portrayed them as peacemakers or defenders of others. A husband claimed that his wife, Ann Jackson, rushed 'to defend me' when they were set upon by adversaries; twenty-three-year-old Alice Tetlow explained that upon hearing that three men were beating her father, she ran home as fast as possible to help him.[66] Assertions of defensive acts generally skip over how women physically enacted such defences, moving abruptly from women's noble intentions to their harsh treatment by assailants. In these tales, selfless heroines become helpless victims. Ann Jackson suffered such grievous injuries in her bid to defend her husband that she 'did lie speechless one night and half a day', 'more likely to die than live'.[67] Alice Tetlow, finding her father 'on the floor,

---

[64] Dalton, *Countrey Justice*, 162; Pulton, *De Pace Regis*, fo. 5v. Husbands, fathers, sons and manservants had equivalent legal provision.

[65] Denise Ryan, 'Womanly weaponry: language and power in the Chester *Slaughter of the Innocents*', *Studies in Philology* 98, 1 (2001), 76; *The Chester Mystery Cycle: Volume I, Text*, eds. R.M. Lumiansky and David Mills (London, 1974), 297–392.

[66] CCRO, MF69/3/144, /145 (November 1646); CRO, QJF 49/3/68 (1620); QJF 81/2/222 (1653). See also QJF 53/3/76 (1624); QJF 53/4/69 (1625); QJF 55/2/138 (1626); QJF 85/4/24 (1658); QJF 87/1/20 (1659); QJF 95/1/70 (1667); CRO, DDX/196, fos. 7r, 17r, 18r, 23v, 24v, 'Examinations touching the death of Roger Crockett, innkeeper, 1572'.

[67] CRO, QJF 49/3/68 (1620).

and all three beating him at once', received a blow to the head 'so that I fell into a sound for the present under their feet'.[68] While the negative implications of women's actual violence were bounded by silence, the silence itself was naturalised by normative discourses about women's incompetence and combative inadequacy. The self-sacrificing woman was most exalted if her subsequent passivity and, indeed, silence were final. Literary accounts presented suicide as the most exquisite feminine self-immolation, but different forms of death for the sake of others could serve just as well (better perhaps, given that suicide was a felony).[69] The 1687 epitaph of a woman killed by a friend's husband when she intervened in their quarrel reads, 'To save her neighbour she has spilt her blood / and like her Saviour died for doing good.'[70]

The positive slant on 'saving' applied to household resources and credit too. Defendants redefined women's actions in 'forcible rescue' (the unlawful recovery from legal custody of goods, livestock or people) and related disturbances according to extra-legal meanings of 'rescue', namely, saving from danger or destruction, giving succour, and effecting deliverance. Margaret Nixon *alias* Buckley allegedly used force to prevent officers from executing a warrant of distraint on her cattle. According to her and her husband, however, she merely took, without force, the reins of the officer's horse and 'desired... with pitiful requests' that the warrant not be served. These 'pitiful requests' positioned Margaret as a conventional female supplicant before rightful authority. Her motivations were similarly orthodox. She wished to 'have saved her cattle from serving', as would any good housewife.[71] Characterising women as preserving the economically and morally reliable household potentially undid the violence of their actions. Yet it required some kind of doublethink on the part of officials who sanctioned the reconfiguration of feminine force as non-violent. Two magistrates, though conceding that Elizabeth Ainsworth had indeed committed an unlawful rescue, opined that she might receive lenient treatment because she had 'only stayed a cow' being driven to the pound, and that 'without any violence in the world'.[72] The 'saving' discourse was not limited to mistresses of households. In certain circumstances, it extended to household inferiors. Sisters acted to protect their brothers and female servants their masters or their masters' goods.[73] A maidservant received 'many blows' and at sword-point was threatened with death for her efforts to stop several men from striking her fellow servants and

---

[68] CRO, QJF 81/2/222 (1653).   [69] D.T., *Asylum Veneris*, 123–6.
[70] Cited in Mendelson and Crawford, *Women in Early Modern England*, 240.
[71] CRO, QJF 49/2/171 (1620).   [72] CRO, QJF 53/2/138 (1624).
[73] For example, CRO, QJF 55/2/138 (1628); QJF 93/4/90 (1667).

making off with her master's goods and livestock. Typically, in her account of events she dwelt not on her efforts but on her suffering.[74]

The implications of the imperative on women to save and to conserve were not purely discursive; they informed action. Revealingly, women participated in over three-quarters of incidents of the withholding or rescue of household goods or livestock. Household ideology and practice informed the manner of female violence in further ways, too. Technically, violence did not breach the peace if dispensed as discipline by the holder of 'natural or civil authority or power'.[75] With rare exceptions, public hierarchies of authority were exclusively male. Women's formal authority to inflict discipline on others was delimited by the household: as mothers and mistresses they were empowered to correct children and servants 'in words of reproof' and 'stripes if needful'.[76] In the absence of other applicable models of female authority, both fictive and descriptive narratives resituated women's domestic authority as a means of legitimating feminine force. In Thomas Harman's account of five dames who beat their friend's unfaithful husband, the women were each armed with a birch-rod – the traditional instrument for flogging unruly children and youths – and their explicit purpose was to punish the man and bring about his reformation.[77] In Restoration Chester, Katherine Huntingdon's roles as peacemaker and care-giver (receiving a sword into safekeeping, staunching the victim's bleeding) merged into that of disciplining matron when the assailant made to escape. 'I took him by the hair of the head' – a classic mark of informal disciplinary action – 'and told him he should not go.'[78] Women often implicitly claimed authority in this manner.

In the semiotics of violence, pulling hair was an assertion of authority and control and was associated with chastisement. Associations of head-hair with honour and, in men, virility, meant that it was a particular indignity for a man to have his hair pulled by a woman. At the same time, hair had an uncertain corporal status, being of the body and external to it. In men's narratives, head-hair was part of the conceptually diffuse body beyond the skin. Hair-pulling acknowledged feminine disorder while maintaining a fantasy that masculine boundaries had remained intact. Knocking men's hats from their heads, and tearing or sullying their clothing, similarly constituted violent

---

[74] PRO, CHES 24/131/1, Examinations re. John Ince (1655). See also CRO, QJF 95/4/90 (1668).

[75] Dalton, *Countrey Justice*, 161–2; Heale, *Apologie for Women*, 33; R.R., *The House-Holders Helpe, for Domesticall Discipline* (London, 1615), sig. A2r.

[76] Cawdrey, *Family Reformation*, 74, 99; *Court of Good Counsell*, sigs. G2r–v; R.R., *House-Holders Helpe*, sig. A2v; Whately, *Bride-bush*, 94–5.

[77] Thomas Harman, *A Caveat for Commen Cursetors Vulgarely called Vagabones* (London, 1567), sigs. F2r–F3r.

[78] CCRO, MF86/65 (February 1668).

affronts with or without the infliction of flesh wounds.[79] Attacks mediated through hair, hat or clothing exemplified the authoritative role assumed by women in dramatising an unsavoury 'truth' about adversaries. As shaming practices, they resembled other means of castigation: public whipping, the pillory and stocks, carting, ducking, ecclesiastical penance, charivari, singing and publishing mocking rhymes, displaying cuckold's horns to a particular dwelling-house, and so on. The castigatory nature of these behaviours can be seen to have informed and legitimated female violence, at least in the eyes of the assailant and her supporters. In 1646, Jane Pickford with some others 'made a libel or rhyme' about John Turner and 'do call him both "rogue" and "thief" and singeth the same openly to strangers to his great disgrace'. Such verses and their performance were customarily intended to admonish and humiliate perceived transgressors of political, religious or social values, including unprincipled or undeserving persons of high status or holding public office.[80] Having named and shamed Turner in mocking rhymes, Pickford proceeded to mark him more permanently. She 'got me by the ear and did bite off the same, and they boasted of it that she had made me a rogue'. Torn, cropped and amputated ears imparted an explicit message to early modern observers: the owner was literally 'ear-marked' for life as one who had been officially punished as a rogue, or a seditious, libellous, fraudulent or perjured person.[81] An ear-mark scarred reputation as well as flesh.[82] By inscribing an indelible punishment upon John Turner's body, Jane Pickford as good as did make a rogue of him. Significantly perhaps, this assumed authority to correct and punish did not structure the physical violence of Pickford's male confederates. Their violence was characterised by conventional codes of masculine combat: one attempted to stab Turner with concealed weapons; the other 'dared me to come forth of my chamber... he having a bill in his hand intending to have killed me'.[83]

Two years later, Turner wanted Pickford bound to her good behaviour again. Though he privileged Pickford's verbal abuses, her previous action underscored her threat to 'mischief me and neither leave me ear nor stump

---

[79] See above, pp. 42–3.
[80] Alastair Bellany, ' "Raylinge rymes and vaunting verse": libellous politics in early Stuart England 1603–1628' in Kevin Sharpe and Peter Lake eds., *Culture and Politics in Early Stuart England* (Basingstoke, 1994), 285–310; Adam Fox, 'Ballads, libels and popular ridicule in Jacobean England', *P&P* 145 (1994), 47–83; Martin Ingram, 'Ridings, rough music and mocking rhymes in early modern England' in Barry Reay ed., *Popular Culture in Seventeenth-Century England* (London, 1985), 166–97.
[81] Pulton, *De Pace Regis*, fos. 1v–2v, 54v–55r; Edward P. Cheyney, 'The Court of Star Chamber', *American Historical Review* 18, 4 (1913), 734, 744.
[82] CDRO, EDC 5/1622/13, *Office* c. *Margaret Dod daughter of Richard Dod*; EDC 5/1620/3, *Mary Griffith* c. *Edward Stones*; EDC 5/1663/63, *Peter Legh* c. *William Halliwell*. See also PRO, CHES 24/117/1, recognisance for John Pike (1624).
[83] CRO, QJF 74/2/46 (1646).

of an ear nor nose nor piece of a nose at all'.[84] The inclusion of the nose as a site of mutilation magnified the sense in which Pickford sought to inflict a performative punishment on Turner. Noses, like ears, were cut off or slit as avenging acts upon those who had unworthily assumed authority. The Star Chamber included nose slitting among penalties for false accusers. Triumphant early modern troops reportedly inflicted nose amputation on the corpses of enemies, prisoners of war and sometimes on civilians.[85] As punishments, cutting off the nose and ears was designed to incite public scorn of the recipient, the degree of scorn and ridicule intended being proportionate to the amount of flesh removed. Ears that were nailed to the pillory when the offender was removed resulted in ripped, and permanently slit, ears. A more serious sentence stipulated that the ears be 'cropped', the tops sliced off. Worst of all, the whole ear was amputated, leaving no 'ear nor stump of an ear'. Much the same applied to noses: they could be slit, chopped (or bitten) off at the tip, or entirely amputated.

The fusion of ears and nose as targets exemplifies a further conceptual implication of feminine violence: castration, which was conventionally understood to be the ultimate usurpation of masculine authority. Historical commentary on early modern nose mutilation has situated it within the idiom of insult. A slit nose – the 'whore's mark' – signified the polluted body and character of the whore or adulterer. The whore's nose represented both her own 'tail' and the penis of her male sexual partner(s). Men's noses, though less prominent in speech about sex, also represented penises.[86] In popular imagination, the size of a man's nose corresponded with that of his penis (and his ears with his testicles). Thus John Bulwer expressed surprise on hearing that Ethiopian men had exceptionally large penises, for he had previously 'read nothing concerning their great noses'.[87] There was also an idea, following Hippocrates, that cutting the vein behind a man's ear made him a eunuch.[88] Nose amputation and castration were directly linked. A 1587 account of Anglo-Welsh battles in the early fifteenth century described Welsh women mutilating English soldiers' corpses. They 'cut off their privities, and put one part thereof into the mouths of every dead man, in such sort that the cullions [testicles] hung down to their chins; and not so contented, they did cut off their noses and thrust them into their tails as they lay on the ground mangled and defaced'. Such abuses, opined the male author, were 'worthy

---

[84] CRO, QJF 76/2/27 (1648).
[85] *Court of Good Counsell*, sig. G2r; Cheyney, 'Court of Star Chamber', 744; Chief Justice Saxey's report to the Privy Council, October 1599, *Calendar of State Papers, Ireland*, Vol. VII (London, 1895), 300.
[86] Gowing, *Domestic Dangers*, 80–1, 103–4; Foyster, *Manhood*, 81.
[87] Bulwer, *Anthropometamorphosis*, 398.
[88] For example, Jonathan Swift, *The Tale of a Tub* (1709; London, 1975), 129.

to be recorded to the shame of a sex pretending the title of weak vessels, and yet raging with such force of fierceness and barbarism'.[89]

In a number of ways, Jane Pickford's threats to cut off Turner's nose and ears intersected with political discourses of authority and rebellion. A political dimension is hinted at by the professed origin of their quarrel in religious differences, and perhaps by Pickford's terms of abuse, which called into question Turner's actions during the wars. She called him 'a traitorly rogue', and 'a murdering thief and said he had murdered a woman and a child at Hankelow'.[90] In the climate of civil war and its aftershocks, women's violence and its meanings were politicised along with men's.

The experience of civil war had various consequences vis-à-vis feminine violence. Women's active defence of towns, castles and households necessitated an extension of positive discourses of feminine force. A Royalist reported during the siege of Chester that 'Our women are all on fire, striving through a gallant emulation to outdo our men and will make good our yielding walls or lose their lives.'[91] In Nantwich, women reportedly braved Cavalier fire time after time to extinguish flames ignited by the shots; some lost their lives.[92] Women showed 'valour' in 'defying the merciless enemy at the face abroad, as by fighting against them in garrison towns; sometimes carrying stones, anon tumbling of stones over the works on the enemy, when they have been scaling them, some carrying powder, others charging of pieces to ease the soldiers'.[93] In actions and words, 'defensive' feminine force was robustly asserted. The Leveller women's petitions to the House of Commons in 1649 and 1653, for instance, drew parallels between the petitioners and exemplary warrior-women who represented a liberating force. For 'our encouragement and example', they declared, 'God hath wrought many deliverances for several nations from age to age by the weak-hand of women.' Just as Deborah and Jael delivered Israel from its enemies, it was by 'the British women' that 'this land was delivered from the tyranny of the Danes (who then held the same under the sword, as is now endeavoured by some officers of the Army)'. Likewise, Scottish women began 'the overthrow of Episcopal tyranny in Scotland'.[94] Their supporters described

---

[89] Raphael Holinshed et al., *The Third Volume of Chronicles... Newly Recognised, Augmented and Continued* (London, 1587), 519–20, 528.
[90] CRO, QJF 76/2/27 (1648).   [91] Cited in Plowden, *Women All On Fire*, xiii.
[92] Thomas Malbon, cited by Hall, *Nantwich*, 161. See also Lucy Hutchinson, *Memoirs of the Life of Colonel Hutchinson* (London, 1968), 146.
[93] James Strong, *Joanereidos: Or, Feminine Valour; Eminently Discovered in Western Women* (London, 1645; 1674), frontispiece; G.S., *A True Relation of the Sad Passages, Between the Two Armies in the West* (London, 1644), 10; John Vicars, *Gods Arke Overtopping the Worlds Waves, or the Third Part of the Parliamentary Chronicle* (London, 1645).
[94] *The Humble Petition of Divers Wel-Affected Women* (London, 1649), 4–5; Strong, *Joanereidos*, sig. E3r. Davies, *Unbridled Spirits*, 80–7, 113–14.

Leveller women similarly, saying that as they went to present their petition, they were like 'whole troops of Amazons... marching with confidence to encounter tyranny, and with abundance of courage exceeding the ordinary sort of women demanding, [in] high terms, freedom for their Levelling brethren'.[95]

Another consequence of civil war was the expansion of the notion of the dangerous adversary outside the home to include women. Women of the opposing party were demonised. Parliamentarians commented on the capture of 120 women at Nantwich in January 1644, observing that the King's army 'seldom march without' this 'female regiment' which was 'weaponed too; and when these degenerate into cruelty, there are none more bloody'. Armed 'with long and sharp skenes, or knives', these women intended 'to play the barbarous cut-throats of such as they should have taken prisoners, or were wounded'. Such 'wicked women' and 'cruel Irish queens' should be 'put to the sword, or tied back to back and cast into the sea'. Even the King's troops 'dare not sleep for fear of having their throats cut by certain Welsh and Irish women which follow the army'.[96] Depictions of murderous, uncontrolled women epitomised what the King's opponents wished to present as the core of the present troubles: the brutality, disorder and treachery of the King's faction and the resultant social chaos and perversion. Typically, such women were defined as other than English, just like the Welsh women who supposedly castrated and stuffed Englishmen in the manner of preparing geese for the table.

Although during the years of civil war and the Republic female opponents were more acceptably constructed as dangerously violent, there was no wholesale discontinuity in the language of violence. Expanded positive and negative versions of violent femininity were assimilated into conventional narratives. A New Model Army lieutenant complained to the Assize bench early in 1648 about the mother and sister of a Royalist soldier whom he killed during the advance upon Beeston Castle. The two women 'will not permit me to pass quietly along the streets, but cast stones at me, calling me "Rogue", "Rascal" and "Murderer", so that my life is daily in danger'.[97] John Turner in 1646 subsumed Jane Pickford's mutilation of his ear into her verbal and symbolic abuse rather than physical assault, which he attributed unproblematically to two male malefactors. In 1648, Turner further

---

[95] Shepherd, *Amazons and Warrior Women*, 66.

[96] *Magnalia Die. A Relation of Some of the Many Remarkable Passages in Cheshire Before the Siege of Namptwich, During the Continuance of It: And at the Raising of It* (London, 1644), 17, 18; J. Isack, *A Famous Victory Obtained by Sir William Brereton, Sir Thomas Fairfax. Sir William Fairfax* (London, 1644), sig. A5r; Vicars, *Gods Arke Overtopping the Worlds Waves*, 144; *A Declaration Sent from Several Officers of His Majesty's Army* (London, 1642), sig. A1. A skene was a type of Irish dagger.

[97] PRO, CHES 24/127/1 (1648), petition of John Turner.

associated Pickford's physical and verbal violence by claiming that 'if it lay in her power, she would not only take [her neighbours'] good names from them (but also their lives)'.[98] In 1653, Samuel Vaudrey reported that Elizabeth Goodyer assaulted him and a bailiff as they distrained her cow. She 'stroke [the bailiff] with a piece of wood or stake, swearing she would be the death of them both, following them, threatening and striking them with a [pitch]fork'. After Goodyer's father and another woman came to her assistance, Vaudrey and the bailiff fled from 'them'. But it was Elizabeth Goodyer 'who was the striker', and who 'ran at the bailiff' with the pitchfork 'and did hit him on the belly to the great peril and danger of his life, who lieth sick and languishing'.[99] In 1659, thirty-year-old Richard Jones described being attacked by the wife and daughter of a man upon whom he served a warrant of good behaviour. One woman grabbed and held him by the hair while the other struck him with a fire shovel, so that the man escaped. 'If the button of the collar of my doublet had not broken', Jones exclaimed, 'I do believe they would have endangered to have throttled me.'[100] Despite stressing the women's verbal abuse and ultimate failure (for Jones did manage to bring the husband before a JP), feminine violence was a force to be reckoned with.

Following the Restoration of Charles II, women's violence became less likely to be discussed so explicitly or seriously. Although some women reportedly continued to use the language of male challenge, their effectiveness was downplayed just as it had been earlier in the century. Women's disorderly speech and other deeds were again privileged over their actual or threatened violence. A constable deposed that Sarah Wright, threatening to 'kill or be killed' if constables entered the house to arrest her son, took him 'by the hair of my head and held me till [her son] was gotten out of my sight'. Yet this violence was subsumed into an account of Wright's general disregard for authority. Being told that the constables were empowered by the Baron of Kinderton's warrant, Sarah Wright replied that 'she neither cared for the warrant, nor for him that granted it, and if he [Peter Venables, Baron of Kinderton] were there himself she would not obey it'.[101] William Steele, the County Sheriff's itinerant bailiff likewise minimised feminine violence in a report to Justices about the resistance he and John Wolmer faced when they went to distrain goods in the Lessonby household in 1668. The report is framed by John Lessonby's actions: at the outset, John refused to hand over any goods; in the end, he wounded the creditor (who was to benefit from the sale of the distrained goods) by throwing 'a great stone' at him in 'a violent manner'. The body of the tale, however, was all taken up with Jane, John's wife. Declaring that 'if any bailiff offered to take any goods there she would

---

[98] CRO, QJF 74/2/46 (1646); QJF 76/2/27 (1648).   [99] CRO, QJF 81/2/225 (1653).
[100] CRO, QJF 87/2/2/114, /39, /40, /25 (1659).   [101] CRO, QJF 93/1/92–/95 (1665).

either kill or be killed', she made to 'take up a pair of iron tongs' but was prevented from doing so by Steele, whom she pulled by the hair of the head, seemingly letting go only in order to grab Wolmer and stop him from carrying her things out of the house. Temporarily overcome, she revived in time to stone the bailiffs as they left with her goods. Steele's narrative contains a tension between Jane's actions and his response. He did not once attribute to her the word 'violent'. When she went to strike Wolmer with the tongs, for example, Steele claimed that 'I took hold of the said Jane and *civilly persuaded* her to forbear to strike.' He was silent about how she was eventually overcome.[102] These oh-so-civil persuasions effectively negated the extent to which Jane Lessonby put up a good fight.

It also became more difficult for women themselves to construct their violence as legitimate within the bounds of Restoration gender codes. 'Merciful[ness], pity and compassion' were endorsed as 'natural' feminine characteristics and 'unnaturally' violent women were condemned: 'Nothing doth more misbecome [the feminine] sex than choler. I have often seen a fair woman melancholy, yet I never heard that any hath seen a fair furious one.'[103] Playwrights increasingly portrayed Amazons as too silly or too quarrelsome to rule themselves.[104] Broadsides undermined the individual warrior-woman with smutty humour. *The Female Warrior* related the tale of a woman who 'in man's attire got an ensign's place' after joining the company 'for the love of a dear friend' (not her husband, note). She was an 'Amazon' whose 'scorn to be controlled' led to her herself becoming the object of scorn. Her 'courage' and 'skill' were vitiated by gambling, drinking and regular bouts of 'gentle exercise', the nature of which became clear when she gave birth to a bastard.[105] The valiant warrior-woman discourse was not vanquished entirely. Female poets evoked it, for example, in the 1670s and 1680s in their defences of the King.[106] For ordinary women, however, the general reinforcement of dominant ideas of feminine passivity in the later seventeenth century meant that discourses of feminine violence were less efficacious in justifying female action than they had been during years of civil war and the Republic.

WOMEN BEWARE WOMEN

Historians have accorded little significance to physical violence between women. Neither did contemporary authors, of course, who much preferred

---

[102] CRO, QJF 95/4/58 (1668); my italic.
[103] Robert Codrington, *The Second Part of Youths Behaviour: Or, Decency in Conversation Among Women*, 2nd edn (London, 1672), 135, 137.
[104] Felicity A. Nussbaum, *The Brink of All We Hate: English Satires on Women 1660–1750* (Lexington, 1984), 44–7.
[105] *The Female Warrior* (London, 1681). [106] Barash, *English Women's Poetry*, 45–6.

to write about women's speech. Unlike mixed-sex or all-male altercations, those between women did not neatly fit categories that facilitated victims' complaints. The rules of combat were applicable to men alone. No accepted concept of sexual threat existed to underscore women's vulnerability at the hands of other women. Notions of incompatible physical difference between female combatants were not culturally reinforced. So what kinds of stories did, or could, women tell about their adversaries?

Female victims and their witnesses discredited violent women in conventional ways. The most common was to draw particular attention to verbal abuses even when the victims had been physically assaulted. We might expect to find this in defamation suits at the church courts, even if defamers allegedly 'fought with me and struck me', gave her 'a blow on the ear' or 'pulled her by the bosom'.[107] But in secular proceedings, too, physical violence was frequently presented as an adjunct to verbal harm rather than *vice versa*. Slanderous words aimed at women, especially those of sexual import, tapped into a far more potent and culturally established discourse of abuse than did physical assault *by* women. Thus, a widow in 1620 presented the blows (and threats to kill) inflicted by two young women as additional evidence of their malice towards her, which was primarily manifested in their calling her a witch.[108]

Female victims had nonetheless to negotiate the inappropriateness of popular constructions that contrasted vulnerable victims with strong and terrifying adversaries. Natalie Davis has noted that in the absence of any 'dependable set of narrative techniques to give drama or intensity to the all-female quarrels', descriptions 'stay matter-of-fact, commonplace'.[109] At a general level, this is true. With few exceptions women's petitions and examinations reported actual violence in little detail. What detail there was tended to be situational. For example, one woman informed a JP that because her daughter had playfully run after a little boy 'with a little frog in her hand', the boy's mother 'struck my child with a distaff and much abused her'; when the girl's mother complained, she too was assaulted.[110] While male violence also arose in the context of everyday social transactions, the language of masculine violence permitted the telling of tales of adventure, honour and manhood. Yet the mundanity of women's stories does more than reveal the absence of any discursive corpus of feminine violence. The very ordinariness

---

[107] CDRO, EDC 5/1597/67, *Margaret Crowther wife of Thomas c. Katherine Finlow wife of John*, depositions and interrogatories; EDC 5/1667/2, *Anne Knutsford wife of Thomas c. Margaret Howell wife of Edward*.
[108] CRO, QJF 49/2/164, /165 (1620). For 'witch' as a term of defamation, see CDRO, EDC 5/1641/15, *Elizabeth Sutton c. Ann Leadbeater*; EDC 5/1661/38, *Jane Eyre c. Jane Oulton*; EDC 5/1667/43, *William and Margaret Moores c. Ann Hickson*.
[109] Davis, *Fiction in the Archives*, 101.   [110] CRO, QJF 81/2/187 (1653).

of women's tales illuminates a particular intensity to women's arguments, which paralleled but was not identical to that of male fights.

Altercations between women, like other interpersonal disputes, arose largely from tensions between (and sometimes within) households over economic resources, space and authority. The force of women's tales of feminine violence is rooted in female competition that was born of household roles and authority. Women's violence was a manifestation of contests for feminine superiority, in much the same way as men's disputes were shaped by competing claims to manhood. Any woman who transgressed household boundaries and encroached on another's capacity for productive housekeeping could violate not only the household unit but also the latter's identity as a woman. Those who imagined the witch as an anti-housewife or anti-mother who destroyed their own endeavours as wife or mother were manifesting in a more extreme form a regular phenomenon in women's quarrels.[111] The same pertained even to unmarried women's work outside the house. Margaret Anion, for instance, snatched Sarah Barrow's basket of cakes, which Sarah was selling in Chester, and 'broke them all to pieces', saying that 'she would teach her for selling cakes'.[112] Teaching somebody a lesson assumed the justifiable punishment of a wayward inferior. And as with their male victims, women's physical assaults upon other women often mirrored accepted methods of (especially domestic) corporal punishment – they hit over the head, struck and boxed ears, pulled head-hair, slapped faces, and so on.[113] Less frequently, they threw dirt in women's faces to signify baseness, or pulled off their headgear and ripped it to shreds with or without further beatings.[114] But it depended: women also thumped and kicked each other's faces and bodies, and knocked each other to the ground, in apparently unisex form.[115] Whatever form it took, where rivalry between women existed, the conceptual usurpation of women's authority, space and resources was always a potential outcome. The stakes were high.

This remained so during and after the war years, when the expanded notion of the violent female informed women's descriptions of their female foes. In 1655 Alice Low told the magistrate that Margaret Kirkham had called her queen, jade, whore and her husband's whore, but also that 'Margaret gave me many furious blows upon my body, and after struck me down to the ground.' Later, Margaret had come to Alice's house 'and abused

---

[111] For witchcraft see esp. Purkiss, *Witch in History*, 91–118, and Gaskill, *Crime and Mentalities*, 57–66. For the competitive nature of women's insults, see Gowing, *Domestic Dangers*, ch. 3.
[112] CCRO, MF69/4/270 (1647).
[113] For example, CRO, QJF 81/3/98 (1653); QJF 83/3/29 (1655); QJF 55/1/69 (1626); CCRO, MF86/137 (1668); CRO, QJF 95/2/93 (1667).
[114] For example, CRO, QJF 93/3/48 (1665); QJF 97/1/85 (1669).
[115] For example, CCRO, MF86/93 (1668).

me with many reproachful and provoking speeches, and struck me between the face and the shoulder, and gave me many threatening speeches, and said that she had not given me so much but she would give me more'.[116] While slander remained a powerful discourse of abuse, women's ability to inflict real harm was far more visible in legal narratives of the 1640s and 1650s. However, female challenges *per se* were not novel. Thus, in 1622, one woman told another who stood in her own doorway with a child in her arms, 'lay down thy child and I shall beat thee, thou arrant whore'.[117] But the civil wars intensified the manner in which women posed mortal threats to other women. At the end of the siege of Lyme, for example, an Irishwoman who was 'left behind' when the enemy vacated the town was reportedly 'slain and almost pulled in pieces by the women of Lyme'.[118] Whether factual or hyperbolic, such accounts suggest how the relationship between women and violence had become unsettled. People did not necessarily believe that women (or men) would carry out their murderous threats. Yet in the context of a bloody civil war and revolution that seemed to strike at the core of hierarchical values, and ongoing political and religious divisions that fractured communities, women's violence could not be discounted as it had been previously. The circumstances of civil wars, revolution and Republican rule enabled some women (particularly if they were relatively vulnerable due to age or status) to tell convincing tales of female oppression.

SCOLDING

Nowadays, distinctions are commonly made between words and actions. In early modern culture, however, verbal utterance was understood absolutely to be a form of action, not merely its weak, binary other. Unacceptable words were categorised severally. William Gearing listed ten 'sins of the tongue': cursing, swearing, slandering, scoffing, filthy-speaking, flattering, censuring, murmuring, lying and boasting.[119] Diverse laws encompassed a variety of forms, processes and penalties.[120] Offensive or threatening speech could constitute a criminal breach of the peace, and the speaker dealt with by recognisance to keep the peace or good abearing or by indictment for

---

[116] CRO, QJF 83/4/70 (1655).
[117] CDRO, EDC 5/1622/31, *Ann Williams wife of Thomas c. Ellen Kelly spinster*. Note that the incident resulted in a defamation suit ('arrant whore') rather than a claim that Williams feared bodily harm.
[118] Vicars, *Gods Arke Overtopping the Worlds Waves*, 254.
[119] William Gearing, *A Bridle for the Tongue: Or, A Treatise of Ten Sins of the Tongue* (London, 1663).
[120] Martin Ingram, 'Law, litigants and the construction of "honour": slander suits in early modern England', in Peter Coss ed., *The Moral World of the Law* (Cambridge, 2000), 139–43, 147–8.

assault. Slanderous words, when alleging specific immoral conduct such as adultery or fornication, were primarily sued in the church courts as private defamation suits but sometimes also as 'office' cases pursued by the ecclesiastical authorities.[121] Slander alleging criminal behaviour, like theft or infanticide, was properly the business of the secular criminal courts. Certain categories of unacceptable speech, including scolding and barratry, were recognised in both canon and criminal law. Particular contexts were legally identified as special cases, such as the verbal abuse of clergymen, brawling (quarrelling loudly and indecently) in the church or churchyard, and disturbing a preacher during sermon time.[122] If the words spoken, or sung in the case of mocking rhymes, had been written down, they attained the status of libel and became a concern mainly of the higher criminal courts.[123] Perjury, false accusation, blasphemy and uttering seditious words, were further classes of verbal misconduct. Their gravity was inscribed in certain of their punishments: ears were nailed to the pillory and ripped, cropped, or chopped off, nostrils were slit, the tongue bored through with a hot iron, cheeks or forehead branded with appropriate letters (such as 'F' and 'A' for 'false accuser', 'B' for 'blasphemer').[124] Words were serious business. As a contemporary remarked, 'it is commonly seen that the stroke of the tongue is more dangerous than the dent of the spear'.[125]

The scold

Not all unruly tongues were women's. Moses Vauts pointed out that biblical treatment 'of the profit and praise, the poison and perniciousness, the plague and punishment of the tongue' made 'no distinction of sex'. Yet Vauts was vexed by women's speech. While he conceded that women might reasonably defend themselves in words, they were never to use their tongues as offensive weapons – an imperative, in Vauts's view, that most women glibly ignored. '[S]o unruly, keen and rancorous' were women that even the Scripture described their words as 'offensive rods, arrows, swords, and poison'. Women's scolding, reviling and railing were acts of 'violence'; 'the *Tongue smiteth*'.[126] That words were female weapons of choice or necessity was a

---

[121] Important works on defamation include Christopher Haigh, 'Slander and the church courts in the sixteenth century', *Transactions of the Historic Society of Lancashire and Cheshire* 78 (1975), 1–13; Martin Ingram, *Church Courts, Sex and Marriage in England, 1570–1640* (Cambridge, 1987), ch. 10; Gowing, *Domestic Dangers*, esp. chs. 2 and 3; Foyster, *Manhood*, esp. ch. 5.

[122] Pulton, *De Pace Regis*, fos. 8v, 18v; 5 and 6 Edward VI c. 4; 5 Elizabeth I c. 21, 3 James I c. 9.

[123] See n. 80 above. [124] Pulton, *De Pace Regis*, fo. 54.

[125] John of Marconville, *A Treatise on the Good and Evill Tongue* (London, 1590), sig. A4.

[126] Moses Vauts, *The Husband's Authority Unvail'd* (London, 1650), 79–80.

familiar early modern theme.[127] Vituperation was attributed to virtually every unsympathetic female stereotype. Witches had a 'scolding tongue'; their 'chief fault' being 'that they are scolds'. The very worst sort of wife – idle, sluttish, adulterous, whorish – was also 'babbling and loud', 'scolding and brawling continually'. Treacherous pamphlet wives who murdered their husbands were likewise portrayed as scolds.[128] Similarly, Bulstrode Whitelocke described as 'reproachful, almost scolding' the behaviour of 'some hundreds of women [who] attended the house [of Commons] with a petition on the behalf of Lilburne' and other imprisoned Levellers in 1649.[129] These were strong words. 'Scold' was 'a strongly negative term, in its destructive impact second only to "whore"... as a pejorative label applied to women'.[130]

While scolding was attributed to various negative female stereotypes, from the later sixteenth century the archetypal scold was not merely loose-tongued and female, but also sexually voracious, economically perverse and physically violent. She was the rotten core of the disordered household and hence of the dissolute community and state. Her political significance was ensured by the force of the household–state analogy.[131] Thus, for Susan Amussen, prosecutions of scolds 'reflected the anxiety of those in authority about the potential for disorder'; scolding 'ceased to be a problem when disorder ceased to be an obsession'.[132] Similarly, David Underdown argued that scolds and certain other categories of unruly female (witches, dominant wives, insolent masterless maidservants) were victims of a 'crisis in gender relations in the years around 1600'. This crisis was a ramification of another: a general 'crisis of order' due to large-scale socio-economic dislocation and an attendant decline in neighbourliness and social harmony.[133] Seen in this light,

---

[127] For example, Bulwer, *Chirologia*, 65; M.P., *Hold Your Hands, Honest Men* (London, 1634); M.P., *Keep a Good Tongue in Your Head* (London, 1634); Henry Smith, *A Preparative to Marriage* (London, 1591), cited in Katherine Usher Henderson and Barbara F. McManus eds., *Half Humankind: Contexts and Texts of the Controversy about Women in England, 1540–1640* (Urbana and Chicago, 1985), 53; John Taylor, *A Juniper Lecture* (London, 1652), sig. A6v; Wiltenburg, *Disorderly Women*, 106, 109–10.

[128] John Gaule, *Select Cases of Conscience touching Witches and Witchcraft* (London, 1645), 5; Reginald Scot, *The Discoverie of Witchcraft* (London, 1584), 34; William Loe, *The Incomparable Jewell* (London, 1634), 14; *Court of Good Counsell*, sig. D1v; *The Araignement and Burning of Margaret Ferne-seede for the Murther of her Late Husband Anthony Ferne-seede* (London, 1608), sig. A4.

[129] Cited in Sharon Achinstein, 'Women on top in the pamphlet literature of the English revolution', *Women's Studies* 24, 1–2 (1994), 132.

[130] Quoting Martin Ingram, ' "Scolding women cucked or washed": a crisis in gender relations in early modern England?' in Jenny Kermode and Garthine Walker eds., *Women, Crime and the Courts in Early Modern England* (London, 1994), 48; Mendelson and Crawford, *Women in Early Modern England*, 69.

[131] *Court of Good Counsell*, sig. D1v.   [132] Amussen, *Ordered Society*, 123.

[133] David Underdown, 'The taming of the scold: the enforcement of patriarchal authority in early modern England', in Anthony Fletcher and John Stevenson eds., *Order and Disorder in Early Modern England* (Cambridge, 1986), 122.

the apparent intensity with which scolds were identified and punished might well suggest a broader agenda to suppress women's speech.[134] The term 'scolding' indeed frequently serves modern commentators as shorthand for all manner of verbal transgressions by women. Hence, 'a scold' was simply 'any woman offering an opinion'; 'any woman who verbally resisted or flouted authority publicly and stubbornly enough to challenge the underlying dictum of male rule'.[135] Such characterisations seem consonant with the scold stereotype chiefly because the figure of the scold encapsulates so many other negative characteristics. But legal evidence encourages us to refine this all-encompassing model.

The scold's impact beyond the household undeniably made her socially dangerous. Alongside the literary preoccupation with the scold's spousal relationship, it was acknowledged that the scold was 'her neighbours' perpetual disquiet', 'sowing discord among them, or betwixt any and her husband by frequent scolding, reviling, tale-bearing, and the like'.[136] From the pulpit, people were instructed that 'St Paul numbereth a scolder, a brawler, or a picker of quarrels among thieves and idolaters', and whereas 'a thief hurteth but him from whom he stealeth..., he that hath an evil tongue troubleth all the town where he dwelleth, and sometime the whole country'. Indeed, those who 'do as much as lieth in them with brawling and scolding to disturb the quietness and peace' of the commonwealth are 'unworthy to live in [it]'.[137] Crucially, this latter conception of damage to local harmony, goodwill and neighbourly relations was at the heart of legal definitions of scolding. Leet jurors were to present 'any common barrators, scolders or brawlers to the annoyance and disturbance of their neighbours', as well as those who eavesdropped in order 'to make debate or dissension among their neighbours'.[138] Upon these grounds, medieval jurors had taken the initiative to report 'common scolds', and ecclesiastical and higher common law courts had followed suit. In legal usage, 'scolding' meant both noisy, quarrelsome behaviour characterised by abusive speech (brawling) and making malicious

---

[134] Underdown, 'Taming of the scold', 116–17, 119–20; Lynda E. Boose, 'Scolding brides and bridling scolds: taming the woman's unruly member', *Shakespeare Quarterly* 42, 2 (1991), 184–5.

[135] E.J. Burford and Sandra Shuhman, *Of Bridles and Burnings: The Punishment of Women* (London, 1992), 19; Boose, 'Scolding brides and bridling scolds', 189. Underdown himself applied the legal definition of the scold, in 'Taming of the scold', 119 and *passim*.

[136] *Twelve Ingenious Characters: Or, Pleasant Descriptions of the Properties of Sundry Persons and Things* (London, 1686), 23; Vauts, *Husband's Authority*, 78.

[137] 'A sermon against contention and brawling' and 'The third part of the sermon against contention', 1623, reprinted in *The Two Books of Homilies Appointed to be Read in Churches* (Oxford, 1859), 137 and 146.

[138] Jonas Adams, *The Order of Keeping a Courte Leete and Courte Baron* (London, 1599), sig. B3v; *The Maner of Kepynge a Courte Baron and a Lete* (London, 1536), fo. 5v.

or false accusations behind someone's back (backbiting).[139] Only individuals who *persistently* brawled or backbit constituted a 'common' nuisance and were liable to prosecution. According to legal criteria, then, not all unwelcome feminine speech was prosecutable as scolding. Nor were prosecutions necessarily the result of declining neighbourly values. They may just as validly have been attempts to foster and maintain local harmony.

Prosecution

Despite the cultural stereotype, scolding was not an exclusively female offence. Early definitions and usage suggest that a scold could be 'a man or a woman'.[140] Only after around 1580 did moral, legal and lexicographical accounts imagine the scold as definitively female and, even then, concerns about scolding continued to be directed at both sexes.[141] Prosecutions of male scolds were far from unknown. Marjorie McIntosh's extensive study of lesser public courts reveals that the proportion of courts whereat men were presented for scolding actually increased from as few as one-seventh in the early years of the sixteenth century to over two-thirds by the 1580s and 1590s.[142] Male scolds were prosecuted in over half of the tribunals examined by Martin Ingram c.1550–1645.[143] One in three scolds prosecuted at the Cheshire quarter sessions in the 1620s were male.[144] Such cases had disappeared by c.1640. Legal outcomes in the 1620s suggest that the figure of the male scold was already less than wholly viable. Only one of five men was indicted, convicted and punished; the grand jury threw out the other four bills. In contrast, over three-quarters of accused women were indicted, nearly all of whom were convicted.[145] Perhaps it was not purely coincidental that in the convicted man's case, the 'common' offence was embellished with a specific allegation of slander, though technically such conduct should have

---

[139] Marjorie Keniston McIntosh, *Controlling Misbehavior in England 1370–1600* (Cambridge, 1998), 32, 58, 60–1.
[140] For example, John Palsgrave, *Lesclarcissement de la Langue Francoyse Compose par Maistre Johan Palsgraue Angloyse Natyf de Londres, et Gradue de Paris* (London, 1530), s.v. 'scoulde'; 'The second part of the sermon against contention' and 'The third part of the sermon against contention', in *Two Books of Homilies*, 141 and 146.
[141] McIntosh, *Controlling Misbehavior*, 197–8. Pulton, *De Pace Regis*, fos. 1v–2r; Jean de Marconville, *Treatise of the Good and Evell Tounge*, passim.
[142] From 14–29 per cent before 1520, to 40–54 per cent between 1520 and 1579, and to 68 per cent in the 1580s and 1590s: McIntosh, *Controlling Misbehavior*, 197–8, 58–9, Graph 3.2.
[143] Ingram, 'Scolding women cucked or washed', 54–5, Tables 3.1, 3.2. Underdown noted the existence of male scolds but provided no figures, 'Taming of the scold', 120.
[144] Fourteen indictments/presentments: nine of women (64.3 per cent) and five of men (35.7 per cent).
[145] Grand jurors returned seven (77.8 per cent) of nine indictments true and two (22.2 per cent) *ignoramus*.

disturbed neighbours generally rather than the plaintiff alone.[146] The disappearance of the male scold related to the semantic shift towards a gendered (female) scold. It might well have a connection to the generally diminishing status of the offence, evidenced in prosecutions dwindling during the seventeenth century. By 1700, formal prosecutions even of women had become 'something of a curiosity'.[147]

Neither the existence of male scolds nor the particularities of the technical definition inevitably invalidate the view that 'scolding' was a catch-all category. However, the low incidence of cases brought would be truly astonishing if such prosecutions really incorporated all, or even a significant proportion of, unruly feminine speech. There were merely fifteen prosecutions of scolds at Cheshire quarter and great sessions in thirty years sampled between 1590 and 1670. In comparison, there were 231 indictments of women for assault/battery and 784 bindings-over.[148] Other regions and tribunals, including manor and church courts, heard similarly few *a priori* scolding cases.[149] The low rate of prosecution in Cheshire is intriguing also because by the late sixteenth century over three-fifths of the local courts where scolding was still presented were in north west and northern England. Elsewhere, scolds were presented at even fewer courts, in line with an overall decrease in the numbers of communities reporting scolding as problem behaviour over the course of the sixteenth century.[150] The 'obsession' with women's speech appears not to have been translated into an 'epidemic of scolding' or its formal prosecution.[151]

However, scolding behaviour also reached the courts *via* alternative routes. One of these was the allegation of barratry. There were actually three sorts of barratry, two of which – causing repeated malicious litigation, and unlawfully detaining land that was in disputed possession – were incommensurate with scolding.[152] But Cheshire barrators were almost always of the third type: disturbers of the peace, common quarrellers or brawlers, maintainers of quarrels and affrays amongst other people, and inventors and sowers of

---

[146] CRO, QJF 55/3/9 (1626), QJB 2/5, fol. 78v.
[147] Ingram, 'Scolding women cucked or washed', 52.
[148] Even if we consider only these offences, prosecutions for scolding constitute just 1.5 per cent of the total.
[149] See Ingram, 'Scolding women cucked or washed', 55–6.
[150] McIntosh, *Controlling Misbehavior*, 181–3. McIntosh's figures for jury presentments did not include actions brought by individuals, whereas the present study includes both. The parallel is nonetheless suggestive.
[151] Quoting Underdown, 'Taming of the scold', 20. For critiques of Underdown, see Ingram, 'Scolding women cucked or washed', *passim*; McIntosh, *Controlling Misbehavior*, 58–65.
[152] See also Ingram, 'Scolding women cucked or washed', 51–2. For definitions, see Dalton, *Countrey Justice*, 36–7.

false reports that caused discord amongst their neighbours.[153] If the alleged behaviour was comparable to scolding, so was the formal proceeding. The wording of indictments for barratry and scolding was usually identical excepting the terms *barractator/-trix* (barrator) and *objurgator/-trix* (scold). Barrators were predominantly male; only one in seven or eight were female. Yet, as with scolding, there was uncertainty in the late sixteenth and early seventeenth centuries about how the offence was gendered. Ellen Roe, for instance, was indicted in 1591 as a 'common barratrix', yet the clerk entered in the Court Book that she was a 'common scold'. Nor was the reconfiguration solely of barratrices into scolds. Alice Meyre's 1620 indictment for scolding was termed barratry by her neighbours. Elizabeth Adams was indicted for barratry upon information that she was a common scold.[154] Some charged that women were common scolds *and* barratrices.[155] Although no man accused of barratry was explicitly termed a scold, William Johnson was in 1622 charged also with being 'a common busybody and a gossip'.[156] Sometimes neither 'barrator' nor 'scold' was ascribed to men, despite their behaviour clearly coming within the remit of both terms. An information against a married couple for keeping a disorderly, unlicensed alehouse stated that the husband was 'a common brawler, his wife a scold, and both disquieters of their neighbours'.[157]

The relationship between scolding and barratry is further illuminated by the frequency with which married couples together were charged with those offences. This occurred usually as strands within a whole web of accusation, counter-accusation, prosecution and counter-prosecution. Richard and Mary Eldershaw were (unsuccessfully) prosecuted for being, respectively, a 'common barrator' and 'common scold and barrator', as well as (successfully) for several related assaults.[158] Similarly, Thomas Cole was convicted of barratry and his wife Mary of scolding at the instigation of their neighbour, George Poole, whom the Coles in turn prosecuted as a barrator and his daughter as a scold. Further accusations flew and several suits for assault and trespass were launched on each side. The Coles' petition to the county bench is instructive in that it attended not particularly to Poole's barratry.

---

[153] Some were *additionally* accused of maliciously initiating lawsuits: for example, CRO, QJF 55/2/120 (1624); QJF 55/2/27, /122 (1626). Others were embroiled in litigation and counter-litigation. For a rare instance of malicious litigiousness being the primary form of barratry, see CRO, QJF 81/2/285 (1653).
[154] CRO, QJF 21/1/4, QJB 2/3 fo. 181v (1591); QJF 49/1/15, /141 (1620); QJF 49/3/13, /81 (1620).
[155] CRO, QJF 49/2/113 (1620); QJF 57/3/10 (1628); QJF 71/1/94 (1642).
[156] CRO, QJF 51/3/45 (1622).   [157] CRO, QJF 53/4/93 (1624).
[158] CRO, QJF 49/2/112, /113, /24–7, /47, /49, /53 (1620); for the counter-suits, see QJF 49/2/19, /21, /22, /53 (1620). See also QJF 95/1/13, /19 (1667); QJF 95/1/21, /22 (1667).

They discredited Poole primarily by alleging that he was an active recusant, who not only kept recusant tenants and suffered recusant women 'to be brought to bed in his house' so they could 'return [home], the child being neither christened nor they churched unless by some popish priest', but also he persuaded others 'to the Romish religion'. The latter was a weighty accusation; it was technically treason.[159] The Coles did, however, draw attention to Poole and his daughter's verbal misconduct: they had 'with most uncivil and opprobrious speeches called [Thomas Cole] thief and cuckold, [Mary Cole] a whore and a murderer, and their children foxes, with many more slanderous and indecent terms'.[160] Prosecutions for barratry and scolding provided the means of dealing with defamatory words when parties perceived each other to constitute persistent nuisances in the context of ongoing interpersonal disputes.[161] Such suits were not necessarily malicious or avenging. They demonstrate yet again how the concept of personal and household credit informed the definition and prosecution of unacceptable behaviour. In the economy of credit that bound social relations in early modern England, the line drawn between individual and community harm was at times exceptionally ill distinct.[162]

Prosecutions for scolding were commonly connected to broader quarrels or tensions manifested in further litigation at the same or different tribunals.[163] At Nantwich Court Leet on 19 October 1664, Roger Davies presented Margaret Lynn for 'a common scold' and for assaulting and battering him, and at the same time he presented her husband for 'a common drunkard'. These presentments had at least one antecedent, for a fortnight before Davies had been fined for assaulting and battering Margaret Lynn.[164] In another cluster of cases, eleven women (and two men) requested that Elizabeth Adams be sworn to her good behaviour. Adams's frequent threats to 'stick them with her knife' and her drunkenness were portrayed as adjuncts to, or examples of, her activities as a common scold, fighter and quarreller who disquieted her neighbours on a daily basis with her 'taleing, cursing and

---

[159] Pulton, *De Pace Regis*, fos. 115v–116r. George Poole took the oath of allegiance at the Michaelmas Sessions: QJB 1/5, fo. 166r.
[160] CRO, QJF 55/1/24–/27, /29, /65; QJF 55/2/8, /18, /23, /151, /159, /161, /83, /84, /95, /118 (1626). This case is discussed in Garthine Walker and Jenny Kermode, 'Introduction' to Kermode and Walker eds., *Women, Crime and the Courts in Early Modern England* (London, 1994), 18–19.
[161] Other examples include Robert Steele's feud with Richard and Joan Jolly, CRO, QJF 53/3/84 (1624), QJF 53/4/49, /102 (1625), QJF 55/2/112, /120 (1626), QJF 55/4/89, /90 (1627), QJB 2/5, fo. 130v.
[162] See also CRO, QJF 79/3/99 (1651).
[163] Ingram, *Church Courts*, 315–16; Ingram, 'Law, litigants and the construction of "honour"', 145.
[164] CRO, DCH/Y/2, 1663–1666, Nantwich Manor Court Files, 24 October 1664 & 3 October 1664.

other ignominious speeches'. Perhaps it was as tale-telling that neighbours conceived Adams's concurrent initiation of a defamation suit in the consistory court against Margaret Rylance. According to Adams, Rylance had accused her of 'playing the whore' with Rylance's husband and had threatened to 'look for a knife to cut thy nose'. Rylance, meanwhile, prosecuted Adams for ambush, assault and battery at the quarter sessions. In cases like this, it is impossible strictly to separate physically violent, verbal and even sexual misconduct.[165]

Available legal options were not restricted to presentment or indictment for a common scold or barrator. Cheaper and more convenient was a recognisance binding the offender to be of their good behaviour. Surety of the peace was less appropriate for scolding and barratry as it chiefly preserved the peace against an individual, and was forfeitable by actual fighting, beating or extreme menacing. Surety of good abearing, however, was 'to provide the safety of many', and was broken by 'rigorous or terrible words', threats 'tending or inciting the breach of the peace', or any other behaviour that 'put people in fear or trouble'. It was expressly granted against, amongst others, 'common barrators, ... common quarrellers, [and] common peacebreakers'.[166] The proportion of women and men who were bound over to their good behaviour rather than to keep the peace was strikingly similar: over thirty-six per cent of women and thirty-eight per cent of men. Sometimes physical violence was subsumed into verbal.[167] But many of these were explicitly concerned with the scold's two main activities of disturbing community harmony through backbiting or brawling.

Numerous men and women were bound over to their good behaviour expressly because neighbours reported explicitly or in so many words that they were common scolds or barrators. Descriptions include 'a very lewd and malicious woman and a common defamer and slanderer of her neighbours' and 'exceedingly troublesome to the peace of her neighbours'; 'a common slanderer' who had slandered divers men's wives, and who should be bound to his good behaviour so as 'not to [cause] harm by insulting words or in any other way a stirrer of strife among his neighbours and between men and their wives'; 'a common barrator', of 'ill life and carriage and for causing debate and sedition between neighbours'.[168] Husbands and wives were described as 'common swearers and cursers and very quarrelsome and contentious amongst their neighbours'; of 'ill fame and report, stirrers-up of needless

---

[165] CRO, QJF 49/3/81, /12 (1620); CDRO, EDC 5/1620/13, Elizabeth Adams wife of Raphe c. Margaret Rylance wife of Hugh, libel.
[166] Pulton, *De Pace Regis*, fos. 18v, 18r, 22r. Dalton, *Countrey Justice*, 160.
[167] For example, PRO, CHES 24/127/2, articles against Edward and Ruth Hall (1648).
[168] CRO, QJF 51/2/67–/69, /126 (1622); QJB 1/6 fo. 115v (1646); QJF 57/1/64, /65 (1628); QJF 57/4/40 (1628).

quarrels, suits, controversies and contentions between' other married couples; of 'evil carriage in slandering their neighbours' from 'inveterate malice', and who, two years later, despite having been meanwhile indicted for barratry, did still 'continually plot together and conspire [with other barrators] to move and stir up suits and debates amongst their neighbours'.[169] Neighbours desired a warrant of good behaviour 'for our own peace and the general peace' against 'a seditious person and a slanderer of his neighbours and of some Justices of Peace,... [and] of so turbulent a spirit that he will neither forbear to use opprobrious and scandalous speeches against his neighbours nor yield himself obedient to the Justices' warrants'.[170] And so on.[171]

In practice, in Cheshire at least, scolding and barratry were not distinct gender-specific behaviours. Some cases seem to reveal a concern about verbal misconduct, while others were utilised within larger frames of dispute in much the same manner as indictments for trespass were often intrinsically about disputed property rights. Either way, both men and women were portrayed as quarrelsome, verbally abusive persons, and whether we count presentments for scolding and barratry, or recognisances to be of good behaviour, women do not seem to have been particularly singled out for harsh treatment. Ingram has suggested that some scolds were a particular type of disorderly woman. This might have been so, but they were more than matched by a particular type of disorderly man who was similarly vilified and prosecuted, even as the terms 'scold' and 'barrator' were becoming increasingly gendered.

Punishment

What, then, of the harsh punishments allegedly meted out to early modern scolds? Nineteenth-century antiquarians discovered in Cheshire a disproportionate number of branks, or 'scold's bridles', recording specimens in the towns of Altrincham, Macclesfield, Congleton, Carrington, Knutsford, Stockport (two), Chester (four) and in the parish of Acton near Nantwich.[172]

---

[169] PRO, CHES 21/4 fo. 187r.; CHES 24/127/2, articles and indictment re. Edward and Ruth Hall (1648); CRO, QJF 81/4/105 (1654); QJF 53/3/84 (1624); QJF 55/2/120, 55/3/90 (1626).

[170] CRO, QJF 53/2/145 (1624). See also CRO, QJF 95/1/142, /72 (1667); QJF 97/2/65, /101 (1669); QJF 95/2/115 (1669).

[171] For example, CRO, QJF 27/3/15 (1597); QJF 53/3/35, /34 (1624); QJF 77/4/45 (1650); QJF 79/1/81 (1651); PRO, CHES 24/105/4/48 (1599).

[172] T.N. Brushfield, 'On obsolete punishments, with particular reference to those of Cheshire'. Part I. 'The branks or scold's bridle', *Journal of the Architectural, Archaeological, and Historic Society for the County, City and Neighbourhood of Chester*, 2 (1864), 41–7; John Corry, *The History of Macclesfield* (London, 1817), 216; Robert Head, *Congleton Past and Present: A History of this Old Cheshire Town* (Congleton, 1887), 62–4; W.M. Taylor, *A History of the Stockport Court Leet* (Stockport, 1971), 28–9.

Branks were iron headpieces with a mouthpiece or 'bit' that prevented the wearer from speaking. On some, the bit was spiked. On one of Stockport's branks, for example, it took the form of a 'bulbous extremity' that sported nine 'iron pins... three on the upper surface, three on the lower, and three pointing backwards'. The unavoidable injuries to the tongue caused by wearing this contraption would have been severer still when the wearer was pulled along by the attached chain.[173] In Newcastle, the branks took the form of an iron crown 'muzzled over the head and face, with a great gap or tongue of iron forced into her mouth, which forced the blood out'. It is notable, however, that the description of a Newcastle woman being subjected to such humiliation and horror sought to exemplify the *extra*ordinary *un*lawfulness of that city's Mayor and Corporation.[174] Despite scattered references to these vicious instruments, there is scant evidence that the branks were regularly inflicted upon women. The records of the Chester Corporation and the Stockport Court Leet are typical in that they contain not a single order or notice to that effect.[175] The suggestion that early modern magistrates purposefully suppressed the evidence of bridling because they knew it was unlawful, is simply untenable in the light of modern scholarship concerning both the magistracy and legal procedures.

In contrast to bridling, other corporal punishments such as the pillory or whipping were regularly inflicted.[176] In a seventeenth-century definition of a cucking stool as 'an engine of punishment... for the bridling of scolds and unquiet women', the women's speech is 'bridled' as a consequence of their shame and humiliation rather than a scold's bridle as such.[177] When contemporaries threatened 'I'll have thee bridled', as one man did to a woman who called him 'Master Fartibag' and 'Master Turdibag' in public, they might not have intended the actual infliction of a scold's bridle any more than William Gouge did when he advised that a woman must not provoke her husband and 'learne first to moderate their passion, and then to keep in their tongues with bit and bridle'.[178] In early modern parlance, emotions such as anger, love and affection and behaviour such as sexual incontinence as well as speech were regularly said to have been or to be in need of bridling.

---

[173] Brushfield, 'On obsolete punishments...' Part I, 45.
[174] Ralph Gardiner, *Englands Grievance Discovered, in Relation to the Coal-Trade with the Map of the River of Tine, and Situation of the Town and Corporation of Newcastle* (London, 1655), 110–11.
[175] Brushfield, 'On obsolete punishments...' Part I, 46; Taylor, *History of the Stockport Court Leet*, 28–9.
[176] For example, CRO, QJB 1/6 fo. 122r.
[177] Thomas Blount, *Glossographia, or, A Dictionary Interpreting All Such Hard Words Of Whatsoever Language Now Used In Our Refined English Tongue* (London, 1656), s.v. 'tumbrell'.
[178] CRO, QJF 81/3/39 (1653); Gouge, *Of Domesticall Duties*, 284–5.

It was about self-restraint in the face of unruly passions of all sorts. A man, as much as a woman, was advised or admonished to 'bridle his lavish tongue' or 'to give the bridle unto his rebellious and untamed affections'.[179] 'Bridling scolds' was as much, perhaps more, a figure of speech as it was a judicial punishment.

Tellingly, use of the aforementioned branks that Newcastle 'magistrates do inflict upon chiding and scolding women' was criticised because it was 'not granted by their charter law, and [is] repugnant to the known laws of England'. The latter stated that 'scolds ought to be ducked over head and ears into the water in a ducking stool'.[180] Here, bridling is presented as an aberration from the norm. The evidence about the practice of ducking presents problems, however. As Underdown noted, references in Court Books to mending or setting up ducking stools, variously referred to as cuck-stools, cucking-stools, or tumbrels, are not proof that such a contraption was possessed, let alone used. To the contrary, Underdown remarked, growing standardisation in legal procedures meant that the presentment of a poorly maintained or non-existent cucking-stool 'with no evidence of actual use in the meantime... is probably an indication that the place never had a cucking-stool at all'.[181] Nonetheless, unlike the scold's bridle, cucking was legally acknowledged as a punishment, although not solely for scolds. There is evidence that some wrongdoers were ordered to be placed on the cuck-stool. Yet being cucked did not inevitably involve ducking in water. References to cucking stools in several late sixteenth-century Cheshire towns stipulate ducking in water in one instance only – in Congleton in 1595.[182] Punishment for first and, in many places, subsequent offences most often took the form of display for a specified number of hours, in the same way as offenders were displayed in the pillory. The connection between cuck-stool and pillory was made by contemporaries.[183]

Usually, however, scolds were neither ducked nor cucked. Court records demonstrate this, and circumstantial evidence points in the same direction. Bridling and ducking are omitted from a 1678 book of plates demonstrating common law punishments.[184] Neither ballads nor pamphlets make much of cuck-stools, paying far greater attention to cuckolding than cucking. The

---

[179] John Lyly, *Euphues and his England* (London, 1580), sig. C5; Sir Henry Wotton, *A Courtlie Controversie of Cupids Cautels* (London, 1578), 62.
[180] Ralph Gardiner, *Englands Grievance Discovered*, 110–11.
[181] Underdown, 'Taming of the scold', 123–4.
[182] John Webster Spargo, *Judicial Folklore in England, Illustrated by the Cucking Stool* (Durham, North Carolina, 1944), 26–7, 30–1, 34.
[183] For example, 'The third part of the sermon against contention', in *Two Books of Homilies*, 145–6.
[184] John Seller, *A Booke of the Punishments of the Common Laws of England* (London, 1678). See also Spargo, *Judicial Folklore*, 45–6, 70.

punishment of scolds was nearly always presented as a husband's, rather than neighbours' or magistrates' preserve. Moses Vauts admitted that 'I bestowed so many slaps with my bare hand alone on [my wife's] mouth, the part offending' when she uttered 'horrid oaths in my face'. In ballads, husbands were advised to strip, chain and beat their scolding wives, or to cut open their tongues in order to bleed the violence out of them.[185] In private and in print, scolds were dealt harsh, sometimes horrific punishments. Yet this was not often sanctioned by legal processes. The routine public penalty for scolding enforced by early modern courts was a monetary fine of 3s. 4d.

The explanation for such a discrepancy between legal procedures and the stereotypical view of the scold lies partly in the ambiguity surrounding women's expected roles and responsibilities. The majority of women prosecuted as scolds or barrators were married. In Cheshire, there were more than twice as many wives as widows, and five times as many wives as spinsters prosecuted for scolding.[186] The prevalence of wives among those identified as scolds or barrators by their neighbours tells us something about the positive as well as the negative assertion of female authority. 'Customary scolding or clamour', as Vauts put it, 'is no argument of [feminine] weakness, but of a stubborn and sinful strength'.[187] Whereas complainants agreed with Vauts that such female strength was condemnable, from a different perspective 'scolding' was a further manifestation of the forceful protection of household concerns.[188] This is somewhat borne out by the facts that a third of wives accused of scolding or barratry acted alongside husbands who were similarly prosecuted and, as we saw earlier, that many accusations of scolding occurred in the context of inter-household disputes. Mistresses of households might well have cause to use words of reproach to their neighbours, words that might easily be redefined as reproachful.

In this chapter, we have seen that women's non-lethal violence differed less from men's than we might expect. Although women constituted a minority of those prosecuted, those women who were prosecuted were just as likely as men to use weapons and to be sworn to their good behaviour as opposed to keep the peace. The conventional view that, unlike men, women fought 'with tongues rather than fists' has been shown to be inaccurate.[189] Female aggression plainly was manifest in deeds as well as words. We can see that women for the most part derived their authority from patriarchal discourses, frequently portraying themselves as the upholders of gendered and social

---

[185] Vauts, *Husband's Authority*, 78, 84; Todd, 'Representation of aggression', 223.
[186] Wives constituted 60 per cent, widows 28 per cent, and spinsters 12 per cent.
[187] Vauts, *Husband's Authority*, 80.   [188] See also Spargo, *Judicial Folklore*, 25.
[189] Quoting Wiener, 'Sex roles and crime', 47.

norms. Yet the meanings of women's violence did differ from that of men. In particular, women's household roles and responsibilities helped shape the nature and form of feminine physical and verbal violence and provided alternative models of feminine force to those of an often misogynist culture. These alternative visions of violence allowed women to construct positively their actions in a number of ways that differed from the conventional, less flexible, depictions of unruly femininity.

One example of this is the figure of the exemplary warrior-women, which presented women with a type of virtuous femininity that was displayed in physical strength and courage. Thus, the apocryphal heroine, Judith, was frequently praised as worthy of emulation. Judith used her beauty to captivate Holofernes, who sought to destroy the Jewish people, in order to come close to him. Then, while he slept, she took his sword and cut off his head. As a show of strength, this cannot be doubted. Decapitating a man was hard work; even skilled executioners were unable always to inflict a quick or clean death. But as a model of feminine violence, we are faced with a conundrum. For female strength and courage was positive only within certain contexts. It was simply not the case that the highest praise bestowable on early modern women was the attribution of masculine courage, strength and determination.[190] In real life, women who killed, whether or not they ascribed to themselves the qualities associated with Judith, were not admired. Neither the legal system nor societal values appear to have had the exemplary warrior-woman much in mind when they dealt with women accused of homicide. Murder, manslaughter and other forms of killing are discussed in the next chapter.

---

[190] See also Jacob Burckhardt, *The Civilisation of the Renaissance in Italy*, trans. S.G.C. Middlemois (New York, 1958), Vol. II, 391–2; Jerry C. Nash, 'Renaissance misogyny, biblical feminism, and Helisènne de Crenne's *Epistres Familières et Invectives*', *Renaissance Quarterly* 50, 2 (1997), 400.

4

Homicide, gender and justice

The history of lethal violence has been dominated by accounts of the incidence of homicide over long periods, within which the paucity of women as defendants is generally taken for granted. Several studies, however, compare men's and women's conviction rates. Pre-modern women are often said to have benefited from lenient treatment relative to men within the criminal justice system. Explanations for such leniency differ. Some historians seem to argue that despite some notable exceptions – the benefits of clergy and belly and the characterisation of husband-killing as petty treason – the law offered both sexes a rough equality in theory, but in practice female offenders benefited from chivalric attitudes on the part of judges and jurors.[1] However, the noted exceptions would seem to undermine the general point about equality before the law even in theory. And it is unclear how the judiciary squared an abstraction of feminine frailty with the alleged acts of the women before them. Others have argued that law itself failed to provide a comparable means of sentencing women and men. Women's ineligibility to claim benefit of clergy led judges and jurors to treat female defendants less severely than males.[2] Yet the view that women were the recipients of peculiar leniency, whether to compensate for the unavailability of clergy or because of chivalric attitudes, is perhaps misconceived. The argument that the sentencing of women was lenient (or harsh, for that matter) judges women's treatment before the courts by the male standards that were embodied in law. I wish to show in this chapter that while these standards operated to the advantage of most men who were charged with homicide, the same cannot be said of women. The nature of homicide law itself precluded men and women from receiving like treatment before the courts.

[1] For example, McLynn, *Crime and Punishment*, 128–9; Wiener, 'Sex roles and crime', 39–40. For the medieval period, see Barbara A. Hanawalt, 'The female felon in fourteenth-century England', *Viator* 5 (1974), 266.
[2] For example, Cockburn, *Calendar of Assize Records: Home Circuit Indictments: Elizabeth I and James I. Introduction* (London, 1985), 114, 117, 121–3; Herrup, *Common Peace*, 143; Jackson, *New-Born Child Murder*, 144.

English common law procedures did not produce records that allow us to reconstruct either fatal encounters or the trials that followed. Despite the emphasis upon *mens rea*, the evidence rarely permits us to assess the intention of killers other than in the manner of 'rank speculation'.[3] In this chapter I do not, therefore, attempt to ascertain the extent to which the guilty were acquitted or innocents led to the gallows.[4] Even the seemingly straightforward 'facts' of a case, as presented and classified by defendants, witnesses, jurors, coroners, magistrates and judges, were contestable. This does not mean that they were inevitably embellishments or manipulations of the truth, although they sometimes might have been. Rather, the precise nature of events was always defined and interpreted from a particular point of view. A very important perspective was that of law itself, with which, as we shall see, the views of historical actors were often but not always in line. It is in the light of plural perspectives that the following analysis occurs. In sections on, respectively, male-perpetrated and female-perpetrated homicide, I shall attend to legal and cultural conceptions of culpability, paying particular attention to the relevance of gender in the way cases were framed and the interpretation and operation of the law. First, though, we need to establish the basic legal distinctions between degrees of culpability in early modern England.[5]

CATEGORIES OF CULPABILITY

Homicide was a heterogeneous offence: 'Even in extreme evils there are degrees', opined Sir Francis Bacon in 1612 at Lord Sanguire's trial for murdering a man who blinded him in one eye during a duel.[6] The legal category of homicide encompassed a range of acts. The ascription of culpability was based upon a tripartite distinction between culpable killing, which was capital, excusable killing, which was pardonable, and justifiable killing,

---

[3] Martin Daly and Margo Wilson, *Homicide* (New York, 1988), 13.

[4] See also Carrie Smith, 'Medieval coroners' rolls: legal fiction or historical fact', in Diana E.S. Dunn ed., *Courts, Counties and the Capital in the Later Middle Ages* (Stroud and New York, 1996), 113. Smith believes 'provided that one retains a firm grip on one's critical faculties, it is possible to assess which verdicts are likely to be more accurate than others'; she neglects to explain the method that permits her to make such judgements.

[5] Evidence in the form of indictments, coroners' inquisitions, grand and petty jury returns, pretrial examinations and informations, recognisances, petitions, warrants and letters are drawn from the period 1570–1689, and pertain to the counties of Cheshire and the City of Chester. Unless otherwise indicated, the source of quantitative data is a sample of 304 individuals – 230 of whom were principal offenders – prosecuted at the Cheshire great sessions between 1590 and 1670. The sampled sessions are those held in alternate years in the 1590s, 1620s, 1650s and 1660s, and all those held in the 1640s. Unless otherwise indicated homicide includes infanticide.

[6] Cited in Jeremy Horder, *Provocation and Responsibility* (Oxford, 1992), 21. See also the list of homicides in *Murder upon Murder* (London, 1635), 435–6.

which deserved acquittal.[7] These categories influenced both the framing of evidence and the decisions leading to conviction and sentencing in early modern England.[8]

By the end of the sixteenth century, two categories of culpable killing existed: murder and manslaughter. Murder was defined legally as intentional, premeditated, cold-blooded killing, and assumed 'malice' on the killer's part. A legal fiction existed whereby the law implied malice if the defendant was thought to be fully culpable despite the absence of literal premeditation. Law thus assumed the presence of malice in hot-blooded killings that were brutal or cowardly. This practice was formalised in the 1604 'Stabbing Statute': when victims died within six months of being stabbed in an unprovoked attack while having no weapon drawn, killers were to receive a murderer's punishment even though they were technically convicted of manslaughter. As with other forms of homicide, accessories to the fact were to be judged in the manner of the principal and punished accordingly. The penalty for murder was death and forfeiture to the Crown of lands and goods.[9]

Manslaughter, the other category of culpable killing, was also 'a fearful crime in God's sight', despite the law being relatively favourably disposed to it.[10] Manslaughter was defined as sudden, unplanned killing where 'the heat of blood kindled by ire...never cooled' in time to prevent the death. The absence of malice had to be demonstrated by way of some recognised excuse or justification. One mitigating notion was 'chance-medley', wherein each party put their own life at risk by voluntarily entering the fight during 'a sudden brangle or falling out'. Another was manslaughter under provocation, whereby the concept of retributive justice by the man of honour permitted immediate retaliation.[11] The defendant's crime was therefore not that he had

---

[7] Baker, *Introduction to Legal History*, 600–3; J.M. Beattie, 'The royal pardon and criminal procedure', *Historical Papers* (1987), 9–22; Thomas A. Green, *Verdict According to Conscience: Perspectives on the English Criminal Trial Jury, 1200–1800* (Chicago and London, 1985), 106–7, 121–4, 145–6; Thomas A. Green, 'Societal concepts of criminal liability for homicide in medieval England', *Speculum* 47 (1972), 669, 675–94; Horder, *Provocation and Responsibility*, 1–54; J.M. Kaye, 'The early history of murder and manslaughter', *Law Quarterly Review* 83 (1967), 365–95, 569–601.

[8] The following discussion draws on Dalton, *Countrey Justice*, 217–30, 263, 266; Coke, *Third Part of the Institutes*, 47–58; Thomas Forster, *The Lay-man's Lawyer, Reviewed and Enlarged* (London, 1656), 8–10, 24–5; Matthew Hale, *Pleas of the Crown: Or, A Methodical Summary* (London, 1678), 40–59; Pulton, *De Pace Regis*, fos. 120, 122–5, 216–40; Zachary Babington, *Advice to Grand Jurors in Cases of Blood* (1676; London, 1680), 175–7, 137–42.

[9] The statutes making murder and stabbing non-clergiable were, respectively, 1 Edward VI, c. 12, s. 10 (1547) and 2 James I, c. 8 (1604).

[10] CCRO, Eaton Hall Grosvenor MSS, Personal Papers, Box 1, 2/52, Sir Richard Grosvenor, 'Jury Charge', *c.* 1625.

[11] CRO, Leicester-Warren of Tabley Collection, DLT/unlisted/16, 'Briefe Notes', Peter Leicester, jury charge, 1660, 57. Coke, *Third Part of the Institutes*, 55. CRO, Cholmondley of Cholmondley Collection: Private Correspondence, DDX X/7, 'King's Pardon, lawyers' opinions and other papers', H. Degge to Thomas Wettenhall, 17 September 1673; William Williams

acted with angry violence *per se*, but that he had done so excessively. Both chance-medley and manslaughter under provocation ascribed some responsibility to the victim for his own death: the killer was thus only partially culpable. Men, but not women, convicted of manslaughter were entitled to plead for the benefit of clergy which, if granted (as it normally was), resulted in branding on the thumb with an 'M' for manslayer, and forfeiture as for murder.[12]

Excusable homicide also took two forms: killing by accident (*per infortunium*) and in self-defence (*se defendendo*). Killing by accident, termed variously misadventure, misfortune and mischance, was a broad category that covered a variety of unintentional deaths (although not killings in the course of an unlawful act). Because the defendant had not intended to cause harm, the victim's death was 'against the will of him who did the deed'. Excusable self-defence had criteria that were more specific: the absolute necessity of the fatal blow to the killer's preservation of his own life, which countered his intention to cause harm. From the fourteenth century, those convicted of excusable killing received pardons 'of course' almost automatically, thereby avoiding corporal and capital punishment and the forfeiture of lands. They still forfeited their goods and chattels 'for the great regard which the law hath of a man's life', as Dalton put it[13] – although defendants' freedom to dispense goods to relatives and friends before the trial regularly resulted in jurors' assessments of offenders having goods of no or little value.

Some forms of killing were legally justified as essential to the maintenance of order and the delivery of justice and therefore carried no punishment. These included the lawful execution of felons, deaths that ensued in the course of administering royal justice (such as those of felons who resisted arrest), and deaths of people who were in the process of committing felonies such as burglary. All these killings were to be undertaken 'with grief and sorrow of mind' but were deemed necessary for the common good.[14] A finding of justifiable homicide led to acquittal.

These conceptual categories of culpable, excusable and justifiable killing underpinned the verdicts and sentences analysed in this chapter.

ORDER, HONOUR AND THE NATURE OF MAN

Murder most foul

From JPs' jury charges to the popular accounts of street literature, murderers were – often at great length – given short shrift. It was 'a wonder' to

to Wettenhall, 23 September 1673; William William's opinion, 15 October 1673; Mr Waterhouse's opinion, n.d.; Mr Attorney's notes on 'what murder is', n.d.
[12] For benefit of clergy, see J.S. Cockburn, *Introduction*, 117–21.
[13] Dalton, *Countrey Justice*, 229.   [14] Dalton, *Countrey Justice*, 229.

Sir Richard Grosvenor 'that there should be so many monsters' in Cheshire, 'who...do thus pollute their souls with the act of so inhumane a crime'. His explanation was that 'whom grace cannot contain within her limits, impiety (with the Devil's assistance) thrusteth on to such infernal stratagems'.[15] Balladeers likewise lamented that 'there's scarce a month within the year, but murders vile are done' by those with a 'devilish desire', 'unnatural will', and 'cruel and monstrous hard heart'; 'their hearts still bent to cruelty, not minding to amend: they cannot see Satan the Devil, that drags them unto all this evil'.[16] Pamphleteer Gilbert Dugdale wrote of a Cheshire case in 1602 that 'After my long being at Chester in the time of this reported trouble, I in my melancholy walks bethought me of the strange invasion of Satan... how that ugly fiend (ever man's fatal opposite) had made practice, but I hope not purchase, of their corruptible lives, and brought them to the last step of mortal misery.'[17] Legal and cultural attitudes converged in attributing full culpability to murderers. Authors of both street literature and lengthy moral tracts, crowds attending hangings, jurors, judges, witnesses and prosecutors appear all to have concurred with jurists' sentiments that murderers deserved to 'be hanged between heaven and earth, as unworthy of both'.[18] The lawful execution of a (normally penitent) murderer provided the powerful form of closure demanded by the didactic and narrative structure of ballads and pamphlets whose themes were sin, divine providence and redemption.[19] In addition to these usually solemn accounts,[20] some were upbeat, telling of multitudes who 'flocked with joy' to see a notorious murderer hanged.[21]

---

[15] CCRO, Eaton Hall Grosvenor MSS, Personal Papers, Box 1, 2/52, Sir Richard Grosvenor, 'A charge to the grand jury', 1624. Gaskill, *Crime and Mentalities*, 203–41; Peter Lake, 'Deeds against nature: cheap print, Protestantism and murder in early seventeenth-century England', in Kevin Sharpe and Peter Lake eds., *Culture and Politics in Early Stuart England* (London, 1994), 257–84; J.A. Sharpe, '"Last dying speeches": religion, ideology and public execution in seventeenth-centuiry England', *P&P* 107 (1985), 147–65; Garthine Walker, '"Demons in female form": representations of women and gender in murder pamphlets of the late sixteenth and early seventeenth centuries', in William Zunder and Suzanne Trill eds., *Writing and the English Renaissance* (London, 1996), 123–39.

[16] *Murder upon Murder* (London, 1635), repr. in *A Pepysian Garland*, ed. Hyder E. Rollins (Cambridge, Mass., 1971), 431–6, at 432, 435; *A Briefe Discourse Of Two Most Cruell and Bloudie Murthers...* (London, 1583), sigs. A5–5v, A7.

[17] Gilbert Dugdale, *A True Discourse of the Practices of Elizabeth Caldwell...In the County of Chester...* (London, 1604), sig. A3.

[18] Dalton, *Countrey Justice*, 266; Pulton, *De Pace Regis*, fo. 123; CCRO, Eaton Hall Grosvenor MSS, Personal Papers, Box 1, 2/51, Sir Richard Grosvenor, 'Jury Charge', c. 1625.

[19] Lake, 'Deeds against nature'; Sharpe, 'Last dying speeches'; Walker, 'Demons in female form'. See also V.A.C. Gatrell, *The Hanging Tree: Execution and the English People 1770–1868* (Oxford, 1994), 106–96. For the same views in a lengthy exposition on sin, see Thomas Beard, *The Theatre of God's Judgements* (London, 1631), 243–343.

[20] For example, *The Cries of the Dead*, c. 1625, repr. in *Pepysian Garland*, 222–8, at 228.

[21] For example, *The Life and Death of M. George Sandys*, 1626, repr. in *Pepysian Garland*, 248–55, at 253.

Doleful or joyous, the point remained the same: in swinging a murderer, justice had been done.

Certainly, murderers were among those whose executions drew the greatest crowds and were accompanied by apparent collective approval. As V.A.C. Gatrell has shown vividly for the late eighteenth and nineteenth centuries, the hangman – who was generally abhorred – might be cheered when he dispensed with murderers.[22] The complexities of crowd behaviour cannot be explained away as evidence of the successful internalisation of 'dominant' notions of the law's might or the wickedness of crime. Individuals or groups might have condemned murderers for different reasons, and, in practice, particular cases were often contested. Yet, whatever else it meant, the crowd's vehemence towards and lack of compassion for murderers suggests a cultural acceptance that murderers should die. For killings classified as murders, the theory of the law *was* practice.

Historians' characterisation of the early modern legal process as one that operated in the favour of offenders to mitigate the 'harshness' of the law is thus inapplicable to cases classified as murder.[23] Murderers comprised two-thirds of all men executed for homicide. Their killings were characterised by premeditation, stealth, betrayed trust and unfair advantage. For example, John Warton cudgelled Thomas Leene from behind and at night after plotting the act with Leene's wife.[24] William Stannop conspired with his lover (they married shortly afterwards) to poison his wife Ann, which he did with a buttermilk drink laced with arsenic. Two days after drinking it, Ann was dead.[25] John Payne led his blind son, Moses, by the hand to the edge of a pit filled with water. To the horror of two men who chanced upon the scene, Payne pushed Moses in and left him to drown.[26] William Gayton butchered James Finlyson with his sword on the Chester to Manchester highway while robbing him of twenty-six yards of expensive cloth and £160 in money. He was 'hanged where the fact was' in chains.[27] Hugh Stringer confessed to having murdered both Ann Cranage and her daughter Cicely.[28] All of the above acts were considered reprehensible. They smacked of greed

---

[22] Gatrell, *Hanging Tree*, 56–7, 70, 74–80, 84, 89, 97–101; Green, *Verdict*, 144; Michael MacDonald, *Sleepless Souls: Suicide in Early Modern England* (Oxford, 1990), 129–30; J.A. Sharpe, *Judicial Punishment in England* (London, 1990), 32–3.

[23] For example, Sharpe, *Judicial Punishment*, 49.

[24] Ellen Leene was also executed; see below, p. 143. PRO, CHES 24/118/3 indictments, recognisance, jury return, CHES 21/3, fo. 126 (1626). See also CHES 24/135/5 indictment, coroner's inquisition, recognisance re. John Boulton and Alice Liverpool, CHES 21/5, fos. 59, 61 (1667).

[25] PRO, CHES 24/129/1 indictment, jury return, recognisance, CHES 21/4, fo. 242v (1651). The new wife was hanged as accessory.

[26] PRO, CHES 24/126/5 jury return, examinations, CHES 21/4, fo. 142v (1645).

[27] PRO, CHES 24/103/3 indictment, jury return, CHES 21/1, fo. 167v (1593).

[28] PRO, CHES 21/1, fos. 192v, 193v (1597).

and self-interest, excessive violence, betrayal and had vulnerable or innocent victims.[29] It is no coincidence that so many murders were domestic, a fact that had gendered implications and which I shall discuss later.

Once convicted, murderers were rarely reprieved.[30] In Cheshire, fewer than one in ten were pardoned, and usually then only on the basis that the conviction was faulty. In other words, the condemned man was not thought by the judge to be a 'murderer' at all. Thus, John Davenport was reprieved because 'the evidence upon his arraignment proving no precedent malice, so as the judges did conceive it to be no murder, and so directed the jury; yet they found him guilty of murder'.[31] Most convicted murderers were not so lucky, and suffered the slow, painful and messy death of being choked on the gallows.

The accounts of lethal violence that were produced by the legal process exemplify the manner in which official and legal discourses informed and converged with individual and lay ones.[32] In the framing of evidence, early modern people assigned degrees of culpability by assessing the perceived motive, intent and circumstances in the light of the categories of culpability described above. As culpability was imagined as a fixed quantity of guilt, deponents frequently constructed the conduct of killer and victim in oppositional terms. If the victim was partially responsible for the lethal blows being struck, the killer was not wholly guilty. In distinguishing murder from manslaughter, the perspectives of the parties could make all the difference. In 1572, for example, Nantwich innkeeper Roger Crockett died six hours after

---

[29] Acts classified as murder were similarly characterised elsewhere. Beattie, *Crime and the Courts*, 77–8, 97–8; Cockburn, *Introduction*, 99; Green, *Verdict*, 107; Maddern, *Violence and Social Order*, 128; Sharpe, *Crime*, 123–5. See also Cynthia Herrup's remark that jurors 'were generally more lenient in crimes carrying punishments over which they had less control, even if the threat to local peace was more severe'. She suggests that juries were more reluctant to return convictions for offences that were considered particularly heinous, such as homicide, than they were for petty larceny. Yet her evidence contrarily demonstrates that murder had the highest conviction rate after petty larceny, jointly with theft without clergy. Manslaughter and grand larceny, which according to Herrup's account should have had higher conviction rates than murder and non-clergiable theft, in fact had slightly lower and significantly lower conviction rates respectively. Herrup, *Common Peace*, 144–5, and Table 6.2.

[30] Cockburn, *Introduction*, 126–7; Herrup, *Common Peace*, 172–3. Across Europe and North America, murder remained the crime most likely to lead to execution even where the use of capital punishment was restricted: Gatrell, *Hanging Tree*, 8–10.

[31] PRO, Signet Office and Home Office: Docquet Books and Letters Recommendatory, SO 3/8 [unfoliated], 'A pardon for the life of John Davenport', September 1626; PRO, CHES 21/3, fos. 125, 131, 143; CHES 24/118/3 indictment, coroner's inquisition (1626). See also SO 3/16/42, 'A pardon to Robert Calcot', July 1666; SO 3/289.

[32] On the process of creating such accounts, see R.F. Hunnisett, 'The importance of eighteenth-century coroners' bills', in E.W. Ives and A.H. Manchester eds., *Law, Litigants and the Legal Profession* (London, 1983), 126–39; John Langbein, *Prosecuting Crime in the Renaissance* (Cambridge, Mass., 1974), 65–77.

being wounded in a fight. The motive attributed to Richard Hassall, Crockett's alleged killer, was revenge: there was a 'deadly mortal malice and hatred' between the two men over the lease of Ridley Field in Nantwich. With meticulous planning, Hassall had sent spies to discover Crockett's movements, instructed servants to ambush Crockett's cousins to prevent them from assisting their kinsman, and personally led the assault on Crockett. Malice was also implied in the attack's cruelty. Crockett was allegedly unprepared and offered no immediate provocation – he did not 'heave up his staff nor draw his dagger or speak evil word to anybody'. Notwithstanding, he was set upon by ten armed men whose ferocity was imprinted in black, blue and green bruises all over his torso and limbs, including the mark of a 'heinous stroke or rather a mortal blow' upon 'his breast or heart'. Crockett received also a dent in the back of his head that 'would shrink down under a man's thumb when it were handled'; his right eye 'was almost stricken out'; 'his blood and brains issued abundantly out of his mouth and nose... upon the ground'. In the light of such murderous premeditation and brutality, there was an expectation and desire that, in all justice, 'somebody must be hanged for Crockett'.[33]

The above version of events was contested, however. Crockett was himself held partly accountable. He had been 'daily in [Hassall's] face' after having 'done him so great a displeasure as to take his living over his head'. Several townspeople had foretold that if Crockett purchased the land, 'mischief and manslaughter' would ensue. 'I would to God it were a fish-pool', one young man had declared, 'for [Crockett] will have his brains knocked out one day about it.' The number and severity of Crockett's injuries were also disputed. By the following morning, it was rumoured that Crockett had received just one blow – 'a little tap' – from a single assailant, Edmund Crewe, who having already left the county (allegedly with Hassall's help) was unavailable to be tried. The widowed Bridget Crockett's response was to display her husband's naked corpse in the marketplace so 'that the truth might appear of his many strokes upon sundry places of his body'. Additionally, a picture 'of the many strokes was drawn' so that 'a just and true trial' might ensue whereby 'it might appear he died not upon any one stroke but by the force and violence of many strokes'.[34] Her adversaries persisted in publishing their version of events, predictably erasing all traces of premeditation and malice and stressing the public nature of the incident. While the men were portrayed as equally culpable in a fight between equals who had each quarrelled with the other,

---

[33] CRO, Miscellaneous Deposits, 'Examinations touching the death of Roger Crockett, innkeeper, 1572', DDX 196, fos. 18v, 17r–v, 1r, 4r, 11r, 14v, 20r, 16r, 21v, 22r, 39r, 2r, 44r, 18v, 8r, 52r, 25r. PRO, Palatinate of Chester: Miscellanea, 'Proceedings relating to the death of Roger Crockett', CHES 38/28/2, fos. 1, 3.

[34] CRO, DDX 196, fos. 18v, 17, 17v, 1, 4, 11, 14v, 20. PRO, CHES 38/28/2, fos. 1, 3.

their wives were presented oppositionally. Hassall's wife, Ann, far from being the evil harpy whom Bridget alleged had shrieked orders to her men to kill Crockett, was the epitome of good womanhood. Being 'great with child' – a condition widely regarded as incongruent with violence, as we know – she knelt at the stricken Crockett's side, and tried to help him, reminding him that 'thou wouldest not do this much for me, if thou sawest me lie in this case'. In contrast, malice was attributed to Bridget Crockett, manifest in her insistence that this was murder, and later her fervent pursuance of the murder charge – she ultimately petitioned the Queen. In this way, Hassall's party effectively rewrote murder as manslaughter. Ultimately, their version – in which Crockett was partly responsible for the incident, Hassall and his men had not behaved maliciously and cold-bloodedly, and the absent Edmund Crewe had dealt the single fatal blow – was officially sanctioned. The verdict was manslaughter, but in the absence of the principal, Edmund Crewe, no one was punished.[35]

Reducing the charge from murder to manslaughter in this way was common practice all over England. In some counties, all homicides were drawn up as murder charges in the first instance. In others, such as Cheshire, the two were already distinguished before the indictment was filed. The majority of Cheshire indictments involved charges of manslaughter, leaving a minority of *a priori* murder cases. We have seen that once convicted, a murderer was unlikely to avoid the gallows. However, the conviction rate for men in murder cases was not exceptionally high, largely because other categories existed into which men's lethal violence could easily be placed. Nearly three-quarters of those tried for murder were either acquitted, pardoned after verdicts of death by misfortune or self-defence, or – most common of all – were branded after they were found guilty of a reduced charge of manslaughter.[36] While there was a consensus that murderers should hang, men who were accused of murder nonetheless had a fair chance of avoiding the gallows.

Manslaughter

Manslaughter was the most common verdict in homicide cases. Convicted men were usually branded as manslayers after pleading benefit of clergy.[37] Many of the incidents in question were probably the spontaneous, unplanned encounters that were presented to the court. Some were expressly defined as chance-medleys, as in the case of Chester beer-brewer, John Garnett, who

---

[35] PRO, CHES 38/28/2, fo. 4, CHES 21/1, fos. 60, 62v, 67.
[36] The figure is 72.5 per cent.
[37] Fifty-one (55.4 per cent) of the ninety-two guilty verdicts were for manslaughter; of these, thirty-nine (76.5 per cent) were branded, ten hanged (19.6 per cent), and two (3.9 per cent) received pardons.

'fell out with Robert Gardner his servant in words' about his debt book. Garnett threw a loaf of bread at Gardner and 'gave him two boxes on the ear' in chastisement, whereupon 'they both closed together and in the closing, Garnett with a shredding knife did strike Gardner', who died forty-eight hours later. The surgeon, whom Garnett sent for that evening (implying perhaps an absence of malice), affirmed not only that Gardner had received the one blow, but that his belly was swollen full 'with a barrel of beer' that might explain his quarrelsome behaviour.[38] The fact that Gardner lived for two days was relevant too: the longer a victim languished, perhaps becoming dangerously ill only after his wounds became infected, the less murderous intent and liability for the death were usually found on the part of the assailant, especially if there were other mitigating circumstances.[39] Lethal weapons in manslaughter cases similarly suggest that many killings were spontaneous or not intentionally lethal. In very few instances were proper arms used.[40] Weapons were normally the everyday implements of non-lethal violence – agricultural tools like pitchforks, shovels or staves, though occasionally men beat others to death with their fists and feet.[41] Ultimately, motive provided a key to distinguishing manslaughter from murder. 'There is no fear that it will be found murder', Henry Ogle stated of a case that lacked any sign of unnecessary cruelty, 'for there was never any acquaintance betwixt them before that instant.'[42]

While manslaughter was generally considered less heinous than murder, some manslayers were deemed deserving of capital punishment. The 1604 Stabbing Statute formalised the view that stabbing or thrusting at an unprepared victim was an act perpetrated only by 'inhumane and wicked

---

[38] CCRO, Coroners' Inquisitions, QCI/10/1–/5, coroner's inquisition, examinations, (1613); he was later pardoned.

[39] Thirty-two of fifty-one victims languished for up to seven weeks. For example, PRO, CHES 21/4, fos. 417v, 423v, 430v; CHES 24/133/1 indictment, coroner's inquisition, jury return, recognisance re. Hugh Smith; seven weeks (1661). CHES 21/4, fos. 146v, 151, 157; CHES 24/127/1 indictment, coroner's inquisition re. William Hooley; three weeks (1648). CHES 21/3, fos. 108v, 111; CHES 24/117/3 indictment, coroner's inquisition, recognisance re. John Lowe; two weeks (1624). A prolonged period of languishment also increased the likelihood of the coroner's inquest returning a verdict of death by natural causes. See, for example, CHES 21/3 fo. 111, CHES 24/117/3 indictment, coroner's inquisition, recognisance re. Randle Smallwood (1624).

[40] For exceptions see PRO, CHES 21/3, fos. 42, 43v, CHES 24/115/3 indictment, coroner's inquisition, jury return re. John Blackwall; sword (1590). CHES 21/4, fos. 418, 419, CHES 24/133/1 coroner's inquisition, indictment, jury return re. William Langley; halberd (1661). As the Latin *cultellus* might signify anything from an arming dagger to a mundane utensil, indictments alleging that the murder weapon was 'a knife' are ambiguous.

[41] PRO, CHES 21/5, fos. 4, 5v, CHES 24/134/1 indictment, coroner's inquisition, jury return (1663).

[42] PRO, Palatinate of Chester Miscellanea, Whitby Papers, CHES 38/48, Henry Ogle to Edward Whitby, 1 February 1625.

persons'.[43] Juries and judges were prepared to convict and sentence accordingly, both before and after 1604. Ten men in the Cheshire sample hanged for manslaughter. Six of them had indeed stabbed their victims, four with swords or rapiers and two with daggers. In one such case, the killing was characterised by additional stealth and unfair advantage: the killer followed his victim up an alley into the courtyard behind the Crown Inn in Nantwich, where he slit his throat.[44] Other manslaughters which were aggravated by the nature of the assaults similarly resulted in a death sentence being passed by the judge: one dark evening, Raphe Lingard used such force that his dagger was embedded in six inches of his victim's flesh; Robert Wade inflicted mortal wounds on Thomas Baker's belly and testicles at one o'clock on an October morning.[45] There is no evidence that clergy was formally disallowed in these cases, suggesting that the 1604 Statute was put into effect. A further three men were hanged after being denied benefit of clergy. This appears to have been the result of a policy decision on the part of the bench. At the May assizes of 1624, two convicted manslayers were denied clergy and a man who had been granted clergy at the previous sessions was also hanged because 'the King denies his reading'. Only one man convicted of a clergiable felony was branded. Perhaps the recently appointed Chief Justice Sir James Whitelocke, and his deputy, Sir Marmaduke Lloyd, wished to flex their judicial muscles with royal approval. Whitelocke was at that time under pressure to move to King's Bench, and consequently might have been particularly scrupulous.[46] In 1626, another convicted manslayer was denied the benefit under Whitelocke and Lloyd's direction.[47] These unfortunate individuals might not have been randomly condemned. Each had acted with accomplices, which could make a killing seem more heinous. As Pulton put it, every accessory present was 'a terror to him that was assaulted, and the occasion he durst not defend himself'.[48] The great majority of convicted manslayers were, however, granted benefit of clergy and were branded.

[43] Pulton, *De Pace Regis*, fo. 124.
[44] PRO, CHES 21/5, fos. 2, 5, CHES 24/134/1 indictment, coroner's inquisition, jury return re. Hamnet *alias* Hamlet Ashton (1663).
[45] PRO, CHES 21/3, fos. 45, 46v, CHES 24/115/4 indictment, coroner's inquisition, jury return (1620); CHES 21/3, fos. 97, 100v, CHES 24/117/2 indictment, coroner's inquisition, jury return (1624).
[46] [Sir James Whitelocke,] *Liber Famelicus of Sir James Whitelocke*, 95–6. On the Home Circuit between 1618 and 1624, only nine men were unsuccessful in claiming benefit of clergy, all in 1623; at least fifty men had been denied it between 1612 and 1618. Cockburn, *Introduction*, 120–1.
[47] PRO, CHES 21/3, fos. 97, 100, CHES 24/117/2 indictments, coroner's inquisitions, recognisance re. Thomas Spruce and Robert Wade (1624); CHES 21/3, fo. 131; CHES 24/118/3 coroner's inquisition, recognisance re. William Bott (1626).
[48] Pulton, *De Pace Regis*, fo. 142.

Manslaughter was a distinctly *masculine* form of homicide. All acts so classified in Cheshire were perpetrated by men. Victims were male too, with three exceptions. John Madder was found to have slain, but not murdered, his wife Ellen by breaking her skull with a hatchet wielded in both hands.[49] Two women were killed by men other than their husbands.[50] Children were occasionally men's victims in cases defined as manslaughter. Ten-year-old Thomas Lynney languished for seven weeks after a Stockport felt-maker kicked him in the stomach. A five-week-old baby boy, carried on his mother's back, was killed during an assault on the mother. A four-year-old boy playing in the hay was mortally wounded by his father's servant at work with a pitchfork.[51] The coroner determined the latter death to be accidental, but the inquest, grand and petty juries each returned a verdict of manslaughter: even a genuine accident might not exculpate the slayer if the accident was thought to have been imprudent and careless. However, these are unusual cases. The scarcity of women's and children's deaths defined as manslaughter reveals more than their low incidence as men's victims *per se*. Early modern legal and societal understandings made manslaughter an unsuitable category for deaths other than those in which both slayer and slain were grown men.

The legal category of manslaughter, or felonious killing, has been described as one that embraced all intentional killings that could not be classified either as murder or as true self-defence.[52] This is not quite so. While women were occasionally convicted of felonious killing in the medieval period, by the later sixteenth century, societal concepts of honour and violence had become conflated with legal ones to make manslaughter a gendered category. Felonious killing had become a mere synonym for manslaughter, which in turn was interpreted overwhelmingly in male terms – those same terms that informed non-lethal masculine violence that we saw in chapter two. Jurists conceived of manslaughter in the terms of a definitively male culture. The words used to describe manslaughter took for granted that it was an 'equal and voluntary' fight, a 'sudden falling out', between men. Women did not enter into 'combat', or 'fetch their weapons and go into the field'. Men, not women, were the subjects who killed 'men [in] duels, tavern and game-house quarrels',

---

[49] Babington, *Advice to Grand Jurors*, 178–9; J.A. Sharpe, 'Domestic homicide in early modern England', *Historical Journal* 24 (1981), 29–48; see also Beattie, *Crime and the Courts*, 86, 105–6 n. 78.

[50] PRO, CHES 21/4, fos. 147, 154, 157, CHES 24/127/1 indictment, jury return, recognisance re. Hugh James (1648). CHES 21/3, fo. 73, CHES 24/116/4 indictment, coroner's inquisition re. George Jackson (1622).

[51] PRO, CHES 21/4, fos. 417v, 423v, 430v, CHES 24/133/1 indictment, coroner's inquisition, jury return, recognisance re. Hugh Smith (1661) – he was pardoned; CHES 21/4, fos. 82v, 84v, CHES 24/125/3 indictment, coroner's inquisition, jury return re. Richard Terry (1640); CHES 21/3, fo. 43, CHES 24/115/3 indictment, coroner's inquisition, jury return re. William Boulton (1620).

[52] Green, *Verdict*, 126 n. 82.

over 'not pledging a health, or something that looks like an affront to his Miss'.[53] Manslaughter under provocation was merely the logical extension of the maxim that, for a man of honour, 'one injury, by another greater than that is taken away'.[54] Thus, in 1601, Thomas Wilkes allegedly slew George Griffin because the latter had said that 'there were boys in Nantwich', meaning Wilkes, who 'would use more brabbling [brawling, noisy quibbling] at a wakes, [a] bear-bait, or in an assembly than any other would that was a man', and that 'Wilkes did strike one Shelmerdyne at Wybunbury wakes was twelvemonth behind his back but would not have stroken him to his face'. A bystander shrewdly observed that Griffin 'had spoken very ill for a boy might be a man, and his friends were known to be men'.[55] Conduct books for gentlemen contained the same message: 'if one man upon angry words shall make an assault upon another, either by pulling him by the nose, or filliping upon the forehead, and he that is so assaulted shall draw his sword, and immediately run the other through, that is but manslaughter; for the peace is broken by the person killed, and with an indignity to him that received the assault'.[56] This discourse of righteous masculine violence was legally sanctioned throughout the sixteenth and seventeenth centuries. Manslaughter was an accepted, if not entirely acceptable, fact of male culture.

As we saw earlier in the case of non-lethal violence, order and honour were contested categories. Legal outcomes relied not only on 'proofs of crime' *per se*, but also on the relative worthiness of competing interpretations. In practice, notions of manhood and masculine honour intersected with law in ways that gave some men advantages over others. Robert Lord Cholmondley, Viscount Kells, was able to use his connections and wealth to avoid punishment for the death of a carter, James Woodall, whom he killed for the latter's 'great affronts' and 'insolence' in not allowing Cholmondley's coach precedence on the highway.[57] Cholmondley's father-in-law was Sir Orlando Bridgeman, not only a former Chief Justice of Chester, but the judge who presided at the trial of the regicides, Lord Chief Justice of Common Pleas and, until shortly beforehand, Lord Keeper of the Great Seal. Cholmondley, while casting events in the light of manslaughter under provocation, instructed his agents in London to procure pardons for a manslaughter conviction, but which would also 'be extensive enough to keep off the danger of the Statute of Stabbing' in order that 'we may be free from their affronts

---

[53] Dalton, *Countrey Justice*, 221–2; Hale, *Pleas of the Crown... Summary*, 56; Babington, *Advice to Grand Jurors*, 92–3, sig. A6v.
[54] Romei, *Courtier's Academie*, 151.
[55] PRO, CHES 24/106/2 indictment, coroner's inquisition, examinations re. Thomas Wilkes (1601).
[56] *R. v Mawgridge* (1707), quoted in Horder, *Provocation and Responsibility*, 30.
[57] CRO, DDX X/7, 'King's Pardon, lawyers' opinions and other papers'. PRO, CHES 38/41, 'Examinations concerning the death of James Woodall'.

at the assizes. I would not be left to the mercy of rustics, who have once affronted me, and may I know not how far further injure me were it in their power.'[58] Cholmondley was in for a shock. The coroner's jury ignored the coroner's opinion that 'there is nothing in all the examinations tending towards any dishonourable killing of the deceased', and returned a verdict of murder.[59] At the assizes, the grand jury followed suit. But the case proceeded no further. Sir Job Charlton, Cheshire's Chief Justice, having discussed the case beforehand with the coroner and Cholmondley's agents, ruled that the offence 'was but errant manslaughter'. Charlton therefore allowed the pardons (which Snell had secured before the sessions) to be pleaded upon the indictment, therefore preventing the gentlemen from being thrown upon, in Cholmondley's words, 'the mercy of malicious and merciless rustics' in a trial by jury.[60] The 'rustics' who served on the inquest, grand and petty juries were representatives of the middling ranks of Cheshire society. They were drawn from 'a broad spectrum of middling freeholders with incomes and status well below that of the magisterial class' – most of them had incomes of less than ten pounds *per annum*.[61] From the perspective of the township, parish or hundred, these men were the local elite. Yet from Cholmondley's aristocratic perspective, they were clownish, boorish, unmannerly 'rustics', and in the case of those who prosecuted him, 'caterpillers', to be treated with contempt.

The correspondence produced by this case demonstrates that the common law *threatened* to apply to all the King's subjects. Bridgeman, the elevated judge – who complained that his anxiety over the case had caused him sleepless nights and the exacerbation of his gout – advised Cholmondley 'to be very humble in his carriage'. Bridgeman refused to write to Sir Job Charlton because 'I think it would do ... more harm than good.' He was certain neither that Charlton would permit the pardons to be pleaded before the trial, nor that the pardons would extend to murder. He believed that his son-in-law had 'taken the worst way in the world for himself by his plea and hath put

---

[58] CRO, DDX X/7, 'King's Pardon, lawyers' opinions and other papers', Cholmondley to Snell, 8 September 1673. Some prosecutions appear to have framed cases according to the 1604 Stabbing Statute in order that the killer would hang. See PRO, CHES 21/4, fo. 416v, CHES 24/133/1 indictment, recognisance re. Robert Garstyd (1661); CHES 21/3, fos. 41v, 43, CHES 24/115/3 indictment, coroner's inquisition re. Thomas Webster (1620).

[59] CRO, DDX X/7, 'King's Pardon, lawyers' opinions and other papers', Griffith, Coroner's certificate.

[60] PRO, CHES 21/5, fos. 130, 130v, 131, 135. CRO, DDX X/7, 'King's Pardon, lawyers' opinions and other papers', Cholmondley to Snell, 22 September 1673; Bridgeman to Snell, 19 October 1673; Cholmondley to Snell, 20 October 1673; Cholmondley to Snell, 8 December 1673; copy of Cholmondley's Pardon. The three gentlemen were pardoned; Cholmondley's servants were tried and convicted of manslaughter but, as the principal was pardoned before judgement, they were discharged without punishment.

[61] Morrill, *Grand Jury*, 17–18, 16, 19.

life and fortune upon this issue whether his pardon extend to murder'. And, 'if the petty jury should find it murder it would be a difficult work for all friends he hath in England to help him off and would rest upon a doubtful point in law'. Even a man of Cholmondley's distinction, then, stood to lose his life and lands. As one of his legal advisers wrote in an apologetic postscript, Cholmondley and the other gentlemen 'are in judgement of law, you know, a little guilty'.[62]

Nevertheless, the resolution of the matter was almost certainly connected to Cholmondley's wealth, status and connections – especially to his father-in-law, Sir Orlando Bridgeman. John Snell, who so diligently obtained the pardons, was the Secretary to the Lord Chancellor. Unlike most accused persons, Cholmondley acted upon the advice of a team of legal experts and reckoned that he had spent, in all, 'almost a thousand pounds' on his defence. Ultimately, perhaps, if violence between men constituted a mechanism for negotiating the hierarchies of power, the powerful were likely to win one way or another. So it was with Cholmondley, who contemptuously dismissed the carter's family's desire for retributive justice. 'I think that what I have is too much, and too good', he opined by way of explanation for the affair, 'for such caterpillars who thirst after other men's fortunes than to thank providence for what He has allotted [to] them, and envy those who are more happily placed and live better than they.'[63] He attempted to reassert his power and status over the prosecutors by paying 'in charity' the widow's arrears on her rent (in the region of £100), 'the man having in his lifetime been a destitute person and had engaged all he had'; he gave 'the other rogue who abused me' thirty pounds. Whether born of compassion, ill-conscience or duty, the impact of such actions was uncertain, as Cholmondley was aware: 'How this may tend to my advantage or disadvantage I know not since my actions though ever so just are rendered ill.' They were, nevertheless, attempts to display extra-judicial mercy and justice. Their meanings might vary. They might be emblems of noble and paternal power that a great man like Cholmondley might seek to imprint upon the bodies of the weak. Alternatively, given his fear of 'rustics', the payment of blood money might hinder further calls for Cholmondley to pay with his own blood.

The Cholmondley case illustrates that just as the law was gendered, it intersected with notions of class and social order. The legal vision of honour and manhood offered a characterisation of positive masculine behaviour that, despite the law's claims to the contrary, was not equally attributable to

[62] CRO, DDX X/7, 'King's Pardon, lawyers' opinions and other papers', Cholmondley to Snell, 8 December 1673; Bridgeman to Snell, n.d.; Bridgeman to Snell, 19 October 1673; Bridgeman to Snell, 24 October 1673; Degge to Wettenhall, 17 September 1673.
[63] CRO, DDX X/7, 'King's Pardon, lawyers' opinions and other papers', Cholmondley to Snell, 8 December 1673.

all men. Male honour was manifest not only in reputation and in physical prowess, but also in the ability to compel others to subordinate themselves. This latter aspect of honour resided, ambiguously, in social status and violence, and in both cases effectively amounted to the domination of one version of manhood over another. Male violence was at once a personal act and a vehicle for cultural expression, and lay at the heart of the way cultural groups defined their masculine identities. While Cholmondley's social position as a gentleman gave weight to his account, the carters' version of events, in which they contrasted Cholmondley's dishonourable and unreasonable behaviour with their own honourable conduct and vulnerability, went some way to levelling the positions of the actors. They claimed that they were the victims of unprovoked violence and were outnumbered three to one, and that Cholmondley had acted cruelly and mercilessly. As James Woodall told his wife before he died, upon Cholmondley's command to lay down his staff, 'I parted with my staff and begged of my Lord for pardon and then he gave me this [mortal] wound' with his sword.[64] Cholmondley's emphasis on the carters' 'insolence' serves further to illustrate the point. He expected subordination. They refused to subject themselves. Regardless of who was most responsible for the altercation, ultimately Cholmondley's view of social order was reinforced. The outcome of Bloore and Woodall's assertion of their manhood resulted in beating, physical defeat and death – all the marks of symbolic emasculation.[65]

The credibility of witnesses and defendants was widely regarded as connected to their social status and general demeanour. The testimony of a man of property was thought to carry the greatest weight.[66] In this sense, the law was not neutral and people knew it. As one braggart was heard to say, 'if he had killed a man, for one hundred pounds he could be saved'.[67] To put a modern spin on it, money talked. In the Roger Crockett case, it was alleged that the coroner, John Maisterson, falsified his report and misled the inquest jury in order to protect his brothers-in-law, Richard Hassall and Richard Wilbraham, who stood accused of murder. Maisterson denied these charges, claiming that they were the malicious invention of Thomas

[64] PRO, CHES 38/41, 'Examinations concerning the death of James Woodall', examinations of John Bloore (30 August 1673) and Catherine Woodall (11 September 1673).
[65] Fletcher, *Gender, Sex and Subordination*, 129–30, 126. Richard Thurston and John Beynon, 'Men's own stories, lives and violence: research as practice', in R. Emerson Dobash, Russell P. Dobash and Lesley Noaks eds., *Gender and Crime* (Cardiff, 1995), 182–3. Roper, *Oedipus and the Devil*, 115.
[66] Cockburn, *Introduction*, 61; Douglas Hay, 'Property, authority and the criminal law' in Douglas Hay et al. eds., *Albion's Fatal Tree: Crime and Society in Eighteenth-Century England* (London, 1975), 42; Barbara J. Shapiro, *Probability and Certainty in Seventeenth-Century England: The Relationship between Religion, Natural Science, Law, History and Literature* (Princeton, 1983), 188.
[67] CRO, QJF 49/3/111 (1620).

Wettenhall, Crockett's cousin, whom he described as 'an envious, crafty and venomous spider seeking to suck innocent blood'. Witnesses on behalf of the prosecution claimed that the defendants had threatened them, which claims were countered by the accusation that Bridget Crockett had bribed witnesses to perjure themselves. Although Bridget petitioned Queen Elizabeth to intervene, and prosecuted Hassall, Wilbraham and the others in Star Chamber, her efforts were in vain. She ultimately had to pay Wilbraham £200 in damages.[68] The Wilbrahams and Maistersons were powerful local families. When Richard Wilbraham died in 1611 at the age of eighty-seven, he left goods valued at almost £1,500, and a great deal of land and business interests in Cheshire and Staffordshire. The Maistersons were another old gentry family – John Maisterson's mother was a Grosvenor.[69] But one cannot discern the degree to which the resolution of Bridget's legal endeavours arose from, predominantly or in combination, patronage, corruption or a defective case.

This is not to suggest a complete disregard for justice on the part of those with judicial or political clout. A man's credit would be damaged among his peers if he were thought to have abused his authority or had behaved unjustly.[70] However, 'just' behaviour included acting on behalf of individuals. Henry Ogle requested that his brother-in-law, Edward Whitby, Recorder of the City of Chester, assist and treat favourably William Tyrer, who was charged with killing a man in 1625, 'in regard I would never be guilty of the sin of ungratefulness if either ability or occasion serve'. Ogle's gratitude stemmed from a previous legal matter. When Ogle's father-in-law had been sued at the Exchequer Court, Tyrer, 'out of his love to me, acquainted me with all informations and proceedings which were against my father-in-law by his malicious adversaries and did deliver me copies both of every information and Article'. Now that Tyrer was 'in some trouble', the honourable course for Ogle was to help him in whatever way possible.[71] Court files are peppered with requests for JPs to 'do what favour you can' for individuals.

Nevertheless, clear evidence of venality and patronage influencing the course of law in felonies is rare.[72] It may be that few persons so accused had influential friends, but that where they did, legal outcomes were stacked

---

[68] CRO, DDX 196, fos. 3, 10, 11, 13v, 14, 41v. PRO, STAC 5/W4/27; STAC 7/16/10.
[69] Jeremy Lake, *The Great Fire of Nantwich* (Nantwich, 1983), 42, 46.
[70] Anthony Fletcher, 'Honour, reputation and local officeholding in Elizabethan and Stuart England', in Anthony Fletcher and John Stevenson eds., *Order and Disorder in Early Modern England* (Cambridge, 1985), 92.
[71] PRO, CHES 38/48, Whitby Papers, Henry Ogle to Edward Whitby, 1 February 1625.
[72] Sharpe found only one such case in seventeenth-century Essex: *County Study*, 125. See also *The Reports of Sir John Spelman*, 2 vols., ed. J.H. Baker (London, 1977), Vol. II, 137–42. See also Wilfred Prest, 'Judicial corruption in early modern England', *P&P* 133 (1988), 67–95.

in their favour. In only two of eighteen cases where grand juries reduced a charge of murder to one of manslaughter, for example, do the defendants appear to have benefited from patronage. Richard Pattrick was prematurely released from prison in order to continue attending to his duties as undersheriff to Sir Robert Cholmondley in 1622, but remained bound to be of his good behaviour for five years.[73] The aptly named William Savage, a Nantwich butcher with a history of violence and drunkenness, likewise had wealthy friends who acted on his behalf, but he was not released from his bond for five years either. Neither man avoided punishment. Both were convicted and branded.[74]

For the most part, however, ideas about manslaughter revolved around the 'typical' male-on-male altercations where the parties were relatively well matched in status as well as ability. In such circumstances, the legal category of manslaughter provided concepts and images that mitigated the responsibility of men who killed. The demarcation of manslaughter from murder was not itself blurred, but the categorisation of lethal encounters between men could depend upon one's viewpoint. This was so in terms of who was understood to have injured whom and how much retaliation was seen to be justified. Matters of opinion, conditioned by class, wealth and gender, could also be crucial in determining which of conflicting accounts most deserved acceptance. Justice was a relative concept. Ideas about voluntary killing being mitigated were inextricably from accepted male behaviours. At the heart of homicide law lay a concession not to human infirmity as such, but to the perceived nature of men alone.

Excusable homicide

Excusable homicide took the form of either self-defence or an accident, and accounted for over a quarter of guilty verdicts returned against male defendants.[75] Before the legal distinction emerged between murder and manslaughter, verdicts of self-defence had provided a means of lessening the punishment for slayers who were not thought to deserve execution.[76] The legal category of self-defence continued to be employed as a means of relativising men's culpability well into the seventeenth century. It addressed male standards of behaviour. Like manslaughter, it was neither intended for

---

[73] PRO, CHES 21/3, fos. 68, 71v, 105v, 109v, 180v; CHES 24/116/3 indictment, coroner's inquisition (1622); CHES 24/116/4 letter, petition (1622); CHES 24/117/2 warrant (1624); CHES 24/119/4 presentment (1628). Quarter sessions juries evidently had no difficulty in finding him guilty of lesser offences: CRO, QJB 2/5, fo. 28v; QJF 51/3/10 (1622).
[74] PRO, CHES 21/3, fos. 67, 68, 72, 107, 109v; CHES 24/116/3 indictment, coroner's inquisition, recognisance, petition (1622); CHES 24/116/4 petition (1623).
[75] Twenty-four of the ninety-two men: sixteen for killing in self-defence and eight for killing accidentally.
[76] Baker, *Introduction*, 597; Green, *Verdict*, 122–3; Green, 'Societal concepts', 677–8.

nor applied to the behaviour of women. Moreover, it affected ideas about the law that the upper sorts could not always control, hence Cholmondley's worries about how 'rustic' jurors would categorise his case. Granted, Cholmondley could afford to purchase his pardon and could perhaps reinforce his power by making a cash payment to the injured parties. Yet, in the context of his being prosecuted, that 'power' had to be purchased. It did not come purely as a matter of course. The power of juries to determine whether a killing was undertaken in hot blood or from necessity invested in ordinary men a great deal of power. Occasionally, class and status relations were destabilised, just as they were on a larger scale when the King was tried and sentenced to death for treason in 1649.

In theory, a defendant who killed in self-defence had 'to fly as far as he can, until he be [impeded] by some wall, hedge, ditch, press of people or other impediment; so as he can flee no further without danger of his life' and so, from 'inevitable necessity' dealt the lethal blow.[77] It is unclear how many cases were what we might call 'true' self-defence. The coroner's and petty juries found that William Mosse shot Edward Devereux (who tried to kill him with a rapier) next to a stable wall; he was subsequently pardoned.[78] Peter Penckton, originally prosecuted for murder, was similarly pardoned 'for that Tydder assaulted him... and drew him out of the house by the hair and parted not with him till the wound was given, so what he did was in his own defence'.[79] William Hulme described how Raphe Wirrall wounded and tried to kill him. He fled backwards, being too afraid to turn and run. The underlying notion – that the defendant was not criminally liable because the victim had forced him to kill – is exemplified by Hulme's claim that he had not killed Wirral at all. Rather, Wirral himself had violently run upon the pike that Hulme held in self-defence![80] In these accounts, 'just desert' had already come to the deceased; it could not therefore be dealt to the defendant.

Other cases appear only spuriously to have met the legal criteria. In 1595, Lawrence Wright was found 'not guilty of homicide but self-defence' because his victim 'did assault him in the footway with an intent to have murdered him' in circumstances that sound suspiciously like a duel.[81] The duel

[77] Pulton, *De Pace Regis*, fo. 122; Dalton, *Countrey Justice*, 229.
[78] PRO, CHES 21/4, fos. 147v, 152v, 156v; CHES 24/147/1 coroner's inquisition, jury return, recognisance (1648).
[79] PRO, CHES 21/4, fos. 161, 179, 241v; CHES 24/147/1 coroner's inquisition (1648); CHES 24/147/2 indictment, jury return (1648).
[80] PRO, CHES 21/1, fos. 166v, 167v, 168; CHES 24/103/3 coroner's inquisition, recognisance, examination (1593). That the victim had slain himself in the course of an attack could constitute a special verdict: Green, *Verdict*, 124.
[81] PRO, CHES 21/1, fos. 180v, 181v; CHES 24/104/2 coroner's inquisition, jury return, examination of Arthur Dudley (1595). One consequence of the legal distinction between murder and manslaughter may have been that few incidents were identified as duels as a means of mitigating the offence. Cockburn has suggested that the growing opposition to duelling in the early seventeenth century might even have had a pejorative effect: 'Patterns of violence', 83–4.

occupied an ambiguous place in discussions of order and disorder. On the one hand, duelling was connected to lawlessness. According to John Selden, it was a way in which men sought redress or revenge 'without judicial lists appointed them'. Sir Francis Bacon, as Attorney General, described duelling as 'that evil which seems unbridled', an affront to the law, and 'a kind of satanical illusion and apparition of honour'. In 1615 the Star Chamber unanimously denied 'that the private duel in any person whatsoever had any ground of honour'.[82] On the other hand, duelling provided a set of concepts of honourable conduct and righteous violence. Selden believed that sometimes there was simply no 'other measure of justice left upon earth but arms'. In the gradual escalation of violence from verbal insult, through blows, to a duel, lay the blueprint for the concept of manslaughter under provocation. The same rules informed that of chance-medley manslaughter, with its emphasis upon combat on equal terms. Despite the stance of some legal commentators, the logic of the duel was consistent with the operation of the law.[83] In Lawrence Wright's case, jury and judge appear to have accepted that killing a man in a duel instigated by the victim was a form of excusable homicide and was therefore open to re-interpretation as killing in self-defence.

As a category, then, excusable homicide might be interpreted broadly. Where there was ambiguity, it could still provide a convenient means of avoiding the full force of homicide law. Edward Griffin, for example, was pardoned for manslaughter on grounds that the coroner's inquest had found the killing 'to be done in his own defence'.[84] John Garnett, the Chester brewer who was convicted for a chance-medley manslaughter after killing his servant with a shredding knife, was subsequently pardoned on the grounds that he 'by misfortune offering correction to his servant and he stubbornly resisting him did without any pretended malice (as has been found) give the servant a blow, whereof he...died'. He was, moreover, reputed to be of 'civil and quiet carriage and conversation', and had the support of both the Bishop of Chester and Sir William Brereton.[85] Thomas Higgins was less fortunate. He had thrown a pair of iron tongs at his stepson after the boy had offended him, and then sent him to the surgeon to get the wound dressed. The

---

[82] John Selden, quoted in V.G. Kiernan, *The Duel in European History*, 11. John Selden, *The Duello*, ch. 4, *Opera Omnia*, Vol III, cited in Arthur B. Ferguson, *The Chivalric Tradition in Renaissance England* (Cranbury, New Jersey, 1986), 144. Francis Bacon, *Charge Touching Duels*, reprinted in James Spedding ed., *The Letters and Life of Francis Bacon* (London, 1868–90), Vol. IV, 399, 409. Kiernan, *The Duel in European History*, 82; Andrew, 'Code of honour and its critics', 412–13.

[83] Babington, *Advice to Grand Jurors*, sigs. A6r–A6v; Beattie, *Crime and the Courts*, 97–8. Lawrence Stone, *The Crisis of the Aristocracy 1558–1641*, abridged edn (Oxford, 1967), 242–50.

[84] PRO, SO 3/8, 'Pardon to Edward Griffin', January 1625.

[85] PRO, SO 3/6/38, 'Pardon to John Garnett', May 1614. CCRO, QCI/10/1–5 coroner's inquisition, examinations (1613).

coroner's inquest returned a verdict of accidental death; but the grand jury redefined the incident as a chance-medley, and he was convicted and branded accordingly.[86] The two forms of excusable homicide were sometimes used interchangeably. The coroner found William Cash guilty of self-defence, but the trial jury convicted him for accidentally shooting Roger Cash with a bow and arrow – from a distance of 'two long buttes', twice that generally used in target practice.[87]

It was, in fact, rare for juries to return verdicts of accidental death when there was a living defendant. Lives were commonly lost in road and work-related accidents, such as drownings that occurred when women fell into the river while washing clothes.[88] Inquest juries also recorded verdicts of accidental death in the absence of evidence that might incriminate an individual. Ellen Jones 'was found dead by her husband and others in her brewing pan in her kitchen with her heels upward, her head being in the water about three inches deep, but upon what occasion she went thither we cannot enquire out according to the evidence given us. So we only find that she accidentally came to her death and by no other way as we can learn.'[89] Occasionally, bizarre incidents led to death: Robert Robinson was mauled to death by a bear (worth £13 6s. 8d.) on Brereton Green.[90]

Individuals were charged with accidental killing when they had unwittingly caused death. Guns discharged accidentally, arrows missed their targets: Richard Banner sent his arrow into the eye of an eleven-year-old boy who watched him practise.[91] Lethal negligence could also be categorised as misfortune. Robert Hurst was found responsible for the death of his nine-year-old brother, Joseph, who slipped and fell under the wheel of a handmill as Hurst worked, and was 'struck, crushed and wounded... in his head and face' by the 'speedy and rigorous motion' of the wheel.[92] Eleanor Smeathers was trampled outside Tarporley church by a horse that Jonathan Downes rode 'like a madman'. Although categorised as an accident by grand and petty juries, the coroner's inquest excused him 'on account of his lunacy'.[93]

[86] CCRO, MF69/2/84, MF69/2/144 coroner's inquisition, examinations (1646).
[87] PRO, CHES 21/3, fos. 155v, 159; CHES 24/102/4 indictment, coroner's inquisition, jury return (1591).
[88] For example, CCRO, QCI/10/11 (1636).   [89] CCRO, QCI/10/10 (1636).
[90] PRO, CHES 21/3, fo. 111v; CHES 24/117/3 coroner's inquisition (1624).
[91] PRO, CHES 24/135/2 indictment, coroner's inquisition, jury return (1665). For accidental shootings, see, for example, CHES 24/127/1 coroner's inquisition, jury return re. Robert Yeardsley (1648); CHES 24/128/2 coroner's inquisition, jury return re. Raphe Done (1649); CHES 24/131/1 coroner's inquisition, jury return re. Raphe Pierson (1655); CHES 21/5, fo. 423v, CHES 24/133/1 coroner's inquisition, recognisance re. Philip Hurry (1661); CCRO, QCI/10/6 re. Robert Basford (1625). Forty per cent of accidental homicides for which pardons 'of course' were granted between 1550 and 1660: Green, *Verdict*, 124.
[92] PRO, CHES 21/4, fos. 417v, 423v; CHES 21/5, fos. 3, 11; CHES 24/133/1 indictment, coroner's inquisition, jury return (1661).
[93] PRO, CHES 21/4, fos. 416v, 419; CHES 21/5, fos. 3, 11; CHES 24/133/1 indictment, coroner's inquisition, recognisance (1661); CHES 24/133/2 indictment, jury return (1662).

Similarly, Elizabeth White 'was run over' by a horse ridden 'very fiercely' by John Edwards, who claimed that the mare 'did run away with me against my will over Dee bridge...I could not rule [her]'.[94] Henry Piggot 'improvidently and by accident' killed Mary Ratcliffe, whom he 'unexpectedly' encountered in a dark porch. During the collision, Ratcliffe received a mortal four-inch-deep wound to the shoulder. The extant information sheds no light on such questions as to what Ratcliffe was doing in the dark porch after sunset, or why Piggot was dashing through with a drawn knife.[95]

It is revealing that in so many incidents for which men were found guilty of killing 'by misfortune', their victims were women or children. This is so in at least five of the eight Cheshire cases where individuals were held responsible for causing death by accident.[96] Indeed, in Jonathan Downes's case, the grand jury originally threw out an indictment for manslaughter before the case was successfully redefined as an accident.[97] Women and children also figure prominently in cases where a charge of accidental death was made by the coroner, but where the defendant was subsequently discharged. Richard Gregory, a tailor, 'full of drink' at nine o'clock in the morning, 'accidentally' dropped a pair of shears on the head of his eighteen-month-old daughter; the grand jury returned an *ignoramus* verdict. In an act which was 'not malicious nor voluntary but by accident', John Netles shot his fifteen-year-old sister Ellen in the belly while 'playing with a loaded pistol'; he was acquitted.[98] Genuine accidents they might have been, yet such episodes were classified as misadventures because available notions of culpability for the deaths of women and children were limited. The deaths of women and children could rarely be credibly presented in terms of righteous violence, equal fights or self-defence. Because homicide law was based upon masculine assumptions of male-on-male combat, the courts found it hard to fit the deaths of women and children into the common categories of killing. There was effectively no provision for the deaths of women and children other than in terms of murder or excusable accident. This is even more striking in the light of how underdeveloped negligence was as a concept in criminal law (as opposed to private law).[99] When men slew men in work-related incidents or in taverns as a consequence of what we would term negligence, they were not charged with negligent homicide. Rather their negligence was subsumed

---

[94] CCRO, MF 86/64, examinations (1662); QCI/11/3.
[95] PRO, CHES 21/3, fos. 174i, 174ii; CHES 24/119/3 coroner's inquisition, jury return, recognisance (1628).
[96] A sixth, Roger Cash, might well have been a young boy, too; see above, p. 133. Cf. the small proportion of female and child victims in manslaughter, above, p. 124.
[97] See n. 93 above.
[98] PRO, CHES 21/5, fo. 61; CHES 24/135/5 indictment, coroner's inquisition (1667). CHES 24/135/1 indictment, coroner's inquisition, jury return (1665).
[99] I am grateful to Tom Green for pointing this out to me.

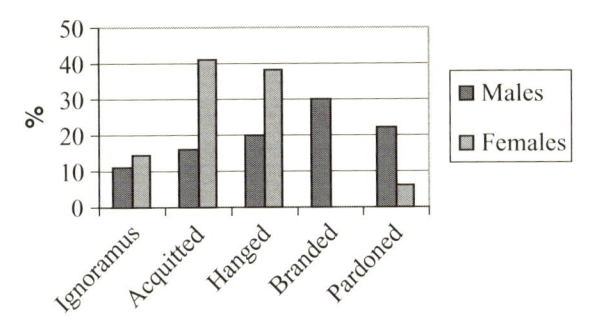

Figure 4.1 Outcomes for defendants in homicide cases

into one or other category of culpable homicide – murder or manslaughter – as seemed most appropriate. The situation as regards women's homicide was, however, rather different, as we shall see.

WOMEN, DISORDER AND DEEDS AGAINST NATURE

Women comprised one-fifth of suspected killers in Cheshire – an average figure for early modern England (one-third in the north east and one-sixth in Surrey, for example)[100] and consistent with the relatively low incidence of women's homicide across the centuries.[101] Women's victims in Cheshire and elsewhere were usually drawn from within their domestic circle – husbands, children, relatives, other household members. Of forty-eight female principal suspects in the sample, five of their victims were husbands, seven were other adults (apparently relatives of theirs or their associates), thirty-one were their own children and five were the children of others. In addition, three women were charged with attempted murder, and fourteen were accused of inciting, aiding and abetting others to kill. Both those whom they helped and their victims were predominantly drawn from women's close circles of household, family and near neighbours.

Women suspected of homicide were more likely than men to be dismissed before formal charges were made.[102] Once the case went to court, as Figure 4.1 shows, grand and petty juries discharged and acquitted a much

[100] Morgan and Rushton, *Rogues, Thieves and the Rule of Law: The Problem of Law Enforcement in North-East England, 1718–1800* (London, 1998), 112; Beattie, *Crime and the Courts*, 82, Table 3.1; Beattie, 'Criminality of women', 84–5, Table 2.
[101] For example, Angela Browne and Kirk R. Williams, 'Exploring the effect of resource availability and the likelihood of female-perpetrated homicides', *Law and Society Review* 23, 1 (1989), 76–94; Daly and Wilson, *Homicide*, 146–9, Table 7.1; James Given, *Society and Homicide in Thirteenth-Century England* (Stanford, 1977), 134–7; Hanawalt, 'Female felon', 257; Frances Heidensohn, *Women and Crime* (1985; London, 1990), 8; Wiener, 'Sex roles and crime', 45, 57 n. 54.
[102] Twenty-nine per cent of men and thirty-five per cent of women.

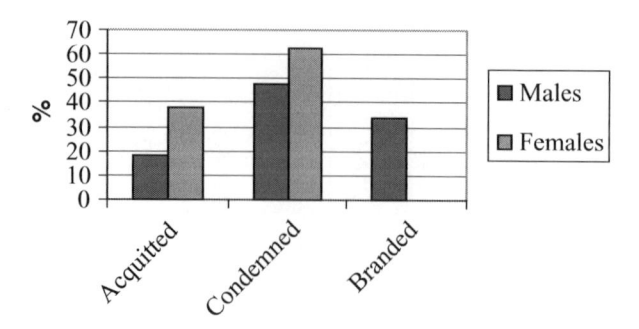

Figure 4.2 Verdicts/sentences for homicide including infanticide

greater proportion of female than male defendants.[103] We ought not too quickly conclude that women received favourable treatment by the courts. For unlike men, who did not often hang for homicide, women who were found guilty almost always suffered sentence of death. Moreover, Figure 4.3 demonstrates that male defendants were also more likely than women to be pardoned. The only form of homicide for which women were pardoned was neonatal infanticide. If the latter is excluded, as in Figures 4.4 and 4.5, the discrepancy between the sexes is even starker. Although half of arraigned women were acquitted, every single convicted woman was executed. This is not explained simply as what happened 'when public horror was mirrored by the official reaction'.[104] In contrast, fewer than one in four convicted men ended their lives on the gallows.[105] Women's homicides characteristically failed to meet the legal criteria for mitigation.

Manslaughter provides a case in point. J.M. Beattie sensibly attributes the predominance of male defendants in manslaughter verdicts to the fact that men were 'much more likely than women to be in taverns, to drink too much, to think their courage slighted, and to feel compelled to give and accept challenges to fight'. But he is mistaken in believing that this 'simply reflects differences in patterns of life' of men and women.[106] It reflects more. Women's conceptual exclusion from the legal category of manslaughter

---

[103] In eastern Sussex, 46 per cent of women (11 of 24) were convicted of homicide compared with 69 per cent of men (24 of 35): Herrup, *Common Peace*, 150, Table 6.4. On the Home Circuit, the figures were similar, 44 per cent of women and 62 per cent of men: Cockburn, *Introduction*, 117.

[104] Quoting Morgan and Rushton, *Rogues, Thieves and the Rule of Law*, 123.

[105] Based on the legal outcomes in the cases of the 49 women and 181 men of 230 principal offenders who were tried for homicide. Available figures for elsewhere are similar. For example, 41 (21.6 per cent) of 190 men arraigned for homicide in Essex hanged: Sharpe, *County Study*, 124, Table 12.

[106] Beattie, *Crime and the Courts*, 97; Beattie, 'Criminality of women', 84; Herrup, *Common Peace*, 150, Table 6.4.

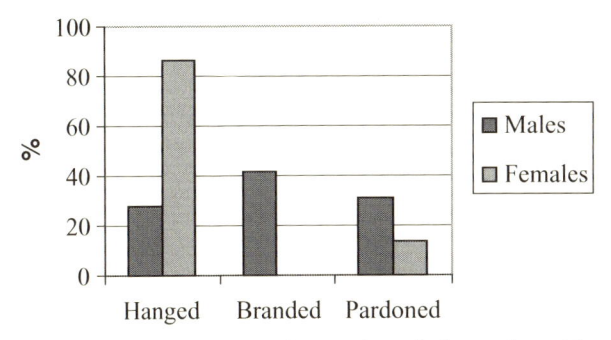

Figure 4.3 Punishments for homicide including infanticide

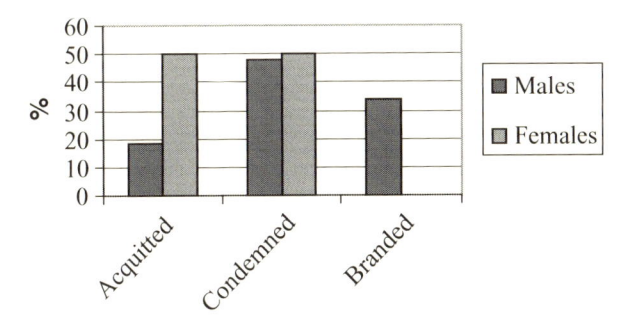

Figure 4.4 Verdicts/sentences for homicide excluding infanticide

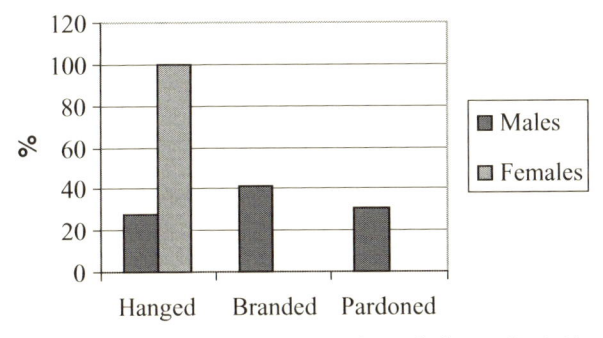

Figure 4.5 Punishments for homicide excluding infanticide

illustrates the limited vision of feminine violence that informed legal provision. A verdict of manslaughter normally carried the non-capital punishment of branding after a plea of benefit of clergy. This penal option was unavailable for women. There was thus nothing to be gained by a jury reducing a charge against a woman from murder to manslaughter, for a conviction of either led to the same end: execution. While benefit of clergy provided a legal fiction whereby its privilege was granted to non-clerics, the punishment of branding was never extended to homicidal women. It is unlikely that this was attributable to the 'few logical problems' inherent in extending benefit of clergy to women.[107] Branding was, in fact, introduced in 1624 as a punishment for women convicted of a limited number of property offences, yet was expressly not conceptualised as an extension of benefit of clergy. Explanations for the reason why women's homicide was institutionalised in ways that appear to have made it more culpable than men's will have to be sought elsewhere.

The petty traitor and the poisoneress

From 1351 to 1828, the wilful murder of her husband by a wife constituted an aggravated form of murder: petty treason, so termed 'because there is subjection due from the wife to the husband, but not *e converso*'. The punishment of being 'burnt to ashes' made brutally clear that husband-murder was more heinous, more sinful and more treacherous than uxoricide. The advantage taken of a victim who ought to have been safe within his own home, the degree of personal treachery, and the aberration of wifely obedience, made spousal murder by women particularly dreadful.[108] Even being cognisant of the fact and present in the house wherein someone else killed their husbands legally constituted petty treason rather than accessory to murder. The construction of husband-killing as treason was based on natural law. As a wife's inferiority and subordination to her husband was ordained by God, in disobeying, let alone killing, their husbands, wives disobeyed God.[109] Hence, John Wing described even the rebellious and undutiful *non*-murderous wife as 'a home-rebel, a house-traitor'.[110] Killing one's husband directly assaulted godly hierarchies; murdering one's wife did not. Servants who killed their masters or mistresses, and ecclesiastics their prelates, were defined as petty traitors for similar reasons. Female servants were burnt; male servants, like uxoricides, were hanged. Petty treason was sometimes understood to extend to parricide, which the relevant statutes omitted,

---

[107] Quoting Sharpe, *Judicial Punishment*, 41.
[108] 25 Edward III c. 2 (1351), 9 Geo IV c. 31, s.2 (1828). Coke, *Third Part of the Institutes*, 19–36; Dalton, *Countrey Justice*, 213–15; Hale, *Pleas of the Crown*, Vol. I, 377–82 at 381.
[109] Margaret R. Sommerville, *Sex and Subjection: Attitudes to Women in Early-Modern Society* (London, 1995), 21–3, 87, 213.
[110] John Wing, *The Crowne Conjugall, or the Spouse Royal* (London, 1632), 297; he used similar metaphors on 198.

ostensibly because 'lawmakers never imagined any child would do' such a deed.[111]

Other than treason, the only crime punishable by burning was heresy, which powerfully reinforced the link with sin.[112] This form of execution undermines the view that law treated women 'leniently'. Contemporaries insisted that the punishment fitted the crime: it was a 'death, though cruel, yet too mild for one that hath a heart so vile'.[113] It is widely held that executioners 'customarily' strangled condemned women first. This was not always so. A chaplain in 1676 who sought to comfort a maid convicted of poisoning her mistress clearly expected the fire to contribute to her death. 'Do not fear the fire', he told her, not because she would be already dead, but because in her penitent state the flames 'can only hurt thy body, it cannot singe thy soul'. In the event, the fifteen minutes of agony he promised if she meditated upon Christ was almost an underestimate because the 'hangman would have set fire unto the furze before she was strangled'. But 'some more charitable and tender-hearted' persons persuaded him to remove the block from under her feet before she was engulfed in flames.[114] Other accounts mention no such mercy and suggest that women did burn alive. Alice Clarke was said to 'suffer by fire', Margaret Fern-seede to die 'presently' after 'the reeds being planted about unto which fire [was] given'.[115] Some women were burnt alive by accident if not by design. The 'fire scorching the [executioner's] hands', 'he relaxed the rope before [Catherine Hayes] had become unconscious, and in spite of efforts at once made to hasten combustion, she suffered for a considerable time the greatest agonies'.[116]

Burning for petty treason is hardly explained by Blackstone's oft-cited claim that concerns about modesty made hanging inappropriate for women.[117] Far greater numbers of women were hanged for other felonies.[118]

---

[111] Coke, *Third Part of the Institutes*, 20. Dalton, *Countrey Justice*, 214.
[112] Heretics ceased to be burnt in 1677; burning remained the legal penalty for murderous wives until 1790.
[113] *A Warning for Wives* (London, 1629), reprinted in *Pepysian Garland*, 299–304, quotation at 303.
[114] *Hell Open'd, or the Infernal Sin of Murther Punished...* (London, 1676), 61, 73–4.
[115] Henry Goodcole, *The Adulteresses Funerall Day in Flaming, Scorching and Consuming Fire* (London, 1635), sig. B2r.; *The Araignement and Burning of Margaret Ferne-seede* (London, 1608), sig. B4r.
[116] William Andrews, *Bygone Punishments* (London, 1899), 101–2, cited in Ruth Campbell, 'Sentence of death by burning for women', *Journal of Legal History* 5 (1984), 45. Some women appear to have been deliberately burnt alive: A.D. Harvey, 'Research note: burning women at the stake in eighteenth-century England', *Criminal Justice History* 11 (1990), 193.
[117] William Blackstone, *Commentaries on the Laws of England*, 3rd edn (Oxford, 1768–9), 4 vols., Vol. IV, 93.
[118] See below, ch. 5.

Nor did burning cause less public exposure than the male traitor's punishment of hanging, disembowelling and quartering. Indeed, in France women were *not* burnt expressly because fire so rapidly consumed clothing to reveal their naked bodies. Ruth Campbell sees burning women as a discriminatory and intimidatory punishment: 'How better to secure their subjugation!' Yet her argument that women were 'a form of property' and so transgressed against property rights in murdering their husbands is flawed.[119] Women were never in common law or popular opinion men's 'property'. Husband-murder was, though, transgressive in violating the premises that underpinned social order.[120]

Spousal murder by wives fulfilled almost all the theoretical requirements of wrongful violence.[121] It was the product and concomitant of disorder and disobedience, it broke moral and natural law as well as the King's peace, and neither motive nor intent fitted any accepted category of excusable or justifiable killing. In short, it defied the principles of hierarchical authority. While the man who murdered his wife was culpable, the degree to which he offended against these principles was extenuated by his position of master of the household. Men who excessively 'corrected' their wives were neither encouraged nor condoned, but their actions could be excused and justified. Thus, only one husband out of eight suspected Cheshire uxoricides was executed, and none of those who beat their wives to death was convicted of murder.[122] Babington counted beating children to death during correction among mere '*errors* and *oversights*'. Beattie's argument that 'a parent or master who used "moderate" methods and a "reasonable" instrument in chastising those over whom they had natural authority would have been acquitted of both murder and manslaughter' may be extended to husbands.[123] Crucial, here, is the notion of natural authority. Men's domestic violence was perceived as an extension of their nature and expected role; women's marital violence was a manifestation of *un*naturalness. Whereas male violence was sanctioned to uphold household order, female violence subverted it. Husband-murder was a 'radical disobedience to social order'; uxoricide was not.

This discourse disadvantaged women accused of husband-murder, as the two most common narratives of murderous wives – wife-beating and female

---

[119] Campbell, 'Sentence of death', 54–5.
[120] For example, *Anne Wallen's Lamentation* (London, 1616), reprinted in *Pepysian Garland*, 84–8, at verse 18.
[121] For these principles, see Maddern, *Violence and the Social Order*, ch. 3.
[122] PRO, CHES 21/4, fo. 97; CHES 24/126/1 indictment, jury return, recognisance re. John Hesketh (1641). For those who used bodily force alone, see CHES 21/4, fo. 99; CHES 24/126/1 indictment, coroner's inquisition, jury return, recognisance re. John Berry (1641); and John Madder, discussed above on p. 124.
[123] Babington, *Advice to Grand Jurors*, 35. Beattie, *Crime and the Courts*, 86.

adultery – exemplify. In the first of these, a wife killed her husband during his violent abuse of her.[124] Beattie has suggested that this narrative of husband-murder, exemplified in two Surrey trial pamphlets, amounted to a 'plausible plea of self-defence'.[125] I would argue, to the contrary, that a self-defence plea was inappropriate in the context of husband-murder and that it was not actually invoked in the narratives in question. As we have seen, homicide law was constructed from the perspective of male force meeting roughly equal force. Women and men were understood to be unequally matched in size, strength and fighting ability, whether through natural aptitude, cultural expectations or practice. Whereas men sometimes killed women with their bare hands, women used weapons to kill men. Yet in law, wielding a knife or a pair of scissors against a man who used mere bodily force or a blunt instrument indicated excessive retaliation. Nor did other strategies employed by women, such as attacking from behind, striking pre-emptively or poisoning, meet legal and social criteria for self-defence. By the male standards embodied in law, these typical forms of violence against husbands were cowardly and villainous. Hence, Alice Clarke's murder of a husband who regularly beat her with cudgels and tied her 'to the bedpost to strip her and whip her' was nonetheless described as 'unmanly'.[126] Far from self-defence providing a mitigating notion for women, the context and manner of women's physical self-defence exacerbated their crimes.[127]

Women failed to meet the legal criteria in other ways also. A history of domestic violence could undermine a woman's claim of self-defence against her husband's life-threatening violence: he had beaten but not killed her before, after all. Moreover, the person who killed in self-defence was supposed not to have provoked the altercation – difficult to sustain perhaps in the light of perceptions of men's domestic violence as 'honest'. In court and fiction, male cruelty was presented as a reasonable response to provocation. Husbands whose wives were not 'mild and modest' were understandably 'drive[n]...to unmanly cruelty'. The repentant Sarah Elston bewailed her former 'rage, unquiet, and evil communication, whereby she had often provoked her husband to be more violent and cruel towards her than

---

[124] For example, Goodcole, *Adulteresses Funerall Day*. Dolan, *Dangerous Familiars*, ch. 3; Wiltenburg, *Disorderly Women*, 216, 218.

[125] Beattie, *Crime and the Courts*, 100–2, at 100. *A Warning for Bad Wives, or the Manner of the Burning of Sarah Elston* (London, 1678); *The Proceedings at the Assizes in Southwark, for the County of Surrey begun on Thursday the 21th of March, and not ended till Tuesday the 26 of the same month* (London, 1678), 3–5.

[126] Goodcole, *Adulteresses Funerall Day*, sig. B1v.

[127] For modern parallels, see Susan S.M. Edwards, *Sex and Gender in the Legal Process* (London, 1996), 363–411; Cynthia K. Gillespie, *Justifiable Homicide: Battered Women, Self-defence and the Law* (Columbus, 1989); Helena Kennedy, *Eve was Framed: Women and British Justice* (London, 1993), ch. 8.

probably he might otherwise have been'.[128] In a ballad, Anne Wallen threw a chisel at and mortally wounded her husband after he struck her. The context: Upon her husband's retiring to bed having returned from 'about the town',

> I fell to railing most outrageously. I called him 'rogue', and 'slave', and all to naught, repeating the worst language might be thought. 'Thou drunken knave', I said, and 'arrant sot, thy mind is set on nothing but the pot.' 'Sweetheart', he said, 'I pray thee hold thy tongue, and if thou dost not, I shall do thee wrong.' At which, straight away I grew in worser rage, that he by no means could my tongue assuage.

No wonder, the ballad instructs, poor John Wallen resorted to violence. The balladeer makes this ballad wife pronounce that her 'dearest husband... ne'er did wrong to any in his life, but he too much was wronged by his wife'. Her deeds, not his, 'are black and foul'; the fault is all hers.[129] In all this, legal and societal understandings of marital violence might have been at odds. While common and canon law defined a husband's cruelty as physical violence, plaintiffs and witnesses clearly recognised mental, verbal and economic cruelty as forms of cumulative violence. Even in petty treason cases, some people 'would partially excuse the woman' if there was a history of domestic cruelty, as long as she had not intended to murder but just to hurt her husband. But in law provocation over time was not yet a viable concept that could be invoked partially to excuse husband-killing. Killing that was a defensive response to cumulative violence was categorised as 'revenge' and was therefore wholly culpable.[130]

For all these reasons, self-defence was an inappropriate mitigating concept for women who killed their husbands. Women very rarely invoked it. Indeed, in both of the Surrey trials Beattie referred to, the women's lethal violence was presented not as self-defence *per se*, but as the other form of excusable homicide – accident, compounded with the notion that the deceased had slain himself during his attack.[131] Both women ascribed a form of nonaction to themselves. One claimed that her husband had 'accidentally' run upon the scissors she held in self-defence, he having already struck her with a fire-shovel as neighbours testified, and by then having a frying pan in his hand. The other said that as her husband beat her, 'the knife stuck in his leg

---

[128] *A Warning for Bad Wives*, sig. A4r. *A Briefe and True Report of Two Most Cruell, Unnatural, and Inhumane Murders, Done in Lincolnshire, by Twoo Husbands upon their Wives* (London, 1607), quoted in Wiltenburg, *Disorderly Women*, 221.

[129] *Anne Wallen's Lamentation* (London, 1616).

[130] For example, *A Warning for Bad Wives, or the Manner of the Burning of Sarah Elston*, sig. A2v–A3r. Goodcole, *Adulteresses Funerall Day*, sig. B2v.

[131] See above, n. 80.

unknown to me'.[132] Neither defence was successful – both women burned at the stake. There was no convenient legal or societal concept of justifiable or excusable homicide for women who killed their husbands. Women were seemingly completely innocent or wholly culpable. Acquittal or death – these were the appropriate verdicts for women.[133] This goes some way to explaining why female defendants were disproportionately amongst both those who walked free and those who were executed in early modern England. Historians who mention only the leniency with which women were treated before the law reveal only part of the story.

The alternative and more common context for husband-murder was female adultery. That murder was adultery's ultimate end was a cultural motif.[134] Thus, pamphlets depicted the petty traitor as a 'filthy desirous woman', 'a graceless strumpet', 'a woman, nay a devil', whose sexual preoccupation with her servant fostered her sin 'till lust had gotten so much power' over her that 'she must needs seek and practise the death of her husband'. She was an adulteress, prostitute and bawd: 'neither being chaste nor cautious' and who cared not 'into what bed of lust her lascivious body was transported'.[135] Tellingly, the only Cheshire women convicted of petty treason were those who had male partners in crime. Ellen Leene allegedly plotted her husband's murder with John Warton, who attacked him from behind with a cudgel. Alice Liverpool stood by as John Boulton shot her husband; nineteen witnesses, including eight women, testified against them.[136] These couples were not necessarily lovers, but to contemporaries, the involvement of another man suggested unlawful love rather than platonic or financial contracts. Indeed, suspicions of adultery and murder could be aroused by the speed of a widow's remarriage, as in the case of Anne Williamson who was acquitted of lacing her husband's beer with arsenic.[137]

Poisoning was placed high on the culpability scale. In 1530, it became a form of high treason punishable by being boiled alive, a purposefully

---

[132] *The Proceedings at the Assizes in Southwark, for the County of Surrey begun on Thursday the 21th of March, and not ended till Tuesday the 26 of the same month* (London, 1678), 4. Beattie, *Crime and the Courts*, 100.
[133] The exception is infanticide, discussed below.
[134] Wiltenburg, *Disorderly Women*, 216–18; Gowing, *Domestic Dangers*, 205.
[135] *A Discourse of Two Cruell Murders... An Other Most Cruell and Bloody Murder* (London, 1577), sigs. B2v–B4r; *Araignement and Burning of Margaret Ferne-seede*, sigs. A3r, A4r. See also *Oh High and Mighty God: The woefull lamentacon of Mrs Anne Saunders* (n. d.), repr. in *Old English Ballads 1553–1625*, ed. Hyder E. Rollins (Cambridge, 1920), 340–8; A.G., *Briefe Discourse of the Late Murther of Master George Saunders* (London, 1573).
[136] PRO, CHES 21/3, fo. 126; CHES 24/118/3 indictment, recognisance, jury return re. Ellen Leene (1626). CHES 21/5, fos. 59, 61; CHES 24/135/5 indictment, coroner's inquisition, jury return, recognisance re. Alice Liverpool (1667).
[137] PRO, CHES 21/3, fo. 156; CHES 24/102/4 indictment, recognisance (1591).

'grievous and lingering death', though the act was repealed in 1547 because it 'was too severe'. The Latin term for poisoning was the same as for witchcraft: *veneficium*. Both were secret, 'most abominable', acts against which there were few defences. Coke believed poisoning to be 'the most detestable of all' murder methods 'because it is most horrible, and fearful to the nature of man, and of all others can be least prevented, either by manhood or by providence'.[138] These sentiments were shared by others: Poisoning was a crime 'where no suspicion may be gathered nor any resistance made; the strong cannot avoid the weak; the wise cannot prevent the foolish, the godly cannot be preserved from the hands of the wicked; children may thereby kill their parents, the servant the master, the wife her husband so privily, so incurably, that of all other it hath been thought the most odious kind of murder'.[139] The poisoner was thus attributed with negative feminine characteristics – weak, foolish, wicked, cunning. Indeed, Reginald Scot wrote that 'women were the first inventors and the greatest practisers of poisoning and more materially addicted and given thereunto than men'.[140] Moreover, the association with women in general was extended to petty traitors in particular. It was in fact the only method of husband-murder where Dalton presents the wife herself killing her husband.[141] Historians have often accepted these associations at face value.[142]

Poisoning did fit the category of non-confrontational methods of killing preferred by women. It was the method women allegedly used in eight (sixty-six per cent) of the twelve Cheshire cases with adult victims. In contrast, only nine (six per cent) of 161 men charged with homicide were suspected of poisoning, and six of these were in league with women. Coroners found moreover that a greater proportion of female than male suicides poisoned themselves, although women most often drowned themselves – men were more likely than women to hang themselves or cut their own throats (see Figures 4.6 and 4.7).[143]

Nevertheless, the gendered nature of poisoning must not be overstated. Poisoning *de facto* implied wilful murder. Therefore inclusion of cases

---

[138] Coke, *Third Part of the Institutes*, 48. See also the comments of Coke and Francis Bacon in *Complete Selection of State Trials*, Vol. II, ed. T.B. Howell (London, 1816), 911, 970–2. Statutes 22 Henry VIII c. 9; 1 Edward VI c. 12.
[139] Anon., *c.* seventeenth century, cited in C.J.S. Thompson, *Poisons and Poisoners* (London, 1993), 109. See also Goodcole, *Adulteresses Funerall Day*, sigs. A2v, B3v–B4v; Beard, *Theatre of Gods Judgements*, 323.
[140] Reginald Scot, *The Discoverie of Witchcraft* (London, 1584), 117.
[141] Dalton, *Countrey Justice*, 214–15. The other two involve a servant or other man killing the husband after compact with the wife. William Lambarde, *Eirenarcha* (London, 1581), 242.
[142] Lawrence Stone, *The Past and the Present Revisited* (London, 1987), 301. See also Sharpe, *County Study*, 129–30 and Beattie, *Crime and the Courts*, 101.
[143] The national pattern was similar: MacDonald, *Sleepless Souls*, 248.

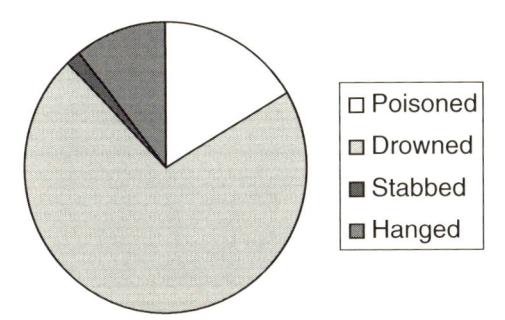

Figure 4.6 Women's methods of suicide

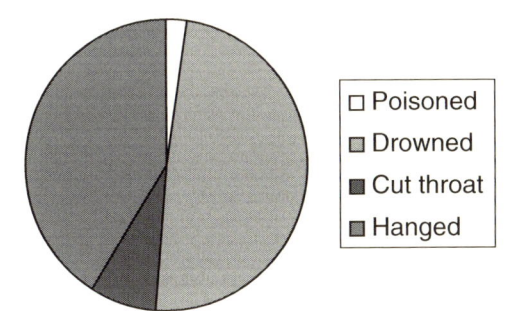

Figure 4.7 Men's methods of suicide

defined as manslaughter, killing in self-defence or by accident is perhaps misleading. Figure 4.8 shows that in killings defined as murder, a significant proportion of men used poison. Moreover, if we exclude infanticide, around three-quarters of suspected women used poison as their weapon. However, if we compare the *type* of murder in which women used poison with equivalent male cases, the gender differential all but disappears. Poison was employed primarily against particular victims, people to whom murderers or their accomplices were intimately connected: spouses, parents, siblings, in-laws and other household members. Poison accounted for eight out of ten such murders allegedly committed or attempted by women; the other two were those cases in which wives procured others to inflict violent deaths upon their husbands. Nine of the twelve parallel male cases were poisonings; the rest were the murders of wives by husbands who used, respectively, a hatchet, a cudgel and bare hands. Poisoning, then, might be best characterised less as an *a priori* feminine method of killing and more as the mark of lethal and treacherous intimacy, the most extreme violation of domestic order.

Though some used mercury, the most popular poison was ratsbane or arsenic, which was tasteless and, when dissolved, colourless and odourless.

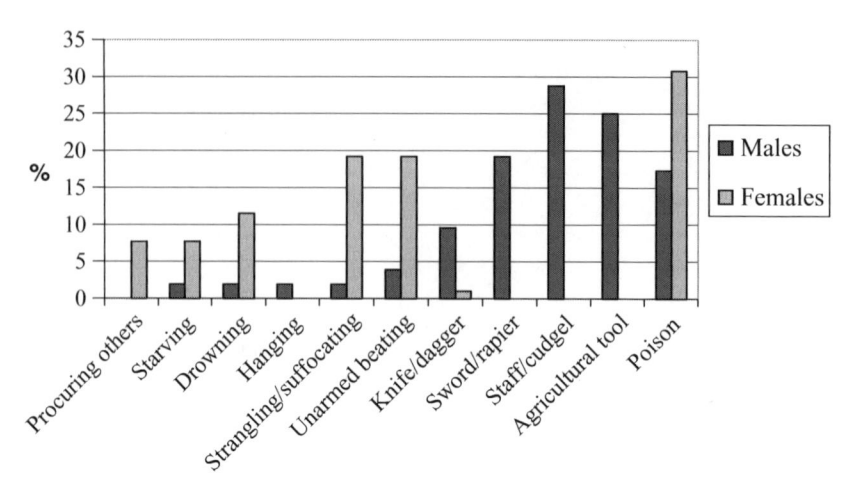

Figure 4.8 Homicide weapons/methods

The symptoms of arsenic-poisoning – searing stomach pains, violent convulsions, diarrhoea, even paralysis of the extremities, sometimes for many months – could easily be attributed to an 'unknown sickness'. Legitimately used for medicinal purposes, there was no reliable test for the presence of arsenic until the nineteenth century. It was the perfect early modern poison.[144] The properties that made poisoning so odious also made it hard to detect. Hence, in no case of poisoning prosecuted at the Cheshire assizes had the coroner viewed the body – these deaths were initially not thought to have been unnatural. Suspicions were aroused when several people became ill, as when Ellen and Henry Edwards were 'suspected to have conveyed and put poison into salt... in the house of Katherine Edwardes of Sutton, widow, so that by eating and putting of the salt so poisoned into meat, four or five persons have been dangerously sick and swelled, and some of them not as yet recovered'.[145] But many alleged poisonings were not prosecuted until long afterwards. Joan and James Sharples had supposedly murdered two years prior to their court appearance. Francis Adshead's wife died eight years before he was prosecuted for 'putting poison in her pot'.[146] In such circumstances, a considerable body of evidence was necessary to persuade a trial jury that the defendant was guilty.

---

[144] MacDonald, *Sleepless Souls*, 227; Kerry Segrave, *Women Serial and Mass Murderers: A Worldwide Reference, 1580 through 1990* (London, 1992), 3.
[145] PRO, CHES 21/3, fo. 110; CHES 24/117/3 recognisance (1624).
[146] For Sharples, see n. 149 below; CHES 21/4, fos. 417, 430; CHES 24/133/1 recognisance re. Adshead (1661).

Consequently, the acquittal rate was high. Poison was the alleged cause of death in each of the unsuccessful petty treason cases, which were also characterised by few witnesses and the absence of an accomplice. Elizabeth Withnail, arraigned at the same sessions at which Ellen Leene was condemned to death, declared that her acquittal was on grounds of insufficient proof. The judge, Sir John Bridgeman, had serious misgivings, asserting that there was 'no want of proof but partiality in the jury'. Although two eminent justices vouched for her good life, conversation and carriage towards her husband while he lived, Bridgeman detained her in gaol for a further six months and then bailed her to appear at the following assizes 'to see if further evidence can be had'.[147] As Thomas A. Green has noted, the aims of the judiciary and jury were not always synonymous: 'The judicial concern with application of the law to set an example, for instance, might make the bench impatient with a jury's merciful desire, in a given case, to overlook the general reasons for concern with a certain sort of behavior.'[148] Perhaps the jury in April 1626 simply found sending two women to be burnt at the stake hard to stomach.

Three female poisoners and one male were convicted and executed. Margaret Stannop helped her lover poison his wife with arsenic mixed with buttermilk. Elizabeth Holme, a minor gentleman's wife, gave her brother-in-law, who died within forty-eight hours, 'an aleberry of arsenic and rosin'. Joan Sharples ministered to Alice Sharples 'arsenic in a medicine drink' from which Alice died a month later. Margaret Stannop's lover hanged alongside her. The husbands of Elizabeth Holme and Joan Sharples, though charged with having 'incited and persuaded' their wives to murder, were acquitted.[149] Evidence might have exonerated these men. But here too may lie the influence of gender. Coverture expressly did not extend to homicide. Even if coercion was present, a wife was to be found guilty.[150] And women who incited and persuaded men to kill their intimates were as culpable as the men who did the deadly deed. Yet the same might not be said of men associated with poisoneresses. Poisoning by women was doubly treacherous. They did more than murder in an underhand fashion, they used their household position as a deadly, secret weapon against those who expected nourishment and

---

[147] The court files contain a warrant 'under the two judges' hands that an attachment should be awarded' against the jurors for their partiality. PRO, CHES 21/3, fos. 126, 146; CHES 24/118/3 indictment, jury return, petition, certificate. For the others, CHES 21/3, fo. 146v; CHES 24/118/4 recognisance re. Jane Marbury (1626); CHES 21/3, fo. 156; CHES 24/102/4 indictment, recognisance re. Anne Williamson (1591).

[148] Green, *Verdict*, 125.

[149] PRO, CHES 21/3, fo. 42; CHES 24/115/3 indictment, jury return re. Holme (1620). CHES 21/3, fos. 41v, 45; CHES 24/115/3 indictment, jury return re. Sharples (1620). CHES 24/4, fo. 242v; CHES 24/129/1 indictment, jury return, recognisance re. Stannop (1651). An aleberry was a drink of ale brewed with spices, sugar and sops of bread; rosin is a solid form of turpentine.

[150] Hale, *Summary*, 434.

succour. As the subversion of household order is implicit in the act, a husband of such a wife might reasonably not be held to rule her.

No natural mother?

Thirty-one women in the Cheshire sample were accused of murdering their newly or recently born infants.[151] New-born child murder, commonly termed infanticide by historians, entered legal discourse in the late sixteenth century as an act connected with the mother's sexual immorality.[152] By 1624, when it entered the statute books, it was established as an offence against morality as much as violent wrongdoing by the poor. The 1624 Act was concerned explicitly with 'the destroying and murdering of bastard children', whose bodies were secretly buried or otherwise concealed by their 'lewd' mothers who, if discovered, avoided punishment by falsely declaring that the child had been stillborn. To prevent such practices, any woman who concealed her bastard infant's death was to 'suffer death as in case of murder' unless at least one witness testified to a stillbirth.[153] Law thus defined poor unmarried mothers as precisely the sort of ungodly, dissolute persons who would perpetrate a heinous, 'unnatural' deed. The assumptions inherent in the statute were echoed elsewhere. Henry Matthews's 'very awful and awakening' 1701 assize sermon at Chester (where three women were on trial for infanticide) meditated upon the passage, 'Then when lust has conceived, it bringeth forth sin, and sin when it is finished bringeth forth death.' Babington in 1676 railed against 'lewd whores, who having committed one sin, to avoid their shame and the charge of a bastard, would commit a greater [sin]'.[154] A 1634 ballad *No Natural Mother but a Monster* delineated a young girl's progression from an 'unbridled will' and 'wild' carriage, through pregnancy, to 'foully... transgress[ing]...against nature' by smothering and strangling her 'poor harmless infant', to her arraignment and execution.[155] A trial pamphlet of 1616 entitled *Deeds against Nature and Monsters by Kinde* told the tale of

---

[151] A further two were suspected of killing their older children, and five more of murdering the children of others.

[152] It was, in fact, a Cheshire case of 1560 which first exemplifed this connection in Richard Crompton's 1584 edition of Anthony Fitzherbert's *L'Office et Auctoritie de Justices de Peace*. Mark Jackson correctly points out that contemporaries did not use the term 'infanticide'. However, usage of the term need not be either 'anachronistic or confusing'. Here 'infanticide' refers only to the killings of newly or recently born infants and not to those of older children. Jackson, *New-Born Child Murder*, 6.

[153] 21 James I, c. 27. The Parliaments of 1606–7 and 1610 had debated similar bills. The Act was repealed in 1803.

[154] Cited in Jackson, *New-Born Child Murder*, 111; Babington, *Advice to Grand Jurors*, 172–5, at 174. See also William Gouge, *Domesticall Duties* (London, 1622), 507.

[155] *No Natural Mother, but a Monster* (London, 1634), repr. in *Pepysian Garland*, 425–30. *A Pittilesse Mother* (London, 1616), sigs. A2v, A3r.

'a lascivious young damsel' who committed infanticide 'that the world might not see the seed of her own shame'. Another pamphlet of 1674 described the 'young wench' as a 'barbarous murderess'.[156]

The latter, though potent, was not the sole child-killing discourse in circulation. Pamphlets alternatively presented a young woman who murdered her new-born babe as a piteous, 'beautiful unfortunate', 'the fairest, most deluded mother in the world'.[157] The 'pitiless mother' who 'most unnaturally' murdered her two children was at once a figure of evil and a victim of feminine frailty. Margaret Vincent, who, desiring 'to have instructions in salvation' had fallen 'into the hands of Roman wolves' had 'the sweet lamb, her soul, ... entangled by their persuasions'. It was 'to save [her children's] soul[s] (as she vainly thought), she purposed to become a tigerous mother and so wolfishly to commit the murder of her own flesh and blood ... never relenting according to nature'. The pamphleteer presented her actions as both pitiless and pitiful, unnatural and natural. The reader is explicitly urged to forgive her.[158] These alternative understandings of murderous mothers, as well as the less sympathetic model embedded in the statute, could attend upon the operation of law.

The context and impact of the 1624 legislation has frequently been misrepresented. First, given historians' assertions that homicides are the least likely of all crimes to remain undetected, the refrain that the 'actual' incidence of infanticide must have been far greater than the numbers of prosecutions is odd. The assumption, as Mark Jackson has signalled, is that accused women were guilty.[159] Effectively, historians extend the concerns of seventeenth-century legislators and moralists to all unmarried mothers, who are portrayed as the hapless victims of a society that forces them to choose between castigation for 'brazen immorality' or murder.[160] Motive, while attributable to such women, is not necessarily indicative of inclination, intent or guilt. Contemporaries knew this. Margaret Yardley, Margaret Goodall and Jane Lightborne were questioned about their infants' deaths, but indictments were not filed,

---

[156] *Deeds against Nature and Monsters by Kinde* (London, 1616), sig. A1r.; *Relation of the Most Remarkable Proceedings at the Late Assizes at Northampton* (London, 1674), sig. A1r.

[157] *Strange and Wonderful News from Durham, or the Virgin's Caveat Against Infant-Murther* (London, 1679), cited in Wiltenburg, *Disorderly Women*, 233–4.

[158] *A Pittilesse Mother*, passim and sig. B2.

[159] Sharpe, *County Study*, 137; McLynn, *Crime and Punishment*, 114; R.W. Malcolmson, 'Infanticide in the eighteenth century', in J.S. Cockburn ed., *Crime in England, 1500–1800* (London, 1977), 191–2. Cf. Jackson, *New-Born Child Murder*, 11–12; Wrightson, 'Infanticide in earlier seventeenth-century England', 10–11.

[160] Beattie, 'Criminality of women', 84; P.C. Hoffer and N.E. Hull, *Murdering Mothers: Infanticide in England and New England 1558–1803* (New York, 1981), ch. 1 and 115, 133, 145–7; Malcolmson, 'Infanticide', 187–8, 207–8; Sharpe, *County Study*, 136–7; Wrightson, 'Infanticide in European history', *Criminal Justice History*, 3 (1982), 6–7.

150   *Crime, Gender and Social Order*

nor were witnesses bound to testify against them.[161] Charges were dropped after coroners' returned verdicts of stillbirth in the cases of Ellen Smith and Aldreda Johnson, and natural death in that of Margaret Walley.[162] It is instructive, too, that coroners so rarely viewed unidentified infant corpses: in the years studied here, only three little strangled or crushed bodies were not positively linked to a suspect.[163] As far as bastardy went, women's options, though narrow, were less restricted in practice than the common characterisation of infanticidal mothers suggests.[164]

The common historiographical view that the 'draconian' and 'barbaric' 1624 Act treated women 'with terrible harshness...desperate injustice and cruelty' similarly requires modification.[165] A consensus has arisen that seventeenth-century women accused of neonatal infanticide were 'frequently convicted and hanged' but from the second quarter of the eighteenth century juries exhibited 'an increasing tendency to acquit'.[166] Although acquittal rates were higher in the eighteenth century than previously, the seventeenth century did not witness vast numbers of successful prosecutions. Between 1580 and 1709, thirty-three women were executed for the offence in Cheshire: one every four years.[167] As Figure 4.9 shows, the sampled years saw successful prosecutions of only ten and the execution of eight of the thirty-one women charged.[168] These figures, though terrible enough in themselves, hardly support the view that '[o]nly an obsession with the classic crimes of horror – infanticide and petty treason – can explain the ruthless treatment of murdering mothers'. Nor do 'the wheels of justice' appear to have ground

---

[161] PRO, CHES 21/1, fo. 167v re. Yardley (1593); CHES 21/1, fo. 169v re. Goodall (1593); CHES 21/3, fos. 67v, 72, CHES 24/116/3 recognisance re. Lightborne (1622).

[162] PRO, CHES 21/4, fo. 108v, CHES 24/126/2 (1641) coroner's inquisition re. Smith; CHES 21/1, fo. 178, CHES 24/104/1 coroner's inquisition re. Johnson (1595); CHES 21/4, fo. 160v, CHES 24/127/1/95 re. Walley (1648).

[163] PRO, CHES 21/4, fo. 243v; CHES 24/129/1 coroner's inquisition re. unknown male infant (1651). CHES 21/4, fo. 260; CHES 24/129/2 coroner's inquisition re. 'a certain young child' (1651). CHES 21/4, fo. 378v; CHES 24/131/6 coroner's inquisition re. unknown female infant (1657).

[164] For women's strategies and discourses of bastardy, see below pp. 227–37.

[165] Lionel Rose, *The Massacre of the Innocents: Infanticide in Britain, 1800–1939* (London, 1986), 1; McLaren, *Reproductive Rituals*, 131; Kennedy, *Eve was Framed*, 102.

[166] Beattie, *Crime and the Courts*, 118–20; Cockburn, 'Patterns of violence', 96–7; Dolan, *Dangerous Familiars*, 124, 131; Hoffer and Hull, *Murdering Mothers*, x; Herrup, *Common Peace*, 173; Jackson, *New-Born Child Murder*, 93, 98. Allyson N. May, '"She at first denied it": infanticide trials at the Old Bailey', in Valerie Frith ed., *Women and History: Voices of Early Modern England* (Toronto, 1995), 23; Sharpe, *Crime*, 109; Sharpe, *County Study*, 135–6.

[167] Over the same period, only eleven persons of both sexes were hanged for witchcraft. Sharpe, *Crime*, 61–2.

[168] In addition to the data contained in Table 4.9, no formal charges were brought against six other suspected women, and of three further women one fled, one died in prison while awaiting trial, and one was sent to Shropshire to be prosecuted.

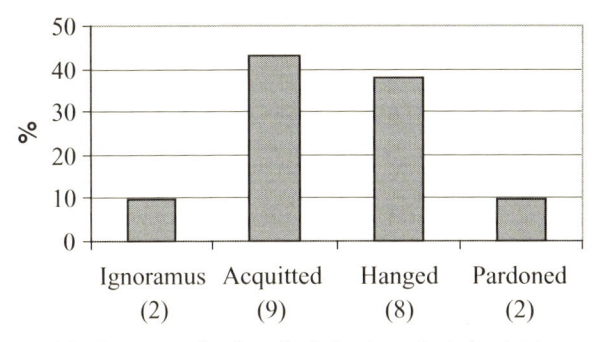

Figure 4.9 Outcomes for female defendants in infanticide cases

| | Ignoramus (2) | Acquitted (9) | Hanged (8) | Pardoned (2) |

'to their inexorable conclusion' in the majority of seventeenth-century cases prosecuted elsewhere.[169] Six of twenty-four cases identified for Norfolk led to convictions, but only two women were executed. In eastern Sussex, seven women hanged of fifteen so accused. In Essex, there was on average only one prosecution each year and a sixty per cent acquittal rate.[170] Although 'the "infanticide wave"... may have resulted in more executions than the more familiar witch craze', neither the incidence of new-born child murder nor its successful prosecution appears to have been 'woefully common'.[171]

A third, related misconception about the 1624 Act is that it reversed the presumption of innocence till proven guilty.[172] This was not quite so. For one thing, the presumption of innocence was not yet strictly formulated for *any* felony.[173] For another, although the Act presumed that a woman who concealed the death of her bastard had murdered it, concealment still had to be proven by evidence. Hiding the pregnancy, birth and even the corpse did not in law imply the mother's guilt.[174] Nor necessarily did the substantial point of concealment of the infant's death, because evidence of stillbirth or death during delivery rendered immaterial the presumption that the mother had murdered it. While it is true that women suspected of concealment were unlikely to produce an eyewitness of the birth and death itself, corpses were always viewed by midwives and other women and by coroners who often were able to testify that a natural death had occurred.

---

[169] Hindle, *State and Social Change*, 142; David Underdown, *Fire from Heaven* (London, 1992), 88, 89.
[170] Amussen, *Ordered Society*, 115 n. 51. Herrup, *Common Peace*, 154, 176, Tables 6.5 and 7.3. Essex: Sharpe, *Crime*, 49; Sharpe, *County Study*, 135; Keith Wrightson, 'Infanticide in earlier seventeenth-century England', 11; Wrightson, 'Infanticide in European history', 8.
[171] Sharpe, *Crime*, 61; F.G. Emmison, *Elizabethan Life: Disorder* (Chelmsford, 1970), 156.
[172] Beattie, *Crime and the Courts*, 113; May, 'She at first denied it', 19; Rose, *Massacre of the Innocents*, 1.
[173] Cockburn, *Introduction*, 107.   [174] Jackson, *New-Born Child Murder*, 33.

Infanticide has been discussed overwhelmingly in terms of the theoretical and practical harshness of the 1624 Act. So certain have historians been of the law's severity that they have been blind to its practical implications.[175] As I mentioned earlier, new-born child murder was the only homicide for which women were likely to be pardoned. This is explained neither by judges' singling out women for peculiar clemency due to chivalrous attitudes, nor by the judiciary's desire to militate against the particular difficulties women faced within the criminal justice system. Rather, in redefining the suspected murder of newly born bastards as a special case, the 1624 Act provided opportunities for mitigation that were evidently lacking for women in standard homicide law. It has been noted that prosecutions for new-born child murder 'confuse[d] together cases of deliberate killing, which may include both premeditated acts and acts of violence caused by mental imbalance, with cases of the attempted concealment of bastard births'.[176] In fact, culpability was ascribed not by conflating these practices but by distinguishing between them.

The most substantive evidence was composed of physical signs that violence had been inflicted on the infant. There was thus little hope that Elizabeth Hall would escape the gallows: her newly-born daughter's throat had been slit with a knife.[177] Guilt was deduced by circumstantial evidence and visible indications of the cause of death. Elinor Pova was 'vehemently suspected' of murdering her baby after his corpse was found at the bottom of Ridley Green pool. His neck was broken, his hands and feet bound with twine and a head lace, and he was weighted down by stones attached by a necklace twisted around his shoulder. The last time he had been seen alive was a few days earlier when Pova had abruptly removed him from his wet-nurse. Pova was hanged.[178] Mary Stockton, too, was suspected of murder after swine rooted out of a hole near her house 'a thing like a child...for it had two feet and a round head'. Mary denied killing the child: she had no clothes prepared because 'she thought she had been eight weeks from her time'; she had not felt the baby stir in the womb for some time; its 'wounds' must have been inflicted by the swine. These wounds, however, secured her conviction. The corpse had 'a cut betwixt its thigh and its body about four inches long and a bruise on the right side of its head which bared the skull, and the skull was bruised and both its stones were gone away and the skin broken or cut'. In one of his first acts as Chief Justice of Chester, Sir George

---

[175] Garthine Walker, 'Widernatürliche Mütter? Die Tötung neugeborener Kinder und das englische Gesetz im siebzehnten Jahrhundert, *Querelles: Jahrbuch für Frauenforschung* 5 (2000), 255–63.
[176] Wrightson, 'Infanticide in earlier seventeenth-century England', 15.
[177] PRO, CHES 21/4, fos. 186a, 199; CHES 24/127/2 coroner's inquisition (1648); CHES 24/128/1 jury return (1649).
[178] PRO, CHES 21/5, fos. 2, 4v, 5, 11v, 12, 21, 21v, 28; CHES 24/134/1 indictment, coroner's inquisition, recognisance (1663).

Jeffreys (who later became 'notorious for his brutality' on a national scale) sentenced Mary Stockton to death.[179]

Just as the presence of violence was incriminating, its absence frequently led to the defendant's exoneration. As early as the mid-seventeenth century, the terms of the 1624 statute were apparently ignored by jurors and judges. The grand jury threw out an indictment against a woman whose one-day-old baby 'came by its death', even though she allegedly concealed the birth, 'buried it and intended to conceal the death'.[180] Petty juries regularly acquitted women whose cases rested on concealment alone and only sometimes on the grounds that they were not guilty 'of the death'.[181] Ann Clough had both concealed her pregnancy and given birth secretly. Precisely how her infant had died she could not say, save that she had had one of her 'fits' during labour 'which did so distract me that I knew not what I did', and that she had not felt the baby move for a week or two before the birth – a common assertion made by women accused of neonatal infanticide. But the crucial evidence was supplied by female witnesses: the body displayed 'neither wound nor blemish', and Ann had openly 'prepared linens for an infant about a quarter of a year before with intent to marry Thomas Wood'.[182] In this case, presumptive evidence suggested that she had not murdered her child.

It was rare for a woman to be executed on grounds of concealment alone. The judge refused to grant Elizabeth Dentith a reprieve in 1669 although she was found guilty only of concealing the death and secretly burying her infant. As a countermeasure to her prosecution, one Peter Dentith had filed an indictment against another woman, Anne Janion, for suffocating and strangling the infant, and Thomas Janion (perhaps the baby's father) for helping her. They were acquitted. However, the evidence presented against them alleged that the child had suffered an unnatural death. Peter Dentith's attempt to save Elizabeth might have been the very thing that brought the full force of the statute upon her neck.[183] Allegations that the fathers of bastards (or their agents) had murdered or assisted in the murder of their

---

[179] PRO, CHES 38/41 'Backford examinations against Mary Stockton' (1681); CHES 21/5, fo. 196v; *Dictionary of National Biography*.

[180] PRO, CHES 21/5, fo. 67; CHES 24/135/5 indictment, recognisance re. Elizabeth Beckett (1667).

[181] PRO, CHES 21/4, fos. 285, 287v; CHES 24/130/1 indictment, coroner's inquisition, jury return re. Jane Hodgkin (1653). CHES 21/4, fos. 285, 287v; CHES 24/130/1 indictment, coroner's inquisition, jury return re. Elizabeth Baxter (1653). CHES 21/4, fos. 360v, 364; CHES 24/131/5 indictment, coroner's inquisition, jury return re. Katherine Hynde, (1657). CHES 21/4, fos. 418v, 419; CHES 24/133/1 indictment, coroner's inquisition, jury return re. Emma Highfield (1661). CHES 24/5, fos. 2v, 6; CHES 24/134/1 indictment, coroner's inquisition, jury return re. Ellen Anderton (1663). Cf. May who states that it was a late-eighteenth-century phenomenon: 'She at first denied it', 23.

[182] PRO, CHES 38/41 'Examinations against Ann Clough' (1686); CHES 21/5, fos. 286, 287v.

[183] PRO, CHES 21/5, fos. 92^{a}v, 92^{b}r; CHES 24/136/4 indictment, coroner's inquisition, jury return, recognisance (1669).

offspring rarely stuck. By the time that Elinor Pova (whose baby was found bound and drowned in Ridley Green pool) stood trial in August 1663, her case had become complicated. Edward Pova, a London clothworker (perhaps her father), was bailed to appear and answer for spreading a 'scandalous report' about the reputed father of her bastard, John Dodd senior, of Crewe. Dodd and his neighbour, Anne Billington (who had initially testified against Pova) were prosecuted for assisting John Dodd, junior, and Pova herself 'wreathe and break' the baby's neck. While Pova was convicted and executed, the grand jury discharged the Dodds and Billington. All three were prosecuted again and arraigned at the next sessions; they were acquitted.[184]

Men were implicated in the deaths of eleven infants in the sampled years. Not one was convicted. As with poisoning, when women and men together were suspected of killing infants, women were invariably held the more accountable. Convictions of men were also elusive due to the means by which men commonly disposed of unwanted bastards: neglect and starvation either within their own households or, upon their instruction, in the home of a hired 'nurse'.[185] In 1624, Anne Benison accused Thomas Cheetham and his wife of 'willful[ly] famishing and starving' her and Cheetham's baby son, Raphe Cheetham alias Benison. The grand jury found the bill *ignoramus*.[186] The same year, two other men were acquitted of having 'famished and starved' a week-old baby, 'not giving the child sufficient nourishment... with the intention of procuring its death'.[187] In 1645, Dorothy Hixon accused miller Richard Hough of sending their baby away 'on pretence to put it to nurse'. Nine days later, being 'much troubled about the child', she found out where it was, 'travelled thither and found the child almost starved, and sore flushed and rubbed with the straw for want of tendering. And a poor woman that came to the door told me that the child had no suck for six days before.' Dorothy put her little daughter to her own breast but she was too late: her baby died, having been 'starved to death'. The nurse explained the death differently. 'The child', she said, 'died a natural death, wanting nothing fit for a young infant to have', but had fallen sick shortly after arrival 'and was full of red pimples and refused both suck and meat.' The coroner's inquest returned a verdict of *morte naturali*. No one was prosecuted.[188] Such infant deaths, where incriminating marks of physical violence were lacking, in the

---

[184] PRO, CHES 21/5, fos. 2, 4v, 5, 11v, 12, 21, 21v, 28; CHES 24/134/1 indictment, coroner's inquisition, recognisance (1663); CHES 24/134/2 indictment, examinations (1664).
[185] Wrightson, 'Infanticide in earlier seventeenth-century England', 16–17.
[186] PRO, CHES 21/3, fo. 99; CHES 24/117/2 indictment, recognisance (1624).
[187] PRO, CHES 21/3, fos. 99, 101; CHES 24/117/2 indictment, jury return, recognisance, petition (1624).
[188] PRO, CHES 21/4, fo. 143; CHES 24/126/5 coroner's inquisition, examinations (1645). This case is discussed at greater length in Walker, 'Telling tales of infant death'.

context of a high rate of infant mortality, could pass as non-suspicious, or at least not suspicious enough.

In general, judges and jurors appear to have applied 'normal' standards of proof for homicide in cases of new-born child murder. After 1624, the statutory definition of the offence made it unlikely that positive evidence (an eyewitness account) of a stillbirth would be forthcoming. Yet from the outset evidence of concealment alone apparently comprised insufficient grounds upon which to send often young, single women to their deaths.[189] This issue of what constituted virtual 'proofs' is important in understanding why the 1624 Act was not rigorously enforced. Perhaps, too, there was sympathy for mothers whose babies died without overt violence, and possibly a lack of concern over the deaths of bastards if enough evidence seemed to exculpate the defendant.[190]

Unlike other female-perpetrated homicides, reprieves and pardons were granted to infanticides.[191] Margery Preston was pardoned in 1595, convicted of 'killing' but 'not of murder'.[192] Ellen Hawarth, found guilty in 1628 of suffocating her child, was declared pregnant by the jury of matrons, reprieved, and quickly pardoned on the recommendation of Sir John Bridgeman and Marmaduke Lloyd, 'for that it did not appear by the evidence she used any violence to the child'. Because the form of the indictment required that the means of death were entered, cases that rested on concealment alone frequently claimed that the child had been suffocated or strangled. This was also the charge against Elizabeth Gee alias Venables, pardoned in 1661 because she was guilty 'of concealment only'.[193] Throughout England, pardons were granted on similar grounds: 'the evidence against her being doubtful'.[194] One woman was pardoned for it 'appears by the certificate of the Lord Chief Justice of the Common Pleas (who gave judgement... at her trial) that she is a very simple woman and in the nature of an idiot'.[195] Idiots and lunatics, and anyone *non compos mentis* at the time of the incident were not legally

---

[189] Babington, *Advice to Grand Jurors*, 130; Barbara J. Shapiro, *Beyond Reasonable Doubt and Probable Cause: Historical Perspectives on the Anglo-American Law of Evidence* (London, 1991), 165, 206–8, 213–16, 50. Shapiro, *Probability and Certainty*, 13–14, 42, 50.
[190] See also Amussen, *Ordered Society*, 115.
[191] I found no pardons recorded for women convicted of any homicide other than infanticide in a sample of royal pardons given in England and Wales for January 1595–March 1597, April 1624–July 1630, January 1661–October 1673.
[192] PRO, CHES 21/1, fos. 180v, 181, 181v, 188; CHES 24/104/2 coroner's inquisition, jury return, recognisance (1595).
[193] PRO, CHES 21/3, fos. 172v, 174b, 178; CHES 24/119/3 indictment, coroner's inquisition, jury return, jury of matrons' return re. Hawarth (1628); PRO, SO 3/9 Pardon to Ellen Hawarth, August 1628. PRO, CHES 21/3, fos. 418, 423v; CHES 24/133/1 indictment, coroner's inquisition, recognisance, jury return re. Gee alias Venables (1661).
[194] PRO, SO 3/8, Pardon to Joan Oliver, April 1624.
[195] PRO, SO 3/9, Pardon for Elizabeth Riddington, July 1628.

responsible for their actions. In the late sixteenth and early seventeenth centuries, few women's homicides were explained in this way. But by the 1660s, such notions had begun to influence judicial decision-making. Hale first gave an account of an infanticide committed by the (married) mother's 'temporary frenzy' in 1668. In Cheshire, one acquittal may have been an early version of temporary insanity mitigating infanticide. In 1661, the coroner reported that Margaret Wyatt had strangled her new-born infant 'at the Devil's seduction'; when she came to her senses and realised what she had done, she had fled in horror before being captured and brought to trial.[196] The insanity discourse became an increasingly common means of interpreting and mitigating new-born child murder, until by the late eighteenth century it had become virtually ubiquitous.[197] In the granting of pardons to women who had been found guilty, we see the power of discourses of infanticide in which the mother who killed was ultimately forgivable.

Paradoxically, the murder of little children, the most vulnerable victims of all, was the only female-perpetrated homicide to which mitigating notions were applied. This was possible because infanticide was sometimes understood by contemporaries in terms of women's responses to unpropitious circumstances. It was acknowledged that the particular social, economic and emotional repercussions of bastard-bearing might drive a woman to allow her child to die, or even to kill it. As long as death was caused by perceivably 'non-violent' means – smothering, strangling, lying upon the infant, or other forms of deadly embrace – it might be forgiven. The manner and form of such killings resounded with notes of negation, almost as if the mother attempted to draw the baby back into her own body as a denial of its autonomous existence. In contrast, when women's violence was interpreted as an assertion, as in inflicting violence with weapons or wilfully killing husbands, no such leeway was permitted. In dominant discourses, husband-murder was always portrayed as an assertion, so much so that self-defence was no feasible plea for women in law. There were few cultural models of positive feminine violence upon which articulations of women's homicide could draw. The positive woman-warrior figure, whom we met in the previous chapter, who fought to protect her family or community from external enemies, was evidently inapplicable in the circumstances of female homicide which invariably involved victims drawn from women's domestic circles. Otherwise, as we saw in the same chapter, discourses of

---

[196] PRO, CHES 21/4, fos. 417v, 423v; CHES 24/133/1 indictment, coroner's inquisition, jury return (1661).
[197] Hale, *Pleas of the Crown*, Vol. I, 36. Jackson, *New-Born Child Murder*, 120–7. Dana Y. Rabin, '"Of persons capable of committing crimes": law and responsibility in England 1660–1800', Ph.D. dissertation, University of Michigan (1996), 148–56.

violence troped women's passive resistance to men's assaults, never their active response.

For men, the situation was different. Homicide law enshrined cultural expectations that men would assert their honour, their manhood, their right to be unmolested and to retaliate to provocation. In short, homicide law embodied male standards of behaviour. Legal distinctions between degrees of culpability, manifest in the categories of manslaughter, provocation and self-defence, were rooted in the idea that violence was a legitimate means of attaining or preserving masculine honour. Women's honour was incongruent with the lethal acts of which women were accused, which lacked the consensual character of much male homicide. In the absence of legal or appropriate cultural languages of righteous feminine killing, the law could not operate similarly for both sexes. One ramification of this was that there was no category of culpability for women's homicide other than murder. No woman in the Cheshire sample was convicted of manslaughter, killing in self-defence, or even killing by accident, and these verdicts were similarly absent or very rare in other counties.[198] While the latter categories attended on the disposition of verdicts and sentences of male defendants, and a child's age was taken into account as a mitigating circumstance, women who killed were almost always held accountable.[199] Unlike their male counterparts, who usually escaped hanging, women who were successfully prosecuted for homicide were invariably executed.

The legal categories of manslaughter and self-defence, and the concepts of chance-medley and just retaliation to provocation, posited men's lethal violence as the inevitable consequence of their nature. This concession to the nature of man served to mitigate the majority of male-perpetrated homicides. Their killings were only exceptionally deemed to be 'unnatural' and wholly inexcusable. Women's homicide was conceived differently, but not oppositionally. While female-perpetrated killings were attributed to woman's nature, notions of what constituted natural and unnatural behaviour were dissolved and naturalised into a pervasive negative feminine stereotype. Women's homicide was seen not to mirror men's, but to be a grotesque

---

[198] For example, in Surrey 1660–1800, no grand jury reduced a murder charge against a woman to manslaughter, although two women were convicted of that crime by trial juries: Beattie, *Crime and the Courts*, 105, 82, Tables 3.3 and 3.1.

[199] Until the age of seven, a child was legally regarded as lacking discretion and understanding and could not be charged with felony. Between the ages of eight and twelve, a child could be prosecuted only 'if it may appear (by hiding of the person slain, or by any other act) that the abundance of his malice doth exceed the tenderness of his years': Pulton, *De Pace Regis*, fos. 125v–6r; Dalton, *Countrey Justice*, 223–4. For examples of the exoneration of children who killed (other children and women), see PRO, CHES 21/4, fo. 91, CHES 24/125/4 coroner's inquisition re. Ludovick Williams (1640); CHES 21/5 fo. 40v, CHES 24/135/2 coroner's inquisition re. John Dale (1665); CHES 21/5, fo. 198, CHES 38/41, 'Examinations against John Shenton' (1681).

exaggeration of it. Thomas Beard opined that if murders 'be strange and monstrous for men, what shall we then say of wicked and bloody women, who (contrary to the nature of their sex) addict themselves to all violence and blood-shedding'.[200] Consequently, the perceived nature of woman served to intensify rather than lessen women's culpability. New-born child murder may have been an exception precisely because the terms of the 1624 Act singled it out as a special case, albeit in ways unforeseen by legislators and moralists. In focusing the attention of jurors and judges so firmly upon the matter of concealment alone, the statute served to deflect the potentially incriminating connection between the images of whore and murderess that epitomised negative femininity. When judged by the male standards that saturated homicide law, women could not receive similar treatment to men before the courts. But when law itself demanded that they be judged by *different* criteria than were men, 'normal' standards of proof appear to have been applied. In turn, this led to fewer guilty verdicts leading to death.

Historians who seek to argue that women's sentencing was 'lenient' or 'harsh' take the sentencing of men as the standard. In doing so, they both deny the gendered vision of homicide law and, in confusing disparity with discrimination, obscure the implications of gender for the administration of criminal justice. Disparity and discrimination are not synonymous. Men and women were not sentenced differently for homicides that were perceived to be alike. All those convicted of acts of particular heinousness such as premeditated murder were liable to be executed. For women, however, the problem was that according to the values of homicide law, their killings nearly always looked like wilful murders. This was so even when they were motivated by fear or desperation and were lacking in what in men would have been defined as malice. In the late twentieth and early twenty-first centuries, lawyers struggle to match women's accounts of homicide to the 'immutable and unyielding' categories of a law that remains quintessentially male. Early modern concepts of gender and order conspired even more than modern ones to eclipse the predicament and experience of women in ways which make the judicial treatment of women and men truly incommensurable.[201]

Homicides made up only a small proportion of male and female crime. Many more times as many men and women were prosecuted not for crimes of lethal violence but for offences against property, which are discussed in the following chapter.

---

[200] Beard, *Theatre of Gods Judgements*, 339.   [201] Edwards, *Sex and Gender*, 363.

5

Theft and related offences

Various forms of theft – petty and grand larceny, housebreaking, burglary, pickpocketing, robbery including highway robbery, and horse-theft – together constituted some three-quarters of felonies prosecuted in early modern England.[1] Everywhere, men were a majority of defendants; of over a thousand offences so prosecuted in Cheshire, more than three-quarters of the suspects were male.[2] Histories of crime have inadequately accounted for this fundamental gender discrepancy. While few studies have dealt with gender *per se*, their methodological and conceptual frameworks have been geared to male offenders, though this usually remains unacknowledged. Conclusions about criminality therefore often apply to men but not necessarily to the significant minority of female offenders. Moreover, the 'low' level of female involvement in property crime is interpreted as a relative numerical insignificance, which in turn leads to an assumption that women's thefts are less significant in other ways too. Hence, female criminality is characterised as petty criminality. Comments about women thieves tend to be underpinned by familiar assumptions. Women were routinely more timid and less likely to operate autonomously than men, frequently being mere accessories to 'real' (male) crooks. They stole items of little value and immediate use, unlike their more ambitious and serious male counterparts. Because women were less criminally inclined than men, contemporaries considered them less criminally dangerous. Consequently, generosity and clemency marked women's treatment within the criminal justice system. This characterisation is not entirely erroneous, but it does require modification. Many assumptions about gender difference are predicated upon an essentialist model that

---

[1] J.M. Beattie, 'The pattern of crime in England', *P&P* 62 (1974), 73–8; J.S. Cockburn, 'The nature and incidence of crime in England, 1559–1625', in Cockburn ed., *Crime in England*, 60–70; Herrup, *Common Peace*, 45–7; Sharpe, *County Study*, 91–2.

[2] Of 1,005 suspected persons in Cheshire in sampled years in the 1590s, 1620s, 1650s and 1660s, 781 (77.7 per cent) were male and 224 (22.3 per cent) were female. Men constituted an even greater proportion of defendants in some southern counties. For example, in Hertfordshire 86 per cent and in Surrey 87 per cent of those prosecuted for theft at assize courts were male: Wiener, 'Sex roles and crime', 40; Beattie, *Crime and the Courts*, 238.

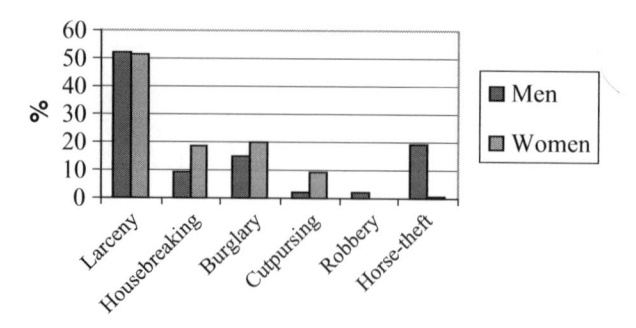

Figure 5.1 Women's and men's participation in property offences

dichotomises masculine/assertive–feminine/passive, and/or a structural view of socio-economic strictures upon women, which overemphasises or neglects certain aspects of the preclusion, minimisation and concealment of female criminality.[3] That women comprised a minority of defendants for property offences is not disputed here. What is questioned is the validity of the supposed relative characteristics of female and male theft and their fates before the judiciary. This chapter explores gendered patterns of theft and related offences such as receiving stolen goods, and reassesses the relative treatment of men and women before the courts.

PATTERNS OF CRIMINALITY

Let us first look to the types of thefts in which women and men engaged. As proportions of their overall activity in property offences, does their criminal activity suggest women's dependence upon men and a relative lack of courage and initiative? Figure 5.1 shows that relative to their overall criminal activity, male and female thieves were almost equally likely to be involved in simple larceny. A significantly higher proportion of female than male thieves acted as burglars, housebreakers and cutpurses.[4] Men had a virtual monopoly on horse-theft and robbery (theft with overt actual or threatened violence against the person, putting them in fear). But it was not the case that women busied themselves with 'easy' crimes. While not entailing the same

---

[3] Beattie, 'Criminality of women', 80–116; Beattie, *Crime and the Courts*, 183–4, 237–43, 436–9; G.R. Elton, 'Introduction', in Cockburn ed., *Crime in England*, 13; R. Gillespie, 'Women and crime in seventeenth-century Ireland', in Margaret MacCurtain and Mary O'Dowd eds., *Women in Early Modern Ireland* (Dublin, 1991), 43–52; Hanawalt, 'Female felon', 265; Ingram, 'Scolding women cucked or washed', 49; Sharpe, *County Study*, 101; Sharpe, *Crime*, 154–6; Shoemaker, *Prosecution and Punishment*, 207–16; Wiener, 'Sex roles and crime'.

[4] See also Hanawalt, 'Female felon', 261.

Table 5.1 *Value of goods stolen by male and female defendants*

Grand larceny			Housebreaking/Burglary	
Men %	Women %	Value	Men %	Women %
21.2	19.0	< 5s.	21.4	17.5
16.3	22.4	5s.–10s.	14.5	15.8
34.0	34.5	10s.–40s.	33.3	45.6
24.6	19.0	40s.–£5	17.9	12.3
3.5	–	£5–£10	3.4	5.3
4.9	5.2	£10 <	9.4	3.5

degree of overt conflict with the victim as robbery, for instance, burglary, housebreaking and cutpursing (removing someone's purse from their waist by cutting the strings, or pickpocketing) all involved a measure of danger and the possible confrontation with angry victims.

Secondly, let us examine the evidence for women and men stealing things of respectively lesser and greater value. Table 5.1 shows the value of goods stolen by men and women in seventeenth-century Cheshire.[5] Clearly, women did not routinely steal goods of little value.[6] Indeed, the general trend for women and men is roughly comparable. Around one-fifth of both female and male larcenists, housebreakers and burglars were charged with stealing items valued at less than five shillings, although men, not women, in fact slightly predominated in this lowest-value category. The highest proportion of thefts by both women and men – generally around a third but rather more in the case of female housebreakers/burglars – were of goods valued at between 10 and 40 shillings. Relatively few suspects of either sex were charged with thefts of between £2 and £5, and fewer still with even higher value thefts. Proportionately, men were not always predominant even in the uppermost categories. The relative monetary values of women's and men's spoils fail to point to a significant discrepancy between them.[7]

---

[5] Based on a sample of the 1620s, 1640s, 1650s and 1660s.
[6] Goods were sometimes devalued to less than 12*d*. before or after indictments were drafted, but women seem not to have been the predominant beneficiaries of this practice. See also Cockburn, *Introduction*, 66–9; Herrup, *Common Peace*, 47 and 47 n. 6; Sharpe, *County Study*, 10, 92, 146. Where large livestock constituted a larger proportion of male thefts, there might have been a greater gender discrepancy in the relative value of thefts; see Barbara A. Hanawalt, *Crime and Conflict in English Communities, 1300–1348* (Cambridge, Mass., 1979), 119.
[7] Garthine Walker, 'Women, theft and the world of stolen goods', in Jenny Kermode and Garthine Walker eds., *Women, Crime and the Courts in Early Modern England* (London, 1994), 86–7. For the 1780s, see MacKay, 'Why they stole: women in the Old Bailey, 1779–1789', *Journal of Social History* 32, 3 (1999), 623–39.

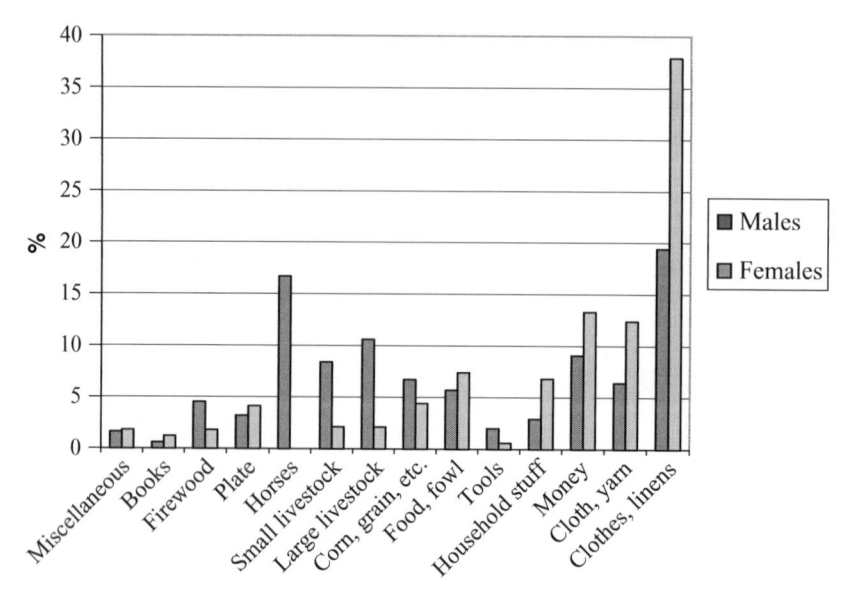

Figure 5.2 Items stolen by women and men

Networks of exchange

There are, however, perceivable differences in what men and women stole. Figure 5.2 shows that men alone were prosecuted for horse-theft, and that livestock featured far more heavily as a proportion of their thefts than women's. In contrast, while clothes and household linens were popular targets for both sexes, they made up a far greater proportion of women's thefts. Women, moreover, disproportionately figured as defendants in the case of stolen clothes and linens: in the 1620s, for instance, women participated in over one-third of larcenies in which these goods were stolen, though only one defendant in five was female. Cloth, yarn and household utensils similarly stand out as feminine targets.[8] We may consider how this evidence fits with the conventional view that men's criminal activity was more daring and women's pettier, that female thieves should be consigned to the 'less terrifying criminal elements'.[9]

The different patterns of unlawful acquisition by women and men are not adequately explained by a model that simply ascribes 'serious' and 'petty' theft to men and women respectively. Part of the problem is that 'seriousness' and 'pettiness' are somewhat vaguely defined. In an unstated circular

---

[8] This was so elsewhere: Walker, 'Women, theft and the world of stolen goods', 87, 101 nn. 20–1.
[9] Sharpe, *County Study*, 101; see also Hanawalt, 'Female felon', 262–4.

argument, women's thefts are perceived by historians to be less serious than men's because they were 'women's' crimes. This makes little sense. Women had no monopoly on the goods they stole, for the same were also frequently stolen by men. Clothes and linens, especially, were extremely valuable commodities in early modern society, with a high re-marketable and use value. Contemporaries did not consider the theft of such items trivial. The cultural as well as monetary value of clothing – apparel signified status, gender, honour and individuality, remember – meant that its theft was often perceived as serious indeed. Its value was known to all. James Gandy listed 'bedding, linen cloth, sheets and other linen and woollen clothes' before the 'hemp, flax, tar and corn' that had perished in a house-fire to his family's 'utter undoing'; magistrates acknowledged the significance of such losses in lamenting that 'these heavy accidents are objects of pity and compassion and may move the hardest heart'.[10] Clothing constituted the largest single category of lawful household expenditure after food and food production.[11] For those without a household of their own, clothes were usually their most valuable commodity. Hence, Ann Hasbie, a twenty-year-old 'work servant' in 1641 'lives upon her own wages for her service and is worth little besides her clothes'.[12] Moreover, the re-marketable value of clothes and linens was evidenced in a thriving second-hand market. Although both men and women stole them, in relative terms women were more than twice as likely to steal apparel, linens, cloth and yarn, and household utensils. The explanation for this discrepancy partly lies in the differing cultural significance of these goods in women's and men's lives.[13]

Clothing, linens, cloth and household goods saturated women's everyday lives in a more immediate sense than most men's perhaps. Women presided over the day-to-day purchasing and maintenance of these things. They were responsible for converting old garments and linens into more serviceable forms and for repairing them, for making up cloth into apparel, napkins and tablecloths for the family, and for most tasks involving household utensils. Ordinary women's marriage portions were comprised primarily of clothing and household stuff, which women often recuperated upon their husbands' deaths, and which they probably regarded as their property for the duration of the marriage.[14] Perhaps because of their intimate knowledge and use of such items, women often appear to have had a more emotional investment in

[10] CRO, QJB 1/6, fo. 135v.
[11] Lorna Weatherill, 'Consumer behaviour, textiles and dress in the late seventeenth- and early eighteenth-centuries', *Textile History* 22 (1991), 298.
[12] CDRO, EDC 5/1641/15, *Elizabeth Sutton c. Anne Leadbeater wife of George*, deposition.
[13] See also Walker, 'Women, theft and the world of stolen goods', 87–99.
[14] Amy Louise Erickson, *Women and Property in Early Modern England* (London, 1993), 86, 62, 223, 226–7.

them.[15] Female victims of theft often gave fuller descriptions of colours and adornment than their male counterparts even when the property in question had been retrieved, making this type of detail superfluous.[16] When clothes, cloth and household utensils were stolen, wives and female servants – not just male heads of households – reported the theft to Justices, gave evidence at trials, and sometimes entered into recognisances to prosecute, despite property laws requiring their husbands and masters to be named as official owners of the goods. Indeed, the good wife was instructed 'to lay a diligent eye to her household-stuff in every room, that nothing be embezzled away, nothing spoiled or lost for want of looking to, nothing worn out by more using than it needful, nothing out of place. For things cast aside are deemed to be stolen, and then there followeth uncharitable suspicions, which breed much disquietness.'[17] Thus Thomas Hodgkinson's wife Margaret prosecuted the woman who stole from a hedge a flaxen sheet that technically belonged to Thomas; Margaret wife of Edward Davenport prosecuted for the theft of a hempen sheet and a pillow bear which were legally Edward's. Similarly, Margaret Lindopp complained to magistrates and was bound over to prosecute the suspected thief even though the bill of indictment named her husband as prosecutor and owner of the stolen goods.[18] Maidservants added small lists of their lost garments and effects to those of their masters and mistresses, and being *femes sole* sometimes entered into prosecution themselves. Two indictments exist for one burglary commited by Mary Smith: one was prosecuted by the husbandman householder, William Brereton, and lists all the goods therein as his, despite the recognisance to prosecute stating that over half of the things were 'belonging to and in the custody of Margaret Brereton his wife'; the other indictment was prosecuted by maidservant, Margaret

---

[15] Amanda Vickery, 'Women and the world of goods: a Lancashire consumer and her possessions, 1751–81', in John Brewer and Roy Porter eds., *Consumption and the World of Goods* (London, 1991), 276, 274, 294; Amy Louise Erickson, 'Common law versus common practice: the use of marriage settlements in early modern England', *Economic History Review* 2nd ser., 43 (1990), 21–39; Beverly Lemire, 'Consumerism in pre-industrial and early industrial England: the trade in second-hand clothes', *Journal of British Studies* 27 (1988), 1–2; Weatherill, 'Consumer behaviour, textiles and dress', 298–301, 306–7.

[16] For example, CCRO, QSF/73/1/8, /13. Similarly, the investment of tailors in the garments they made was reflected in detailed descriptions; for example, PRO, CHES 24/132/3, examination of Thomas Greenehall (1659). For contemporary comment on women's penchant for colourful clothing, see John Brinsley, *A Looking-Glass for Good Women, Held Forth By Way of Counsell and Advice to Such of That Sex and Quality, As In The Simplicity of Their Hearts, Are Led Away to the Imbracing or Looking Towards Any of the Dangerous Errors of the Times, Specially that of the Separation* (London, 1645), 9–10; James Norris, *The Accomplished Lady or Deserving Gentlewoman* (London, 1683), 38; Joseph Swetnam, *The Araignment of Lewd, Idle, Froward and Unconstant Women* (London, 1615), 7.

[17] Dod and Cleaver, *Godly Forme of Household Government*, 2nd edn (London, 1630), sig. F5r.

[18] CRO, QJF 79/1/5, /22, cf. /21 (1651); CRO, QJF 83/1/3 (1655); CCRO, QSF 73/1/11, /12 (1620).

Olton, spinster, for several items of clothing, a remnant of new cloth, and a pair of scissors, 'being her goods'.[19]

Women's close relationship with clothing and linens often placed them in the thick of identifying stolen goods, too. Yeoman William Steele reported that a thief had 'stripped' his hedge and had stolen several linen clothes belonging to his wife, his children and his servants. It was his wife who went along with constables to search the house of the suspect, Ellen Wickstead, and who recovered the clothes.[20] In another case, Mary Weedall, a barrow-maker's wife, was able to recognise five slippings of yarn as John Rogerson's, 'for that I dressed the same, and comparing them with some others of the same yarn' of Rogerson's, 'being parcel of the number of twenty slippings I received from John Rogerson's wife, find them to be of the same reel'.[21]

Women had a high profile in the networks within which clothing, cloth and household goods were pawned, sold and exchanged.[22] Women had important roles in alehouses and inns where small-scale pawning was commonplace and in the retail trades that dealt in textiles, clothing, small-wares and food.[23] Women also had a high profile amongst petty chapmen and pedlars, both as independent traders and in partnership with male family members. While women constituted a minority of named pawnbrokers and salesmen, wives and daughters were actively involved in the trade itself.[24] Just as less reputable horse dealers dealt in stolen horses, the seedier side of the second-hand market embraced stolen clothes and utensils. Women had a high profile among those suspected to receive or to buy stolen clothes, linens and household stuff.[25] The lower end of the second-hand trade, 'with

---

[19] PRO, CHES 21/3, fo. 144r, CHES 24/118/4, indictments and recognisances re. Elizabeth Chaddock, Ann Bate and Mary Smith. See also CCRO, QSF 73/1/11, /12 (1645), QSF 73/1/17–/19 (1645); PRO, CHES 24/134/1, recognisance to prosecute Sarah Merret *alias* Stanley *alias* Danson (1663).

[20] PRO, CHES 38/41, 'Examination re. Wickstead', 1681.

[21] PRO, CHES 38/41, 'Examinations taken at Leftwich, 24 February 1682', examination of Mary Weedall. See also CHES 38/41, 'Examinations against Mary Dowkin', 1678. Walker, 'Women, theft and the world of stolen goods', 93–4.

[22] Madeline Ginsburg, 'Rags to riches: the second hand clothes trade, 1700–1978', *Costume* 14 (1980), 121–35; Beverly Lemire, 'Consumerism in pre-industrial and early industrial England: the trade in second-hand clothes', *Journal of British Studies* 27, 1 (1988), 1–24; Beverly Lemire, *Dress, Culture and Commerce: The English Clothing Trade Before the Factory, 1660–1800* (London, 1997), 95–120; Margaret Spufford, *The Great Reclothing of Rural England: Petty Chapmen and their Wares in the Seventeenth Century* (London, 1984).

[23] Alice Clarke, *The Working Life of Women in the Seventeenth Century* (1919; London, 1982), 197–209; Peter Clarke, *The English Alehouse: A Social History, 1200–1830* (London, 1983), 145–7, 138–9, 229; Peter Earle, *The Making of the English Middle Class: Business, Society and Family Life in London, 1660–1730* (London, 1989), 160–3, 166–74.

[24] Lemire, *Dress, Culture and Commerce*, 104–11; Spufford, *Great Reclothing*.

[25] For example, PRO, CHES 21/1, fo. 169r re. Alice Foster (1595); CHES 24/104/1 recognisance re. Alice Latham (1595); CHES 24/104/1, recognisance re. Margaret Richardson (1595); CCRO, QSE/5/107 (1597); CCRO, QSF/73/1/1 (1628); QSF/73/1/11 (1629); CRO,

no barriers inhibiting entry in to [it], with commodities readily available and so easily exchanged', was attractive to women as well as to men. Dealing in stolen clothes and utensils was one of the 'wayward but necessary improvisations of working women'.[26] The significance of pawning and the second-hand market must not be underestimated. Royal proclamations identified such activities as the very 'ground and nursery of burglaries, robberies, felonies and frauds'.[27]

Women's role as receivers of stolen goods should not be associated with their position as dependent household members as conventional histories of crime suggest. Rather, it should be contextualised in terms of women's own economic activities and interactions.[28] For example, when, in the summer of 1669, Aurelia Savage had clothes and linens to the value of 9s. stolen, she had a good idea of where they might have turned up, even though she had identified no suspect. Sure enough, she found some of her goods at the Fishers' alehouse in the possession of Elizabeth Fisher and two of her maidservants. Elizabeth promised to compensate Aurelia for two aprons and a napkin no longer in her custody, presumably sold. Although Arthur Fisher hovered in the background, evidently aware of what was going on, Elizabeth was clearly the dealer. It was she who was prosecuted by recognisance; and when the Fishers later refused to provide the thief, Jane Care, with food and money during her imprisonment, Care threatened to 'open such a door against Elizabeth Fisher as should not please them'. Other incidents in which stolen goods turned up at the Fishers' alehouse tell a similar story. Hearing of Aurelia's success in recovering her goods, Ellen Sadler subsequently asked Elizabeth Fisher whether Care had brought her stolen yarn there. Perhaps, said Elizabeth, who then protested ignorance of what had become of it. Another woman then took it upon herself to make a search of Elizabeth's household; she discovered the yarn, and promptly returned it to Ellen.[29] Although Elizabeth Fisher's maidservants were not officially prosecuted, they too were obviously aware of what kind of trade was going on. In another case, both Ellen Aspenall and her husband Thomas were bailed 'for clothes found in their house which were supposed to be stolen' by two burglars,

---

QJF 97/1/35 (1669). Beattie, *Crime and the Courts*, 189–90; Beverly Lemire, 'Peddling fashion: salesmen, pawnbrokers, tailors, thieves and the second-hand clothes trade in England, c.1700–1800', *Textile History* 22, 1 (1991), 67–82.

[26] Lemire, 'Peddling fashion', 67–8, 74, 76; Lemire, *Dress, Culture and Commerce*, 121–46. Michael Roberts, 'Women and work in sixteenth-century English towns', in Penelope J. Corfield and Derek Keene eds., *Work in Towns, 850–1850* (Leicester, 1990), 93–5, at 95.

[27] *A Proclamation for the Better Discovery and Prevention of Burglaries, Robberies, and Other Frauds and Abuses...* (London, 1630).

[28] Walker, 'Women, theft and the world of stolen goods', 91–3. See also Beattie, *Crime and the Courts*, 189–90; Gillespie, 'Women and crime', 49; Hanawalt, 'Female felon', 256–7, 261, 266–7; Shoemaker, *Prosecution and Punishment*, 133, 171–2.

[29] CRO, QJF 97/2/ 82, /133 (1669).

but the grand jury returned a verdict of true bill against Ellen alone and discharged Thomas.[30] Similarly, Ellen Cowper and her maids were implicated when stolen clothes were allegedly pawned at her house. Witnesses and magistrates were interested only in the activities of Ellen and her maidservants, and not at all in Ellen's husband, Robert.[31] As Michael Roberts has remarked, early modern 'household incomes ebbed and flowed across the threshold between cash and kind, and in the management of the associated pawns and credit dealings women were the experts'.[32]

Women's participation in cases where clothes, linens and household goods were stolen reflects women's preoccupations and duties in social and economic life. The world of stolen clothes, linens and household goods was populated by women as well as men – stealing, receiving, searching, passing on information and goods, deposing and prosecuting. This was in large part because women's lawful networks of exchange and interaction served their unlawful purposes too. Established networks for the disposal of goods was one important aspect of gendered criminal behaviour.

The same applies to horse-theft. Horse-stealing is usually viewed by historians as a calculated, daring and organised crime.[33] There is an assumption that the gender of suspects – nearly always men – needs no explanation for acumen and bravado are masculine characteristics. It is possible, however, to contextualise the maleness of horse-thieves. Successful horse-theft relied upon virtually identical mechanisms of exchange as the lawful trade in horses. In illegal and legal trade, horses changed hands remarkably quickly in private deals and at horse fairs.[34] Horse-thieves, like dealers, operated within a network of contacts that were distributed over a considerable geographical area. This was reflected in prosecutions: typically, one Cheshire horse-thief in 1648 was charged alongside men hailing from Derbyshire and Staffordshire.[35] Moreover, thieves mingled with reputable dealers at many markets and fairs. Horse dealers themselves had a reputation for untrustworthiness, and many certainly traded in stolen horses: such traffickers constituted 'one end of a continuum of the trade'.[36] Hence, Acts of Parliament

---

[30] PRO, CHES 21/1, fos. 153v, 155v (1591).
[31] CCRO, QSF 73/1/11, /12 (1620). See also PRO, CHES 21/4, fo. 136v, CHES 24/126/4, recognisances re. Margery wife of William Ellis and Alice wife of William Clarke (1642).
[32] Roberts, 'Women and work', 95.
[33] Beattie, *Crime and the Courts*, 167–70; Herrup, *Common Peace*, 168–70; Sharpe, *Crime*, 152.
[34] This and the subsequent paragraph draw heavily on Peter Edwards, *The Horse Trade of Tudor and Stuart England* (Cambridge, 1988), 52–3, 55–6, 84, 87–8, 105 ff.; P.R. Edwards, 'The horse trade of the Midlands in the seventeenth century', *Agricultural History Review* 27, 2 (1979), 90–100.
[35] PRO, CHES 24/128/1, indictment of Thomas Fisher et al. (1648).
[36] Edwards, *Horse Trade*, 139.

regulating the horse trade were overtly concerned with criminal activity.[37] The horse trade, then, provides a general context for horse-theft. The buying and selling of horses was very much a male activity. Female horse dealers were only occasionally known. Many dealers in fact came to the trade *via* other male occupations involving horses: postmaster, carrier, carter, hackney-man, coachman, groom, postilion, horse-breaker, blacksmith, farrier, and so on. Although some women rode on horseback, of course, horseback riding itself was culturally identified with manhood, being closely aligned with military service, masculine prowess and sportsmanship.[38] This male world of the horse and horse dealing was duplicated in the overlapping world of horse-theft.

The connections between dealing in horses and stealing them for profit nevertheless suggest something of women's participation. Horse dealing was frequently 'a family tradition', a form of household economy with a gendered division of labour. This took men beyond the household. They travelled extensively around the country. Younger males usually learnt the trade by accompanying their fathers or uncles to fairs in order to acquire experience of the business and to meet and build up contacts with other dealers.[39] Thus, buying horses as well as selling them was normally a male activity.[40] Women meanwhile remained in the family holding. However, their responsibilities extended to attending to horses in various ways. Recipes for horse-medicine, similar to those used for human healing, were concocted in the kitchen by mistresses of households and female servants. Some housewifery manuals explicitly included sections on 'horse medicine' and also on day-to-day care such as feeding.[41] Evidence suggests that it was sometimes women who transformed equine appearance by obliterating or painting on blazes and stockings, cutting manes and tails, and altering earmarks to prepare stolen horses for sale.[42] In practice, then, women in legal or illegal horse

---

[37] For example, Statutes 2 & 3 Philip & Mary c. 7 (1555), 31 Elizabeth I c. 12 (1589). See also *Complete Justice*, 114–15.

[38] See, for example, Thomas De Grey, *The Compleat Horse-man and Expert Ferrier* (London, 1651); Gerard Langbaine, *The Hunter: A Discourse of Horsemanship Directing the Right Way to Breed, Keep, and Train a Horse, for Ordinary Hunting* (London, 1685); Gervase Markham, *How to Chuse, Ride, Trayne, and Dyet, both Hunting-horses and Running Horses* (London, 1606); Nicholas Morgan, *The Horse-mans Honour, or, the Beautie of Horsemanship* (London, 1620); John Vernon, *The Young Horse-man, or, The Honest Plain-dealing Cavalier* (London, 1644).

[39] Edwards, 'The horse trade of the Midlands', 96, 100; Edwards, *Horse Trade*, 84.

[40] For example, PRO, CHES 21/1, fo. 192r (1597).

[41] S. I. *Here Begynneth the Proprytees and Medycynes for Hors* (London, 1502), xxii ff.; Nicholas Maltbey, *Remedies for Diseases in Horses Approoved and Allowed by Divers Very Auncient Learned Mareschals* (London, 1588); John Partridge, *The Widowes Treasure* (London, 1588), sigs. O1v–O3v; Gervase Markham, *A Way to Get Wealth, by Approved Rules of Practice in Good Husbandry and Huswifrie* (London, 1631), 218.

[42] See Edwards, *Horse Trade*, 112.

trading households had much to do with horses, quite apart from the buying, stealing or selling. At least some women whose menfolk regularly stole horses must have been apprised of the fact and have been involved both before and afterwards. Yet the logistics of horse-theft and legal classification highlighted men's illegal behaviour and made women's almost invisible.[43]

The theft of large and small livestock likewise depended on networks of exchange that were predominantly male. It was not usual for women to sell cattle or sheep at market; that was men's work. Stockmen and drovers, like horse dealers, were itinerant, spending much time on the road buying and selling their wares.[44] Butchers, known for their entrepreneurship in acting as wool merchants, horse dealers or a variety of other economic activities, also featured as the stealers of livestock and the recipients of stolen beasts.[45] Often this was the consequence of practical considerations: thieves could not themselves 'break up' the deer they had poached on Lady Cholmondley's estate, so they asked a butcher to do it. For his pains, they gave him a shoulder of venison.[46] Within the context of male networks and organisation, it is unsurprising that men predominated among those who stole cattle and sheep (see Figure 5.2). In contrast, women were more likely to steal those commodities that they were responsible for marketing: 'butter, cheese, milk, eggs, chickens, capons, hens, pigs, geese, and all manner of corn'.[47] It is no coincidence that the proportion of women who stole food and fowl was higher than that of men, and that the discrepancy between proportions of women and men who stole corn was significantly smaller than for many other commodities (see Figure 5.2).[48]

Here, too, the nature of early modern household organisation implicates women in what were formally men's crimes. When stolen sheep, fowl or other small livestock were brought home for consumption by men, they

---

[43] For exceptions, see CCRO, MF/69/3/143, indictment returned *ignoramus* of Mary Nuttall for stealing a horse from an unknown person (1646); *Calendar of State Papers: Domestic. Charles I*, Vol. XLVI, 199, December 1661, 'Warrant for a pardon to Mary Dixon of Whittlesea in the Isle of Ely for horse-stealing'.

[44] For example, Joan Thirsk, *The Rural Economy of England: Collected Essays* (London, 1984), 146–7, 176.

[45] Edwards, *Horse Trade*, 89. For example, PRO, CHES 21/4, fo. 147v, CHES 24/127/1/53, /35 (Thomas Cooke, two black heifers; 1648); CHES 21/4, fo. 179r, CHES 24/127/2, indictment re. William Walmsley (two ewes; 1648); CHES 21/4, fo. 208v, CHES 24/128/1, indictment re. Raphe Hoome (six sheep; 1649); CHES 21/4, fo. 154r, CHES 24/127/1/219, /222, /370 (Thomas Davenport and Rowland Orrell, for receiving fourteen stolen sheep; 1648). See also CRO, QJF 73/3/73 (1645); CCRO, MF69/2/82 (1646).

[46] CRO, QJF 51/2/40 (1622).

[47] Anthony Fitzherbert, *The Booke of Husbandrye*, 2nd edn (London, 1562), fo. 60r. No swine were stolen in the Cheshire sample; pigs were associated with women because, as consumers of whey, they were often kept as a sideline of dairying.

[48] This applied also to the medieval period, when women's household responsibilities were much the same: Hanawalt, *Crime and Conflict*, 120–2.

were prepared for the table by the household's women and not the men who stole them. It was, for instance, the mistress of the house who converted ill-gotten geese into 'a whole goose (which had been roasted in the oven), ... a quarter of a goose which was baked in a pie', and another part 'boiled with the giblets'.[49] After Charles Brown was suspected of stealing a sheep, his mother was spotted coming out of the house and, looking 'very ghastly around her' to see if she was being observed, she attempted to remove the evidence of the theft by hiding some sheep's suet and tallow under a clod of earth.[50] When David Bartington and Thomas Gatcliff stole a goose, they delivered it to Bartington's mother, who hid the creature in the loft and afterwards killed it, roasted it and served it up for Sunday dinner.[51] Mary Wettenhall was implicated when her husband was suspected of theft. She threw a stolen sack with a stolen loaf of bread inside it into a ditch in her back yard when searchers came by. On another occasion, she hid a blanket stolen by her husband under the bed and tried to cozen the searchers by fetching three other blankets down from the chamber for them to inspect.[52] Even without explicit references to women as partners or accessories – such as Isabel Goulding who was 'privy to the taking of a cow' by three men – women were undoubtedly knowing partners in many unlawful activities perpetrated by men.[53] Sometimes women instigated such crimes. John Oldfield, his sister Elizabeth Henshaw and her daughter Sarah stole three lambs, each of them carrying one away; Elizabeth 'sticked and killed' two of the lambs, John did the third. Although Elizabeth's husband allegedly aided and abetted them, he himself denied all knowledge of the crime, blaming Elizabeth alone; she backed him up, saying that he had known nothing of it.[54]

Patterns of male and female thieving were rooted in cultural context. Opportunities for stealing particular things were culturally disposed. Situating thefts within terms of the opportunities open to each sex is not to privilege opportunism, although that was part of the story of theft, of course. Rather it is to acknowledge that occasions for men and women to steal arose frequently from gendered activities and knowledge. Part of this involved gendered networks of exchange that facilitated the disposal of certain commodities over others. The marketable, use and cultural values of all goods were not the same for both sexes.

Criminal associations

The conventional assumption that women were dependent criminals – dependent upon men's guidance – may be challenged by analysing the

[49] CRO, QJF 81/4/91 (1654). [50] CRO, QJF 75/4/138 (1648).
[51] CRO, QJF 91/4/45, /41–/44, /11 (1663). [52] CRO, QJF 103/1/141, /138 (1675).
[53] PRO, CHES 24/127/1/230 (1648). [54] CRO, QJF 51/4/60, /31 (1623).

criminal associations of women and men. Participation in burglary (breaking into a house at night with the intention of committing a theft or other serious offence) and housebreaking (the same undertaken in the daytime) might prove particularly illuminating in this respect. These activities were more likely to involve premeditation and more than one perpetrator than simple theft. They might thus be expected to reveal a significant proportion of female participation with females acting as accomplices to male principals.

At first sight, evidence would seem to support the common view. Of ninety-seven men prosecuted in Cheshire during the 1620s, for example, almost a third were solitary agents in comparison to fewer than one in eight of forty-seven women. A different picture emerges upon closer inspection, however. While roughly a third of men worked alone, another third had male partners, and a fifth operated in mixed-sex groups where men predominated. Fewer than ten per cent of male burglars and housebreakers took part in enterprises where women were actively involved. Women displayed a different pattern of activity. Only a quarter of women committed crimes with male partners or in mixed-sex groups in which men predominated. The proportion of female criminals who worked alongside men was clearly larger than that of males who committed crimes in the company of women, yet few women actually acted as accomplices to men. Approaching half of female burglars and housebreakers in the 1620s were in league exclusively with other women, mainly working in pairs. If we include those operating in groups in which women outnumbered men, almost two-thirds worked solely or largely with other women. The majority of suspected female burglars and housebreakers during the late sixteenth and seventeenth centuries committed crimes alone or in league with other females rather than with men. In the 1640s, for instance, nearly a quarter of women burglars/housebreakers acted alone, while about a third combined with other women and a further third in groups involving other women as well as at least one man.[55] The significance of female associations is reinforced when we consider the wider networks involved in criminal activity. Ann Heywood, for example, was in 1648 accused of burglary with two other women, and four of her five other accessories were female too.[56] In 1595, Congleton spinster Ann Davenport burgled a house of over sixty-three pounds' worth of clothes and linens along with a male accomplice, but two women were indicted as accessories to the

---

[55] Beattie says that many female burglars in his study associated with men, but he does not provide statistical evidence: 'Criminality of women', 92. Hanawalt states that 46.6 per cent of medieval women prosecuted for burglary acted with an accomplice, 'usually a male'. Over half of the women thus acted alone, and some with other women. Even if all of the 46.6 per cent had involved male accomplices, the majority of women were not working with men: 'Female felon', 262.

[56] PRO, CHES 24/127/2, indictment re. Ann Heywood (1648).

crime and furthermore three women were suspected to have received the stolen goods.[57]

Larceny prosecutions tell much the same story. In the 1590s, a mere one in ten females were suspected of thieving alongside men. In the 1620s and 1640s, only about a third of female suspects were thought to have had male partners in crime. In the 1650s, the figure had dropped to six per cent, and in the 1660s' sample, no woman accused of larceny had a male accomplice. These figures for Cheshire are confirmed elsewhere. In early modern Kent, only a quarter of women defendants in property offences were prosecuted alongside men; women were just as likely to work with female partners, and twice as many were prosecuted for carrying out thefts alone.[58] Maidservants, in particular, were well placed for pilfering goods out of the household, and were often suspected. Sarah Brown deposed that one week a shilling in money and some perfume had been taken out of her box, the following week six slippings of yarn, two pewter dishes, part of a flitch of bacon and a pillow bear from her child's cradle had gone missing, and the week after that a blanket from the cradle and a petticoat that was part of her 'wearing clothes' had disappeared. She suspected eighteen-year-old Elizabeth Hill, maidservant to another family member who dwelled in the same house, for Hill often came into Brown's chamber despite being warned against doing so. In the constable's presence, a shilling and part of Sarah's perfumes were found in Hill's box.[59] Rather than criminal culture being particularly masculine, many women appear to have operated within a culture of criminality that overlapped with and coexisted alongside men's.[60]

A similar vision of criminal culture is indicated by the stories that women and men told when they were caught red-handed with stolen goods. Sometimes these tales were idiosyncratic. Jane Davies conceded that linens missing from the chamber in which she had slept had indeed fallen 'forth of her bosom' the next morning; her explanation was that Roger Chetwood must have 'put [them] into my bosom while I was asleep'![61] More commonly, people's descriptions of how they had come by and disposed of goods reveal that even imagined criminals were gendered. One well-rehearsed (though rarely

---

[57] PRO, CHES 21/1, fos. 177r, 177v, CHES 24/104/1, indictment and recognisances re. Ann Davenport (1595).

[58] Figures calculated from *Calendar of Assize Records: Kent Indictments. Charles II, 1660–1675*, ed. J.S. Cockburn (London, 1995); *Calendar of Assize Records: Kent Indictments. 1649–1659*, ed. J.S. Cockburn (London, 1989); *Calendar of Assize Records: Kent Indictments. Charles I*, ed. J.S. Cockburn (London, 1995); *Calendar of Assize Records: Kent Indictments. James I*, ed. J.S. Cockburn (London, 1980); *Calendar of Assize Records: Kent Indictments. Elizabeth I*, ed. J.S. Cockburn (London, 1979).

[59] CRO, QJF 89/2/29 (1661).

[60] Walker, 'Women, theft and the world of stolen goods', 83–5. MacKay, 'Why they stole', 623–39.

[61] CRO, QJF 81/3/50 (1653).

efficacious) excuse proffered by suspects was that they had purchased from or been given the goods by an anonymous stranger.[62] Men tended to blame unknown men, women tended to blame unknown women. A man who was so poor that he earned what living he could 'selling twigs' in Stockport claimed to have bought five pecks of barley and beans and a handful of oatmeal from 'a stranger'.[63] Other culprits were 'a boy whose name he knows not', an anonymous 'young man' wearing green breeches, and an unnamed boy whom the suspect met on the highway.[64] A young boy, whose father had put him through a hole he made into a shop in order to rob it, had been told that if caught he was to say that it was an unnamed pedlar who broke into the shop and put him in.[65] Women said that they had purchased the goods in question from a woman 'whose name she knew not';[66] 'a woman whom she never saw before nor knew, neither did she know where to find [her]';[67] 'a woman who was a stranger to me' (although they had sat and drunk together long enough to consume two quarts of ale);[68] 'two women travellers who lodged in my house, but I knoweth not [their] names... nor the place of their abode';[69] a 'strange woman' who hailed from 'a great way off', who 'desired me to carry one of her geese to Nantwich and sell it, and she would give me twopence'.[70] Depositions and examinations wherein named individuals were mentioned likewise suggest that male and female patterns of criminality followed general patterns of sociability and economic exchange, in which much male and female interaction occurred in gendered, if overlapping, circles.

It is worth noting that there existed one category of perceived criminal that was wholly male. Disbanded or absconding soldiers and sailors were routinely classified as potential thieves. Some contemporaries believed that impressment took the form of scouring 'prisons of thieves' and 'streets of rogues and vagabonds'.[71] When pressed men were no longer needed for military service it was thought that they would naturally revert to their criminal lifestyle. The problem was a real one. Demobilised troops were permitted to beg on their way home from service, and some clearly did engage in petty thievery in the absence of other means of subsistence.[72] The conduct of soldiers on their way to or from service abroad was said to be lamentable. One

---

[62] For a summary of common excuses, see Herrup, *Common Peace*, 146–9.
[63] CRO, QJF 51/4/54 (1623).
[64] CCRO, QSF/73/1/11 (1629); QSF/73/1/21 (1629); QSF/73/2/50 (1629).
[65] CCRO, MF/69/3/147 (1646). [66] CRO, QJF 75/4/80 (1647).
[67] CRO, QJF 79/3/74 (1651). [68] CCRO, QSF/73/2/71, /72 (1645).
[69] PRO, CHES 38/41, 'Examinations taken at Leftwich, 24 February 1682'.
[70] CRO, QJF 83/4/25 (1656). See also QSF/73/1/9; QSF/79/2/14, /63; QSF/73/1/11, /12; QSF/73/1/21; QSF/73/2/50; QSF/73/2/52.
[71] Barnaby Rich cited in A.L. Beier, *Masterless Men: The Vagrancy Problem in England, 1560–1640* (London, 1985), 94.
[72] Beier, *Masterless Men*, 93–5.

MP told the House of Commons that soldiers returning from La Rochelle in 1628 had stolen sheep, disturbed markets and fairs, engaged in highway robbery and burglary, and raped and murdered local people.[73] Civil war created further opportunities for soldiers in service to act wrongfully towards civilians. Court records for the civil war years teem with complaints such as that a 'party of horse' (that is, the cavalry) stole John Cottgreave's bay nag and that a Mollington man had 'a black bay nag' stolen by the King's soldiers quartered on him.[74] Not long before Royalist Chester succumbed to the Parliament, several soldiers under Captain Werden's command in Colonel Gamull's regiment forced their way through the doors of Ellen Woodcock's lodging in Chester, 'took me by the arms, and rifled me of my money, writings, and a gold ring together with some linens of my husband's'. Returning to her house after they had put her over the city walls, 'they seized upon my goods and divided the same amongst them and some of them lived in my house until this city was reduced to the Parliament's obedience'.[75]

War provided new opportunities for thievery for non-soldiers too. Raphe Pike, for instance, was 'a notorious plunderer and receiver of plundered goods' who confessed to having sold 100 plundered cattle.[76] Plundered goods were not restricted to men. It was reported that after the capture of 120 women with the King's forces at Nantwich, 'some poor women in the town took some of the best of their clothes from them, which they had got by plunder'.[77] Mary Bennett, widow, hostess of the Golden Lion Inn in Chester, was examined in 1646 about pawning and selling the property of Lady Ann Crosby, which had been left in her custody. Bennett said that it was Parliament soldiers (whose names she knew not) who had broken open the Lady's trunks when they took Foregate Street. She admitted that she had afterwards sold some of the clothes and linens on her own behalf and some others on behalf of one of her maidservants 'to some country people whose names she remembereth not'. Being asked about the provenance of the cloth out of which suits of clothes had been made up for her two sons, she replied that 'I bought two livery coats off a soldier', but being pressed about the soldier's name, she changed her story, saying that her late maidservant, Alice Walker, had bequeathed them to her. The tailor who had converted a coachman's sleeved cloak and another cloak into 'two suits of apparel' for Bennett's sons said that Bennett had told him she had bought them 'in the Common Hall since this City was reduced to the Parliament's obedience'. Her son, John, contrarily said that his mother sold two beds, a

---

[73] Sir Walter Erle cited in Carl Bridenbaugh, *Vexed and Troubled Englishmen, 1590–1642* (Oxford, 1968), 269.
[74] CCRO, MF69/2/78 (1646); MF69/2/88 (1646). See also MF69/2/130 (1646).
[75] CCRO, MF69/2/104, /107, /123 (1646).   [76] CCRO, MF69/2/86, /82 (1646).
[77] Cited in Hall, *Nantwich*, 166–7.

carpet, a covering for a cupboard, and one piece of 'stripe stuff hanging', but that the livery coats had been given to her by Alice Walker who had had them from Harry Wyggers (who later denied that he had sold Alice Walker any such things).[78] Whatever the truth of the matter, examining the criminal associations and networks of men and women in the above ways reveals that female criminality was not simply a subsidiary of male criminality, even when soldiers were involved, but existed alongside it.

The evidence for household and kinship playing a part in structuring criminal associations suggests likewise. A good many of those thefts carried out by pairs or groups of people involved members of households or kin, wherein household hierarchies rather than straightforward gender ones might determine who was most or equally implicated. In 1595, Peter Dewsbury, Thomas Dewsbury, widowed Alice Dewsbury and Roger Shawe (probably the Dewsburys' servant) were all suspected of involvement in the theft of two valuable heifers; Thomas Dewsbury was additionally prosecuted (and convicted) of burgling a house and stealing thirty-seven shillings and eightpence worth of clothes; Alice Dewsbury was indicted also as an accessory, knowing of the crime both before and afterwards, to Jane Dewsbury *alias* Watson and Ann Dewsbury for stealing a sheep; Ann and Peter Dewsbury had been convicted of felony at the previous sessions of October 1594.[79] Members of this husbandman's family were involved in a range of unlawful activities, but it is impossible for us to determine relative culpability or who might have instructed or encouraged whom to commit the crimes. The extent of family and household operations is undoubtedly greater than traceable associations suggest, as persons with different surnames could easily be related by blood or marriage, or were servants or apprentices in the households in question. We discover from a deposition that John Rudland was 'commanded' to steal slate from a neighbour's barn by Sarah Noden, his dame, who bid him 'deny the truth and not confess that she bade him to go into the barn as aforesaid' if he testified, but there is nothing otherwise in the record to connect these individuals.[80] Commentaries on crime and the law described as 'a lamentable spectacle' 'almost a whole family confederates in villainy', being 'two brothers and their sister, and one that pretended to be her husband', yet in practice such arrangements were probably the most common of criminal organisation.[81]

---

[78] MF69/1/41, /40, /55, /63 (1646).
[79] PRO, CHES 21/1, fo. 177v; CHES 24/104/1, recognisance re. Peter Dewsbury et al., jury return re. Peter Dewsbury and Thomas Dewsbury, jury return re. Jane Dewsbury, indictment of Thomas Dewsbury, indictment of Peter and Thomas Dewsbury, indictment of Jane Dewsbury and Ann Dewsbury (1595).
[80] CRO, QJF 89/1/91 (1661).
[81] Anon., *A True Narrative of the Proceedings at the Sessions-House in the Old-Bayley, April 11, 12, & 13, 1678* (London, 1678), 7.

Wives and husbands operated together even in activities that were primarily considered to be in the 'male' domain. For instance, the wife of Darcy Lascelles, a 'notorious highwayman' prosecuted in Cheshire in the late 1660s, was implicated in his robberies, although in quite what manner it is difficult to say. She certainly accompanied or met up with him on his unlawful forays into the countryside, and apparently had on one occasion thirty-four ill-gotten guineas 'quilted in her sleeve'.[82] Ann Dean had taken up with horse-thief, highwayman and cattle-rustler, Hugh Tunnycliff, in the 1590s – they passed themselves off as man and wife although they were each already married – and she might well have been one of those 'others' who committed felonies 'by his privity' about whom the Chester authorities expressed concern.[83] When women and men were suspected to work together in crime, the male was not inevitably the senior partner. Even when husbands and wives were both implicated in dishonest dealings, the woman might carry out the burglary itself while her husband took a back seat as in the case of Margaret Cally, who in 1590 broke into her employer's house on several occasions and stole a large number of clothes, linens and household goods, some of which were later sold in London.[84] Similarly, in 1622, both Barbara Smith and Thomas Smith were initially suspected of breaking into a house and taking nearly twelve shillings' worth of clothes and linens, but in the event, Thomas was not even prosecuted. Barbara was convicted and hanged.[85]

In all, an analysis of gendered patterns of criminality does not lead us to conclude that the difference between women's and men's criminality was as fundamental as has been assumed. Considering theft in the context of male and female work and networks of exchange does not entirely explain away discrepancies between what women and men stole, but it does offer a more satisfactory understanding than a mere reliance on stereotypical female and male characteristics. Female theft should not be interpreted in terms of pettiness or lack of bravado any more than male theft should be seen as inevitably profound and courageous.

BEFORE THE COURTS

Various studies have shown that for felonious property crime men had a higher conviction rate than women. This has conventionally been interpreted as evidence that women were considered less criminally dangerous than men,

---

[82] *Calendar of State Papers: Domestic. Charles II*, Vol. CCLIV, Major Anderton to Williamson, 21 June 1669; Ralph Hope to Williamson, 4 January 1669; Hope to Williamson, 24 February 1669, 374, 145, 208,
[83] CCRO, QSE/5/103, /97, /100–/102 (1597).
[84] CCRO, QSF/40/3, /4, /38, /54, /57–/63, /65, /92 (1590).
[85] PRO, CHES 21/3, fo. 71v, CHES 24/116/4, recognisance, indictment and jury return re. Barbara Smith (1622).

more inferior, dependent and in need of protection; hence women were objects of judicial clemency.[86] The conviction rate for property offences in late sixteenth- and seventeenth-century Cheshire was indeed higher for men, although women were not far behind – two out of three arraigned women and seven out of ten men were found guilty.[87] However, the reliability of comparative figures depends upon precisely what is being compared. Aggregating all forms of theft produces a misleading impression of the relative treatment of men and women because both sexes were not always equally represented in all the relevant criminal activities. In Cheshire in the 1590s, for example, nearly two-thirds of male defendants were convicted but just under half of female ones; of these, over half of the men but fewer than a third of the women were executed. However, in that decade, few women but many men were prosecuted for aggravated forms of theft – burglary, robbery, horse-theft.[88] This impacted upon the disposition of verdicts and sentences, for the latter non-clergiable crimes had a high conviction and execution rate. When men's and women's fates before the courts for grand larceny are compared, we shall see that a different picture emerges. Before we conclude that female offenders were recipients of peculiar leniency on the parts of jurors and judges, then, we must ensure that like is compared with like. In the following discussion, I shall compare the verdicts and sentences for specific categories of offence and consider legal outcomes in particular decades and even individual sessions. By comparing very specific categories, we might discern more accurately the relative judicial treatment of men and women.

Larcenists

Larceny was by far the most common property offence committed by both men and women, and as such is the most representative of their experiences before the courts. Larceny was defined legally as the 'felonious and fraudulent taking and carrying away by any man or woman, of the mere personal goods of another' neither from the person nor by housebreaking. Grand larceny, wherein goods stolen were valued at one shilling or more, was a capital offence with forfeiture of all goods to the Crown.[89] Petty larceny, wherein stolen items amounted to no more than eleven pence, was punished

---

[86] Elton, 'Introduction', in Cockburn, *Crime in England*, 13; Hanawalt, 'Female felon', 256; Herrup, *Common Peace*, 149–51; Sharpe, *County Study*, 95 and Table 5; Wiener, 'Sex roles and crime', *passim*. For general execution rates see Cockburn, *Introduction*, 125; Herrup, *Common Peace*, ch. 7; Sharpe, *County Study*, 96, 109, 134, 136; Sharpe, *Crime*, 64–5.
[87] 66.2 per cent of women; 71.5 per cent of men.
[88] As many men were charged with committing these crimes alone as there were women for all property offences.
[89] However, forfeiture was rarely applied in practice for juries systematically assessed offenders as having 'no goods'.

corporally, by whipping. From the distinction between grand and petty larceny, a legal fiction arose: in cases of grand larceny, juries were permitted to undervalue the goods stolen in order to find a verdict of petty larceny, thereby removing an offender from the reach of the death penalty.[90] This applied to both sexes. A second legal fiction attendant upon grand larceny proceedings was the benefit of clergy. In cases where the stolen goods did not exceed forty shillings in value, a convict who demonstrated an ability to 'read' by citing certain lines of a well-known psalm, escaped the gallows and was instead branded on the brawn of the left thumb with a 'T' (for thief). Women were not eligible to claim this benefit, although branding without the reading qualification was introduced as a punishment for women in 1623.[91] This inequity had a visible effect on judicial decisions.

The case for judicial leniency towards women charged with grand larceny is poor. Granted, late sixteenth- and seventeenth-century trial juries devalued women's thefts to less than a shilling proportionately more often than they did men's, most probably because of women's ineligibility to plead the benefit of clergy.[92] But in all else women came off worst. First, grand juries returned a smaller proportion of *ignoramus* verdicts in cases against women, which meant that women were disproportionately put on trial.[93] Secondly, petty juries found arraigned women guilty relatively more often than they did men.[94] Thirdly, once convicted, women were almost twice as likely to be sent to their deaths on the hanging tree.[95] Instituting branding as a punishment for women did little in the long term to ensure that women escaped the gallows. Despite a decrease in the numbers of women sentenced to hang for larceny immediately after branding was introduced, in the period between 1624 and 1670 fewer than one in three female larcenists were branded as an alternative to hanging, compared with over half of their male counterparts.[96]

Of course, the entire context in which the theft occurred or that surrounded the case, and not merely gender, was important in determining the outcomes

---

[90] Coke, *Third Part of the Institutes*, 107, 109, at 107; Pulton, *De Pace Regis*, fo. 129r. Juries had depreciated the value of the stolen property since the reign of Edward III: Sir William Holdsworth, *A History of English Law*, 5th edn (London, 1966), Vol. III, 367.

[91] Branding had been a means of punishing male felons since 1490; it was extended to women under the 1623 Act concerning benefit of clergy.

[92] 45.5 per cent of women and 37.1 per cent of men were found guilty of petty larceny only and whipped. These and the following figures are calculated from sampled years in the 1590s, 1620s, 1640s, 1650s and 1660s.

[93] *Ignoramus* verdicts were returned in 20.3 per cent of cases against men and 12.3 per cent of cases against women.

[94] 26 per cent of male and 22.8 per cent of female defendants were acquitted.

[95] 31.8 per cent and 16.6 per cent respectively of convicted women and men were sentenced to hang.

[96] Overall, 30.3 per cent of women; 50.6 per cent of men. Walker, 'Crime, gender and social order', 186–7.

of trials. When motivation was believed to be hunger, the courts were generally sympathetic. John Robinson, for instance, was whipped in 1622 for the theft of bacon and cheese. The fact that he did not take any of the other things of far greater value from the house worked to his advantage. He himself claimed not to have eaten for a day and two nights before the incident and never to have stolen anything previously in his whole life.[97] Thomas Jones, a Shropshire labourer, was branded after explaining the theft and sale of six swine that he found at the roadside in terms of his being very poor and hungry; he was 'constrained' by the need for relief.[98] Conversely, aggravating characteristics were present in the thefts of those larcenists who were condemned to die. In the 1640s' sample, for instance, only one male and one female larcenist were so sentenced. John Stanway was charged with a total of seven offences: five burglaries of which he was convicted of three, and horse-theft, as well as grand larceny of six sheep and an iron chain.[99] Larceny no doubt contributed to the judge's view of Stanway as an undesirable, but it was his convictions for three burglaries that ensured the judgement of death in Stanway's case. Jane Miller, an unmarried maidservant, was sentenced to hang for stealing forty shillings in cash out of her master's chest. Here, the violation of the trust placed in her and the lack of respect for her master's goods and his right to be unmolested in his own home made Miller's theft particularly heinous. Even here, death was not inevitable. Miller was afterwards reprieved by the judge and remained in prison at Chester for three and a half years until at last she benefited from the general royal pardon of 1652.[100] Other thefts wherein profit or premeditation were thought to have been prime motivators were also treated seriously. Hence Hugh Baguley, a shoemaker who had stolen four pieces of tanned leather worth thirty shillings, presumably out of which to make shoes to sell, fled rather than risk being found guilty and executed. The same applied to Leonard Banister, whose occupation as a petty chapman selling small wares up and down the country meant that he could easily sell things he had stolen, even though on this occasion he was suspected of stealing only one pair of stockings.[101] Butcher John Bennet, who was tried on five separate counts of theft of cattle whose meat he intended to sell, was convicted and hanged.[102]

[97] CRO, QJF 51/4/61, /34 (1623). See also QJF 53/4/66, /118 (1624).
[98] CRO, QJF 53/4/66, /118 (1625).
[99] PRO, CHES 24/127/1/6–/12; CHES 21/4, fo. 146r (1648).
[100] PRO, CHES 24/127/2, indictment re. Jane Miller; CHES 21/4, fo. 179v (1648); CHES 21/4, fo. 267r (1652).
[101] PRO, CHES 24/118/3, indictment re. Hugh Baguley, CHES 21/3, fo. 129r (1626); CHES 24/118/4, indictment of Leonard Banister, CHES 21/3, fo. 146v (1626).
[102] PRO, CHES 24/117/3, indictments and jury return re. John Bennet, CHES 21/3, fo. 108r (1624).

The value of goods stolen in larceny had some impact on the judicial treatment of women and men, too. Generally, the lower the value, the greater the likelihood of devaluation and a finding of petty larceny for both sexes. In the 1620s, for example, no defendant, male or female, who stole goods worth between one and ten shillings was hanged for larceny alone; only those who were convicted of multiple thefts including aggravated offences were sentenced to death. A death sentence was also rare for thefts of goods worth between ten and forty shillings although for this category of theft women were more likely to be whipped on reduced charges and men more likely to be branded.[103] However, this discrepancy in punishment cannot lead us to conclude that women were generally being treated leniently, for juries reduced charges against over two-thirds of the men but only half of the women. In practical terms, this meant that women were proportionately more often left to face the threat of capital punishment.[104] The death penalty was most in evidence where goods were valued in excess of forty shillings. Even here, branding remained more common for men than for women (despite the fact that such offences were ostensibly non-clergiable).

By examining in detail individual sittings of the courts, it becomes possible to identify contradictions in the wider view. Such anomalies tend to be overlooked, or subsumed within an aggregate of offences. Many of the women who were hanged could have been saved from the gallows, for instance, if the grand or petty jury had decided to reduce the charge against them. In October 1591, fourteen men and five women were put on trial for grand larceny. Of these, one man and four women were sentenced to death. Five of the remaining men had their charges reduced to petty larceny by the petty jury, which was an option the jury could have selected in the cases of at least three of the female offenders. One of the women, Ellen Burton, was subsequently pardoned for having stolen a silver spoon worth 3s. But Alice Tomlinson and Elizabeth Smythe were both hanged for the theft of a gown and other clothes valued at 3s. 4d. The value of Tomlinson's and Smythe's spoils is significant, for 3s. 4d. was the very sum that was acknowledged to have been rendered by inflation the latter-day equivalent to the one shilling threshold between petty and grand larceny.[105] Yet there was no undervaluation of goods stolen by these two women. Meanwhile, at the same sessions, John Williamson and Richard Jennings were whipped for stealing clothes worth 4s. 7d. and 3s.

---

[103] Relative male and female felons who were whipped, branded and hanged were respectively 16.7 per cent, 75 per cent, and 8.3 per cent; and 37.5 per cent, 50 per cent, 12.5 per cent.
[104] For grand larcenies of less than forty shillings in value, 52.9 per cent of women were whipped, 29.4 per cent were branded, and 17.6 per cent were hanged; the comparative figures for men were 65 per cent, 27.5 per cent and 7.5 per cent.
[105] David Dean, *Law-making and Society in Late Elizabethan England: The Parliament of England, 1584–1601* (Cambridge, 1996), 192.

respectively, having had the charges against them reduced. It is simply not possible to deduce why women were treated more severely than the men at this assize court.

Overall, the evidence for grand larceny does not support the view either that women received especial judicial clemency relative to men or even that they received equitable treatment.

Burglars and housebreakers

While contemporaries might have believed that 'smaller rogueries...deserved the brand' rather than hanging, there was a consensus that aggravated thefts such as housebreaking and burglary merited more severe punishment. The law was said 'most prudently' to punish housebreaking with theft of goods worth five shillings or more and all burglary with death.[106] These offences were removed from the scope of benefit of clergy in the sixteenth century and consequently had a higher rate of execution than grand larceny. Moreover, the state regularly proclaimed that a reward of ten pounds was in store for anyone who apprehended a burglar or housebreaker who was subsequently convicted.[107] Whereas larcenists were often thought to have acted upon simple opportunism, the motives attributed to burglars and housebreakers were the more sinful compulsions of 'greedy covetousness and unquenchable desire of lucre'.[108] Burglary and housebreaking were also perceived to be far more violatory than larceny 'since every man's house ought to be his castle, and greatest place of security'. Indeed, it was technically burglary even when a building's barriers were merely broken rather than fully trangressed, such as when a pane of glass was smashed and goods hooked out of the window without the thief actually entering the house.[109] Burglary was particularly heinous as it was a night-time offence committed in darkness when occupants of the household were most defenceless: 'nor could any one sleep in peace, were there not some extraordinary restraints put upon their desires who live in the world like perfect beasts of Troy, and to gratify their lusts and debaucheries are ready to devour (if it lay in their

---

[106] *A Narrative of the Sessions, Or, An Account of the Notorious High-way-men and Others, Lately Tryed and Condemned at the Old-Bayly* (London, 1673), 5–6.

[107] For example, Parliamentary Ordinance, 8 November 1649; *A Proclamation for Discovery of Robberies and Burglaries, and for a Reward to the Discoverers* (London, 1661); *A Proclamation for the Apprehension of Certain Notorious Robbers* (London, 1668). These proclamations extended also to highway robbers.

[108] *Narrative of the Sessions, Or, An Account of the Notorious High-way-men and Others*, 3; Beard, *Theatre of Gods Judgements*, 438.

[109] Hence, Margery Barker, a Congleton spinster, was sentenced to hang after removing eight yards of serge 'forth of the shop window' of a mercer; she had also cut a woman's purse. PRO, CHES 21/1, fo. 177r, CHES 24/104/1, indictments, recognisances and jury returns re. Margery Barker (1595).

power) all their fellow creatures'. Such 'beasts' were commonly imaged as male: tales of notorious burglaries rarely included female protagonists; the dangerous 'rogues, vagabonds and sturdy beggars' whom public discourse imaged as would-be burglars were predominantly male too.[110] The threat and damage associated with the boundary violation that these offences entailed were associated with masculine action.[111] Thus one pamphleteer insisted (erroneously) that burglary was 'rarely if ever attempted' by women and pronounced Martha Harman's breaking into a house 'a matchless piece of female impudence'. Another account of three female burglars described them as having 'grown so courageous in villainy', but was unable to explain their possession of such a male attribute other than, paradoxically, in terms of women's innate sinfulness: 'because from the female sex sprung all our woes and bad inclinations at first'.[112]

The evidence for the way such gendered stereotypes informed conviction and sentencing in housebreaking and burglary is inconclusive. On the one hand, men did have a significantly higher conviction rate than women: over three-quarters of men arraigned for housebreaking were convicted, compared to under two-thirds of female defendants.[113] This might be related to the fact that women constituted overall a minority of such 'dangerous' criminals, which together with the persistence of the stereotype of the male burglar would make women defendants seem less of a threat to social order. Certainly, at times when women became more visible as offenders the discrepancy between conviction rates and punishments for men and women diminished. In the 1620s, for instance, despite men being more numerous among those initially suspected of housebreaking, precisely the same number of men and women were arraigned. The trial jury not only convicted all but one of each sex, but also reduced the charges to larceny for exactly the same number.[114] On the other hand, this apparent equity masks the disadvantages faced by women before branding was enacted as a punishment for women in 1623. Before the Act, the absence of an alternative punishment for women meant that they were disproportionately more likely to hang than men for housebreaking for there was nothing to be gained by juries reducing the charges against them. In contrast, few women were hanged for that offence

---

[110] *Instructions to be Observed by the Several Justices of Peace in the Several Counties within this Commonwealth, for the Better Prevention of Robberies, Burglaries, and Other Outrages* (London, 1649); *Complete Justice*, 29; Parliamentary Ordinance, 8 November 1649.
[111] See above, pp. 33–74.
[112] *The Confession and Execution of the Eight Prisoners Suffering at Tyburn on Wednesday the 30th of August 1676* (London, 1676), 5; *A True Narrative of the Proceedings at the Sessions-House in the Old-Bayly, at a Sessions of Peace There Held; Which Began on Wednesday the 23rd Of this Instant August, and ended on Fryday the 25th 1676* (London, 1676), 3.
[113] 77.6 per cent of men; 63 per cent of women.   [114] The grand jury behaved accordingly.

once branding became a viable option.[115] Throughout the period, daytime breaking into outhouses or dwelling-houses when no one was in tended to be punished less severely than when people were present who could be put in fear.[116]

For the more serious offence of night-time burglary, juries were tougher on women as well as on men: they convicted almost three-quarters of the women who were tried. Sentencing followed accordingly, although overall women remained less likely to be hanged than men. Housebreaking and burglary were non-clergiable crimes. For women to benefit, juries would first have to find them guilty of either housebreaking for goods worth less than five shillings or grand larceny. The introduction of branding as an alternative punishment for women might have encouraged victims to prosecute – the numbers of women prosecuted for burglary greatly increased relative to men in the years immediately following the change in the law – but it did not lead to female burglars being routinely let off the hook by well-disposed juries reducing charges against them.[117] Women whose spoils amounted to less than ten shillings were most likely to be found guilty of larceny only and branded.[118] Nonetheless about three of every four women and four of five men were convicted of burglary in the 1620s.[119] Overall, there was less of a discrepancy between male and female conviction rates and sentences for burglary and housebreaking when women were more visible as criminals.

Here too, however, gender interacted with other categories in informing decisions. The correlation between the value of the items and the sentence passed applied also to burglary and housebreaking, though to a lesser extent than with larceny. The number of felons hanged for burglary and housebreaking increased proportionately with the value of goods stolen, and almost all those whose charges were reduced to larceny had stolen goods valued at less than forty shillings (which was the qualification laid down by statute). Thus when in 1624 Mary Williamson, Joan Read and Patience Baylie were convicted of burgling over ten pounds' worth of Raphe Leycester of Toft's goods out of Toft Hall, Leycester's gentry status as well as the value of their

---

[115] In the sample of assizes held in 1626, 1628, and the autumn sessions of 1624, and sampled years of the 1640s, 1650s and 1660s. See also Beattie, 'Criminality of women', 95.
[116] For example, PRO, CHES 21/5, fo. 2r, CHES 24/134/1, indictment, jury return and order re. Sarah Merrett *alias* Stanley *alias* Danson (1663).
[117] Women accounted for 13.6 per cent of those accused of burglary in the five sessions before the 1623 Act introducing branding as a female punishment came into effect, which is not dissimilar to the 10.2 per cent in the 1590s. In the five subsequent sessions examined for the 1620s, women constituted 39 per cent of accused burglars. For the decade as a whole, 28.2 per cent of the total accused were female defendants.
[118] For example, PRO, CHES 24/118/4, indictment re. Ann Bate, Elizabeth Chaddock and Mary Smith, CHES 21/3, fo. 144r (1626); they were prosecuted for two burglaries of goods worth respectively 6s. 2d. and 2s. 2d., convicted of housebreaking for 5s., and branded.
[119] 72 per cent of women; 80.4 per cent of men.

spoils marked their case as particularly abhorrent to the judge. Williamson, Read and Baylie were uncommon in having had the charge against them reduced by the petty jury. But it did them no good. The three women and their male accomplice, who was unusually denied benefit of clergy on grounds that he 'did not read', were all hanged.[120] Confessing to one's crimes did not necessarily lead to clemency. Thomas Nevill pleaded guilty to the charge of burgling a shop and stealing at least fifty pounds' worth of goods, as well as stealing two horses, and breaking out of gaol. 'Nor could he be persuaded otherwise'; 'his reason was, because he knew it would be proved against him', and given the value and nature of his crimes, 'he had no hopes of life'.[121] Nevill's pessimism was well founded. He was indeed hanged. In contrast, convicted burglar Thomas Janson was reprieved by the judge. Janson's credentials for mercy might well have included poverty: Nathan Janson, his accomplice in another offence (housebreaking) for which they were acquitted at the same sessions, was described as 'a poor boy', and during one of the burglaries Thomas had stolen merely sixpence worth of food, which he ate rather than sold. Dalton and others interpreted the legal category of burglary as not applicable 'to poor persons that upon hunger break and steal under the value of 12d'. Perhaps also relevant was the fact that Thomas Janson had burgled a stable – technically, the boundaries of the dwelling-house in cases of burglary extended to all outbuildings, but everyone knew that breaking into an outhouse where people were not expected to be asleep was less outrageous than entering the dwelling-house itself.[122] Nonetheless, Thomas Janson's story does not end happily. After his reprieve, he turned his expertise in breaking into places to breaking out of prison. He was recaptured in Lancashire, brought back to Chester, and sent to his death on the gallows after the following great sessions.[123]

Youth was a further category that influenced judicial decisions. In September 1624, four men and four women were found guilty of burglary. The women each applied for benefit of belly, but failed the pregnancy test. All eight offenders were thus sentenced to hang. Yet Barbara Deane was reprieved, whipped and set at large at the instigation of the jury and acquiescence of the Chief Justice of Chester. It comes as no surprise that the jury of matrons discovered she was not pregnant, for Deane was only a child, perhaps as young as seven years old if the indictment against her which describes her as 'an infant' is legally precise. Whatever the case, she was probably not

---

[120] PRO, CHES 21/3, fo. 97v, CHES 24/117/2, indictment, recognisance and jury return re. John Williamson et al. (1624).
[121] *The True Narrative of the Proceedings at the Sessions-House in the Old-Bayly which Began on Wednesday the 26th of this Instant May, 1680* (London, 1680), 3.
[122] Dalton, *Countrey Justice*, 226; *Complete Justice*, 31; Forster, *Layman's Lawyer*, 11.
[123] PRO, CHES 21/5, fos. 59r, 67v, CHES 24/135/5, indictments and jury return re. Thomas Janson (1667).

more than thirteen years of age – the clerk who drew up the jury return noted that she was 'a young wench'.[124] Jurists were of the opinion that an offence could not be classified as burglary if the offender was under the age of fourteen, partly because the sense of violation and fear was diminished along with the offender's age. In Barbara Deane's case, her young age rather than her sex saved her life. Much evidence suggests that children and adolescents were the most likely candidates for leniency from grand and petty juries in early modern England for a range of felonies.[125] In the case of 'a very young youth' who had 'childishly and innocently pleaded guilty' upon his indictment for stealing some silk ribboning from his master, the court 'ordered him to be brought back to the bar to plead on his bill' so that he could plead 'not guilty' and be acquitted.[126] A fifteen-year-old servant girl was brought to trial after her mistress found several garments marked with her own name in the girl's trunk, but 'because nothing else could be laid to her charge and the maid young enough to be taught more honesty', the jury returned a partial verdict of guilty to the value of 10*d.* in order that she be whipped instead of branded or hanged.[127] 'Hugh Jones, a boy not above twelve years of age', was caught red-handed picking a woman's pocket, 'but he being young, the jury by the direction of the [judge] brought him in guilty but to the value of ninepence', thereby allowing him to be whipped for petty larceny and discharged.[128] Pardons were granted on similar grounds. Thomas Pace, for instance, was pardoned for horse-theft, 'the evidence against him being uncertain and he being a young man and this his first offence'; John Hobbes pleaded a pardon on account of his being under twenty-one years old as well as for the sake of his innocent wife.[129]

Cutpurses and pickpockets

Cutpurses and pickpockets figured among 'the caterpillars of this nation' condemned in rogue literature. Unlike other categories of felon, in popular imagination cutpurses and pickpockets were frequently female: 'Of this

[124] Dalton, *Countrey Justice*, 226; *Complete Justice*, 31.
[125] Herrup, *Common Peace*, 129 and 129 n. 49. Cf. Sir William Blackstone who maintained that criminal responsibility was 'not so much measured by years and days, as by the strength of the delinquent's understanding and judgement', *Commentaries*, Vol. IV, 23. See also *A True Narrative of the Proceedings at the Sessions-House in the Old-Bayley, at a Sessions there held on the 1st and 2nd of June 1677* (London, 1677), 2.
[126] *A Narrative of the Proceedings at the Sessions, Held in Justice-Hall at the Old-Baly. Shewing the Several Crimes of the Mallefactors* (London, 1676), 3.
[127] *A True Narrative of the Proceedings at the Sessions-House in the Old-Baily: begun the 28 and continued till the 31 of August 1678* (London, 1678), 3.
[128] *The True Narrative of the Proceedings at the Sessions-House in the Old-Bayly which Began on Wednesday the 8th of this Instant December 1680* (London, 1680), 3.
[129] PRO, SO 3/14 March 1629, 'A pardon for Thomas Pace...'; *Calendar of State Papers: Domestic. Charles II*, 216 (1661).

sort there be as many women as men.' The secret nature of the acts, being undertaken without the victim's knowledge and without overt violence to the person, was compatible with negative feminine traits in much the same way as were poisoning and witchcraft. Women practitioners were frequently described as whores, 'who when they are wapping [copulating] will be sure to geld the man's pocket'.[130] Prosecutions tell a similar story. In Cheshire, women and men were prosecuted in equal numbers. In Surrey, women outnumbered men by two to one (probably because figures for cutpursing and pocketpicking included those of prostitutes who stole from their clients' pockets while the latter slept or were drunk).[131] The labels 'cutpurse' and 'pickpocket' were used interchangeably, though technically they described different types of thief. Cutpurses cut the strings by which purses were attached to their owners' girdles, whereas pickpockets surreptitiously removed purses, boxes, money, watches and other valuables from people's pockets. Both could be extremely skilled: during a lengthy civil trial at the Cheshire great sessions in 1663 'the High Sheriff, sitting in his charge, in the face of the court, had his watch stolen out of his pocket'![132] They were also by definition premeditated acts. This was reinforced by suspicions that before pickpockets 'put in a man's pocket but a middle and a forefinger... they jog the pocket, either to know whether there be any money there, or to jumble it all into one corner thereof, that they may make but one diving'.[133]

Characterised by secrecy, deception and violation of the person's physical boundaries, one might expect cutpurses and pickpockets to have high conviction and execution rates. Certainly, the perceived seriousness of their crime made it one of the first offences to be removed from benefit of clergy in the sixteenth century.[134] Yet despite the distinguishing features, most sixteenth- and seventeenth-century defendants, male and female, charged with these crimes, did not end their lives on the gallows.[135] There are several reasons why this was so. Pickpockets and cutpurses were infrequently prosecuted. Compared to other categories of offender, they might not have appeared to the courts as threatening the fabric of social order. In fifteen years sampled for eastern Sussex by Cynthia Herrup, a mere four cutpurses were convicted, only two of whom were hanged.[136] Over a twelve-year period in later seventeenth-century Surrey, only two persons (both women) were sentenced

---

[130] *The Catterpillers of this Nation Anatomized, In a Brief Yet Notable Discovery of Housebreakers, Pick-pockets, etc.* (London, 1659), 4. See also, for example, Pietro Aretino, *The Fifth and Last Part of the Wandering Whore...* (s.n., 1661), 13–15; *The Lawyers Clarke Trappand by the Crafty Whore of Canterbury, or A True Relation of the Whole Life of Mary Manders* (London, 1663), 2.
[131] Beattie, *Crime and the Courts*, 180.
[132] *Calendar of State Papers: Domestic. Charles II*, 330, T.T. to Williamson, 7 November 1663.
[133] *Catterpillers of this Nation Anatomized*, 4.   [134] Statute 8 Elizabeth I c. 4 (1566).
[135] See also Sharpe, *County Study*, 102.   [136] Herrup, *Common Peace*, 169, Table 7.1.

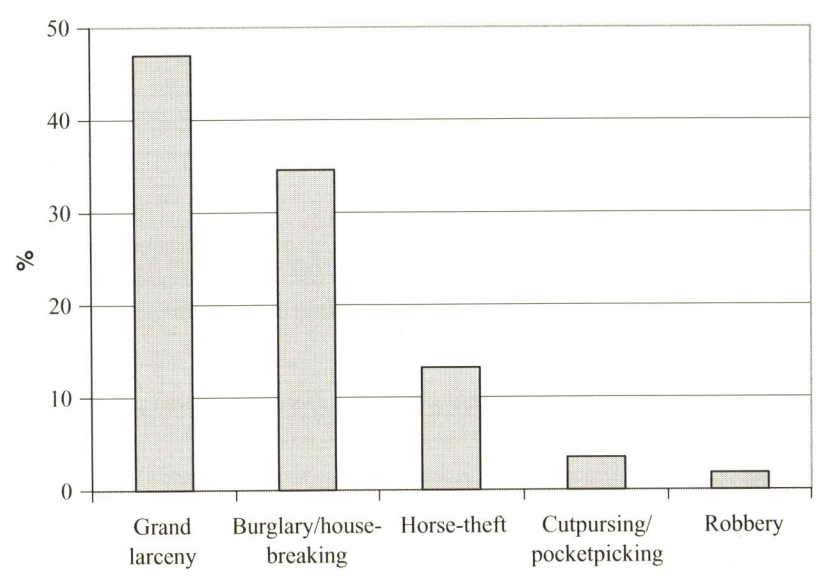

Figure 5.3 Categories of prosecuted property offences

to death for the offence and both were pardoned. In comparison to the numbers of those condemned to die for other crimes in the same period – in Surrey, twenty-five for robbery, thirty-five for burglary or housebreaking, and twenty-eight for horse-theft – cutpursing has a very low profile in terms of both convictions and proportions of convicts actually hanged.[137] In the thirty years of Cheshire court records sampled for quantitative analysis in this present study, only twenty-four individuals were officially prosecuted as cutpurses or pickpockets – an average of well under one prosecution per year. Figure 5.3 shows how small a proportion this was of prosecuted property offences. However, the infrequency of prosecutions cannot alone explain why cutpurses fared better before the courts than other uncommon thieves such as robbers.

Nor does the monetary value of cutpurses' spoils correspond neatly with judicial decisions, although it was understood that if the amount stolen was less than a shilling 'it will not amount to felony unto death'.[138] Offenders often offered as a mitigating notion the fact that a stolen purse contained little. Elizabeth Owen, for instance, in 1588 claimed that she had 'never cut any purse before this time but one with seven pence in it'.[139] More often than not, there was no obvious relation between the amount stolen and the

---

[137] Beattie, *Crime and the Courts*, 454, Table 9.1.
[138] Dalton, *Countrey Justice*, 229; *Complete Justice*, 55.   [139] CCRO, QSE/5/2 (1588).

outcome of a trial. In April 1622, for example, a Staffordshire labourer, William Heath *alias* Aston was charged with picking a man's pocket, and two women, Elizabeth Anglisey and Elizabeth Jackson, were arraigned as cutpurses. William Heath *alias* Aston, who had stolen 5s. 6d., pleaded his clergy and was branded after the petty jury found him guilty of the reduced charge of grand larceny. But Elizabeth Anglisey was convicted and hanged, even though the purse she stole from Hester Williamson contained only 11d.[140] Elizabeth Jackson meanwhile was whipped despite being acquitted, her treatment most likely in line with a policy that known cutpurses who 'be not convicted of felony be dealt with as rogues and so punished'. At another sessions of the assizes, this time in 1649, Priscilla Daniel, a labourer's wife, and Ann Hyde *alias* Ostler, who was unmarried, were together indicted for stealing out of a man's pocket a purse (itself worth sixpence) containing eighteen shillings. Priscilla was acquitted; Ann was found guilty and sentenced to hang. It may have been that although they were suspected to have been partners in crime, Priscilla 'not being in [Ann's] company when the fact was committed, could not be found guilty', as was the practice in some other pickpocketing trials.[141] For the record, neither of the men who were prosecuted for cutpursing in Cheshire in the 1640s was arraigned: one was discharged after the grand jury returned an *ignoramus* verdict; an indictment was not filed against the other.[142] Comparing verdicts and sentences for individuals at particular court sessions illuminates the problems that historians face in trying to identify and explain patterns of judicial decision-making.

Pamphlet accounts of trials help us to build a fuller picture of the sorts of considerations taken into account by juries and judges. A woman was indicted at the Old Bailey 'for cutting a gentlewoman's pocket, and taking from her a box and five shillings and three groats'. When the woman was searched, 'a box like [the gentlewoman's], and the same sum... in it' had been found in her possession. But the gentlewoman could not and 'would not swear that was her box, nor that her money, every like not being the same'. The suspect was therefore acquitted.[143] In another trial, a young man was accused of stealing a box and 21s. 6d. out of a 'young maiden's' pocket while she was 'dancing with the milkwoman', and delivering it immediately to another boy who ran away with it. 'But our young practitioner was not so

---

[140] PRO, CHES 21/3, fos. 66v, 67r; CHES 24/115/4, indictments, recognisances and jury returns re. Elizabeth Jackson, Elizabeth Anglisey and William Heath *alias* Aston (1622). For the policy of punishing as rogues known cutpurses upon their acquittal, see Order re. cutpurses, Eaton Hall Grosvenor MSS, Quarter Sessions Papers, Box 1/2/33.

[141] *The True Narrative of the Proceedings at the Sessions-House in the Old-Bayly which Began on Thursday the 15th of this Instant January 1679* (London, 1680), 2.

[142] PRO, CHES 21/4, fo. 88r, CHES 24/125/4, indictment re. Thomas Gasconye (1640); CHES 21/4 fo. 153r, CHES 24/127/1, recognisance re. John Edge (1648).

[143] *Narrative of the Proceedings at the Sessions, held in Justice-Hall*, 6.

much Master of Art as to perform the exploit clearly, for he was seen by the girl diving into her pocket and seen by another deliver away the prize.' He was convicted.[144] This young fellow was unfortunate. For in many comparable cases, cutpurses and pickpockets were either acquitted or found guilty on a reduced charge.

Part of the reason why this might have been so lies in a contradiction in attitudes towards the offence. On the one hand, cutpursing has been termed one of 'the most feared [offences] and most widely regarded as serious', which explains its non-clergiable status. On the other hand, the historian who described it thus was able also to maintain that it was a 'very trivial' crime, one that was not regarded as sufficiently serious and threatening to prosecutors or the courts, which is why it 'put few people in danger of being hanged'.[145] This contradiction is not explicable primarily in terms of the crime being viewed as less serious over time. Secret boundary violation continued to be conceived as very harmful into the eighteenth century. Successful cutpurses – those who imperceptibly stole purses, picked pockets and got away unnoticed – were viewed as dangerous criminals throughout the early modern period. Hence, 'known' cutpurses, when they were finally caught, tended to be treated without clemency. Paradoxically, however, in many cases, the very fact of having been discovered and prosecuted militated against offenders being labelled as particularly dangerous. Whereas, in comparison, prosecuted burglars were nearly always caught after *successfully* carrying out a burglary, prosecuted cutpurses were generally, by definition, failures. What made their crime so terrible – its secret nature and violation of the person – did not really apply to them if they were caught or observed in the act. Richard Owen, for instance, 'a young fellow with no hair on his face', was seen pressing against people in Chester's salt market holding a cudgel, which immediately marked him out as 'a knave and worthy to be a suspect'.[146] Although their intentions were bad, such offenders had managed neither secrecy nor true violation, for the knowledge of the victim and prevention of a successful theft kept the victim's boundaries intact. This was reaffirmed by the capturing of the offender and the return of the purse or box and was confirmed by law itself. For in order for the offence to qualify as a non-clergiable felony, 'the thief must have an actual possession of the thing severed from the person of the owner'.[147] Hence, most prosecuted cutpurses, male or female, were not treated severely. Many more were never brought to trial, like the 'boy in the blueish jerkin' who cut the purse of an apothecary's wife. He begged her to let him go and not to prosecute him, saying that he

---

[144] *A Narrative of the Proceedings at the Sessions in the Old-Baily, June the 1st 1677* (London, 1677), 1–2.
[145] Beattie, *Crime and the Courts*, 423, 181.   [146] CCRO, QSF/73/2/52 (1628).
[147] *Complete Justice*, 55; Dalton, *Countrey Justice*, 229.

would pay her back when he next came to Chester, but that if he never came there again he hoped she would forgive him.[148]

Robbers

While the violence of cutpursing was concealed, the legal category of robbery, which included most notoriously highway robbery, was theft that involved overt threatened or actual violence against the person. To qualify as robbery, the victim of the crime 'must be put in fear', 'though that thing taken be but to the value of a halfpenny'.[149] Lewis ap Jenkyn described his ordeal at the hands of three highwaymen: they 'set upon me with their swords drawn... and rent my cloak in pulling me off my horse and then bound my hands and feet... When they had bound me, they turned me grovelling with my face downwards to the earth, and when they had robbed me they rode away.'[150] If prosecutions are an accurate guide, robbery was in practice an overwhelmingly male activity. All the principals suspected of robbery in the Cheshire sample were male. Robbery was constructed in masculine terms in both condemnatory and romanticised discourses. Popular accounts that implicated women in robbery were extremely rare. In one, 'six men and a bloody woman', the latter described as 'pitiful, a scrubbed, lousy creature', robbed a minister. She allegedly encouraged one of her male confederates to cut their victim's throat, crying out 'Kill the rogue!' or 'Kill the dog!' He did so, and they left the minister for dead, lying in the road stripped of his clothing.[151] We heard in an earlier chapter about the cook-maid armed with nothing more than a black pudding who amusingly held up some pathetic tailors.[152] A ballad relating the tale of Susan Higges, a Buckinghamshire woman who, weaponed and in male attire, supported herself by highway robbery for twenty years, also side-stepped the issue of the physical threat posed by women. Only when Higges was recognised by a female victim was she forced to resort to actual violence. She killed the woman, but Higges's identity was discovered because, providentially, she could not afterwards wash the woman's blood from her face.[153] Such tales, ambiguous about women's role in robbery as they were, are the exceptions that prove the rule. Robbers who appeared in court or in published accounts were nearly always men.

[148] CCRO, QSF/69/2/53, QSF/69/1/52 (1622).
[149] *Complete Justice*, 227, 226; Pulton, *De Pace Regis*, fos. 131v–132r.
[150] PRO, CHES 24/103/3, deposition of Lewis ap Jenkyn (1593).
[151] *An Exact Narrative of the Bloody Murder and Robbery Committed by Stephen Eaton, Sarah Swift*, et al. (London, 1669); *A Perfect Narrative of the Robbery and Murder Committed near Dame Annis So Cleer* (London, 1669), 13, 20, 23, 25.
[152] See above, pp. 82–3.   [153] *A True Relation of One Susan Higges* (London, 1640).

The figure of the highway robber in particular was constructed predominantly as the epitome of those negative characteristics of manhood gone awry that were commonly attributed to violent male opponents in order to discredit them.[154] The absence of honourable manhood was evident in robbers' 'very untowardly' treatment of victims who had only small amounts of money on them, their indiscriminate targeting of poor and rich no matter what the consequences for victims, and their cheating of each other when they divided their spoils.[155] Highwaymen typically robbed in pairs or groups and thus unfairly outnumbered their victims: James Whitney worked 'with a notorious crew'; Lewis Deval with 'a knot of highwaymen', Richard Dudley with 'a gang'; Hugh Tunnycliff with 'a great number of companions', 'a pack' of 'confederates'.[156] Highwaymen did not even have the courage of their convictions: 'for though they swear to shoot you if you yield not, 'tis but to fright you, for they dare not do it'.[157] Penitent John Clavell directly contrasted his previous 'foul offences' as a highwayman with the 'brave and noble actions' of his reformed self.[158]

Furthermore, whereas the man of honour was recognisable by an open countenance, highwaymen 'obscure the due proportions of [their] faces' with 'false beards, vizards, hoods, patches, wens, mufflers, and false periwigs, all unnatural'. They 'muffle their faces with their cloaks, or else cloak or coat hides all their clothes; they have a handkercher or scarf, which with their hand they'll rear up to their eyes, over their faces just when they bid you stand [and deliver]'. In highway robberies in Cheshire, Darcy Lascelles was described as having 'a vizard or covering over his face, in black clothes', and the three men who set upon Lewis ap Jenkyn had 'scarves and such like things over their faces'. Their dissemblance was further manifest in the 'uncertainty

---

[154] See above, pp. 23–49.
[155] *A True Narrative of the Proceedings at the Hertfordshire Assizes, this Instant July 1676* (London, 1676), 4; *Catterpillers of this Nation Anatomized . . . A New Discovery of the Highway Thieves*, sig. C2r.
[156] Anon., *The Penitent Robber, or The Woeful Lamentation of Captain James Whitney* (London, n.d.); *The Life of Deval. Shewing How He Came to be a Highway-Man; and How He Committed Several Robberies Afterwards* (London, 1969), 3; Anon., *A Narrative of the Life, Apprehension, Imprisonment and Condemnation of Richard Dudly the Great Robber* (London, 1669), 2; CCRO, QSE/5/100, /102 (1597). See also Anon., *A True Relation of a Great Robbery Committed near Andiver in Hampshire* (London, 1648), 2; Anon., *The Great Robbery in the West: Or, The Innkeeper Turn'd Highway-man* (London, 1678); Anon., *The Highway Mans Advice to his Brethren* (London, n.d.); Anon., *A New Ballad of Three Merry Butchers and Ten High-way Men* (London, n.d.); Anon., *The Notorious Robber's Lamentation or, Whitney's Sorrowful Ditty* (London, n.d.).
[157] *Catterpillers of this Nation Anatomized . . . A New Discovery of the Highway Thieves*, sig. E1v; Anon., *The Devils Cabinet Broke Open: Or, A New Discovery of Highway Thieves* (London, 1657), 3.
[158] John Clavell, *A Recantation of an Ill Led Life: Or, A Discoverie of the High-Way Law* (London, 1628), sig. A8r. Clavell was pardoned for his robberies on condition of banishment from the realm, PRO, SO 3/8, April 1626, 'A pardon to John Clavell . . .'.

of [their] attire, ... [their] non-residence, and changeable names'.[159] This was perceived as a real problem: highway robbers had the outward appearance of gentlemen, wearing gentlemen's apparel, sporting gentlemen's arms (swords and pistols), and riding quality horses (usually stolen from previous victims). Such a masquerade disguised their actual social position among 'the baser sort of people'. Thus it was opined that Lascelles, 'as he pretends his name to be, is no better than he should be', despite the fact that he had managed temporarily to pass himself off as a gentleman at his lodgings.[160] Highway robbery was, in short, 'ignoble', 'base', an 'art... void of honour'. It involved neither 'worth nor valour', and was censured by 'good and brave men'. Within this dominant discourse, robbery was decidedly not the behaviour of a true gentleman.[161]

The association between robbery and dishonourable manhood is made explicit in satirical works. Such unmanly men were ironically described as 'knights of the road'. The vernacular translation of Thomas More's *Utopia* pokes fun at the false manhood of the gentleman turned robber, who 'being daintily and tenderly pampered up in idleness and pleasure, was wont with a sword and a buckler by his side, to jet through the streets with a bragging look'.[162] However, far from being 'of stouter stomachs, bolder spirits, and manlier courages' than craftsmen and ploughmen with their earthy masculinity, idle gentlemen who had hitherto been retainers in rich men's households were 'effeminated', their 'stout and sturdy bodies... now either by reason of rest and idleness be brought to weakness or else by too easy and womanly exercises be made feeble and unable to endure hardness'.[163]

At the same time, such accounts were produced in dialogue with a competing cultural construction of robbery in which the dashing highwayman was admired for his bravery. Here, the representation of the robber was more ambiguous. On the one hand, it was suggested that his motivation, inspired by the Devil, was 'to covet other men's applause'. On the other, he retained an element of the 'Robin Hood' about him, robbing only the rich.[164] Richard Hainam, for instance, was known as 'the grandest thief in

---

[159] *Catterpillers of this Nation Anatomized... A New Discovery of the Highway Thieves*, sigs. B2v, D3v, D1v; PRO, CHES 24/135/6, examination of John Brown (1667); Clavell, *A Recantation of an Ill Led Life*, 12–15.
[160] *Calendar of State Papers: Domestic. Charles II*, Vol. CCLIV, 145, Ralph Hope to Williamson, 4 January 1669.
[161] Clavell, *A Recantation of an Ill Led Life*, sigs. A2, B2v, 21; *Catterpillers of this Nation Anatomized... A New Discovery of the Highway Thieves*, sigs. A6v, A8r.
[162] Thomas More, *Utopia*, trans. Ralph Robinson (London, 1551; 1597 edn), sig. D2v.
[163] More, *Utopia*, sig. D3v. For an alternative interpretation of the discourse of the gentleman robber, see Gillian Spraggs, *Outlaws and Highwaymen: The Cult of the Robber from the Middle Ages to the Nineteenth Century* (London, 2001), 1–12.
[164] The Robin Hood tradition was in fact more usually a means of critiquing structures of power than it was a representation of the robber. Stephen Knight, *Robin Hood: A Complete Study of the English Outlaw* (Oxford, 1994).

Europe', having robbed many great personages including kings, dukes and ambassadors, but when he robbed a poor man, 'he delivered him his moneys again', saying, 'There, honest man, take your moneys, I come not to rob the poor.'[165] 'Captain' James Hind was said to have robbed unpopular figures such as usurers as well as wealthy and foolish gentlemen.[166] Nevertheless, admiration of such men was usually condemned as vulgar, 'base and nought':

> Those that will now brave gallant men be deem'd,
> And with the *common people* be esteem'd,
>   ... if they look for fame,
> And mean to have an everlasting name
> Amongst the *vulgar*, let them ...
> ... bid our wealthy travellers to *stand* [and deliver]:
> Emptying their full cram'd bags ...
> And though there's boldness shown in such a case,
> *Yet to be tossed at Tyburn's a disgrace,*
> No, 'tis their credit, for the *people* then
> Will say: *'tis pity, they were proper men.*[167]

In any case, printed accounts of actual robbers' daring exploits nearly always ended the same way, with the robber's 'just reward', his execution.

The discourses of highway robbery that stressed negative masculine characteristics were not sympathetic to the condemned highwayman's plight. Neither were the law or legal personnel. It has been suggested that the judiciary harboured a 'special sympathy for the gentleman who felt himself driven to turn robber', which suggests that highwaymen were dealt with leniently.[168] Analysis of court records does not bear this out. If gentlemen robbers were exonerated, it was not because of a romantic notion of the gentleman-*robber* but because they were *gentlemen*. It was their status, not their behaviour, that helped them towards exoneration. Gentlemen were considered by contemporaries more likely to be capable of reformation than their social inferiors. And there was certainly a view from some quarters that the purpose of justice towards highwaymen was 'to judge the past, new ills to prevent'; 'were the bench of men's repentance sure: none should the strictness of the law endure'. So said reformed highwayman John Clavell in the 'recantation' he penned after his pardon.[169] Highwaymen of less prominent

---

[165] *The Witty Rogue Arraigned, Condemned and Executed* (London, 1656), sigs. A2v, A1r, A4r, D3r.
[166] *No Jest Like a True Jest, Being a Compendious Record of the Merry Life and Mad Exploits of Captain James Hind, the Great Robber of England* (London, 1657), sigs. A6r–v, A7v.
[167] George Wither, *Abuses Stript and Whipt: Or, Satirical Essayes* (London, 1613), 191–2. Original italics.
[168] Spraggs, *Outlaws and Highwaymen*, 6–7.
[169] Clavell, *A Recantation of an Ill Led Life*, sig. A6r.

social position could expect less happy treatment by the courts. Thus, even when many 'women of good quality' interceded on behalf of a mere innkeeper turned highwayman, 'not so much for his sake, as out of charity to his poor innocent wife and children, for she [his wife] was generally reputed a very good, careful, industrious and pious woman, and hath no less than nine very hopeful children', 'the nature of his crime excluded him from mercy in this world'.[170] Darcy Lascelles, styled as 'gent' but 'no better than he should be' (his relative, John Lascelles, who was suspected to have harboured him between robberies, was a yeoman), was hanged at Chester on 16 June 1669. This was in spite of his having been granted a temporary stay of execution after he turned informer regarding a supposed conspiracy against the King.[171]

Hanging Darcy Lascelles did not have the desired deterrent effect, however. Sir Geoffrey Shakerley wrote from Chester to Sir Joseph Williamson that 'Notwithstanding Lascelles was executed on Wednesday last, seven or eight men coming to the fair were robbed yesterday of seven score pounds by three highwaymen in the road from Warrington. The thieves got upon Delamere Forest and evaded the hue and cry.'[172] A great many robbers, like the latter ones, in fact remained at large, and so were never officially prosecuted. But when they were brought to trial, robbers, especially highwaymen, faced high levels of conviction and execution. One reason for this was that robbers frequently were apprehended only after committing several robberies, which meant that their offence was aggravated from the outset. Additionally, their spoils were often considerable. Lascelles and his confederate, for instance, took £328 in cash from one man on the high road between Chester and Whitchurch in October 1666.[173] Even without the violence which robbery entailed, and its non-clergiable status, such circumstances made hanging the likely outcome of a trial. If statistics for robbery and highway robbery are included in general comparisons of the judicial treatment of men and women, it will appear that men fare far worse because the sample of robbers will invariably be all-male. As we have seen, however, when like is compared with like, the answer to the question of whether women were treated more leniently than men is not an unequivocal 'yes'.

---

[170] *Great Robbery in the West*, 5.
[171] *Calendar of State Papers: Domestic. Charles II*, 145, 272, 333, 351, Hope to Williamson, 4 January 1669; John Armytage to Lord Arlington, 9 April 1669; Secretary Trevor to Sir Job Charlton, 18 May 1669; Trevor to Charlton, 1 June 1669; PRO, CHES 24/135/5 recognisance of John Lascelles to give evidence (1667); CHES 24/136/3, warrant to sheriffs of the City of Chester for the execution of Darcy Lassells, CHES 21/5, fo. 86r (1669).
[172] *Calendar of State Papers: Domestic. Charles II*, 378, Sir Geoffrey Shakerley to Sir Joseph Williamson, 23 June 1669.
[173] PRO, CHES 24/135/5 recognisances re. Darcy Lascelles; PRO, CHES 21/5, fos. 60v, 68v (1667).

Horse-thieves

Formally prosecuted defendants for stealing horses were nearly always men, as was noted above, though occasional references to female horse-thieves exist. The theft of horses had long been a non-clergiable felony, and from 1597 it was excluded from the scope of general pardons.[174] Its legal status has led historians to state that contemporaries considered horse-theft 'particularly obnoxious', but precise reasons why it should have been so characterised are rarely elaborated upon.[175]

Horse stealing was one of the most lucrative criminal activities in early modern England. Horses were expensive commodities whether they were sold legally or illegally. In the 1590s, even the rock bottom price for 'a flea-bitten ambling gelding' was as much as £3 2s., which was equivalent to the weekly income of a labouring household.[176] In the early part of the period, horses were predominantly owned by the gentry and aristocracy, and the Crown was particularly concerned about the provision of horses for military service. Thus, the theft of these animals was an affront to the elite and potentially damaging to the state. However, the later sixteenth and seventeenth centuries witnessed a huge expansion in the social base of horse ownership and in the uses to which horses were commonly put. Horses were increasingly used for draught, mill-power, commercial haulage and personal transport. By the later seventeenth century, many quite modest smallholders possessed at least one horse. The nobility still owned far more horses, of course. Local gentry usually possessed between ten and twenty horses, while the richer gentry and aristocracy had up to one hundred, many of which were kept for the leisure purposes of hunting, hawking, dressage and racing.[177] My point here is that the particular odiousness of horse-theft diminished as horse-ownership ceased to be restricted to the upper sorts of people. Because in the late sixteenth and seventeenth centuries, the non-clergiable status of the offence did not correspond with popular ideas, horse-theft had a much higher acquittal rate than most other felonies. Overall, towards one-half of defendants were found not guilty by trial juries. This is significant in the light of the fact that only around one-quarter of men accused of grand larceny and burglary were likewise acquitted, for instance.[178] Again, the fact that

---

[174] Statute 39 Elizabeth I c.28.
[175] Quoting J.G. Bellamy, *The Criminal Trial in Later Medieval England* (Stroud, 1998), 136.
[176] CCRO, QSE/5/133 (1599).
[177] Joan Thirsk, *Horses in Early Modern England: For Service, For Pleasure, For Power* (Reading, 1977), 5–7, 23; Keith Thomas, *Man and the Natural World: Changing Attitudes in England, 1500–1800* (London, 1983), 26.
[178] In the Cheshire sample of male defendants, 43.7 per cent of horse-thieves, 26 per cent of larcenists, and 23 per cent of burglars were acquitted. In the 1620s, four of eight men tried for horse-theft were acquitted; in the 1660s, six of the seven men tried were found not guilty.

only two women were suspected of stealing horses in the court sessions sampled for this study (one was not formally prosecuted, the other was acquitted along with her husband) means that aggregating horse-theft with other felonies would produce a skewed picture of the relative treatment of men and women before the courts.

Moreover, a relatively large proportion of suspected horse-thieves were not brought to trial, either because complainants did not file indictments against them or because grand juries returned verdicts of *ignoramus*. In many cases, by the time stolen horses had been tracked down to their new owners, the thieves had long since departed and were not to be found. In such circumstances, the original owners had the prerogative to buy back their animals. Thus, in November 1646, two men deposed that they had known the bay nag now in William Bridge's possession since it was a colt. They could definitely identify it as John Cottgreave's nag that had been stolen from him 'by a party of horse' over a year before, although they were not able to say whether the thieves were the King's soldiers or Parliament's. Cottgreave paid Bridge 26s. 8d. for the horse 'and so the business was ended'.[179]

Discourses of horse-theft, like those of robbery and larceny in fact, intensified almost as soon as did the fighting between the King and Parliament.[180] This is hardly surprising given that the prices of horses rose along with the 'insatiable demand' for horses as mounts and draft animals in the civil war years and that soldiers had the legal right to capture horses from the enemy. In the process of goods and chattels being commandeered by the King's or Parliament's forces, the line between lawful and unlawful seizing of property could be blurred. Hundreds of people tried to recover their horses, 'especially when soldiers subsequently disposed of them to third parties who happened to be civilians'.[181] Parishioners in the hamlets of Burton and Puddington claimed that yeoman Thomas Hickson had stolen horses from three individuals in December 1646, whereas Hickson claimed that he had taken the

---

[179] CCRO, MF69/2/78 (1646). See also CCRO, MF69/2/88 (1646).
[180] For discourses of robbery, see, for example, Anon., *A Great Robbery in the North, neer Swanton in Yorkshire; Shewing how one Mr. Tailour was Robbed by a Company of Cavaliers* (London, 1642); *Speciall and True Passages Worth Observation, From Severall Places of this Kingdome, September 23, and 24 . . . IV. From Yorkshire, that the Cavaliers, and Malignant Party of That County, Doe Still Persist in Robbing and Spoiling the Kings Subjects, &c. . . .* (London, 1642); *A Proclamation for the Better Government of His Majesties Army, and for the Preventing the Plundring, Spoyling, and Robbing of His Majesties Subjects, under any Pretense Whatsoever, upon Pain of the Punishments Herein Declared* (London, 1642); *Mercurius Rusticus, Or, The Countries Complaint of the Murthers, Robberies, Plundrings, and Other Outrages Committed by the Rebells on His Majesties Faithfull Subjects* (London, 1643); Anon., *A Proclamation Commanding the Due Observation of the Desires of the Commissioners for the Contribution of the County of Oxford, and for Punishing all Stragling Souldiers and Others, Robbing, and Plundering the Country* (London, 1644).
[181] Ian Gentles, *The New Model Army in England, Ireland and Scotland, 1645–1653* (Oxford, 1992), 129–30.

animals in his capacity as a commissioner for the King.[182] A gentleman along with a 'trooper in the sheriff's troop' were similarly charged with 'unlawfully [taking] a grey mare'.[183] Arbitrators heard in 1646 how 'at the first Battle of Middlewich when Sir Thomas Aston and his forces were routed', Thomas Chrymes lent Master Robert Bromfield a gelding furnished with saddle, bridle, holsters and pistols (which Chrymes had taken from Major John Marbury's ensign) on condition that Bromfield return the horse at Northwich or Nantwich or wherever they happened to march to. Chrymes never saw the horse again. When the two men met a month later and Chrymes demanded that the horse be returned, Bromfield claimed that he had sold it for forty-six shillings after it had fallen lame; subsequently, Chrymes again demanded payment for the horse to which Bromfield replied that 'when he had payment from Major Marbury for that horse he [Marbury] took from him [Bromfield], he [Bromfield] would pay [Chrymes] afterwards'. The two men came to blows over it.[184]

Civil war provided other sorts of unlawful opportunities, too. For example, a man had 'two iron grey mares and one flea-bitten nag' stolen from his stable by thieves who pretended 'to shelter themselves from the Parliament forces'. They 'hid themselves in my garden while my Lord Rivers and the Lord Cholmondley's troops passed by (whom [the thieves] pretended to be the Parliament forces)'.[185] Confusions over horse-ownership and commandeering of horses for military service led to a huge increase in numbers of complaints of horse-theft in the 1640s, along with a corresponding increase in cases that never came to trial. For those who were arraigned, however, two-thirds were acquitted in these years. The remaining third all hanged. The civil wars thus created a particular context in which the pattern of judicial decision-making in cases of horse-theft differed somewhat from the general pattern in the seventeenth century.

Benefits of belly and clergy compared

So far in this chapter, the benefits of belly and clergy have been mentioned only in passing. Benefit of belly has often been discussed by historians in one or more of three related ways: first, as if benefit of belly were in practice a rough female equivalent of benefit of clergy; secondly, as if benefit of belly provided a usually successful route by which clemency might be sought by and granted towards women; thirdly, as if the granting of such pleas reflected

---

[182] PRO, CHES 21/4, fos. 153r, 153v, CHES 24/127/1, petition of Thomas Hickson (1648).
[183] PRO, CHES 21/4, fo. 149r, CHES 24/127/1/234 (1648).
[184] CRO, QJF 74/1/56 (1646).
[185] CCRO, MF66/2, /3 (1643). See also Edwards, 'The horse trade of the Midlands', 99–100.

a general sympathy towards women.[186] In certain respects, belly and clergy were similar. Both involved 'tests' that were administered after conviction by others than the trial jury or judge. An especially composed jury of matrons judged upon physical examination whether a convicted woman was pregnant, while the prison ordinary conducted the test of 'literacy' required for clergy. Women arraigned for felony were supposed 'only for one time [to] have the benefit of their belly', just as men were permitted to have benefit of clergy only once.[187] A simple overview of judicial outcomes would seem to support the comparability of the two mechanisms. In late sixteenth-century Cheshire, for instance, where just over half of arraigned women and men received sentence of death, around a third of each pleaded their belly and clergy respectively. Yet to assume parity of treatment is optimistic. Women fared rather worse than men because benefit of belly was far less comprehensive than that of clergy. The comparison between the outcomes of pleas of the two benefits is starkest when women and men were indicted together for their part in the same offence. Thus, Ellen Watson and Thomas Harrison were indicted for burglary in 1639: she was declared 'not pregnant' and hanged; he had his charge reduced to grand larceny, pleaded his clergy, was branded and discharged.[188] In the first place, as Cynthia Herrup has remarked, the test for benefit of belly was 'more complex, more humiliating and probably less open to manipulation than the test administered for benefit of clergy'.[189] Unlike the latter, benefit of belly had not become a legal fiction, granted for the most part indiscriminately to anyone who pleaded it. Juries of matrons returned verdicts of 'not pregnant' against the majority of women they examined. In the years sampled for 1620s' Cheshire, twenty-four women claimed that they were pregnant; the matrons concurred in only one in six cases.[190] Twenty of the twenty-four women were left to suffer sentence of death.

Moreover, even women who were reprieved upon matrons finding them to be 'quick with child' were not always pardoned. Of the four women whom Cheshire juries of matrons declared were pregnant in the quantitative sample from the 1620s, two were eventually hanged. In the 1590s, three of the four women who were supposedly pregnant when they were convicted of property

[186] Cockburn, *Introduction*, ch. xi, sects. ii, iii and iv (Table II), esp. 114; Thomas A. Green implies that women often avoided the gallows through false claims of pregnancy or by conceiving during their imprisonment: *Verdict*, 118 n. 50; Sharpe, *Crime*, 68–9.
[187] *Complete Justice*, 292; T.E., *Lawes Resolutions*, 207.
[188] PRO, CHES 21/4, fo. 80r.
[189] Herrup, *Common Peace*, 143 n. 16. The fullest discussion of the role of the jury of matrons can be found in James C. Oldham, 'On pleading the belly: a history of the jury of matrons', *Criminal Justice History* 6 (1985), 1–64.
[190] For example, Joan Parre, convicted of cutting a purse containing 3s. 11d. and 3 farthings in 1626 was sentenced to hang, reprieved after successfully claiming benefit of belly and was discharged in 1628 after being pardoned. PRO, CHES 21/3, fos. 143v, 172r (1626, 1628); CHES 24/118/4, indictment, recognisance, jury return re. Joan Parre (1626).

offences were hanged between six months and one year after their plea had been accepted. The fourth was pardoned two and a half years later, being the only one beside whose name the clerk had made a marginal note that she 'is delivered'. So a valid claim of pregnancy did not itself ensure a woman's life. One woman who was reprieved in the 1660s was also pregnant, her child being born three weeks after her trial; she was sent to the gallows six months later. Another, Anne Dickenson *alias* Sarah Merrett, had already been branded for housebreaking in 1663 when she was convicted again and sentenced to hang the following year; this time she successfully pleaded pregnancy. The judge deferred her execution until after she was delivered, but denounced her as 'a most wicked woman', and charged the gaoler to keep a watchful eye on her. She 'wilfully refused' to name the father of her child at the birth, despite the public midwife's efforts, saying that 'she would be racked to death first, and many words to that purpose'. In 'pursuance of the judge's order', the gaoler had the baby taken away from her, baptised and put to a wet-nurse. 'And shortly after', the gaoler stated, 'Anne Dickenson *alias* Sarah Merrett according to the sentence passed on her at the last great sessions was executed.'[191] Katherine Read was reprieved in 1621 upon a jury of matrons finding her quick with child; she was hanged a year later.[192] Elinor Ratcliffe was reprieved in 1623 not due to pregnancy but because she was nursing her infant. The court's generosity may have been as much due to sparing the expense of a wet-nurse as it was to any consideration of the well-being of mother and child. Ratcliffe, too, was hanged six months later. In practice then, benefit of the womb was hardly the 'generous provision' that some have claimed it to be.[193] It would seem that women's best chance of life came not from pleading benefit of belly but in the form of a general pardon, as was the case in 1627 when several women were pardoned whether they had been found pregnant or not.[194] But general pardons were not granted in tandem with the assizes. In any case, pardons sometimes came too late. Isabel Naylor, who robbed a house of £38-worth of goods, was reprieved after the matrons pronounced her pregnant in 1625; she gave birth to her child in prison, but she died in prison, too, before the pardon could take effect.[195]

---

[191] PRO, CHES 21/5, fo. 2r, CHES 24/134/1, indictment, recognisance, jury return and order re. Sarah Merrett *alias* Stanley *alias* Danson (1663); CRO, QJF/93/1/122 (1665). Merrett appears to have taken the pseudonym 'Anne Dickenson' after a woman of that name was tried alongside her in 1663.
[192] PRO, CHES 21/3, fo. 66v (1622).
[193] PRO, CHES 21/1, fos. 152v, 167, 177, 180, 182v, CHES 21/4, fos. 20, 28; CHES 21/3, fos. 81, 88. Hanawalt, 'Female felon', 265.
[194] PRO CHES 21/3, fos. 41v, 45, 49v, 66v, 117, 158, 158v, 165, 172, 187 (1627); PRO, SO 3/9 November 1627, 'A pardon for Isabel Nealor et al.'.
[195] PRO, CHES 21/3, fos. 125r, 143r (1626), 172r (1628); CRO, QJB 1/5, fo. 217r (1628); PRO, SO 3/9 November 1627, 'A pardon for Isabel Nealor...'.

The reality for even those women who were lucky enough to be granted their benefit of belly was in sharp contrast to that of male felons whose benefits of clergy resulted almost universally in avoidance of the gallows.

Unlike women who claimed benefit of the womb, few men who applied for benefit of clergy were turned down. The minority who were unsuccessful had either been branded previously, or their reading was disallowed, presumably for reasons other than their ineloquent delivery of the text.[196] Benefit of clergy was used as a standard method of mitigating the death sentence; benefit of belly was not.

The use of pardons does not appear to have been particularly favourable to women either. Although general pardons affected men and women equally, those that were conditional on other factors, such as entry into military service did not extend to women. In the 1620s, five of thirteen condemned men who had committed property crimes escaped death by this means; a further seven were pardoned unconditionally apart from being bailed, and one more was discharged as the court ruled that his bill had been insufficiently drafted. Not one of the reprieved men was hanged. We have already seen that women reprieved after successfully claiming pregnancy were not pardoned as a matter of course. Women who failed the pregnancy test but who were subsequently reprieved by the Chief Justice did not fare much better. Of four such women, one was discharged because she was a minor, another was pardoned after four years of incarceration, and the other two were hanged six months after the reprieve was granted. An extensive study of the use of pardons, which would examine why and to whom they were granted, may well show that women were generally luckier than the few who appear in the Cheshire records of this study. Nevertheless, the fate of Elinor Ratcliffe and women like her should remind us that to generalise about women being regular beneficiaries of mercy might be to perpetuate a myth.

What of the extension of benefit of clergy to women that was introduced in 1623? In fact, it was not benefit of clergy *per se* that was extended to women but merely branding as a form of punishment. Women did not have to cite the 'neck verse' in order to be branded rather than hanged.[197] It was

---

[196] Six of thirty-nine men who pleaded benefit of clergy in the 1620s' sample were denied it. One of them had been branded previously, but was reprieved and pardoned; the rest apparently could not read. Another man read successfully and was branded, but the King 'denied his reading', and he was condemned at the next sessions: CHES 21/3, fos. 66v, 71, 97, 97v, 108, 144. Cockburn found for the Home Circuit assizes between 1559 and 1589 that no man was denied clergy because he failed the reading test: 'Trial by the Book?', 77. For benefit of clergy see Cockburn, *Introduction*, ch. xi, sect. ii.; Sharpe, *Crime*, 67–8; Leonora C. Gabel, *Benefit of Clergy in England in the Later Middle Ages* (New York, 1969), ch. 5; Herrup, *Common Peace*, 48–50.

[197] Barbara Kreps's comment that only educated women had recourse to benefit of clergy is therefore erroneous: 'The paradox of women: the legal position of early modern wives and Thomas Dekker's *The Honest Whore*', ELH 69 (2002), 89.

simply that for first-time clergiable offences, a woman was to be 'branded and marked in the hand upon the brawn of the left thumb with a hot burning iron having a Roman "T" upon the said iron; the said mark to be made by the gaoler openly in the court before the judge'. She could also be further punished by 'imprisonment, whipping, stocking, or sending to the House of Correction' for up to one year at the discretion of the judge or justices.[198] Legal handbooks written after 1623 continued to state that 'No woman can have benefit of clergy because no woman is in capacity to be a priest.'[199] In the 1660s, Cheshire JP Sir Peter Leycester annotated his manuscript handbooks to the effect that branding was the routine sentence for thefts by women of goods worth between one and ten shillings.[200] Yet an anomaly remained, for the comparable ceiling for men's thefts was forty shillings, thereby allowing men far greater scope for avoiding hanging for felony. It was only in 1691 that branding came to be administered to women for thefts of stolen property valued at up to forty shillings, although still without the reading qualification.

The feme covert

The issue of husband and wife criminal partnerships, which has been raised on several previous occasions in this chapter, deserves further attention. Conventionally, historians have taken the legal status of the *feme covert* at face value. The maxim that husband and wife were one person and that person was the husband is reinforced by interpretations in which married women's agency is subsumed into that of their husbands. Frank McLynn, for instance, while acknowledging that many female pickpockets and shoplifters were independent criminals, sees women who acted with men very much as dependent and passive, 'corrupted by their partner's example', or 'so browbeaten by their husbands that they went along meekly with their evil schemes'.[201] It was, after all, a wife's duty to 'submit and subject herself to her husband, ... to be a help unto him, ... to obey his commandment in all things, which he may command by the authority of a husband'.[202] The criminal law certainly made a concession to wives who might have been so commanded. When 'a wife stealeth by the compulsion of the husband, it is no felony in her'; 'if a

---

[198] 'An Acte concerning women convicted of small felonies', 21 James I, c.6 (1624). Forster, *Lay-man's Lawyer*, 276–7.
[199] Forster, *Lay-man's Lawyer*, 276.
[200] CRO, DLT/unlisted/16, Leicester–Warren of Tabley Collection, 'Concerning endictments', 33. DLT/unlisted/18, Leicester–Warren of Tabley Collection, 'Briefe Notes', 'Of the thinges which Justices of Peace have power to heare and what not', 20; 'A charge to the grand jury 1660', 75.
[201] McLynn, *Crime and Punishment*, 125–6.
[202] Dod and Cleaver, *Godly Forme of Household Government*, sig. H2v.

man and his wife commit a felony jointly, it seemeth the wife is no felon, but it shall be wholly judged the husband's fact'; when 'the wife receiveth the husband being a felon, and relieveth him, she is no accessory', 'for a woman cannot be an accessory to her husband insomuch as she is forbidden by the Law of God to betray him'.[203]

We find manifold examples of legal practice following theory in this respect. Printed reports of court sessions frequently explained the relative treatment of wives and husbands in these terms. A woman whose husband fled after they had committed a felony together was exonerated because 'our merciful laws, in favour of marriage, are pleased to suppose the wife's act to be done by coercion by the husband, and that he by flight had acknowledged his own guilt'.[204] Flight was usually understood to denote guilt.[205] The fact that the husband had fled and the wife had not could therefore be interpreted as a sign of her innocence. Another woman, who was apprehended riding upon a stolen mare for which theft her husband was convicted, defended herself against the charge of horse-theft 'by alleging herself his wife, and consequently what she did was done by his coercion'. Hence, the reporter opined, she 'could not be found guilty'.[206] A man and woman were tried for a burglary, but 'the house being broken in the daytime, it was esteemed a felony, the man was found guilty [on the reduced charge of grand larceny and branded], the other acquitted being his wife'.[207] Hannah Bolton, her husband and another man were charged with robbing an ale-wife of a considerable amount of plate, household stuff and clothing; 'the two men were convicted, and the woman by reason of her marriage [was] acquitted' despite 'having been all [three] old offenders' and previously branded on the thumb.[208] The implication of such statements is that wives were routinely exonerated due to their covert status.

In Cheshire, some wives seem similarly to have escaped conviction and punishment for their parts in property offences. Katherine Baker was indicted with her labourer husband Edward for stealing ten measures of malt valued at eighteen shillings; a recognisance notes that *'they* confessed' to the crime. Yet Edward's name alone is entered in the official record of the great sessions and only he was subjected to being flogged after the petty jury's verdict of

---

[203] *Complete Justice*, 263–4; T.E., *Lawes Resolutions*, 206; Dalton, *Countrey Justice*, 236, 252.
[204] *A True Narrative of the Proceedings at the Sessions-House in the Old-Bayly, October 10, 11 and 12* (London, 1677), 7.
[205] PRO, CHES 24/118/3, recognisance re. Richard and Thomas Bailey (1626).
[206] *True Narrative of the Proceedings at the Sessions-House in the Old-Bayly, April 11, 12 and 13, 1678*, 7.
[207] *Narrative of the Proceedings at the Sessions, Held in Justice-Hall at the Old-Baly*, 8.
[208] Anon., *The True Narrative of the Proceedings at the Sessions-House in the Old-Bayly which Began on Wednesday the 8th of this Instant December 1680* (London, 1680), 2.

guilty to the reduced value of ten pence.[209] Adam Johnson's wife was not officially charged as an accomplice even though witnesses deposed that it was she who took the stolen cloth to be dressed, and insisted that it be dressed in her presence.[210] Margery White was acquitted even though her supposed husband was convicted and branded for the theft of two felt hats in 1595.[211] Chester labourer Thomas Mossley was hanged for the theft of over forty-four pounds' worth of plate, linens and clothes from a gentleman's house; his wife Katherine was acquitted as an accessory.[212] Eleanor Harrison and her husband Thomas were together prosecuted on three occasions. Her husband was acquitted in 1640 for the theft of a communion cup and other church ornaments out of Taxal church, which meant that Eleanor and two male accessories were likewise acquitted. The following year, Eleanor was a second time acquitted though Thomas was convicted and branded for housebreaking and stealing goods worth three (reduced from nine) shillings. On the third occasion, in 1642, Thomas and a male accomplice were hanged for a burglary; Eleanor was again acquitted along with two other female accomplices.[213] It is easy to assume that Eleanor had benefited from coverture in these verdicts – note, though, that the situation is muddied somewhat by the fact that other accomplices not married to the principal were similarly acquitted. We ought not, though, to be too hasty in supposing that wives whose names were not inserted into official documents necessarily avoided punishment. Dorothy Elston and her two children were not listed as offenders in the Cheshire Crown Book – only her husband's name was entered – yet all three languished alongside William Elston in prison 'in great misery and almost famished', 'they being charged with felony' in stealing sixty-five sheep and eight kine.[214]

The legal and practical position of married women was ambiguous. Marriage was a conundrum: 'that united state of man and wife; whereof two persons become but one, *which still are two*'.[215] This was acknowledged

---

[209] PRO, CHES 24/116/3, indictment and recognisance re. Edward and Katherine Baker, CHES 21/3, fo. 66v (1622); my italic.
[210] CRO, QJF 53/4/1, 2 (1624).
[211] PRO, CHES 21/1, fo. 180v, CHES 24/104/2, indictment and jury return re. George and Margery White. She is entered in the Crown Book as Margery White his wife, but as Margery White *alias* Smith, spinster on the indictment. See also PRO, CHES 21/3, fo. 110v, CHES 24/117/3, indictment re. John and Katherine Sanderson (1624).
[212] PRO, CHES 21/3, fo. 42r, CHES 24/115/3, indictment and jury return re. Thomas and Katherine Mossley (1620).
[213] PRO, CHES 21/3, fos. 88v (1640), 105v (1641), 115r (1642), CHES 24/125/4, indictment and recognisance re. Thomas and Eleanor Harrison (1640), CHES 24/126/1, indictment and jury return re. *idem* (1641), CHES 24/126/3, indictment, jury return and recognisances re. Thomas Harrison et al. (1642).
[214] PRO, CHES 21/3, fo. 66r, CHES 24/116/3, petition re. William Elston, his wife and children (1622).
[215] Ste. B., *Counsel to the Husband: To the Wife Instruction* (London, 1608), 1–2; my italic.

in legal theory and court records attest to women's practical accountability for their crimes. Despite the historiographical emphasis to the contrary, 'in matters criminal and capital causes, a *feme covert* shall answer without her husband'. This meant, first of all, that even when husbands and wives acted together, the husband was not automatically held to be accountable for the woman's actions. Women could be held responsible for acting at the suggestion of or in league with their husbands, if coercion was absent. When wives and husbands together were under suspicion, wives were not routinely discharged on the grounds that they had acted in accordance with their husbands' commands. Women were held to account in other circumstances also. If goods stolen by a husband were found secreted in his wife's possession, 'she shall be culpable with her husband of his felony'.[216] Isobel and Adam Byrum were both prosecuted for together plucking the wool from twenty-four sheep belonging to a Nantwich widow in 1620. They were both convicted; Adam pleaded his clergy and was branded, Isobel was unsuccessful in her claim of pregnancy and was hanged.[217] Margaret and Gruffin Vaughan were both sentenced to be hanged for a joint burglary in 1622.[218] Paradoxically, in the 'crime wave' of the 1620s, when women were most visible as offenders, wives who acted with their husbands were more likely to be hanged for the offence than wives who had acted independently.[219]

The *feme covert*'s ability for independent action in criminal matters meant secondly that 'woman by herself without the privity of her husband may commit felony to become either principal or accessory'. If a husband kept company with a felonious wife in full knowledge of what she had done, he became an accessory to the fact. Victualler William Johnson was suspected to have received from his wife Elioner three ruffs that she had stolen from a local gentleman.[220] But if a wife 'steal goods or receive thieves to her house, *et cetera*, and if the husband so soon as he perceive it waive and forsake their company and his own house, in this case the woman's offence makes not [his]'.[221] In 1598, the Chester jury convicted Anna Browne of stealing a cloak worth five shillings, but stated categorically that 'we clear her husband' from the charge of aiding and abetting her.[222] Wives who acted without their husbands' knowledge were fully accountable for their crimes. In practice, this was manifest in the majority of cases where married women were suspected

---

[216] T.E., *Lawes Resolutions*, 207.
[217] PRO, CHES 21/3, fo. 41v, CHES 24/115/3, indictments, recognisance, jury return, jury of matrons' return re. Isobel and Adam Byrum (1620).
[218] PRO, CHES 21/3, fo. 71r, CHES 24/116/4, indictment and jury return re. Gruffin and Margaret Vaughan (1622).
[219] 55.6 per cent of wives acting in league with husbands were hanged as opposed to 33.3 per cent of wives who acted independently.
[220] PRO, CHES 24/117/3, recognisance re. Elioner Johnson (1624).
[221] T.E., *Lawes Resolutions*, 206.   [222] CCRO, QSF/47/22 (1598).

of felonious activity in which their husbands were not implicated at all. This is important to note because historians' consideration of judicial treatment of wives tends to limit discussion to those wives who might qualify as *covert* in acting with their husbands. Crucially, married women more often than not were brought before the courts *without* their husbands and alone faced the full force of the law.[223] Only a minority of these women were styled as both wives and spinsters on indictments in an attempt to circumvent coverture and thus to ensure legal accountability.[224] Just one in eight who were prosecuted independently of their husbands (and one in ten wives who were suspected alongside their husbands) were described as married spinsters. Margaret Foster, for instance, a tinker's wife, was so styled in 1624, when she was charged with burgling a butcher's dwelling-house and taking a child's coat worth a shilling, a pewter dish valued at sixpence, and four herrings.[225]

Whether wives were prosecuted with their husbands or not, they had a lower conviction rate than spinsters. Fewer than half of the married women tried were found guilty as opposed to more than two-thirds of women styled as spinsters.[226] Single women were also more likely to be given secondary punishments. In 1624, the judge ordered that Elizabeth Fairhurst and Katherine Woods be whipped as well as branded for thieving, probably because they had wandered from as far away as Wigan, Lancashire into Cheshire, and so were punished as rogues as well as felons.[227] Once convicted, however, a similar proportion – nearly half – of married and unmarried women were sentenced to death on the gallows.[228] Yet we must not too hastily suppose that guilty wives and spinsters were treated equitably. Although wives and unmarried women were reprieved at roughly the same rate, wives were more successful by far in being pardoned than were their single counterparts. Proportionately, twice as many married as unmarried women were pardoned.[229] The higher conviction rate of unmarried women was partly related to contemporary fears about young single

---

[223] The husbands of 43.7 per cent of the married women suspected were also under suspicion; the husbands of 56.3 per cent of married women were not included in the complaints.

[224] J.H. Baker, 'Male and married spinsters', *American Journal of Legal History* 21 (1976), 255–9; Valerie C. Edwards, 'The case of the married spinster: an alternative explanation, *American Journal of Legal History* 21 (1977), 260–5; Carol Z. Wiener, 'Is a spinster an unmarried woman?', *American Journal of Legal History* 20 (1976), 27–31.

[225] PRO, CHES 21/3, fo. 98v, CHES 24/117/2, indictment and recognisance re. Margaret Foster (1624).

[226] 46.2 per cent of married women and 69.7 per cent of spinsters were convicted.

[227] PRO, CHES 21/3, fo. 108r, CHES 24/117/3, indictment and recognisance re. Elizabeth Fairhurst and Katherine Woods (1624).

[228] 44.4 per cent of married women and 43.5 per cent of unmarried women were sentenced to hang.

[229] Of married women sentenced to hang, 37.5 per cent were pardoned; the equivalent figure for spinsters is 16.7 per cent.

women living beyond the bounds of a patriarchal authority that should have constrained them. But it was undoubtedly also bound up with the status of married women. Rather than coverture denying women's accountability, it might well have been that the responsibilities of married women to their households and families meant that the courts were less keen to see them removed. Motherless children and bereft husbands did not do well in early modern society.

We may conclude that marital unity was a fiction, not a description. The courts did not always treat husband and wife as one person. Yet the ambiguous status of married women and their responsibilities to their families meant that in practice they received better treatment before the courts than did single women, who were more often subjected to the full force of the law.

Legal categories of property offence encompassed a wide range of behaviour. One indication of the less tangible factors at play can be seen in popular perceptions of ownership and 'right action' that were drawn upon and manipulated in examinations taken before magistrates and petitions to the sessions bench.[230] Just as notions of social order in early modern England were constantly renegotiated by deponents and supplicants in cases involving violence, narratives about property offences were likewise dependent upon a certain amount of ambiguity regarding legality and probity. Notions of what moveable property belonged to whom were generally based upon the practicalities of the household in early modern England. Although technically the ownership of property was weighted towards men, popular perceptions of ownership did not strictly adhere to legal definitions. Women as well as men clearly felt uninhibited in claiming the right to protect goods and chattels that they deemed to be theirs, either as their own personal possessions or as part of the property of their household. This was commonly manifest in disputes over inheritance and in instances where household and family members physically defended property from bailiffs and constables who attempted to serve warrants of distraint. But tensions within as well as between households resulted in prosecutions for theft that could take many forms.

Much criminal justice appears to have been dispensed in a manner that is difficult to reconstruct given the sources available to us. Juries based their decisions upon the facts of a case, the relevant legal rules and their perception of a defendant's character. The disparate treatment of the women and men who came before them implies that the sex of an offender was one

---

[230] By 'right action' I mean the moral superiority on which testimonies drew in order to place the examinant in a stronger position than his or her adversary.

variable but not necessarily the primary consideration. The impression of randomness in judicial decision-making is largely the result of the fact that 'the idiosyncratic pressures of acquaintance and dependence, of prejudice and superstition, are largely unrecoverable', as Herrup has pointed out.[231]

In recent years, juries and their verdicts have been the focus of a great deal of research. The debate has centred around the notion of jury lawlessness: that is, whether jurors were instruments of the state, their criteria for returning guilty verdicts in capital cases being predominantly based on the requirements of exemplary punishment; or whether their decisions were more informed by community norms, in which case the jury was a mitigating force which saved defendants from the full force of the law. Proponents of both views have arguably misrepresented the social context of the jury system, as both use a quantitative model to discern patterns in judicial decision-making that effectively treats 'the jury' as if it were a static and homogenous entity.[232] In Cheshire, both grand and petty jurors were drawn from 'a coherent social group, the middling freeholders'. Assize jurors in other counties were perhaps drawn from a broader social group than the lowest rank of gentlemen who served in Cheshire, yet despite local differences, jurors everywhere were drawn from 'the better sort' and might have shared a range of social attitudes.[233] Juries were nevertheless made up of individuals. In the courtroom, moreover, they dealt with other individuals – individual defendants, victims, justices, judges, witnesses and members of the wider community who often intervened successfully on behalf of the accused. The Cheshire magistrate, Sir Richard Grosvenor, located his critique of the grand jury precisely in these terms when he lamented the 'three main enemies which hinder the perfection of this service': 'the first is fear to offend great men our superiors; the second is favour and affection we bear towards our friends

---

[231] Herrup, *Common Peace*, 142, 144–5.
[232] Beattie, *Crime and the Courts*, chs. 8–10; Cockburn, *Introduction*, chs. 6 and 8, and conclusion; J.S. Cockburn, 'Twelve silly men? the trial jury at Assizes, 1560–1670', in J.S. Cockburn and Thomas A. Green eds., *Twelve Good Men and True: The Criminal Trial Jury in England, 1200–1800* (Oxford, 1988), 158–81; Green, *Verdict*, ch. 4; Hay, 'Property, authority and the criminal law'; Herrup, *Common Peace*, ch. 7; Herrup, 'Law and morality in seventeenth-century England', *P&P* 106 (1985), 102–23; P.J.R. King, 'Decision makers and decision making', *Historical Journal* 27 (1984), 25–58; John H. Langbein, 'Albion's fatal flaws', *P&P* 98 (1983), 96–120; John H. Langbein, *Prosecuting Crime in the Renaissance: England, Germany, France* (Cambridge, Mass., 1974), 104–28; P.G. Lawson, 'Lawless juries? The composition and behaviour of Hertfordshire juries, 1573–1624', in Cockburn and Green eds., *Twelve Good Men and True*, 117–57; Joel Samaha, 'Hanging for felony: the rule of law in Elizabethan Colchester', *Historical Journal* 21 (1978), 763–82.
[233] In Cheshire, grand and petty jurors came from the same social group. Morrill, *Grand Jury*, 6, 9–10, 11, 12, 15–20. See also Herrup, *Common Peace*, 97–103; Stephen K. Roberts, *Recovery and Restoration in an English County: Devon Local Administration, 1646–1670* (Exeter, 1985), 67–81, 89; Joel Samaha, *Law and Order in Historical Perspective: The Case of Elizabethan Essex* (New York, 1974), 49–52.

and neighbours; the third is foolish pity extended where not deserved'.[234] Indeed, as Herrup has noted, since the grand jury should have weeded out cases which rested upon suspicion alone, the status of circumstantial evidence could result in many instances in which the decision rested upon the conflicting words of the individual parties and their witnesses. A defendant's attitude could itself lead to conviction if it suggested improbity on his or her part. And petty jurors often mitigated charges when it appeared that the crime was the consequence of necessity, immaturity or anything else that indicated that profit was not the motivating force. So, while gender partly informed the expectations of jurors, it cannot be properly disentangled from other phenomena.[235]

A gender analysis of theft and related offences has nevertheless shown that thefts by women and men were in many respects far less different than some commentators have assumed. Women committed certain offences that involved courage and initiative, such as burglary, housebreaking and cutpursing. Their spoils were not necessarily of less value and more mundane than men's. Both male and female patterns of theft make most sense when situated in the wider context of the activities and networks that pertained to women's and men's 'lawful occasions'. While men and women were both most likely to commit crimes either alone or with others of their own sex, the most common criminal associations revolved around household or familial relationships.

We are able to build up a picture of the relative treatment of men and women before the courts by comparing like with like rather than aggregating all offences. For larceny, the case for judicial leniency towards women is poor. For housebreaking and burglary, women had a lesser conviction rate except at times when they became more visible as offenders, when the gender discrepancy all but disappeared. Cutpurses and pickpockets of either sex had a low conviction rate, partly because the crime was infrequently prosecuted and partly because those prosecuted had proved themselves inept. The various characteristics of robbery and horse-theft, in contrast, related to male conviction rates in particular ways that did not pertain to women. The relative judicial treatment of men and women is therefore more complex than simple comparisons of all offenders would suggest. Benefit of belly and benefit of clergy must also be distinguished. Their administration worked on very different premises and their outcomes were incomparable. Benefit of belly

---

[234] CCRO, Eaton Hall Grosvenor MSS, Quarter Sessions Papers, Box 1/2/51, Jury Charge, undated, c.1625.

[235] Herrup stated similarly that in eastern Sussex 'neither the gender nor the stated social position of a defendant or a victim had a statistically significant relationship to the behaviour of petty juries', despite her general claim that the rate of conviction for women was low: *Common Peace*, 148–51; see also 155, 157–8 and Table 6.4.

was not synonymous with leniency towards women. Nor was the legal fiction of coverture. Although some women seem to have benefited from the idea that they could not be punished if they had been coerced by their husbands to commit unlawful acts, plenty more were convicted alongside husbands or prosecuted independently. Compared to unmarried women, however, wives do seem to have been pardoned more often. This is likely to have been in part a consequence of the negative repercussions of making a household mistressless. It was married women's responsibilities rather than their lack of accountability that distinguished wives' and spinsters' fates before the courts.

In the next chapter, I consider further issues connected to notions of responsibility and authority before the law.

6

Authority, agency and law

'Remember that authority is a touchstone which trieth every man's metal, and that justice is the summary and absolute beauty of all virtues. Abide this touch, blemish not this authority, stain not this virtue.' Thus Cheshire magistrate Sir Richard Grosvenor in 1636 advised his son 'in the public deportment as you stand in relation to authority, being a Justice in Commission of the Peace'.[1] Grosvenor, a magistrate and leading member of the county elite, seemingly had a clear notion of the manner and form that authority and justice should take. But neither were rigid concepts. Both were open to interpretation. On the one hand, authority was equated with official and legal supremacy, the institution or individual in possession of the power to command and enforce obedience. On the other, in any given situation, authority might be ascribed to persons who were not in positions of formal or structural power. Authority was closely associated and invested with notions of rights and morality. Justice, too, invoked notions that complicated its relationship with judicial administration and the exercise of power. It was measured upon a scale of conformity to truth, fact and moral righteousness.[2] These were slippery concepts. No single criterion existed whereby one might gauge the nature of justice. After all, the infliction of punishment might lead the victim of a crime and the judiciary to believe that justice had been done, yet the convicted person might not share this view.

Each of the previous chapters has broached the issue of how and with what practical implications order, culpability and authority were articulated. Here, I wish to develop those strands of argument and explore further the related concepts of authority and responsibility, justice and law. I shall suggest that notions of lawfulness and unlawfulness were drawn from a range of specifics, and that people ascribed to themselves degrees of lawfulness, honesty and authority accordingly. First, I shall look briefly to the law as an expression

---

[1] CCRO, Eaton Hall Grosvenor MSS, Box 1/2/22, Personal Papers, Memoranda Book, Richard Grosvenor to his son, 10 August 1636, 37–55, at 51, 55.
[2] 'Fact' in this context was an alleged act that required proof. Barbara J. Shapiro, *A Culture of Fact: England, 1550–1720* (London, 2000), 8–33.

of elite authority. Next, I shall consider in turn aspects of popular legalism and popular resistance. Law is shown to have been multivocal. Not only did law itself draw on traditions of various sorts but also legislation implicitly contained the voices of the people as well as that of the legislators.

On the surface, these themes fit neatly into Keith Wrightson's explanatory model of 'two concepts of order' in which the concept of order is shown to have been ubiquitous but not monolithic. However, Wrightson's juxtaposition of a legislative/elite concept of order with an alternative village-based one may be limiting. As he himself notes, order was a mutable concept that might have 'different implications in different situations'.[3] Historians of crime have tended not to develop this latter aspect of Wrightson's argument. Instead, an historiographical emphasis on social polarisation tends to be underpinned by a consensual model of the relationship between ordinary people and the law. The concepts of lawfulness and order to which the people adhered was the result of the 'permeation of the law into the wider culture'.[4] We are constantly reminded that much litigation was between people of similar social status, that it was used to settle disputes, and that a high level of popular participation in administering the legal process resulted in ordinary people accumulating 'first-hand knowledge of how the law operated, albeit on a lowly level'. The law entered people's manifold ways: in marriage settlements, disputes and settlements over property and inheritance as well as debt, matters pertaining to the poor laws, and numerous other forms. The people, therefore, are seen to have accepted and to have respected the law. '[L]aw-mindedness came imperceptibly to colour social relationships and ideals.' Law had become an integral, 'internalised' part of 'popular culture' and 'a powerful cement of society'.[5] Law itself is presented as a homogenous and static entity, one that was the property of, and in the gift of, the ruling elite. Law was a means by which 'the people at large participated in the "great tradition" of their social superiors'.[6] Although the middling and lower orders are credited with having concepts of lawfulness and order,

---

[3] Keith Wrightson, 'Two concepts of order: justices, constables and jurymen in seventeenth-century England', in Brewer and Styles eds., *An Ungovernable People: The English and their Law in the Seventeenth and Eighteenth Centuries* (London, 1980), 21–46, at 22.

[4] Sharpe, 'People and the law', 247, 248, 267; Martin Ingram, 'Communities and courts: law and disorder in early seventeenth-century Wiltshire', in J.S. Cockburn ed., *Crime in England, 1500–1800* (London, 1977), 116.

[5] Sharpe, 'People and the law', 246, 256; Christopher Brooks, 'A law-abiding and litigious society', in John Morrill ed., *The Oxford Illustrated History of Tudor and Stuart Britain* (Oxford, 1996), 143. See also Herrup, *Common Peace*, 195–205; Ingram, 'Communities and courts'; Alan Macfarlane, *The Justice and the Mare's Ale: Law and Disorder in Seventeenth-Century England* (Cambridge, 1981), 197; J.A. Sharpe, ' "Such disagreements betwyx neighbours": litigation and human relations in early modern England' in John Bossy ed., *Disputes and Settlements: Law and Human Relations in the West* (Cambridge, 1983), 167–87.

[6] Sharpe, 'People and the law', 256.

these concepts are seen to have been injected by, imposed from, or otherwise shared with the conventionally defined political nation. Within this view, the people themselves are accorded little agency. In this chapter, I will scrutinise this characterisation of the people's relationship to law.

As E.P. Thompson noted, any analysis of authority, power and the law must offset that of the 'cultural hegemony' of the ruling class with a consideration of 'the images of power and authority, the popular mentalities of subordination'.[7] Thompson, however, tended to oppose authority and resistance, structure and agency. If we are to go beyond simple oppositions between 'control' and 'consent' or 'structure' and 'agency' we must first define some terms. As Anthony Giddens argues, without agency there would be no human history, and without structure in the form of institutions or discourses, agency would be purposeless.[8] Structure and agency are, then, inseparable. Activity can either reproduce or undermine structure, so historical analysis is required to determine how things work out in practice. The degree to which people are *conscious* of their ability to 'choose otherwise' varies historically, according to the ideas available to them, their education, their social position, and so on. The physical and social constraints on people's ability to choose to behave as they wish also vary historically.

Furthermore, we should not equate agency simply with the desire for change, since even maintaining the *status quo* in reproducing institutions and discourses requires the conscious choices and activities of people. First, the everyday choices made, values enacted and ends pursued by ordinary people in cultivating crops, choosing marriage, exercising a skill and supporting a household involve a form of 'private' agency and knowledge that characteristically are inscribed within and reproduce existing social structures. Secondly, individual or even collective agency in pursuing 'public' goals, such as is seen in religious movements, political struggles and military conflicts, is typically inserted into dominant formal structures rather than seeks to transform social relations. These are just as valid forms of agency as the final type, that of collective projects that seek to create or remodel whole social structures.[9] However, not all agency is conscious and goal-directed. Agency is also at work in the unconscious, unintended or unforeseen consequences of human action.[10] We might therefore identify several possibilities for the existence of agency in addition to behaviour that consciously sets out to change the *status quo*. These include purposeful activity that consciously

---

[7] E.P. Thompson, 'Patricians and the plebs', in E.P. Thompson, *Customs in Common* (London, 1991), 42–3.
[8] Anthony Giddens, *Social Theory and Modern Sociology* (Oxford, 1987), 219–21.
[9] For these categories of agency see Perry Anderson, *Arguments Within English Marxism* (London, 1980), 19–20.
[10] Giddens, *Social Theory and Modern Sociology*, 223.

seeks to preserve the *status quo*; behaviour that inadvertently reinforces the *status quo*; behaviour that is directed consciously at private (individual or collective) goals but which unintentionally undermines dominant institutions or discourses; and behaviour that aims to change or restore a group's position within a generally agreed framework.

In our particular case, we find that people appeal, for example, to the notion of the integrity of the household or to traditional rights. Whether or not such appeals reinforce or challenge conventional structures is a matter for investigation. The household and popular legalism may constrain individuals and position them in particular ways, but they may also constitute a resource that people can use for other purposes.

AN ELITE MECHANISM

It hardly needs to be said that law was frequently called upon to enforce or affirm the authority of elite individuals and groups. George Booth, for example, baronet, knight and magistrate, desired the bench that one of his tenants be continued in bond to keep the peace, 'in regard he uses threatening speeches against my officer whom I employ in my business in that place'. Booth was confident that his wish would be granted.[11] Secular and ecclesiastical officials regularly used legal mechanisms against those who were disrespectful towards them or with whom they otherwise disagreed. In effect, the law was used as a political tool to control public speech. Speaking out against a magistrate, mayor or minister, for instance, could by definition be construed as 'scandalous', 'seditious' and 'infamous' whatever the precise nature and tone of the words spoken.[12] Figures of local authority had a greater purchase on the concept of a threatened social order than ordinary complainants who had to rely on more general notions of a broken communal peace. An official complainant's adversary was presented as not merely abusing him personally, but as potentially or actually disrupting the entire social order. Here we have a clear convergence of power and self-conscious agency designed to reproduce the existing social order.

Thomas Parnell, Mayor of Congleton, in 1620 reported 'two very irregular persons refusing to be obedient to the rule and government of th'officers of [Congleton], common quarrellers, disturbers of the peace and such persons as former mayors and constables were doubtful to intermeddle with in cases where they deserved punishment'. At Parnell's investiture as mayor, the two men, accompanied by 'great numbers of other rude, barbarous, and uncivil persons, some by their incitations and others emboldened by their lewd misdemeanours raised an uncivil tumult in the public assembly for the election

---

[11] CRO, QJF 49/3/121 (1620).   [12] For example, CRO, QJF 49/1/74 (1620).

of the new charter...made public shouts and raised unfitting oppositions drawing [Parnell] by violence from taking his oath, pulling him from the book making public proclamations at that instant both in the Common Hall and after at the High Cross...that [Parnell] was no mayor, neither was there any mayor in the town'. That evening, the two ringleaders allegedly assaulted with knives and candlesticks the former mayor and other notables including the schoolmaster and the preacher. In a symbolic as well as physical gesture of disrespect, they cut one fellow's hat into pieces and tore his clothes. These and further incidents might have been part of a factional struggle for control of the Congleton Corporation; the events sound suspiciously like an election riot. But Parnell's elected position, however much disputed, meant that his use of the language of tumult had a great force before the law.[13]

In 1661, Edward Warren, JP, informed the clerk of the peace that Thomas Wasse 'has taken that desperate oath of the peace' against Stockport's mayor, constables and an alderman. On the one hand, the incident shows that ordinary people resorted to law to protect them from those who abused their office. On the other, it is clear that the forces of authority coalesced against those who spoke or acted against them. Warren insisted that the officials concerned were 'men of good and civil conversation, and of good estates and repute'. The alderman, moreover, was nearly eighty years old, and hardly constituted a mortal threat. Wasse, in contrast, was 'a constant troubler of the peace' who had been previously bound over. His grievance was presented as a manifestation of his own misbehaviour. He now swore the peace in retaliation for being punished for 'abusing' the mayor 'in his authority sitting in his court with the aldermen and constables about him'. Warren concluded his letter with the overriding concern of the authorities: 'The practice...is a mischievous example. For those offenders who you, I, or any Justice of peace shall punish may for the like revenge swear the peace against such of us.' Accordingly, Wasse, rather than the officials about whom he complained, was bound over to be of good behaviour.[14] Disrespect that went unpunished obviously undermined the local elite's position. Justices took such incidents extremely seriously.

JPs were particularly sensitive to derisive comments made by those beneath them. Mary Janson, furious when a constable came to her house with a warrant from Edward Legh to search for stolen goods, exclaimed that the magistrate 'had utterly undone both her and her children' and that she cared for him 'no more than for a fart of her arse'. She was bound by recognisance not explicitly because she was suspected of receiving stolen goods but because she was of 'evil fame and very bad behaviour and hath lately spoken

---

[13] CRO, QJF 49/3/63 (1620).
[14] CRO, QJF 89/3/85 (1661). See also, QJF 89/2/31, 32 (1661); QJF 89/2/49 (1661).

and uttered divers opprobrious and scandalous words against Edward Legh of Baguley'.[15] Thomas Percival was bound over for uttering 'threatening and disgraceful words' to two gentlemen, Peter Mainwaring and Hugh Mainwaring, Steward of Witton Court;[16] Henry Low was bound likewise for 'abusing Doctor Foster in words'.[17] These people were bound not to the peace, but to their good behaviour, a sanction that was used when the culprit was believed to constitute a threat to social order generally rather than to an individual alone. The bench's sensitivity to abusive words spoken to gentlemen and officials was heightened during and after the civil war years, when county justice was administered by many lesser gentlemen whose families had no history of public office, and when sectarianism created another level of potential abuse.[18] Thus in 1651 a man was hauled before magistrates for calling Colonel Henry Bradshaw (who had been among the militant faction under Sir William Brereton during the civil wars and was now associated with establishing a Presbyterian classical system of religion in the county) 'plow chorle' or 'plough hog', meaning thereby that he was base and low-bred. Another who commented sarcastically on Bradshaw's plain apparel not befitting his status as 'the King's elder brother' quickly excused himself by saying that he had uttered the said words 'only by way of discourse, and not forth of any malicious, evil or malignant intent against the keepers of the Liberties of England or the present government'.[19] The bench's concern was extended to those who held lower positions. When the head constable of Bucklow Hundred complained in 1645 that Richard Eaton 'did intemperately revile him with uncivil and abusive speeches', the bench declared that it conceived 'officers to be worthy of regard and protection'. Eaton was forced to acknowledge his 'error and rashness' in open court and bound to be of good behaviour.[20]

Early modern hierarchy was believed to be propped up by a visual and public display of patronage and paternalism on the part of the gentry, and deference on the part of their social inferiors. This was apparent in the gentry's public role in administering law.[21] Magistrate Peter Legh wrote to the bench on behalf of two of his tenants, James Hey and his mother who would, he assured them, appear 'in humble manner to submit themselves to your

---

[15] CRO, QJF 95/2/49, 85, 87 (1667).   [16] CRO, QJF 53/3/42 (1624).
[17] PRO, CHES 21/3, fo. 129v (1626). See also CRO, QJB 1/5, fo. 172v re. Lawrence Leicester (1627); QJB 1/5, fo. 211r re. Raphe Leicester (1628); QJF 75/4/131 (1647); QJF 87/1/58 (1659); QJF 91/1/93 (1663).
[18] For example, CRO, QJF 75/4/131 (1647); PRO, CHES 127/1 re. Edward Bostock (1648).
[19] CRO, QJF 79/1/38, 78 (1651). On Bradshaw, see Morrill, *Cheshire*, 52, 264–5.
[20] CRO, QJB 1/6, fo. 94r (1645). See also QJF 73/3/103 (1645).
[21] Thompson, *Customs in Common*, 47–9; E.P. Thompson, *Whigs and Hunters: The Origins of the Black Act* (London, 1975), 219–69; Hay, 'Property, authority and the criminal law'.

fine'. He requested that the Justices at sessions 'impose some reasonable fine upon the indictment'. Hey, his mother and another woman had been convicted of a riotous affray upon John Rowbotham. Yet Legh's patronage effectively rewrote events to turn the Heys' misdeed into that of their victim's. 'Consider the smallness of the offence', Legh wrote, 'and the troublesome nature of Rowbotham in vexing them with this troublesome suit' at Macclesfield court as well as at the quarter sessions.[22] Magistrates manipulated fluid notions of order in the same way that their lesser neighbours did. But the word of a magistrate in such cases was invested with authority in every sense of the word: social, moral, legal and political. Their position *vis-à-vis* the administration of the law was dependent upon maintaining this all-encompassing authority. Their patronage of their neighbours and tenants served to reinforce this, both in the act itself, and in the manner in which their wishes were expressed to the bench. Just as in the examinations and petitions of the protagonists, in the letters of magistrates and other gentlemen seeking favours on behalf of others, versions of events were written or rewritten in order to present the recipient of such favour as worthy. Fines were reduced ostensibly because the adversary was 'troublesome', because the protagonist was 'innocent' or 'ignorant', or because the business was 'small'.[23] There seemed to be no tension in questioning the findings of the legal process because the administration of justice was understood to be discretionary. The elite framed their requests with a language that compounded legality and discrimination – what they wanted, after all, was a 'lawful favour'. Such terms are, however, multivocal. While seeking favours for poorer tenants or neighbours bolstered paternalism, it also might inadvertently have legitimated resistant behaviour. The lower orders appear to have seen patronage as something that they deserved even when they had committed a wrong.

Justices of the peace were not necessarily neutral, impartial arbiters. They often did fix cases in their own interests. Randle Mainwaring, for example, asked the Clerk of the peace to mitigate a fine imposed on one of his brother's tenants for killing a hare in the snow, as the man's rent was in arrears. Payment would be even less likely to be forthcoming if the fellow had to cough up for a fine.[24] Humble litigants to equity courts not infrequently referred to the 'terrifying' use of the common law against them by magistrate landlords or those who had other influence on the county bench. The refrain

---

[22] CRO, QJF 55/1/66 (1626).
[23] For example, CRO, QJF 55/2/59 (1626); QJF 55/2/99 (1626); QJF 55/2/147 (1626); QJF 55/2/98 (1626); QJF 55/1/76 (1626); QJF 55/2/44 (1626); QJF 49/1/108 (1620); QJF 49/1/140, cf. QJF 49/1/18, /43, /110 (1620); QJF 49/1/148 (1620).
[24] CRO, QJF 55/2/61 (1626). See also Richard Grosvenor's concerns, CCRO, Eaton Hall Grosvenor MSS, Box 1/2/22, Memoranda Book, 51–2.

of the Levellers that 'no man should be his own governor' attended to the real concerns of ordinary people.[25] This is not to say that all paternalism was feigned. Richard Grosvenor's concerns were probably genuine when he advised his son that 'when poor snakes shall be brought before you to examine, beware that you fear [frighten] them not; neither triumph over nor trample upon the misery of such... And in your examinations labour to discover the truth, but entrap not poor, simple men in their own words.'[26] But his words acknowledge that law and its procedures were inherently biased in favour of the ruling class.

Law nonetheless provided a handy tool for those of less notable status but who nevertheless stood in positions of authority over others. A woman who was pregnant with her master's child said that her master forced her to name another man as the father of the child by threatening 'to lay her in the House of Correction or to drive her out of her country'.[27] One man seems to have procured spells of incarceration for his 'disorderly' ex-servant in both the House of Correction and the county gaol because he was consumed with jealousy, believing that the servant had been having an affair with his wife.[28] In such cases, the law operated as an extension of household authority. The law and the mechanisms of 'justice' provided an arena in which power relations could be extended and played out. This applied in both structural and conceptual terms. The potential tension inherent in the failure of heads of households to exert sufficient influence over household members was usually avoided by emphasising the extremity of the threat that such miscreants posed to the entire community. Such malefactors were inherently 'evil'. The extent of the disorder thus served to enforce rather than to undermine the authority of the complainant.[29] Nevertheless, official authority was usually the last resort when order within the household was subverted or undermined. (For the most part, there appears to have been resentment of 'public' or official interference in 'private' or household matters. For example, when Oliver Pollett threatened to kill his wife and her brother, after he found her drinking in an alehouse, the alehouse keeper announced that he would fetch the churchwarden as the nearest JP, Sir Thomas Mainwaring, was not then at home. Pollett replied that 'he cared not a fart for the churchwarden nor for [the JP] neither, for he [Oliver]... would whip his wife to Sir Thomas's

---

[25] *Puritanism and Liberty Being the Army Debates (1647–49): From the Clarke Manuscripts*, ed. A.S.P. Woodhouse (1938; London, 1992), 339.
[26] CCRO, Eaton Hall Grosvenor MSS, Box 1/2/22, Memoranda Book, 52.
[27] CRO, QJF 97/1/105 (1669).
[28] CRO, QJF 49/2/144 (1620); QJF 49/3/80 (1620); QJF 49/4/26 (1621).
[29] For example, QJF 49/1/151 (1620); QJF 49/2/150 (1620); QJF 49/2/161 (1620); QJF 97/3/126 (1669). For the inverse of this in complaints made by the parents of adolescents in service against masters, see QJF 57/1/24 (1628); CRO, QJB 1/5, fo. 110v; QJF 57/2/40 (1628).

gates and from thence home with an iron whip, [and] what had Sir Thomas to do with that?')[30]

The law itself was not a homogenous entity, as the sheer number of alternative jurisdictions suggests. In the Westminster and local courts to which custom and equity were central, notions of law were by definition specific to particular jurisdictions or communities. By extension, the law's scope was far from uniform. Different bodies of law were frequently at variance with each other. An extreme version of this is found when civil war brought common and martial law into conflict.[31] But different or overlapping types of law were pitted against each other throughout the early modern period. Attempts by landlords to evict or otherwise intimidate or oppress their tenants under common law were sometimes countered by those tenants' appeal to equity. There were indeed many instances of equity courts overturning common law verdicts in favour of tenants.[32]

Law was also dynamic. In a period that experienced the Reformation of the Church, civil wars, regicide, republican rule and the Glorious Revolution, along with less immediately tangible but equally significant processes of social differentiation and local elite formation, lawfulness and unlawfulness were defined and redefined many times and in many ways. In the middle decades of the seventeenth century, even what constituted treason and sedition underwent change. Particular speeches had different implications depending upon where and in whose company the speaker was and the precise date on which the words were uttered. To confuse matters further, during the civil wars, 'laws of war came into conflict with laws of peace that punished taking arms against authority as treason'.[33] During the first civil war, opponents on both sides were treated as enemies rather than as traitors; during the second, however, 'the military crime of breach of faith and the civil crime of treason mingled. Exemplary justice, long a staple of discipline *in terrorem* within one's own army, was extended to defeated enemies.'[34] Treason was redefined further with the 1649 Treason Act, which declared that any plot or force against the republican government, 'the Supreme Authority of this nation', was now deemed high treason. In practice, this compounded martial and civil law, effectively voiding the legitimating nature of the former. When Colonel John Morris was prosecuted under this Act for

---

[30] CRO, QJF 91/3/44, /37 (1663).
[31] Barbara Donagan, 'Atrocity, war crime and treason in the English civil war', *American Historical Review* 99, 4 (1994), 1139.
[32] E.P. Thompson, 'The grid of inheritance: a comment', in J. Goody, J. Thirsk and E.P. Thompson eds., *Family and Inheritance: Rural Society in Western Europe, 1200–1800* (Cambridge, 1976), 328–60.
[33] Donagan, 'Atrocity, war crime and treason', 1139.
[34] Donagan, 'Atrocity, war crime and treason', 1161.

his part in the Royalist taking of Pontefract in 1648, he attempted to defend himself by evoking both martial and common law. According to the laws of war he had 'not done any unsoldierly and base act'; according to common law, his actions constituted no offence under the law of treason then in effect. His defence, like that of so many others, was unsuccessful.[35]

Certain concerns of the bench changed over time too and informed practice.[36] Up to the 1620s, Justices in Cheshire seem not to have been particularly concerned about the numbers of alehouses *per se*, but focused on suppressing only those that were disorderly or unlicensed. That changed in the early 1630s with directives to restrict licensed alehouses to two or three in market towns, one in villages, and none in hamlets.[37] The tempo of the campaign for alehouse regulation increased after the first civil war, when the bench became particularly vexed by the proliferation of 'unnecessary' alehouses.[38] Thus, a township that had had thirty-one alehouses could suddenly find itself reduced to a mere three. The keepers of those three, of course, had to be thought 'sufficient' by the authorities. While John Beckett senior was 'an honest man, and fit to keep an alehouse', Robert Ellams, who refused to subscribe to the Solemn League and Covenant, was considered unfit and was prohibited from selling ale.[39] This new emphasis on 'unnecessary' alehouses was not due solely to the invigoration of the bench by the Deputy Lieutenants (who in Cheshire operated as a committee, although no formal County Committee was established as they were elsewhere).[40] Feeling against alehouses was strong among Puritan laymen as well as magistrates and preachers. In 1647, a quarter sessions order concerning alehouse licensing ordered the local JPs to seek the advice of 'ministers and others of the better sort', while constables certified that many 'well-affected' persons desired the number of alehouses to be reduced.[41] Fifty-five inhabitants of Astbury parish, for instance, in 1646 entreated the bench to 'bend your strength, power and authority towards the speedy suppression of this growing evil, which, if not prevented will like a gangrene endanger the whole body'. They were quite specific about the 'evil' that alehouses presented. Their petition:

---

[35] Donagan, 'Atrocity, war crime and treason', 1162, 1159–61.
[36] This varied from county to county. Magistrates' responses to the 1631 Book of Orders, for instance, are said to have resulted in more effective enforcement of social policies in counties such as Essex, Somerset and Warwickshire, while in Cheshire the administrative achievement was allegedly 'unimpressive': Hindle, *State and Social Change*, 8.
[37] For a summary of these concerns, see Hindle, *State and Social Change*, 152–3.
[38] For example, QJF 74/2/33, /34, /36 (1646); QJF 74/4/27 (1647).
[39] CRO, QJF 74/2/30, /35 (1646). See also QJF 74/2/72 (1646).
[40] Morrill, *Cheshire*, 82–3.
[41] For example, CRO, QJB 1/6 fos. 134r–134v, 135r–135v, 138v–139r (1647); QJF 75/1/48, /49, /77, /102 (1647).

sheweth that the Captain of our salvation is highly dishonoured, youth greatly corrupted, men's estates occasioned to be embezzled by an excessive number of disordered and unlicensed alehouses: the nurseries of all riot, excess, and idleness; the dens, shops, yea thrones of Satan; the sinkers of sin, which like so many common shores or receptacles refuse not to welcome or encourage any (on days set apart for His worship and public humiliation through the kingdom) in the most loathsome pollutions they are able to invent and put in practice.[42]

JPs' concerns were not solely moral. Idling in the alehouse at times of divine service constituted a problem for the purse as well as the soul. Absence from church in favour of tippling meant the avoidance of paying the poor rate and other dues, which in many parishes were collected in church after divine service as all inhabitants were supposed to be present.[43] More pressingly at times of dearth such as during the 'famine' of 1647–8, beer-brewing depleted stores of grain, a problem to which magistrates were particularly attentive.[44] A petition in 1648 from thirty-nine 'religious and well affected' inhabitants of Hale suggests how moral and practical concerns about alehouses were entwined. On the one hand, they 'have willingly during the late troubles endeavoured to contribute what lay in our power that might any way promote the work of the Reformation within this kingdom', but 'to our great grief' the profane sin of drunkenness had continued, 'which is indeed the basis and foundation of many other horrid iniquities'. Alehouses were 'fit stalls and receptacles for all the unclean birds that flock unto them'. On the other, 'many doleful and hideous lamentations... flow from the mouth of poor people who sadly complain that they cannot buy corn in the markets for money, by reason of those many maltsters who do engross the best and most part of barley that comes to be sold'.[45] Early in 1648, the poor of Nantwich petitioned at quarter sessions, lamenting that the price of grain was so high that 'where there are four or five in a family, a fortnight's getting by their trades and labour will not serve to provide them victuals for a week'. They requested that something be done about 'malt-makers, bread-bakers, alehouse-keepers, badgers, and forestallers', whose activities resulted in 'the affamishing and great oppression of the poor whose children cry out for bread and are like to perish for mere want'.[46] Being 'sensible of these miseries', the court was 'willing to take all occasion to lessen the unnecessary number of alehouses at all times but especially in these times of dearth and scarcity', when converting 'so great quantities of barley into malt to the nourishing and increase of riot and drunkenness' was 'needless waste'.

[42] CRO, QJF 74/1/76 (1646). See also QJF 75/1/33 (1647), which refers to the 'evil rule' kept in certain alehouses.
[43] Morrill, *Cheshire*, 244. For example, QJF 79/4/82 (1652).
[44] CRO, QJF 77/3/43 (1649). Paul Slack, 'Dearth and social policy in early modern England', *Social History of Medicine* 1 (1992), 1–17.
[45] CRO, QJF 75/4/42 (1648).   [46] CRO, QJB 1/6 fo. 167v (1648).

Despite their measures, unnecessary alehouses constituted a 'still growing evil'.[47]

In all the above ways and more, law was called upon by members of the early modern elite to maintain their hegemony over the lower orders. Yet we have seen that rigorous maintenance of law conflicted at times with the exercise of patronage, that elites themselves could be divided on the application of the law, and that law itself was not unitary. Although I have not elaborated upon this, the voices of the ruled are also evident in many of the examples above. The very idea that social order had to be upheld by legal processes recognised that society had no 'natural order'. If it had, there would be no need for the elite to use the law to maintain order.

PLEBEIAN USE OF THE LAW

The law in early modern England was not merely a force by which the powerful could regulate others. Ordinary people used the law for their own ends. The most obvious manifestation of this is in the sheer extent of litigation. In theory, the peace that miscreants broke with unruly and disorderly behaviour was not only the King's but was also 'common' to every member of the community, however humble. Moreover, law entered ordinary people's everyday lives in matters relating to, among other things, marriage, christening, burial, inheritance, the ownership of tenancies and freehold property, moveable goods, debt, taxation and the poor laws. As one student of the subject has remarked, 'Through frequent contacts with the legal machine, whether as litigants, local government officers, witnesses, jurors, sureties, or, indeed, as malefactors, the everyday culture of the English, the way in which they acted and expected others to act, were informed by notions derived and at times adapted from the law.'[48] This applied to women as well as men, although the lesser visibility of women in the legal process has meant that their relation to the law has conventionally been neglected by historians of crime and law. We now know that women's lesser involvement in administering law and as litigants did not preclude knowledge of law and the legal process. This was so even in areas that might be considered exclusively male domains. Women in north west Derbyshire displayed a sophisticated knowledge of mining law despite being called upon as deponents only rarely in the barmote courts.[49] When widows became eligible for war pensions in the mid-seventeenth century, they demonstrated a knowledge of both the law itself and the means by which the system might be worked, which made

---

[47] CRO, QJB 1/6 fos. 134v (1647), 167v, 161v, 179v (1648), 219v–220r, 227v (1649); QJF 76/1/59 (1648); QJF 79/2/113 (1651).
[48] Sharpe, 'People and the law', 256. See also Sharpe, *Crime*, 45, 144–5; Ingram, 'Communities and courts'.
[49] Wood, *Politics of Social Conflict*, 171–3.

them fierce rivals of the maimed soldiers with whom they competed for limited funds.[50] Women were active too in important quasi-judicial capacities, such as sitting on juries of matrons or as those who searched for witches' marks.[51] To understand more fully the ways in which law imbued the culture of ordinary women and men we must broach not only the way they used the law in material terms, but also the ways in which they conceptualised it. We must consider whether people evoked law in an attempt to change society or to advance their own interests.

Poor women and men often stressed that they could not afford 'to spend money to defend' themselves or to sue those who had wronged them.[52] Instead, they took advantage of another legal mechanism: petitioning the quarter sessions or assize bench was a cheaper alternative or addition to prosecution by other means. A Justices' order cost 2*d*., compared to recognisances and indictments at several shillings.[53] For instance, in 1665, after Thomas Jackson had obtained permission to build a little cottage on common land, a landowner in the parish prosecuted him at the Westminster courts to prevent him from doing so. Jackson responded by petitioning the quarter sessions bench, alleging that he was 'molested by Master Edmund Pershall' because he refused to 'turn and become his tenant'. He complained of the great charge that he was put to by the prosecution, and asked the bench to confirm their previous order. Jackson used petitioning at quarter sessions as a countermeasure in an ongoing legal struggle that was being played out in another jurisdiction.[54] Appealing to the bench was a popular means of countering legal suits. Prudence Beswick successfully turned to JPs when Richard Badcock and, at his expense, his servant Mary Barrow, 'did threaten by means of suits... to drive her out of the parish'. The reason for Badcock's animosity was that she had previously brought him before a magistrate for chopping up her gate for firewood.[55] Similarly, Anne Cleaton claimed in 1669 that four men had 'wrongfully' cast her husband into prison, thus leaving her in 'a very deplorable condition being as a widow', although neither she nor her husband had ever been indebted to them. On the contrary, she had previously sued them 'for the great abuses done to me and my child', since which time through their 'inveterate malice against me and

---

[50] Geoffrey L. Hudson, 'Negotiating for blood money: war widows and the courts in seventeenth-century England', in Jenny Kermode and Garthine Walker eds., *Women, Crime and the Courts in Early Modern England* (London, 1994), 146–69.

[51] J.A. Sharpe, 'Women, witchcraft and the legal process', in Jenny Kermode and Garthine Walker eds., *Women, Crime and the Courts*, 106–24. See also the role of women in extra-judicial capacities regarding theft in Walker, 'Women, theft and the world of stolen goods', 81–105.

[52] For example, CRO, QJF 55/3/95 (1626); QJF 79/2/137 (1651); QJF 83/2/188 (1655); CHES 24/118/4 petition of John Gorst (1626).

[53] CRO, QJF 95/1/150 (1667).   [54] CRO, QJF 93/1127 (1665).

[55] CRO, QJF 71/2/69, /85 (1642).

my husband', they had threatened 'me and mine after such sort that I dare scarcely pass out of my house for fear of bodily harm and the burning of my house'.[56] Cleaton's credentials were measured against those of her adversaries, underscored by the fact that the law could be abused by malicious people who desired to destroy her household: her husband had been removed, her physical dwelling was in danger, and her own capacity to leave the house and tend to her everyday duties as mistress of the household was curtailed. In another case, a widow accused the farmers of the excise for beer and ale of harassment. They made her pay more than the amount they had agreed upon, and then demanded payment although she had ceased to brew and sell ale.[57] Petitions were used regularly as a means of countering mistreatment by social superiors and officials. Such petitions were often successful. If direct orders were not made, the cases were frequently referred to the nearest JPs for arbitration. Quarter sessions files are peppered with such evidence. In this sense, indeed, the law 'did not belong to one group of men [sic]'.[58]

Popular knowledge of the law is also evident in the ways in which ordinary people adapted their complaints to new legislation or the expressed concerns of the bench at any given time. An example is in popular responses to official interest in swearing and blaspheming. Throughout the sixteenth and early seventeenth centuries, moralists had lamented people's propensity to swear, and swearing had long been a sin within the jurisdiction of the ecclesiastical courts.[59] The extent of central and local government concern varied over time. Many MPs believed that swearing was a purely moral offence that should continue solely within the jurisdiction of the Church, but Acts against common swearing were passed in 1601, 1604, 1610, 1621 and 1624.[60] The latter was a general prohibition on 'all profane swearing and cursing' upon pain of one shilling for every oath or curse. If the offender refused or was unable to pay the fine, he or she was to be set in the stocks (or whipped if under the age of twelve years).[61] There is little evidence that Cheshire

---

[56] CRO, QJF 97/1/125 (1669).   [57] CRO, QJF 95/4/140 (1667).
[58] Anthony Fletcher and John Stevenson, 'Introduction' to Anthony Fletcher and John Stevenson eds., *Order and Disorder in Early Modern England* (Cambridge, 1985), 15.
[59] For example, Stephen Hawes, *The Conversyon of Swerers* (London, 1509); Thomas Becon, *An Inuectyue Agenst the Moste Wicked [and] Detestable Vice of Swearing, Newly Co[m]piled by Theodore Basille* (London, 1543); Miles Coverdale, *A Christe[n] Exhortacion Unto Customable Swearers* (London, 1552); Edmond Bicknoll, *A Swoord Agaynst Swearyng* (London, 1579); Jean de Marconville, *A Treatise of the Good and Evell Tounge* (London, 1592); Abraham Gibson, *The Lands Mourning, For Vaine Swearing: Or The Downe-fall of Oathes* (London, 1613).
[60] Joan Kent, 'Attitudes of Members of the House of Commons to the regulation of "personal conduct" in late Elizabethan and early Stuart England', *Bulletin of the Institute of Historical Research* 46 (1973), 49, 71.
[61] Statute 21 James I c. 20.

magistrates were keen to enforce such legislation. However, as swearing fell within the summary jurisdiction of magistrates, there might have been more activity than formal court records suggest, perhaps at Justices' monthly meetings. In the mid-seventeenth century, though, official feeling against swearing had a higher profile. During the civil wars, both sides denounced soldiers' 'unlawful oaths and execrations', which were punishable by loss of pay and other discretionary penalties. In the 1650s, stamping out common swearing among the populace impacted on the public agenda in a new way. Given that magistrates had become exercised about it, people now found it most convenient to mention the number of profanities uttered by those they complained about. Hence, in 1653, Randle Kemp reported that upon charging John Johnson to be obedient to the state when Johnson resisted Kemp's attempt to distrain his nag, Johnson swore six times 'by God's flesh and wounds' that he cared for no state nor would obey them. In 1655, Edmund Shelmerdine was fined eight nobles for swearing 'by God' at least ten times during a quarrel.[62]

One of the most interesting aspects of popular use of legalistic language is the mutability of notions of authority at the point at which they intersected with those of lawfulness. As we saw in the case of patronage, law and morality were not always clearly linked. A claim of lawfulness might be made in opposition to another's claim of authority. This could be so even when that authority was legal. Anne Bailey told Justices that she had endeavoured to persuade the widowed Anne Hyde to obey Sir Fulke Lucy's warrant when she heard that Hyde had been sent for and had not gone, saying 'I advise you to get up early in the morning and go to him lest you come in further trouble.' To this, Anne Hyde answered: 'she would not go and she would not abide a second and a third warrant, and ere she would go to him Sir Fulke should draw her at a horse's ... tail, and when he had her he must take heed of hurting her, or [words] to that effect'. We are not dealing here simply with an orderly woman trying to bring a disorderly one into line. Of course, Bailey's words firmly positioned the magistrate's warrant within the social and political hierarchy; after Hyde's outburst Bailey told her that 'she must obey the King's laws'. This is perhaps unsurprising given that Bailey was recounting her speech before a magistrate – Sir Fulke Lucy himself, in fact. But in her own relation of the incident, Bailey originally told Hyde to obey the warrant not because the King's laws or magistrates' precepts must be obeyed *per se*, but because if Hyde disobeyed, she would get into trouble. Moreover, Anne Hyde's alleged words signal the fragility of the authority of individual

---

[62] CRO, QJF 81/2/151 (1653); QJF 83/1/73 (1655). For other examples see QJF 81/2/22 (1653); QJF 81/4/24 (1654); QJF 81/4/30 (1654); QJF 83/2/78 (1655); QJF 87/1/101 (1659); QJF 85/3/88 (1667); QJF 85/4/25 (1668).

gentlemen. While the structures and ideology of the law undoubtedly bolstered and maintained the role of the gentry in local society, concepts of lawfulness were not homogenous. Hyde's defiance was not merely part of a 'hidden transcript';[63] her refusal to appear before him was public and open. But, being told by Bailey that she must 'obey the King's laws', Hyde did not disagree. She answered that indeed 'she must so do'. Her disobedience was not to the King, for she claimed that she had done nothing wrong. Hence 'she would not go [before Sir Fulke Lucy], she had said nothing to any and she would not go. She would choose her Justice of peace and not go to Sir Fulke Lucy.' Anne Hyde does appear to have chosen her Justice: four days later she appeared before Sir John Arderne.[64]

Competing notions of lawfulness informed the rhetoric in which depositions and examinations were couched over a range of common law offences. Both men and women complained that the litigation against them circumscribed their own abilities to use the law to defend themselves or to carry out their 'lawful business' or 'lawful occasions'. They also invoked the 'laws of God and man' or sought 'remedy by law' against adversaries who prosecuted them at common law.[65] People regularly drew on notions of lawfulness and legal form in order to sanction behaviour that might otherwise be, or which was by others, construed as unlawful. Hence, in 1669, a 'great number' of Cheshire Quakers symbolically sanctioned their own unlawful activities by threatening to set in the stocks the constable who tried to break up their illegal meeting and arrest the preacher.[66] In this case, a mechanism of law enforcement was evoked in a critique of law itself. In many instances, however, law was resisted only as it applied in particular circumstances, not in general. When people openly defied the law and its officers they frequently presented their actions as 'right' and 'just' in opposition to individual legal officials to whom they attributed unlawfulness or injustice. In cases where abusive or accusatory words were spoken, alleged defamers frequently said that they would 'justify' the words, meaning that they would prove the truth of what they said in court.[67] Two brothers who were obstructed by the warrener when they coursed rabbits in Colonel Legh's warren in 1665 demanded 'what orders he [the warrener] had to take them up for coursing for they would justify what they did and would kill and carry away rabbits in spite

---

[63] For the concept of the 'hidden transcript', see James C. Scott, *Domination and the Art of Resistance: Hidden Transcripts* (London, 1990).
[64] CRO, QJF 97/1/100, /49, CRO, QJB 3/1, fo. 211v (1669). Hyde is also referred to as Anne Parker. For similar cases, see QJF 95/2/66 (1667); QJF 97/3/49 (1669).
[65] CRO, QJF 89/3/231 (1661); QJF 49/1/149 (1620); QJF 49/2/161 (1620); QJF 55/2/111 (1626).
[66] CRO, QJF 97/2/37 (1669).
[67] For example, CRO, QJF 95/2/57 (1667); QJF 95/1/95 (1667).

of the best in Adlington for they had orders of the sheriff of the shire'.[68] This latter case might or might not have been one in which the central issue was the recent enclosure of a rabbit warren upon ground that had hitherto been common land. Certainly, the use of legal language and force was a vital component of anti-enclosure and other activities pertaining to the protection of common rights. But differing notions of both law and unlawfulness underpinned claims on both sides in many kinds of dispute and not only those that may be categorised in terms of conflict between the people and their rulers. Again we see that notions of lawfulness were evoked to legitimate unlawful behaviour, yet in doing so, the system itself remained challenged only in as much as it applied to the individuals concerned. People's use of the law is seen frequently to reinforce the social system rather than to undermine it.

There are several legislative and administrative areas in which the law can be seen as an overt means whereby the elite aimed to control the actions of the lower orders in the early modern period. For instance, between 1576 and 1610 there were thirty-five parliamentary bills concerning drunkenness, inns and alehouses, nine against the profanation of the Sabbath, nine on bastardy and six against swearing.[69] If we add to this the numerous other pieces of sixteenth- and seventeenth-century legislation that combined to create the evolving poor law, the extent of moral, social and political control over the lower orders that was encapsulated in the law was far-reaching. Paul Slack has argued that by paying the poor rate, householders became visible members of respectable society, distanced from the destitute and disorderly: 'They had a vested interest in maintaining settlement rules, enforcing the laws against bastardy and unruly alehouses, and restricting relief to the evidently deserving.' Yet, as Slack points out, the lines that demarcated the respectable from the non-respectable were fluid. Moreover, the law and the courts formalised charity; they constituted a mechanism by which the benevolence of the elite could be demonstrated and the deference that confirmed social hierarchy could be maintained. Keith Wrightson has thus argued that the law in this respect provided 'in its balance of communal identification and social differentiation, a powerful reinforcement of habits of deference and subordination'.[70] This, however, is not the whole story. Ordinary people responded to these measures in a number of ways that complicate the view that the law was an effective means of social control.

In this section we have seen that individuals used elite notions of the law largely to offset the actions of their peers or to forward their own individual position in the face of interference by legal officials. While conscious agency

---

[68] CRO, QJF 93/4/82 (1665).
[69] Paul Slack, *Poverty and Policy in Tudor and Stuart England* (London, 1988), 130.
[70] Slack, *Poverty and Policy*, 130; Keith Wrightson, *English Society*, 181.

and a sophisticated knowledge of the law and its contradictions was involved, neither was used regularly in attempts to transform social norms. Bastardy, however, is somewhat different.

Bastard bearers

The laws against bastardy were weighted against the poor. The 'bastard child of persons able to keep it and not like to be chargeable to the parish' did not come within the scope of the relevant statutes.[71] The application of the law was particularly weighted against women. While both parents might be ordered to maintain a child, with the father contributing a greater amount, women were more likely to be whipped, incarcerated in Houses of Correction, or punished further.[72] The reason for this lay partly in the material fact that single women who bore children were unlikely to be able to support both themselves and their offspring.[73] (Conversely, when the mothers of bastards were given financial assistance, it might be lower than the going rate for putting the child out to nurse.)[74] The relative severity with which female bastard bearers were treated was also in part due to early modern conceptualisations of culpability for sexual offences. The Jacobean statute compounded lewdness with poverty to depict a particularly disorderly type of woman; a later Caroline statute defined the mother as 'lewd' while exonerating the 'putative' father from any such negative connotation.[75] Thus in 1668, Jane Nevat was bound by recognisance under condition that 'she shall not hereafter transgress or offend in the same kind and nature', while the fathers of her two illegitimate children were not required to enter into similar bonds.[76] In 1643, a gentleman petitioned on behalf of the inhabitants

---

[71] CRO, DLT/unlisted/19, 'Cases related to Sessions', 156; DLT/unlisted/16, 'Precedents', 59, no. 60. Statutes 18 Elizabeth I, c. 3. and 7 James I. c. 4. For bastardy, see Peter Laslett, Karla Oosterveen and Richard M. Smith eds., *Bastardy and its Comparative History* (London, 1980); Peter Laslett, *Family Life and Illicit Love in Earlier Generations* (Cambridge, 1977).

[72] Anne Lawrence, *Women in England*, 47, 82. For example, CRO, QJF 89/3/112 (1661), QJF 89/4/150 (1662); QJF 89/4/131 (1662).

[73] The relative material wealth and earning potential of single men and women is also reflected in the lesser amounts which women were typically ordered to pay towards the costs of the maintenance and education of their bastard offspring. In one case, in which the mother was 'so poor that she could be procured no sureties to be bound for her', it was ordered that while she kept the child for its first five years, the father was to pay to her the sum of thirty shillings annually; thereafter, he was to keep the child and she to pay him a mere 6s. 8d. annually, CRO, QJF 51/2/51, /52 (1622).

[74] For example, Alice Hawkshawe was awarded 6s. 8d. quarterly to keep a child for whom the deceased father had agreed to pay John and Ellen Blackhurst 40s. annually for its maintenance. CRO, QJB 1/6, fo. 67r (1642).

[75] Statutes 7 James I, c.4; 14 Charles II, c.12; CRO, DLT/unlisted/18, Peter Leicester, 'Briefe Notes' (1660), 122–3.

[76] CRO, QJF 95/4/82 (1668).

of Daresbury about a young woman who refused to name the father of her child, thereby forcing the expense of its maintenance onto the parish: 'Mary Picton...who liveth in the said town hath been abroad in the country and played the whore in plain terms, and returned to the town and there bore a bastard child, her mother being a midwife and who entertained her.' While the father was wanted in order to provide financial support for the child, the petition requested that Mary alone be punished for she 'hath not received any punishment for her fault' and 'exemplary punishment will cause others [not] to offend in the like nature'.[77] On the surface, then, the law may be understood to have been a means of controlling and punishing poor women's disorderly sexual behaviour.

The extent to which the Cheshire bench in practice applied punishments to female bastard bearers differed over time. For the most part, women were not whipped or sent to the House of Correction. Rather, they, just like the reputed fathers, were forced to enter into bonds concerning the financial arrangements for the child's upkeep until it was old enough to get its own living. It seems that the father was imprisoned and the mother whipped usually only after an initial order by the bench had been disobeyed. In the middle decades of the seventeenth century, however, JPs regularly ordered the whipping and incarceration of women.[78] (They did not, however, act on the demand of one supposedly falsely accused man to banish the lewd and incestuous woman from the township.)[79] At this time, magistrates also clamped down on males, although primarily in financial terms.[80] In general, though, bastard bearers in Cheshire were not treated as harshly as they were in certain other parts of England. Moreover, the view that the law discriminated against women must be tempered by the use which bastard bearers themselves made of the law. Granted, it was difficult for people to invest their own words with authority and legitimacy when they had committed an unlawful, immoral, dishonest act. This was especially so, perhaps, for poor women who were pregnant with or had borne illegitimate babies. There were, nonetheless, means by which the mothers of bastards attempted to assume lawful, moral and honest personae before the courts.

One of these was the transference of liability onto the father of the child by the complaint being mediated through the woman's own parent or guardian. This was sometimes a strategy to shift the focus away from the female bastard bearer, but at others simply reflected the girl's age or the financial implications

---

[77] CRO, QJF 71/4/19 (1643).
[78] For example, CRO, QJB 1/6, fos. 87r (1643), 182v–183r (1648); QJF 81/2/280 (1653); QJF 83/4/122 (1656); QJF 83/4/132 (1656); QJF 85/3/148 (1657).
[79] CRO, QJF 75/1/65 (1647).
[80] For example, CRO, QJF 75/4/40 (1648); the record had been removed into the file for 1648 from that for 1641, when the recognisance was taken. CRO, QJB 1/6, fos. 183r–183v (1648).

Authority, agency and law

for the petitioner.[81] In 1620, William Rafe appealed to the bench at quarter sessions after his daughter, Elizabeth, became pregnant by George Smallwood.[82] As with so many other bastardy cases, this case was not instigated by a parish elite concerned with the size of their poor rate. William Rafe used the courts to transfer his own responsibility as father of the child-bearing Elizabeth Rafe onto George Smallwood, the father of the bastard child. Speaking as the head of the household in which Elizabeth lived, he was able to align himself with good order, bypassing any culpability on his daughter's part. Smallwood 'hath got with child a daughter of mine'; Rafe was therefore able to appeal to the law 'upon complaint thereof', requesting 'some good order for relief of the child and the discharge of the parish'.[83] Consequently, Smallwood was ordered to pay to Elizabeth Rafe 26s. 8d. annually towards the child's maintenance for twelve years. Yet at the next quarter sessions, William and Elizabeth Rafe jointly filed another petition, asserting that 'Smallwood hath utterly refused and still doeth refuse notwithstanding he hath been thereunto diverse times required, contrary to all equity and right, and in contempt and breach of the said order.'[84] Smallwood's wrongful act is presented on two counts. First, he had defied the magistrates' order. Secondly, he had transgressed natural justice. In saying that Smallwood had acted 'contrary to all equity and right', William and Elizabeth Rafe drew upon notions of lawfulness and justice that went beyond the confines of the regulative business of the common law courts. Elizabeth Rafe expected payment from Smallwood because it was her natural right to have it, not merely because the law stipulated that putative fathers ought to maintain bastard children to keep the poor rates down.

This language of equity and natural law comes up regularly in these petitions, and not only when the complaint was mediated through others. A 'very poor' widow with an already great charge of other children, Margaret Hinkley, drew upon similar notions when she appealed to the courts after John Cowper refused to take their child from her as he was ordered to do, 'although the time is now expired contrary to his promise and to equity and conscience'.[85] Notions of equity could provide another means whereby

---

[81] See also CRO, QJF 49/3/154 (1620); QJF 51/1/120 (1622); QJF 74/1/38 (1646); QJF 75/1/112 (1647); QJF 77/1/31 (1649); QJF 89/2/216, /217 (1661); QJF 93/2/155 (1665); QJF 93/2/164 (1665). For a sister's petition and the charges she had been put to, see QJF 71/2/41 (1642).

[82] Smallwood was servant to Brereton of Ashley, an active JP. Rafe had originally gone to Brereton, who bound Smallwood over to appear at the first sessions after the birth of the child.

[83] He also said that he was 'a very poor man, and not able any longer to keep either his said daughter or the child', who was by then about 'three months' old. Claims of poverty were essential to the success of such petitions. CRO, QJF 49/1/137, /61, /127 (1620).

[84] CRO, QJF 49/2/ 67, /176 (1620).

[85] CRO, QJF 51/2/119 (1622). Hinkley evaded the question of her own responsibility by attributing the cause to her 'hard fortune' rather than a lapse of morals.

women might transcend the 'lewd', disorderly stereotype of female bastard bearers. Equity had evolved as a legal category to provide remedies in situations in which precedent or statutory law might not apply or be equitable. In the sixteenth century, it was formalised as a body of law practised in equity courts such as the Courts of Requests and Chancery, which was primarily concerned with the protection of property rights.[86] Evidently, it also provided a resource upon which people drew in other jurisdictions and for other purposes.

Women also transferred responsibility onto the fathers of their children by inverting the stereotypes of bastard bearers.[87] Alice Whisshall complained before magistrates that it was not she, but John Cotton, who was 'of very ill behaviour' which he 'hath showed himself towards me'. She told them, moreover, that Cotton 'hath heretofore used the like behaviour towards one Isabel Moore (a woman of honest parentage) by begetting her with child, and used her so basely that he caused her to refuse her country by the lewd behaviour he showed to her'. Furthermore, Cotton 'doth utterly deny to be father to the said child begotten on me, and doth accost me with very opprobrious speeches'.[88] Women presented themselves as honest, lawful and abused by an implicit juxtaposition of male dishonour and female honour.[89] The dishonourable conduct of men is a constant refrain in the examinations and petitions. The father's refusal to afford the woman 'any penny towards' her maintenance 'in the time of her lying in childbed' or for that of the child was condemned as dishonourable when it led to mother and baby being 'affamished and utterly undone'.[90] Katherine Turner, a 'very poor woman', presented the father of her child, 'a rich man', as having taken unfair advantage of her youth and innocence – she was only fourteen when she first entered his service and was 'corrupted' 'through his daily diabolical practices'. She being 'young and fearful', he was able 'through his subtlety and threatening speeches in the time of these distractions' to cause her 'to compound for the maintenance of the child and take only ten shillings *per annum* and that if I refused so to do, that he would cause me committed to prison during my life'.[91] Frances Moore had lived 'without any stains' and had been 'a just and upright servant' until she fell pregnant through Thomas Whittingham's 'allurements and future promises... to her utter undoing' and 'perpetual disgrace'. Not only had he 'brought her to this poor and weak condition, but

---

[86] For women's use of equity courts, see Stretton, *Women Waging Law*.
[87] The fathers of illegitimate children were sometimes, though rarely, described as 'lewd'. When such terminology was applied to men, it seems to have implied their ongoing dissolute lifestyle. For example, CRO, QJF 51/2/72 (1622).
[88] CRO, QJF 49/1/142, /64 (1620).   [89] See also CRO, QJF 49/2/159 (1620).
[90] For example, CRO, QJF 71/1/35 (1642); QJF 49/2/156 (1620); QJF 79/3/148 (1651); QJF 85/3/158 (1657).
[91] CRO, QJF 75/4/128 (1648).

instead of relieving her with any manner of comfort, doeth plot and devise...to work the disgrace, ignominy, and shameful reproach', which 'she doubteth not but it shall all return to his own disgrace'.[92] Whereas in cases of sexual insult it seems that women publicly gauged their honesty and honour by comparison with other women, in bastardy cases women's honesty was often gauged according to the dishonesty and dishonour of the men whom they held responsible for their pregnancy.[93] While it is true that these female tales of male sexual misconduct were intended to shift culpability onto the man concerned, they nevertheless reveal something about alternative ways in which female honesty could be imagined.

One of the most common claims that women made in bastardy narratives was that the man in question had broken a promise of marriage. This was enough to provide conceptual legitimisation of a woman's claim that she was the injured party.[94] Men were castigated for 'pretending love to me', for their 'fair pretences' and 'deluding promises'.[95] In 1622, Anne Williams laid culpability almost entirely upon her fellow servant, Thomas Prince. He 'with many cruel protestations and vows promised me marriage, in so much that being overcome with his most lewd tongue I consented unto my utter undoing unto his most unfortunate will in all, and now being with child by him, and he going under sureties for his appearance...at this sessions, for the answering of this so great a wrong committed against me, which unto my shame and utter overthrow I have, and am, to sustain at his hands, unless your worships commiserate'. Williams begged the Justices to 'be merciful unto me' for 'my state is so very poor I am not able to maintain myself'. But she did not merely request mercy, she demanded justice: 'that *in all right*, since he hath this undone me, he may be bound in good sureties for my maintenance in my time of weakness and for taking the child after my delivery'.[96] Sometimes the link between legality and honesty is even more explicit. Many women referred to contractual promises, having had the banns read out in church, or having arranged wedding days with the local minister. Alice Deane told magistrates that John Brownefield 'swore that he wished the devil might take his soul if he did not marry her...and on midsummer's day last she swore the same to him'.[97] Elizabeth Ditchfield said that Jeffrey Williamson asked her to marry him after their child was born. Afterwards, 'informing his parents of the said Williamson's speeches, they all agreed upon

---

[92] CRO, QJF 76/1/51 (1648).
[93] Laura Gowing, 'Language, power and the law: Women's slander litigation in early modern London', in Jenny Kermode and Garthine Walker eds., *Women, Crime and the Courts in Early Modern England* (London, 1994), 26–47.
[94] Men's denials of such allegations suggest this too: '[he] denies he ever promised her marriage, or at any time wronged her in thought, word or deed', CRO, QJF 89/2/191 (1661).
[95] CRO, QJF 74/1/32 (1646); QJF 83/4/132 (1655); QJF 74/1/42 (1646).
[96] CRO, QJF 51/3/112 (1622).   [97] CRO, QJF 89/4/76 (1661).

the agreement,...Williamson and Ditchfield went and thus publicly asked in the church according to law, and the day [was] appointed for the marriage'. But once Ditchfield had taken the child from the wet-nurse (whom Williamson was paying) to nurse it herself, Williamson called the marriage off. She insisted that she had been duped: 'by this means [he] supposeth to discharge himself of the child'.[98] Another woman, Katherine Lockett, said that she feared the father, Thomas Torkington, would not take the child as he should 'according both to the law and honesty'. Lockett reinforced her own legality and honesty at Torkington's expense by emphasising the non-sexual implications of dishonest acts. Not only did Torkington faithfully promise her marriage, and 'continued this suit for a long time', until 'through his many persuasions so far wrought under colour of marriage with me that he begot me with child'; but he then refused to take responsibility. Lockett 'in end was forced to flee to the consistory [court]...for relief', where she arranged to affiliate the child 'with the hands of seven honest women'. After Torkington and another man, a piper,[99] 'did solicit the greatest part of the women for the affiliation not to be present at that time', Lockett arranged for another affiliation to take place. She, then, had acted within the law; Torkington attempted to pervert it.[100] The bench responded positively to such petitions, passing orders according to its view of 'the unjust behaviour' of the father and 'the shame that he hath brought upon the poor woman' as well as the material expenses he put her to by not keeping the child or providing for her period of lying-in.[101]

By aligning themselves with legal process, women accessed a concept of honesty that could eclipse the shadow that their sexual activity might otherwise have cast upon their testimonies. This was so even when the tales which women told seem bitter and desperate.[102] Anne Dawson swore that John Dunbarr was the only man she had ever lain with, and that 'I never deserved the like or was at every time guilty of the like abominable sin and transgression but only with him...merely and only occasioned through his false deceitful and most desperate allurements.' She told Justices that Dunbarr 'hath kept my company in the way of love, or as a suitor for the space of

[98] CRO, QJF 49/1/139 (1620), QJF 49/2/104, /106–7 (1620).
[99] This connection might itself have implied disorderliness and unlawfulness.
[100] CRO, QJF 51/4/163 (1623), QJF 51/4/113 (1623). See also QJF 55/1/88 (1626).
[101] CRO, QJB 1/6, fo. 153r (1648).
[102] The court files contain many poignant tales of men's broken promises of marriage. Some women told their stories simply, merely stating the alleged bleak facts of what had happened. Margaret Gibbons said that John Key 'did promise her marriage and that he would make her as good as he could' in 1661, but after she became pregnant he said he would have no more to do with her; CRO, QJF 89/1/112, /114 (1661). Alice Oliver alleged that Thomas Mason had promised to marry her, but the morning after the baby was born he left saying that he was going to fetch her clothes 'but did not return to her again though she stayed almost a fortnight'; QJF 89/2/152, /153, /57 (1661).

three years last past', often promising to marry her, and 'as often times attempted me, hastily affirming and declaring that he would marry me, or otherwise set far and plentifully provide for me that I should never want, if I would but yield and consent he might have the carnal use and knowledge of my body'. It was 'by and through which deceitful promises I did for want of grace permit and suffer him to have [his way]' on three occasions. When she told him she was pregnant 'and moved him to take some course about it', Dunbarr endeavoured to persuade her to name some other man as the father of the child, for which he offered her four nobles a year.[103] Dawson avoided the taint of corruption by refusing his money. By using the law to rightfully affiliate her child, she ascribed to herself a lawfulness, an honesty, at Dunbarr's expense which his rejection of her would otherwise have destroyed. In such cases, women's honesty was not solely mediated through their sexuality; it could not be if their words were to have any force. Women who presented themselves as wronged by men who 'pretended love and great affection', or who seemed 'zealous and right' in their promises of marriage, drew upon particular constructs of righteousness, namely marriage and contract.[104] Women who claimed that they had resisted the attempts to bribe or coerce them to name innocent men as fathers of their illegitimate children also aligned themselves with law and honesty,[105] as did the many women who made other complaints against the men whom they accused as the fathers of their children.[106] In law, women had access to a public voice in which to consolidate those claims. In cases like these, law provided a means through which women reinforced their dignity, and re-inscribed their honesty, albeit within certain conventions that might themselves be constraining.

The contiguity of differing and contrasting notions of credit was another feature of these narratives. Men, with their economic, social and sexual advantage, appear to have used the language of credit to a greater degree than women did. The term 'credit' was, of course, a loaded one: it could apply to both economic and social worth. Undermining women's reputations by accusing them of lewd behaviour was a common means whereby deponents

---

[103] CRO, QJF 89/2/190 (1661).
[104] CRO, QJF 89/2/192 (1661). See also QJF 73/3/111, /112 (1645); QJF 74/1/42 (1646); QJF 75/6/123 (1648); QJF 89/2/191 (1661); QJF 89/3/76 (1661); QJF 89/4/75 (1662); QJF 95/4/55 (1668); QJF 97/1/57 (1669); QJF 97/1/93 (1669).
[105] For example, CRO, QJF 81/2/152 (1653); QJF 97/1/57 (1669).
[106] Women used the courts against men in a variety of circumstances. For additional cases of men's refusal to pay maintenance, see: CRO, QJF 49/2/149 (1620); QJF 49/3/74 (1620); QJF 55/1/88 (1626); QJF 57/4/13 (1628); QJF 75/1/95, /96, /109 (1647); QJF 75/4/91, /89 (1648); QJF 75/4/120 (1648); QJF 77/3/20 (1649); QJF 85/1/114 (1657). For men who fled or who might flee, see: QJF 51/3/96 (1622); QJF 53/2/96, /97 (1624); QJF 89/3/233 (1661). To ensure that the father was held responsible or for relief, see: QJF 51/4/105 (1623); QJF 89/1/245 (1661). For a complaint against a parish that withheld ordered relief, see QJF 75/1/60 (1647).

sought to elevate, in contrast, men's credit in order to give weight to denials of fatherhood. One young man's mother insisted that Ann Elcock's 'naughty carriage' in carrying herself 'wantonly towards himself in a manner not fit to be named' was 'the cause of committing that foul act', and therefore Elcock should 'bear an equal share in the burden which her folly hath brought upon them'. (The Justices, incidentally, disagreed and placed the greater economic burden on the fellow.)[107] Arthur Blackemoore likewise offset his own credit against that of Jane Briscoe. Blackemoore claimed to be a gentleman with an inheritance worth forty marks *per annum*. His accuser was in comparison 'a woman of very ill behaviour', who 'hath had divers bastards', and who before the birth of the child 'alleged another to be father by whom she had a former bastard'. Moreover, he claimed that she kept him bound from sessions to sessions by pretending that she believed he would flee the county, and that she had not proceeded against him by 'course of law' as she should have done. Nevertheless, Blackemoore's credit in monetary or social value did not outweigh that given to Briscoe's testimony. He was not released from his bond.[108] It is difficult to know how much one can make of such decisions taken by the bench. Most likely, magistrates and parish elites were primarily concerned to ensure that bastard children were financially supported outwith the poor rate.[109] By claiming superior credit, therefore, men may be seen to have played into the hands of the bench.

The petition of Robert Bertles *alias* Pedley suggests alternative ways in which the concept of credit could be used. Bertles reported that Mary Ryle was 'a most lewd woman for she hath had three base children since the death of her husband'. His own credit in the community was presumably little: he had only recently arrived in the parish of Mobberley, and he was a poor man. It was his lack of substance in wealth and repute that Bertles believed led Ryle to name him as the father of her child. Such a man did not have the means, in any sense of the word, to counter accusations. Bertles merely claimed that he was most 'wrongfully and unjustly' charged, and asked the bench to treat him favourably.[110] In another case, John Turner said that he 'did earnestly solicit' the mother of his bastard child to marry him when he discovered that she was pregnant. She, however, refused and landed herself employment as

---

[107] CRO, QJF 77/2/64 (1649).
[108] CRO, QJF 49/2/156, /163, QJF 49/3/58 (1620). See also QJF 71/1/31 (1642); QJF 75/1/65 (1647); QJF 75/4/78, /82 (1648); QJF 81/2/308 (1653).
[109] See also CRO, QJF 51/1/117 (1622); QJF 49/3/88 (1620); QJF 51/3/99 (1622). Constables who allowed the apprehended father to escape were sometimes held responsible for the maintenance of the child, as sometimes were those who had acted as sureties for absconding fathers. For example, QJF 57/3/52 (1628); QJF 51/2/135 (1622); QJF 74/1/38 (1646). Some others were successful in getting poor relief towards the child's maintenance, for example, QJF 91/2/93 (1663).
[110] CRO, QJF 55/1/47 (1626). See also QJF 55/3/95 (1626); QJF 95/4/68 (1668).

wet-nurse to a 'noble family...where she lives in great plenty'. Moreover, 'she has a £20 portion left her by her friends, besides her great wages and gifts, and refuses to pay anything at all towards the maintenance of the child'. In contrast, Turner was worth only £5 a year, and was likely to suffer 'great want and misery and the child to starve'.[111]

Credit, or lack of it, was not always used to women's disadvantage in bastardy cases. Elizabeth Peacock stressed that William Cross not only had reneged on his promises to marry her but also that he refused to support the child in any way, and had lied to the bench about his economic worth. He in fact possessed a messuage and lands worth sixteen pounds *per annum* while she had 'nothing for the payment of my maintenance but what I have by living as a servant under my mother'.[112] Elizabeth Rowson complained that ever since her child was born well over three years before, John Martinscrofte had not observed an order to pay her thirty shillings annually. Even if he now paid, she said, it 'will not near maintain the said child', because 'I am grown very weak in body, and very poor and weak in estate for that I have sold much of my apparel to maintain myself and the child.' In comparison, Martinscrofte was worth fifty pounds *per annum*. Rowson therefore demanded that the Justices order an increase in the maintenance payments and that 'I may have the child'. Martinscrofte was duly ordered to pay her fifty shillings annually in future, 'and all arrears past'. Rowson presented Martinscrofte as an unlawful, untrustworthy man, in stark contrast to her self-representation.[113] Ellinor Bosier similarly contrasted her own and Philip Johnson's credit when she requested an order be revoked by which she was to contribute 13s. 6d. annually in favour of an original order that laid the entire charge on Johnson. Her justification was 'that Johnson is a man much given to this filthy vice, and is a very rich man, and I but poor, and nothing to maintain myself but by my service, and never spotted with any the least light behaviour until I was thus defamed by his lewd abusing of me'.[114] These women, like so many others, used the concept of credit to place culpability upon the man, despite their circumstances.[115]

The wives of men who were accused of fathering illegitimate children also called upon the legal process for their own ends. Some time after Anne Button bore Richard Pancket's illegitimate child, she married Davie Jones, a Nantwich labourer. According to a former order, the child was living with Pancket, and Button was supposed to give him 12s. per annum towards its

---

[111] CRO, QJF 89/2/213 (1661). See also QJF 71/2/46 (1642); QJF 74/1/60 (1646); QJF 74/2/49 (1646).
[112] CRO, QJF 74/1/32 (1646). [113] CRO, QJF 89/1/230 (1661).
[114] CRO, QJF 75/4/91 (1648).
[115] See also QJF 74/1/67–/69 (1646); QJF 75/4/82 (1648); QJF 93/3/50 (1665); QJF 95/3/137 (1667).

maintenance. However, after Button's marriage, it was not Richard Pancket, the child's father, but his wife Margery who appealed to the bench to make Button's husband financially responsible for the child. Margery Pancket complained that '*I* hath kept the child hereunto and now of late came not by aid according to the order'; and she informed magistrates of Button's marriage, saying that 'Jones... will not take the child or yield to the order.' She wanted a new order to compel Jones and his new wife to keep up the payments. With the exception of the stock final phrase, requesting the JPs' 'tender consideration', and the assurance that in return she would pray daily for them, Margery Pancket's petition was devoid of sycophantic and deferential language. Her position in her household, and the parallel between herself as good housewife and Button as a disruptive force on that household economy, provided her with the authority she felt necessary to petition Justices on her own behalf.[116] In another case, Elizabeth Swindells went not to the man upon whom she had falsely fathered her child, but to his wife, asking her not to be angry and seeking her forgiveness. Again, it was the wife of the accused man, not the man himself, who presented the case to magistrates.[117] The concerns of the law and the construction of formal legal documents tend to preclude many references to the authority of women in bastardy cases. It is therefore all the more interesting that women themselves felt that they had a right to seek redress through legal means.

Both men and women used contrasts of rich and poor, honest and dishonest, lawful and unlawful in their examinations and petitions concerning bastardy. The legal process, as an arena in which various kinds of conflict were played out, offered women as well as men a language and a set of concepts of order, honesty and lawfulness upon which they could draw in order to invest their words and actions with some kind of authority. This is the case for a vast array of concerns. Yet the fact that such language and concepts were available to women who had borne, or who were about to bear, illegitimate children is revealing, for in the female bastard bearer we have a potent personification of disorder and dishonesty. That such women used legal language and metaphors to reinforce their tales before Justices of the peace illustrates that notions of the law did not belong only to the respectable male householder. Rather, they constituted an available resource for a much wider range of sorts of people. However insignificant women's involvement in litigating or administering the law might have been, even poor bastard bearing women had some purchase upon the 'popular consciousness' which 'formulated its own ideas about the law'.[118]

---

[116] CRO, QJF 49/2/174 (1620). See also QJF 95/4/59 (1667).
[117] CRO, QJF 97/1/57 (1669); QJF 97/1/104, /105 (1669).
[118] Sharpe, 'People and the law', 248.

In women's actions in bastardy cases, we see women defending themselves against culpability in the sense of one set of ruling ideas – namely, that bastard-bearers were lewd and dishonest – by appealing to another set of established notions about honesty, contract and credit. In an attack upon the double standard of sexual behaviour, men are pronounced guilty of deceiving women and acting dishonourably thereafter. These assaults upon the double standard at the same time reaffirm female weakness and vulnerability. The implication is that men – including those sitting on the bench – should protect women, for women outside of marriage are weak. Thus the marital household is also evoked as a positive force for women. While women are calling upon conventional notions, the effect is nonetheless potentially subversive in that the idea that women are to blame in bastardy cases is generally undermined.

Poor cottagers

Another area in which the poor might be expected to have come into conflict with the law was the building of cottages on commons and wastes. Legislation of 1589 made it illegal to erect such buildings without a licence from quarter sessions or assizes, as well as the consent of the lord of the soil.[119] Consequently, petitions to Justices of the peace requesting such licences constituted a dialogue between elite attitudes to poor cottagers and those of the poor themselves – the courts were again sites of negotiation. To be granted a licence in part reflected acceptance of the petitioner among the 'respectable' poor. Petitioners also usually claimed that they were legally entitled to build a cottage on the common land of a particular parish, especially after the Settlement Act of 1662. Petitions requesting licences to erect cottages, then, reveal something of popular notions of entitlement and rights, as well as of legality and respectability.

Petitions to magistrates for licences to build cottages fall into two categories: those that simply plead respectable poverty, and those that assert a range of additional reasons that either explain the petitioner's poverty or imply further reasons for their entitlement. The latter type was most common, and it is on these that the following discussion will primarily focus. Both types of petition included much that was formulaic. Petitioners, on their own initiative and/or encouraged by a clerk or scrivener, emphasised certain legally relevant themes: that they and/or their wives, children or other dependants had been born in the parish or township in question, or how long they had resided there; how many children they had, especially if they were 'small' and could not yet get their own living; their own age if they

[119] Slack, *Poverty and Policy*, 63.

were 'old'; that they had hitherto supported themselves and their families by their hard labour but were now too poor to pay what was referred to as the racked rent.[120] Reasons given for poverty varied from 'impotence' due to old age or sickness to circumstances such as fire conspiring against them, to being 'labouring' poor who had unfairly been cast out by evil landlords. After 1645, poverty was also explained by disabling injuries sustained while fighting for Parliament or having been plundered by the enemy.[121] Petitioners thereby presented themselves as deserving.[122] All of these reasons were common to male and female petitioners – female petitioners were usually widowed, and therefore additionally put their poverty down to their husbands' deaths.[123] Beyond these basic themes were further means by which petitioners constructed their worthiness.

One of the ways in which cases were promoted was by invoking the consent and goodwill of the community. Over the seventeenth century, petitioners became increasingly likely to procure the signatures of as many parishioners of repute as possible. They also placed greater emphasis upon the courtesy and helpfulness of their neighbours. Widowed Margaret Carter said that her dead husband's master promised to help her himself and get his friends to help too in building a cottage for her to live in. Twenty-six people, including seven women, who put their names to James Woods's petition stated that they 'shall be ready to put their helping hands to the cote's erection'. The seventy-nine-year-old John Watson 'hopeth to have the good will and... furtherance of the neighbours towards the erection of his cote being both loved and pitied by them'. James Richardson said that his neighbours had encouraged him to apply for permission to build a cottage in their parish.[124] Other people told Justices that from the charity of well-disposed friends and neighbours they had been given small poles, timber and other necessary building materials.[125] In some cases, these details of the love and help of the community were no doubt intended to override the concerns of legislation. After the Act of Settlement – or as Slack has more appropriately termed it, the Act of Removal – was passed in 1662, consensus and neighbourliness became even more important in substantiating claims of entitlement to erect

---

[120] For example, CRO, QJF 49/1/134 (1620); QJF 53/3/52 (1624); QJF 55/4/9 (1626); QJF 81/2/315 (1653); QJF 89/1/238 (1661); QJF 89/2/223 (1661); QJF 89/4/140 (1662); QJF 93/4/126 (1665); QJF 95/1/157 (1667); QJF 95/2/150 (1667); QJF 95/3/140 (1667); QJF 97/1/129 (1669).
[121] For example, CRO, QJF 74/1/71, /70, QJB 1/6, fo. 100r (1646).
[122] For contemporary perceptions and distinctions of poverty, see Slack, *Poverty and Policy*, ch. 2.
[123] Examples may be found in QJF 49/1/150 (1620); QJF 53/4/86 (1624); QJF 89/4/134 (1662); QJF 89/2/231 (1661).
[124] CRO, QJF 71/2/64 (1642); QJF 89/2/225 (1661); QJF 51/2/110 (1622); QJF 89/2/207 (1661).
[125] CRO, QJF 89/2/223 (1661); QJF 89/2/233 (1661).

a cottage on commons.[126] The hardening of official attitudes to the poor was also reflected in the increasing rate of denial of requests for licences. After the first civil war, the Cheshire bench began to qualify their granting of licences, stipulating for how long a cottage was to remain standing before it was to be pulled down – usually for a term of two lives (those of husband and wife) on condition the recipients behaved themselves well, but occasionally until such time as all the household's children had attained the age of sixteen.[127] The bench also began categorically to order that other poor people in a township were to pull down cottages that had been unlawfully set up.[128] Magistrates tended nevertheless to grant requests for licences. By the 1660s, however, the bench displayed a harder attitude; supplications were by then twice as likely to be unsuccessful as they had been in the 1620s.[129] This may reflect the local gentry's increased sense of security and power in the 1660s, a repercussion of the gentry's consolidated position as rulers in the provinces.[130]

Having the patronage of wealthy landowners or respected parishioners was a common means by which poorer people ascribed their own claims with authority, mediated though they were through the authority of others. A supportive petition asked that a woman be allowed to erect a cottage as 'for many years she lived and behaved peaceably amongst us... [despite having] little maintenance and a great charge'.[131] Richard Bathoe said that he had the 'free consent and the good liking' of parishioners and the lord of the manor. Jasper Griffin 'moved divers gentlemen freeholders and charterers within the manor', and was given consent 'upon the entreaty of the said gentlemen'. One man was 'much pitied' by gentlemen who allotted him a piece of land upon which to build a cottage; another said that consent was given 'in commiseration of his poor estate, knowing him honest'.[132] Certificates by lords of manors sometimes explicitly stated that the petitioner 'is a true and painful workman never addicted to any dissolute or disordered courses'.[133]

---

[126] The increased importance of named signatories might also have been a consequence of a more marked social differentiation in the later seventeenth century. Keith Wrightson, *English Society*, 140–2, 222–8. If this were so, then the middling sort would have been more easily identifiable as appropriate supporters of the respectable poor. See also Steve Hindle, 'Aspects of the relationship of the state and local society in early modern England, with special reference to Cheshire, c. 1590–1630', Ph.D. thesis, University of Cambridge (1993), 418, 422–3.
[127] For example, CRO, QJF 74/1/47, /78, QJF 74/2/19, QJB 1/6, fos. 101v–102r, 102v, 107r (1646).
[128] For example, CRO, QJB 1/6 fo. 108r (1646).
[129] In the 1620s, roughly one-sixth of petitions were refused. By the 1660s, this figure had increased to roughly one-third.
[130] Hindle, *State and Social Change*, 9.
[131] CRO, QJF 89/2/215 (1661). See also QJF 89/2/214 (1661).
[132] CRO, QJF 57/2/38 (1628); QJF 51/1/122 (1622); QJF 49/1/165 (1620); QJF 55/2/115 (1626).
[133] CRO, QJF 53/2/162, /110 (1624); QJF 85/3/153 (1657).

One gentleman asserted that although 'I am an enemy to all such erections where they can be avoided', the poor man in question had been 'thrust out of his dwelling' by his landlord, and 'having lived there long and being still painful in his profession of marling', he 'in all charity' should be permitted to erect a cottage.[134] Court orders granted licences on similar grounds, 'he behaving himself well' or 'pitying his misery'.[135] Thus, licences for cottages were given within a rhetorical framework that linked ideas of order, neighbourliness and Christian charity.[136] This rhetoric, however, should not be taken at face value.

In drawing on notions of good will or charity, either by neighbours or by the bench, petitioners placed themselves in a particular position before the law and those members of the county elite who administered it. They were poor supplicants, who presented themselves as needy of the beneficence of the authorities. Yet some petitions, while not disregarding the tactical language of deference, nevertheless indicate that the poor believed that they had some purchase on the law itself. A petitioner in 1642, who was unable to continue working as a weaver being afflicted with the 'falling sickness', successfully claimed a licence to erect a cottage 'as the laws of the land and your Christian charity have provided in such condition'.[137] When John and Elizabeth Maddock petitioned the bench in 1622, they said that they needed a cottage in which to leave their two children while they 'went forth to their labours to earn their sustenance'. They informed the bench that they were both born and bred in Astbury parish, and that they believed they would not become a burden to any if they had the court's assistance. Assistance is a different concept from charity; it does not invest the elite with the same type of moral and material control over the licence that the Maddocks sought. Moreover, they asked for an order enabling then to build a cottage on the commons there 'as to law and justice'.[138] Asking for a licence according to justice as well as law incorporates the notion of entitlement.

The experience of civil war created a new category of entitlement: that of one whose losses had been incurred in service to the state. While maimed soldiers were already granted pensions on such grounds (although they received no monies during the first civil war),[139] the civil wars saw a broadening of the scope of those to whom the state was perceived to owe assistance. Geoffrey L. Hudson has shown how war widows carved out a niche for themselves as petitioners for and recipients of limited pension funds.[140] But petitioners for

---

[134] CRO, QJF 77/4/62 (1650).   [135] CRO, QJB 1/5, fos. 26r (1620), 174r (1626).
[136] Hindle, *State and Social Change*, 147–8.
[137] CRO, QJF 71/2/71, QJB 1/6 fo. 77r (1642).
[138] CRO, QJF 51/2/115 (1622).   [139] CRO, QJF 74/2/67, QJB 1/6, fos. 108v–109r (1646).
[140] Hudson, 'Negotiating for blood money'.

cottages soon appropriated the concept for their purposes. In 1646, William Cheshire, 'a labourer in husbandry affairs', was given permission to erect a 'little piece of building' in a convenient place on the grounds that he and his wife had been 'since these times of eminent dangers... constantly ready for any service or design for King and Parliament [a common euphemism for the Parliamentary side in the civil war]' and that 'by reason or against reason of my service through the malice of some evil people neighbouring near unto me, when the enemy [the King's troops] came over the county [I] was robbed, plundered and my wife so abused which is and so I think will prove the cause to work a continual weakness upon her, which is to me great hindrance'.[141] Alexander Bancroft had for three years served as a soldier in Colonel Duckinfield's regiment under the command of Sergeant Major Henry Bradshaw, and he, his wife and three children sustained 'great losses' at the hands of Colonel Goring's Royalist forces. Bancroft, too, was granted a licence.[142] Robert Lewis, trained soldier for his township but 'refusing to serve under the array', had been imprisoned in Halton Castle 'where he endured great misery', and after his release took up arms for the Parliament; all the personal estate of his lately deceased father had been taken from him by the Cavaliers; the sequestrators now had possession of his father's tenement (the lease had expired) on account of his landlord's delinquency. In response, the bench ordered that Lewis was to enjoy his father's tenement 'upon the ancient or old rent'. Their expressed reason was that 'it is thought fit... for the encouragement of such as have been or hereafter shall be sufferers and do good service to the state'.[143]

Throughout the early modern period, the language of equity and 'right' was frequently used in cottage petitions, often to great effect. John Vemstone claimed in 1622 that he had his 'right' to a messuage and tenement taken from him by his master, who gave it to another servant.[144] It was therefore unfair that he and his family should be driven from place to place. He wanted an order to build a cottage on wasteland according to the statute 'made and provided for the relief of habitation of poorer people'. Vemstone's petition indicates a sense of his entitlement, which the bench appears to have agreed was justified: the clerk noted that it was to be discovered 'if Mr Legh did give his Cottage away'.[145] Jane Jackson said that she had been 'defeated of

---

[141] CRO, QJF 74/1/70 (1646).   [142] CRO, QJF 75/1/47 (1647).
[143] CRO, QJB 1/6, fos. 114r–v (1646). See also QJF 74/2/44 (1646); QJF 74/2/82 (1646); QJB 1/6, fo. 140v (1647); QJF 79/1/95 (1651); QJF 79/2/133 (1651); QJF 79/2/136 (1651); QJF 85/2/175 (1667).
[144] This man was also called Vemstone and was perhaps a relative. The issue may have been a much narrower one of disputed property rights than at first appears.
[145] CRO, QJF 49/2/173 (1620).

her right' to a tenement in Church Hulme by one Gandy, thereby putting her and her three children into 'distress and want': she therefore merited a licence to build a cottage. Again, the Justices agreed.[146]

Petitioners frequently claimed that they had been cast out by an unjust landlord or were victimised by individuals. They sought recourse to the courts to offset such actions.[147] Roger and Elizabeth Pott argued that they needed habitation because of 'the injurious dealing' of Master Hugh Wardle, 'who hath brought diverse violent suits against us in wrongful manner; whereby through his powerfulness, he hath not only impoverished us by expense, but hath likewise wrested from us part of a tenement in Merton where Elizabeth was born and for which we paid a great sum of money long since', from which now 'we are to be cast forth by Master Wardle'.[148] A widow complained that George Venables of Agden had 'enclosed the commons' there, 'and now not only seeks to hinder me of those liberties and easements I formerly quietly enjoyed of his ancestors, but also seeks to avoid me into another parish, having taken down part of my building and converted the same to his own use, and threatens to pull down that which remains'.[149] Others were successful after claiming that they had been cast out 'by an obdurate landlord' or 'in most lamentable manner'.[150] One widow said that her family had been 'unconscionably' thrown out of their cottage. She evidently presented her case well: the bench ordered that she was to be allowed back in until 'Sir Roland's mind is certainly known'; if he was unwilling, then she was to have a cottage on wasteland.[151] William Smith said that he was cast out of his cottage 'by order of law', after his landlord contracted with a stranger. The copyhold had expired with the last of the three lives for which it had been leased, but Smith implied that this was itself unfair as two of the lives had been lost in the civil wars. Smith was granted a licence to build a cottage.[152] One widow even implied that the relief she was given after a former supplication was a form of mistreatment: the churchwardens told her that the habitation she was allotted was upon the order of Thomas Savage, esquire, 'which I supposeth Master Savage would never have confined me unto, it being in the same room with a man and his wife, and where the rain falleth upon me and my poor children', while there were three perfectly

---

[146] CRO, QJF 53/2/172, /110, /112 (1624).
[147] For additional examples to those cited below, see CRO, QJF 53/1/69 (1624); QJF 55/2/117 (1626); QJF 55/3/87 (1626); QJF 79/1/166 (1651); QJF 85/2/154 (1657); QJF 93/1/132 (1665); QJF 95/1/145 (1667).
[148] CRO, QJF 71/1/24 (1642). See also QJF 71/1/24, QJF 71/2/35, QJB 1/6 fo. 76v (1642).
[149] CRO, QJF 74/2/58 (1646).
[150] For example, CRO, QJF 77/4/63 (1650); QJF 53/2/155, /113, /16, QJB 2/5 fo. 45r (1624); QJF 89/3/230, QJB 2/5 fo. 40v (1661).
[151] CRO, QJF 53/2/167 (1624); QJF 55/2/130, QJB 1/5 fo. 160v (1626).
[152] CRO, QJF 89/2/205, QJB 3/1 fo. 33r (1661). For a similar case, see QJF 89/2/207 (1661).

good cottages in the parish standing empty. The bench ordered that more convenient house-room be found for her.[153] Another frequent and related complaint was that the inhabitants of a parish would not allow the petitioner 'to take housing for his money'. These adversaries might be the general inhabitants, individual characters or 'some persons of authority or interest'. Faced with such opposition, a cottage on the commons might be the only way of providing a family with harbour. Petitions that stress this usually asked either for some cheap rented housing in the parish to be found for them or for a licence to build a cottage on common land.[154] Many poor men and women presented themselves as deserving not merely on grounds of their 'impotence' but because they were mistreated. The moral imperative was one way of conceptualising entitlement. Amongst ordinary people just as amongst their rulers, notions of equity underwrote their understandings of the law.

Morality was also a legitimising notion in petitions that emphasised extreme need. One man claimed that he 'hath been enforced this week or thereabouts to lie in the streets with his poor wife and three small children', saying that if habitation was not provided they might 'starve... for lack of harbour and succour'. An elderly couple lived in 'a poor booth they had made under a tree'. A widow and her two small children had been sheltering in a hollow tree, and now even that had fallen down. One family were living in a cow-house; another slept under hedges; yet another had no habitation 'but what they had digged in the earth covered over with clods upon Blackden heath', which, the petitioner added, was 'very uncomfortable'.[155] These latter two cases reveal how difficult it could sometimes be to procure a licence, especially after 1662, for neither was successful. The petition in which the supplicants were living on Blackden heath was presented jointly by John Hurdesfield and Francis, his son. They would appear to have had many of the necessary credentials to be given a licence: John and his wife were aged fifty and sixty respectively; both John and Francis had been born in the parish and had lived there all their lives; they had never been a burden on the poor rate, and their want of a dwelling was allegedly due to the lack of available accommodation for their money. Moreover, Francis's wife was heavily pregnant: with winter approaching, both she and the child would be in 'much hazard' if they continued in their makeshift abode on the heath. The minister and churchwardens of Blackden certified that the contents of the petition were true, and offered the additional information that one of the men was a trained soldier there, and 'the other carrying the arms of a neighbour';

---

[153] CRO, QJF 71/4/20, QJB 1/6 fos. 86r–v (1643).
[154] For example, CRO, QJF 89/4/139 (1662); QJF 89/1/229 (1661); QJF 75/1/81 (1647).
[155] CRO, QJF 49/1/154 (1620); QJF 51/3/98 (1622); QJF 89/2/233 (1661); QJF 55/2/130 (1626); QJF 95/3/136 (1667); QJF 95/2/148 (1667).

they were both 'faithful subjects'. Yet patronage by the minister, an appeal to the charitable disposition of the bench, and their supposed good names, did not move the Justices, who refused to give the family any help or licence whatsoever.[156] Although a man might state truthfully that he and his family were forced to sleep outdoors exposed to the elements, the primary concern of Justices was not always the material state of the petitioner. Except during and immediately after the civil wars, when the uncertain political situation resulted in the bench exhibiting their paternalistic nature by turning down scarcely any petitioners for cottages, the crux of the matter seems to have been the causes of petitioners' destitution and wider claims to entitlement.

While some petitioners professed knowledge of the law, others manipulated elite perceptions of plebeian ignorance in order to stake their claims. William Wiswall in 1626 presented a petition in which he explained that eighteen months previously 'tempestuous weather' had destroyed his cottage on 'little heath' (the common) in Woodchurch. For twenty years he had lived in that cottage, which had stood there for 'time out of mind', and he had erected a new cottage four or five yards from the old site with the consent of both the chief lord of the common and the charterers. However, a year later he was indicted for building without a licence, 'whereby being a simple man and misled by some of his neighbours', he confessed. Now, he wished to traverse the bill. The fact that Wiswall obtained the consent of the appropriate authorities before he rebuilt his cottage, and the way in which he presented his case which he was now pursuing in his petition, do not suggest that he was a man completely ignorant of the legal process. Nor does his confession necessarily suggest this: he was indicted for building a cottage without it being assigned the statutory four acres of land, which his original cottage might not have had. Assuming the position of a poor, ignorant man – whether he was such or not – allowed Wiswall to bend the legal rules. The bench ordered that if the new cottage was built with the consent of the lord there, Wiswall was permitted to traverse the indictment 'notwithstanding his confession'.[157]

Wiswall's indictment was presumably not the result of a broad community bias against him. It is more likely that he was indicted as part of an interpersonal dispute between him and Robert Greene, the man who prosecuted him. We may assume that many poor cottagers did have the permission, if not always the encouragement, of other members of their communities to build small dwellings on commons and wastes. Nonetheless, despite relatively few complaints at quarter sessions against prospective cottagers, several instances of such conflict are apparent. Consensual opposition to those who desired

---

[156] CRO, QJF 95/2/148, /149 (1667).
[157] CRO, QJF 55/4/10 (1627); QJF 55/1/17, QJB 2/5, fo. 71r (1626).

to build on wasteland often dissuaded Justices in sessions from granting a licence. Yet faced with opposition from substantial villagers, the law could provide a forceful counter-measure. Raphe Parker erected a cottage in the lordship of Over Whitley in 1626, having received permission from the bench and the consent of the lords there, and the order being made known to the inhabitants there, 'divers of which gave their consent'. According to Parker, shortly afterwards, 'Notwithstanding the said order', Thomas Turner *alias* Stockton and William Haukinson 'by the instigation of certain others' came to the cottage while Parker was thatching it, 'and violently pulled it down, and afterwards cut the timber in pieces, and although I did gently acquaint them with the order, and desired that they desist from so outrageous and wicked a deed in disobeying the said order, they said they cared neither for Justices nor nobody else'. The petition began by establishing Parker's lawfulness and entitlement to build the cottage, and throughout stressed Turner and Haukinson's offence against law and order rather than against him as an individual. Parker's allegedly 'gentle' reprimand served to keep him on the right side of the line which demarcated orderly from disorderly behaviour.[158] Likewise, when Ann French, whose husband had been killed fighting 'the rebels in Scotland', had her licensed cottage pulled down not once but three times by her adversaries 'in contempt of all authority' that had officially sanctioned its erection, the bench opined that it 'much misliketh such presumption and cruelty especially against a poor woman and children there born and bred'. The miscreants were commanded to build the cottage up again at their own expense or else forty shillings a-piece would be 'levied of their goods to the use of the poor woman'.[159] In a similar case, the bench opined that it 'much misliketh such cruelty and the threatenings' of those that pulled a cottage down.[160] Such cases demonstrate both that the law concerning the building of cottages on commons and wastes was contested terrain and that poor cottagers might have better claims on the law than even their more affluent adversaries.

In anti-cottage petitions, the same ideas of community consensus were used as in those requesting a licence to build, but they were inverted. The inhabitants of various townships thwarted the attempts of would-be cottagers. John Wilson, it was said, was 'a man of very evil behaviour and wasteful to make that away which he getteth by his hard labour with drinking'; his wife was a 'very able woman, but will not work'. Moreover, Wilson allegedly frequently threatened to desert his wife and children, saying that the inhabitants

---

[158] CRO, QJF 55/3/30, /85, /115 (1626). For a similar case, see QJF 89/3/215, /12, QJB 3/1 fo. 41v (1661).
[159] CRO, QJB 1/6, fo. 92v, QJF 73/3/93 (1645).
[160] CRO, QJB 1/6, fo. 154r (1648). See also QJF 81/2/295 (1653); QJF 81/2/299 (1653); QJF 83/1/125 (1655).

there 'will relieve them whether we will or not, 'fore he will bring them to the constable's house and there leave them'. They therefore wanted not only that Wilson should not be permitted to erect a cottage there, but that he should enter into a bond on condition that he would not desert his family and that 'he and his wife may work being able to work'. The Justices took this on board and ordered that unless Wilson provided sureties for the discharge of the parish, he was to be sent to the House of Correction and punished 'as a sturdy wandering rogue'.[161] In another case, the inhabitants of Chelford complained about two lesser gentlemen who permitted ten or eleven servants' cottages to be built, 'most to the great hindrances of us their neighbours'. These gentlemen held lands which were 'but 20s. ... and 25s. 8d. of the old rent', and rented the cottages to disorderly persons. The inhabitants requested that the bench disallow any further cottages to be built given that help ought to be directed to those poor who already lived there.[162] In 1645, nine cottagers claimed that when the lord of the soil had granted the commons to the use of another fellow, they had 'made an agreement... to buy his estate out', they 'not being able to subsist without the benefit of the common in respect of the smallness of their livings, the best of them valued but as cottagers'. Thus, the waste lands upon which someone now intended to build 'only properly belong unto us', and the erection of a cottage would be 'a great prejudice unto us'.[163] Inhabitants also justified their obstructive behaviour by emphasising the 'obnoxious and hurtful' or otherwise disorderly behaviour of potential cottagers. Such claims were frequently bolstered by others that cottagers had no legal claim to settle there, that they had previously 'wandered abroad', or that they had erected or rebuilt a cottage without 'warrant or ... due course of law'. The implication was that such people would breed up a charge upon the parish poor rate.[164] The lack of consent of other inhabitants seems to have carried some weight with JPs. Such petitions were often successful.

It is clear from the preceding discussion that the content and emphasis of men's and women's petitions for cottages were similar. Something may nevertheless be said about the relative position of men and women. Certain men were able to use a language of skill and special rights which was exclusively male. When Thomas Webster applied for a cottage licence in 1620, he was merely going through the motions to sanction his right to build a cottage on wasteland in Lymm, where he had lived for 'divers years now last past, by reason there is a quarry of stone there'. Webster was a freemason, and like other extractive workers, not only did his occupation exempt him from the 1589

---

[161] CRO, QJF 49/1/165, QJB 1/5 fo. 69v (1620).   [162] CRO, QJF 51/1/113 (1622).
[163] CRO, QJF 73/3/106 (1645).
[164] For example, CRO, QJF 49/2/175 (1620); QJB 1/5 fo. 36r (1620); QJF 57/2/37 (1628); QJF 49/1/158 (1620); QJF 95/2/147 (1667); QJB 3/1 fo. 134v (1665).

Act but certain local customs also allowed special rights to quarry workers and miners. His skilled status enabled his elite patrons to give added weight to their pleas on his behalf. These 'worshipful worthy friends' included three JPs, who wrote not only to the lord of the manor who gave his consent for the cottage to be erected, but also to the Clerk of the peace, saying that they 'doubt not of [his] kindness' towards Webster in encouraging the Justices at the sessions to grant the licence. For Webster was 'a very good workman', who, by having a cottage near the quarry, 'hopes not only, by his own pains and labour to maintain himself and family, but also to do very much good in the country about him in the affairs of his occupation'.[165] Skilled groups such as blacksmiths were similarly almost universally successful in their attempts to be granted permission to build smithy houses as well as cottages on commons. Skilled workmen did not only request somewhere to live, but also a place from which they could 'apply [their] trade'. They were given that permission on particular grounds: 'knowing him to be a good workman in his trade of blacksmith'.[166] Only a few men could make such explicit claims; men drawn from the labouring poor were largely excluded from this sphere of entitlement and reciprocal good.[167]

Women did not have a comparable purchase on the language or concept of such contributions to the good of the community. Very rarely did a woman claim 'I am a midwife and very helpful to any hath occasion to use me. I have likewise a daughter who is a bone-lace weaver and doth instruct diverse children thereabouts in her trade and calling.'[168] Most women, like men, could merely hope that they would persuade the community and the bench that they were not likely to become chargeable to the parish. Thus, petitioners who drew upon notions of entitlement other than impotence often stated that their and their wife's hard labour would be sufficient to maintain their families if they no longer had to pay 'rent upon the rack'.[169] Even this was more difficult for lone women to do. Martha Henshall said that she had taken 'extraordinary care and pains' to maintain herself and her five children since her husband's death; and her petition was subscribed by thirteen inhabitants of her township, including the rector, churchwardens and two female neighbours.[170] Henshall, though, was unusual; on the whole, it was difficult for widows to make such claims when they had a family to

---

[165] CRO, QJF 49/1/160, /159, QJB 1/5 fo. 31v (1620). See also QJF 85/3/156 (1657).
[166] For blacksmiths, see for example, CRO, QJF 75/1/85, QJB 1/6 fo. 132r (1647); QJF 77/1/45, QJB 1/6 fo. 210v (1649); QJF 89/3/215, QJB 3/1 fo. 41v (1661); QJF 89/4/148, /149 (1662); QJF 97/1/56, /135 (1669); QJF 97/3/112, /114, /115, QJB 3/2 fo. 10v (1669).
[167] An exception may be found in CRO, QJF 53/2/162 (1624).
[168] CRO, QJF 75/4/106 (1648).
[169] For example, CRO, QJF 51/2/115 (1622); QJF 51/3/98 (1622); QJF 55/2/131 (1626); QJF 89/4/139 (1662).
[170] CRO, QJF 89/2/231 (1661).

support. Poor women, after all, because their potential wages were relatively low, constituted a large proportion of those receiving poor relief.[171] Although a language of female skill and labour existed, it corresponded neither to financial independence nor to the same rhetoric of communal good gauged in economic terms. Thus, the widowed Anne Lowe requested that her four children be kept upon the parish because she, 'not having anything in the world to subsist upon not so much as a garden place but hath laboured and endeavoured as much as in her lieth which falleth far short to maintain such a family'. If they granted her request, she swore that 'having some little end she will be content to work day and night towards their maintenance'.[172] Although women stressed their hard labour, they tended to end their petitions with words of desperation even when they had attributed their poverty to the mistreatment of others or had drawn on other notions of entitlement. The petitions of widows and spinsters nearly always culminated in claims of impotence by virtue of their economic disadvantage. Isabel Harper said that since the death of her husband she was unable to maintain herself and her children, nor to provide house-room for them 'for want of means'. Margaret Dutton was 'overburdened' with the charge of her four children after the death of her mother, with whom she had lived. Frances Holford said simply that she would become a charge on the parish if she were not allowed to repair and continue living in 'my poor cote'. Jane Jackson, the widow who said that she had been 'defeated of my right', asked not only for a cottage, but also for a weekly allowance.[173] Anne Smith, a single woman, explained that since the death of her parents, her brother 'doth enjoy that whole estate both real and personal which was my father's and mother's'. She was now 'unable to work for my living by reason of my great age [sixty-four] and infirmities which do greatly grow upon me daily, and utterly unable to travel and being removed from place to place causeth great sorrow and grief of heart'. She wanted the Justices to allow 'me to have some place of abode to rest in and some weekly maintenance from my brother or out of that liberty where I was born'.[174] This is not merely a reflection of women falling more easily than men into the category of impotent poor who were considered to be appropriate recipients of poor relief. Rather, excluded from a language of skill that had positive economic implications, women and men of the poorer sorts used the language of rights, entitlement and natural justice as a way of reinforcing their claims.

Again, as in the previous section, the agency of the poor represents the attempt to use the law, especially where it intersected with broader expectations

---

[171] Slack, *Poverty and Policy*, 75–6, 180.   [172] CRO, QJF 89/3/36 (1661).
[173] CRO, QJF 49/1/150 (1620); QJF 89/2/218 (1661); QJF 95/1/151 (1667); QJF 53/2172 (1624). See also QJF 53/4/86 (1624); QJF 53/2/147 (1624).
[174] CRO, QJF 89/3/234 (1661).

of the elite's behaviour, to further individual aims. There is, however, a hint of collective assertion of the rights of the poor, in that they are 'entitled' to certain favours from the gentry and parish. Thus, although the supplications of poor people for licences to build cottages on commons and wastes endorses conventional class hierarchies, it contains a germ of the notion of collective rights.

RESISTANCE: FORCIBLE RESCUES

When people openly defied the law and its officers, they did not always perceive their actions to be, or present them as, unlawful. Resistance was often portrayed as 'right' and 'just'. John and Anne Maddocke refused several demands for half a crown towards 'Royal Aid and Additional Supply', and beat one of the constables who eventually managed to distrain three of their pewter dishes. Their case suggests a conflict between differing notions of lawfulness and righteousness. First, in their verbal abuse they aligned themselves with lawfulness in contrast with the constables, whom they denounced as 'out-comeling knaves'. Maddocke threatened to have those fined 'for putting in two such knaves to be constables'. Secondly, Maddocke was in fact one of the assessors for the tax. He had not wanted to be one, 'but was one, and assessed himself in the said half crown which he refused to pay'![175] Elizabeth Goodyer, to whom bailiffs gave the opportunity of paying her outstanding fine to avoid distraint of her goods, bade them 'kiss her arse and [dis]strain if they durst, calling them "beggarly rogues", saying she would see them both hanged before she would never [sic] pay any'.[176] Her abusive language positions them as thieves who should hang for taking away her property. John Newport 'violently' rescued cattle from a bailiff, saying 'the cows I bought and paid for in the market and I will be killed before I'll lose them'. His own claim of lawful ownership underlined his rejection of the law in saying that he cared not for the sheriff or his warrant, 'nor would [he] obey the law'.[177] As lawfulness and law were clearly not synonymous in popular conceptualisations, it follows that resistance to the law might not always be seen in simple terms of blatant disorder. Rather, as we shall see, resisting distraint was often undertaken in the name of the economically and socially reliable household, which rested at the heart of conventionally defined political relations.

'Forcible rescue' – the recovery of distrained goods and chattels, or the removal of a person or goods from legal custody – was a misdemeanour

---

[175] CRO, QJF 95/4/99 (1668). 'Out-comeling' referred to someone who hailed from outside the community. Royal Aid was a quarterly tax payable between 1665 and 1668 to help pay for building a navy; Additional Supply was to assist in the expense for the Dutch war and was similarly payable quarterly.
[176] CRO, QJF 81/2/225 (1653).   [177] CRO, QJF 97/1/113 (1669).

punishable by a fine set at the discretion of Justices of the peace.[178] Not all rescuers were formally indicted. Some were bound by recognisance, others were referred to arbitrators or ticked off by magistrates. As a category of offence, rescue has scarcely been addressed by historians of crime. Rescues would seem to reveal nothing but the obvious: people wanted to keep hold of their goods, and wished to protect relatives and friends from the law's force. Yet probing the apparently obvious actually illuminates a broader interpretative framework for disorder, and challenges common historiographical assumptions about resistance to the law. Moreover, the nature of and meanings ascribed to the household meant that practical disputes over material resources were also contests over cultural capital; that ideas about household, gender and law worked together in constructing particular meanings; that ambiguities and tensions arising from such intersections meant that in particular contexts people were able to use dominant ideas in various ways.

Distraint of household goods and livestock arose from several circumstances, most commonly non-payment of taxes, unpaid debt or breach of contract. Civil litigation over debt and breach of contract was incredibly common. In the 1580s, suits concerning debt or breach of contract were prosecuted at the Sheriff's Court in Chester at an annual rate of over two-and-a-half lawsuits for every household in the city.[179] Nor was this the exclusive venue for suits of this type. The 'speedy justice' of borough and hundred courts could be initiated at three or four pence. Manor courts were even cheaper: at Nantwich Court Leet, for instance, costs were regularly assessed at only one or two pennies. Even 'poor artificers' and the 'very meanest' women and men could thus afford to sue for debts of a few pence.[180] Although the initial plaint usually sufficed to achieve settlement, the scale of litigation was so great that by the later sixteenth century almost all households were likely to have either experienced or witnessed an arrest, attachment or distraint of goods for auction.[181] Not all those who had their property distrained responded with violence and forcibly rescued those goods back

---

[178] JPs could punish offenders by fine and imprisonment, but rarely employed the latter.
[179] Muldrew, *Economy of Obligation*, 232–4.
[180] Muldrew, *Economy of Obligation*, 4, 248. In the Chester Portmote Court in the 1620s, the cost of bringing to judgement a suit for 15s. was 2s. 6d., CCRO, QSF/71/8 (1624–5), verdict in Edmund Heywood v. John Francis senior. CRO, DCH/Y/1/1, Nantwich Manor Court Book 1636–1653 (unfoliated): for example, Ellen Yates, spinster v. Thomas Madder, in a plea of debt for 6s. 8d., the jury found for the plaintiff 2s. 8d. part of the debt and awarded costs of 1d. and damages of 1d.; Mary Catherall v. Richard Weaver and Mary his wife, in a plea of debt for 5s. 6d., the jury found that the defendants owed the whole amount and awarded the plaintiff 1d. costs and 2d. damages (28 April 1651). CRO, DAR/H/62, Arderne Collection, Legal Papers, Tarporley Manor Court Papers, 17 October 1653: William Whally sued for a debt of 8d. and the defendant confessed; John Bostock sued for a debt of 13d. and damages of 8d. and was awarded the whole debt and 4d. damages.
[181] Muldrew, *Economy of Obligation*, 273.

again.[182] Of those who did, some attempted to justify their actions by claiming that the distraint itself had been unjust. In certain circumstances, such as vexatious litigation or the wrongful seizure of goods by unscrupulous bailiffs, forcible rescue could be entirely legal: 'he that will attempt by force and violence to take away another man's goods wrongfully from him, may justly by force and strong hand be resisted'.[183] If 'a man shall distrain with force, for a rent (be it due, or not due) this doeth countervail an entry with force'.[184] However, even without these conditions, many people strongly resisted distraining officers.

At the spring assizes of 1622, Randle and Frances Holbrook, Margaret Wilkinson and her husband Raphe, and the Holbrooks' servant Thomas Doughtie, were successfully prosecuted by Matthew Smallwood for a forcible rescue. Smallwood had obtained a county court judgement against Randle Holbrook for a debt of £14, upon which the Sheriff's bailiffs distrained two oxen, two cows and a heifer. The defendants apparently did not dispute the legitimacy of the original debt, the county court judgement or the distraint. They rescued the livestock because the bailiff had allegedly acted unscrupulously. Randle Holbrook's father explained to the bench that

The bailiffs serve the execution on their cattle which were their only stay for milk, having many young ones. The bailiff, to do them a mischief, drives the cattle out of the liberty to a pound not known. This made my children and their servant to take home their cattle and to provide money to pay the debt and costs whereupon the indictment grew. And they have paid Master Birkenhead the Prothonotary and all is well. Only the fines are feared ...

[Please assuage their fines because] my children are poor and not yet grounded in substance, neither with much understanding.[185]

Whatever the verisimilitude of this account regarding the particulars, it hints at some general truths. First, even middling households could rely for their subsistence on the chattels in question. The Holbrooks' two milch kine were allegedly 'their only stay for milk'. If these were their only dairy cows, the heifer was significant as an investment to be sold or to increase their stock. Local people needed no reminding of oxen's indispensability in husbandry: Cheshire people mainly did 'all their labour' with them.[186] The losses involved in the distraint and potential auctioning of these beasts were

---

[182] In Cheshire and elsewhere, defendants rarely responded to this or other forms of legal action with violence; nor did the majority of plaintiffs have defendants bound over to keep the peace against them as a precautionary measure. See Ingram, 'Communities and courts', 118; Muldrew, *Economy of Obligation*, 285.
[183] Pulton, *De Pace Regis*, fo. 6; Dalton, *Countrey Justice*, 188.
[184] Dalton, *Countrey Justice*, 178.
[185] PRO, CHES 24/116/4 petition of Randle Holbrook, senior; CHES 24/116/3 indictment of Randle Holbrook et al., PRO, CHES 21/3 fo. 68r (1622).
[186] *King's Vale Royal* (London, 1656), 28.

considerable, for cattle were expensive in real and relative terms. Sir Thomas Wilson expected 'yeomen of meaner ability' to be able to keep between six and ten milch kine in addition to a few plough-horses and several young beasts for stock.[187] But younger sons of gentlemen, like Randle Holbrook junior, who had no or little land of their own were often as economically fragile as husbandmen, despite the raised social credit afforded by their household of origin. One tenant farmer described how his family were nearly starved because of 'the great losses I sustained the last year by the death of my cattle, losing two kine and two young beasts in a short time, being all or part of my stock and maintenance'.[188] Inventories confirm the importance of livestock: one Cheshire husbandman's cow and heifer (£3 6s. 19d.) were worth far more than all his other possessions – tools, furniture, clothes, linens, household goods – together (£2 7s.).[189] Early modern people were well aware that it was not merely the poorer sorts who potentially paid the material costs of distraint.

Secondly, the cost was counted in more than the material value of the goods taken. The removal of possessions to be sold at public auction in execution of a judgement potentially damaged a household's reputation. There was nothing intrinsically shameful about having proceedings initiated against one for debt. It was a common means by which creditors chased repayment or renegotiation.[190] But where a case proceeded to judgement or, worse, to distraint of goods or imprisonment, a question mark was raised over the indebted household's honesty and credit. Distraint had negative associations: an inability or obstinate refusal to pay one's debts, the failure to secure sureties (to undertake that the debt would be repaid), not appearing in court after attachment. Each implied that economic and social credit was lacking.[191] The repercussions of such loss could be socially and materially devastating. One man was 'in so much debt that he doth neither go to church [n]or market'.[192] Another assumed a false name on arriving in Chester because 'he was afraid of troubles in regard he is much indebted', and donned an apparent disguise. Asked by the suspicious Mayor 'wherefore he wears a periwig having much hair of his own upon his head, he answered that he wore the same to regain his hearing, which was much impaired before he

---

[187] *The State of England, 1600*, by Sir Thomas Wilson, ed. F.J. Fisher, Camden Soc., 3rd ser. (1936), 16–25.
[188] CRO, QJF 79/1/109, /108 (1651).
[189] Inventory of William Jones of Nantwich, husbandman, in Lake, *Great Fire of Nantwich*, 23.
[190] By the late 1580s, the Sheriff's Court in Chester heard some 3,500 cases annually; the average rate of litigation in that court alone was over two-and-a-half suits per household per year: Muldrew, *Economy of Obligation*, 232–4.
[191] Muldrew, *Economy of Obligation*, 285, 202, 261, 274–5.
[192] CRO, QJF 51/4/167 (1622).

made use thereof'![193] Comical though this may seem, the loss of social credit was no laughing matter. It could launch a household onto a desperate spiral of debt and downward mobility.[194] As one 'careful' ballad wife warned her 'careless bad husband', their indebtedness would lead to his imprisonment, whereupon even his friends 'will all forsake your company, and on you turn their back'. What nonsense, the husband exclaimed, 'Go wash your dishes, or go spin, and do not talk to me.' The careful wife pointed out that as they were so deeply in debt, their children ragged and barefoot, and her household linens too threadbare to pawn, it would not be long before 'I shall not have a dish to wash, or any other thing that will hold flesh, or fish'. Her counsel fell on deaf ears. The family was propelled with gathering momentum towards the grim, inevitable conclusion: 'We shall all famish, starve, and die, and so there is an end.'[195] The danger of downward mobility was especially acute for fragile households – Randle and Frances Holbrook, remember, were allegedly 'poor, and not yet grounded in substance' – but it was not restricted to them. In this context the cry of women, that they would 'kill or be killed' before any bailiff removed their possessions to sell them at auction, was not merely an excessive display of force and emotion.[196] Losing one's goods and chattels really could seem a matter of social and cultural death.

Thirdly, parties could reach an agreement even after judgement. Distraint served not as a punishment (although some might have viewed it as such) but as a practical measure. Thus in October 1649 Richard Smith informed John Scragg that a bailiff had served an execution on Scragg's cattle, saying that if Scragg 'would come and satisfy the debts he might have his kine again, otherwise sale would be made of them'.[197] The Holbrooks settled with Matthew Smallwood after rescuing their cattle. As the dispute was resolved, the rescue became largely irrelevant as far as the creditor was concerned.[198] This is one reason why the courts often lowered or waived the fines in cases of rescue. Even abused bailiffs recommended that defendants be treated leniently. Adam Goodier prosecuted the (unfortunately named) Swindells – husband, wife and son – at quarter sessions for attacking him with bill-hooks and pitchforks in rescuing the brass pan which he had distrained in execution of a county court judgement for a debt of 19s. and 4s. 1d. costs. Although the grand jury found the bill 'true', Goodier requested the

---

[193] CCRO, MF/86/46 (1667).   [194] Muldrew, *Economy of Obligation*, ch. 9.
[195] *A Carefull Wives Good Counsell to a Carelesse Bad Husband, in a Dialogue*, in I.A., *The Good Woman's Champion, or, A Defence for the Weaker Vessell* (London, 1650), sigs. A6v–B2v.
[196] CRO, QJF 95/4/58 (1668).   [197] CRO, QJF 77/4/92 (1649).
[198] This was usually so when the plaintiff was the creditor.

bench, 'Let this, I pray you, pass; he hath contented me for it.'[199] Individual fines were not large – usually between 2s. 6d. and 6s. 8d. – but could be daunting if several individual household members were involved, especially during years of dearth.[200] The Holbrooks were prosecuted during a period (1621 to 1623) of crop failures and low livestock prices.[201] After hearing Holbrook senior's petition, the bench agreed that 'Consideration shall be had of this petition upon setting down of the fines.' Lowering or waiving fines was an acknowledgement of the financial burden of payment; of the fact that debts might arise from agreements into which both parties entered with good faith; that debts could remain outstanding due to problems further down the chains of credit in which households were necessarily bound. Failure to meet obligations could be a repercussion of both dearth and, in corn-growing regions, bumper harvests which drastically lowered the price of corn – good for the poor, but difficult for small producers. The mitigation of fines helped threatened households to remain materially intact, and so safeguarded the security of credit chains that were essential to social and economic life.

In sum, distraints and attachments threatened not only the household's material resources but also its social credit. Unsurprisingly, some people were overly zealous in their attempts to prevent it while there remained the possibility of settlement or renegotiation of terms with the creditor. Rescuing goods and chattels could seem like the best, or the only, option for the good of the household. What was being resisted here was more than a particular legal order. Resisters were not part of a subculture but attempted to hang on to a life in the mainstream.

Women – wives, widows and spinsters – were particularly active in resisting attempts by constables and bailiffs to distrain goods or collect taxation. This was so even when the goods or money in question belonged to their friends or relatives in other households. This area of female concern over household goods was widely acknowledged, in spite of the male bias of formal court sources. The county under-bailiff arrived at Humphrey Worthington's house and attempted to seize three brass pots belonging to Margaret Golden, a widow. Mary Worthington, Humphrey's daughter, asked him 'by what authority' he did so, to which he cryptically answered 'that which would bear him out'. He then proceeded to charge Mary to keep the

---

[199] CRO, QJF 57/3/8 (1628). Goodier regularly filed indictments for rescue and for assault, for example, QJF 55/1/54, QJF/55/2/21, /22 (1626).

[200] PRO, CHES 21/5 fo. 7v, PRO, CHES 24/134/1, indictment of Anthony Bostock, Joan Mason and Joan Barnes (1663). The values of fines were set at the discretion of the bench and did not rise over time with the rate of inflation; fines of 2s. 6d. continued to be imposed through the 1660s and afterwards.

[201] Peter Bowden, 'Agricultural prices, farm profits, and rents', in Joan Thirsk ed., *The Agrarian History of England and Wales, Vol. IV. 1500–1640* (Cambridge, 1967), 631.

peace, and said that if any of the women present 'spoke a word, he would knock them down'. Presumably, Mary did not keep quiet, as he hit her with the end of his staff and 'bade her keep off'.[202] Henry Cherry was beaten with sticks by five women – four of them married – when he tried to distrain three cows that belonged to one of them. Cherry was Bailiff of the Royal Forest of Macclesfield, and acted upon a writ issued out of the Manor and Forest Court. He went away empty-handed and filed an indictment against them.[203] When two constables went to Edward Hankinson's house to demand payment of an assessment, Edward's wife, Mary, 'bid them come in if they durst, and with that locked the door'. They returned later in Edward's absence and Mary 'bid them get out of her house, for she would pay them none'. When they tried to execute their warrant, Mary, her daughter Susannah and her son William 'fell upon' the constables 'and carried them out of the house by force'; Mary and Susannah first dealt with one constable, and then Mary and William dealt with the other. Later, Mary allegedly declared spuriously that 'the assessors had no right to assess any lay unless her husband joined with them, and that it was an easy thing for the Justices to sit on their arses to cause the poor commonalty to pay lays needlessly'.[204]

Mary's apposition of household and official authority is interesting. Her claim that she was within her rights to withhold payment in her husband's absence is an acknowledgement that, as head of the household, her husband was officially responsible for household goods and moneys. This was evidently a fiction; she did not defend her property merely because it was not hers to part with. Rather, the idea of spousal authority permitted an indignant legitimisation of her actions, as did aligning herself with the 'poor commonalty'. Official action was said to fly in the face of the people's rights and paternal authority. While ideas about 'the people' constituted the term as a masculine construct, in political discourse and in many popular uses of the term, women spoke in terms that simultaneously acknowledged exclusion and inclusion. Women, as senior members or 'joint governors' of households, had a stake in claiming the rights of 'the people'; yet, as Mary Hankinson did, they often removed themselves to a supporting rather than leading role in legitimating those claims. The 'poor commonalty' no less than 'the people' was constituted of households, not individuals. As a political unit, the household was a gendered concept: it was unashamedly male. Women's actions did not, however, sit easily with that particular rhetorical and legal construction.

The household context of rescues is reflected in their form. In rescues of goods and chattels, people acted mostly in twos or threes, often in groups

---

[202] CRO, QJF 95/4/35 (1668).   [203] CRO, QJF 51/3/22 (1622).
[204] CRO, QJF 91/3/90, /86–/89 (1663).

of four or five, but seldom more.[205] Tellingly, middling households in early modern England had, on average, between four and six inhabitants.[206] Most rescues appear to have included participants who lived under the same roof or were otherwise related; frequently these were spouses, or parents and children.[207] It is worth noting that seemingly unrelated defendants might also be bound in ties of household, kinship and mutual support as well: stepchildren, household servants, servants in husbandry, apprentices, various other relatives (whether inhabiting the household or not). In particular, bonds between parents and grown-up children, and between adult siblings, 'were routinely recognised between households' and 'could involve a powerful sense of obligation'.[208] Indictments rarely reveal the nature of relationships such as that of two married women Margery Ryley and Anne Holland, who together rescued household goods distrained out of Margery's household; the two women were sisters.[209] Moreover, occupational and personal obligations overlapped when the workplace was located within or adjacent to the dwelling-house. When constables tried to remove a pewter dish in lieu of unpaid taxes in 1668, Jane Pickin, the mistress of the house, and William Wilson, a journeyman there, together prevented them.[210] One must not overstate the case, however. Family and household ties are evident in the vast majority of cases, but do not preclude additional associations. Household rescuers were frequently joined by friends or neighbours. For instance, the bailiff for the Liberty of Weaverham in 1649 told of how, after he had distrained two cows out of a close of John Scragg's for debts owed, Scragg accompanied by one William Hazelhurst (who claimed the cows were his) and their two wives came after him, and the four of them 'took the two kine by violence from me, using many threatening speeches, with the offer of blows unto me'.[211] It has been suggested that early modern people tended to rely on nuclear family members and other close relatives in matters involving

---

[205] Of 217 people indicted for rescue in Cheshire, a mere 19 (under 9 per cent) acted alone. 7 out of 10 indictments for rescue of goods and chattels named 2 or 3 defendants; 93.1 per cent of cases involved groups of between 2 and 5 defendants. Proportions of the total are as follows: 2 defendants 41.4 per cent, 3 27.6 per cent, 4 10.3 per cent, 5 13.8 per cent; 7 3.45 per cent, 8 3.45 per cent.

[206] Peter Laslett, *The World We Have Lost – Further Explored* (London, 1983; 1988), 96, Table 7.

[207] Eighty per cent of groups prosecuted for rescue of goods and chattels included household/family members. For example, CRO, QJF 55/2/34 (1626) mother and son; QJF 57/3/8 (1628) husband, wife and son; QJF 95/2/122, /123 (1667) husband, wife, two sons and a daughter.

[208] Keith Wrightson and David Levine, *Poverty and Piety in an English Village: Terling*, ch. 4, 188–97, at 194; Laurence, *Women in England*, 88–9.

[209] CRO, QJF 79/4/4 (1651).

[210] CRO, QJF 95/4/54 (1668). See also QJF 53/4/101 (1625) labourer, QJF 53/1/7 (1624) maidservant.

[211] CRO, QJF 77/4/92 (1649).

family property, but on neighbours and friends for support in other things.[212] Rescues of goods and chattels would seem to fall somewhere between the two.

The significance of household in rescues of goods is highlighted further when compared to its lesser role in rescues of persons from legal custody. In general, arrest and public attachment were potentially as destructive of social credit as distraint was. The direction of physical authority against the body indicated that, in some quarters at least, the captive's word or goods carried very little credit. The meanings of arrest were, of course, variable according to why a warrant had been issued. Failure to provide sureties for the peace was an altogether different matter from being suspected of a heinous felony, yet both could result in imprisonment. Rescuing a felon was so grave an act that it was itself felonious. Arrest could obviously have far-reaching implications for the household (the removal of labour, or the payment over a term of years for the upkeep of a bastard, say). As one would expect, household members and close family were frequently among those who helped individuals escape from the clutches of constables. There were, however, differences in the patterns of rescues of persons and those of goods, which may be understood in terms of the context in which each typically occurred.

Most warrants for distraint, and therefore most rescues of goods, were executed in or near the household. This in itself goes some way to explaining the prominence of household alliances among rescuers of goods and livestock. Moreover, in sparsely populated pastoral areas where farmhouses and labourers' cottages were scattered over large parishes or in arable areas where there were few populous townships (as in the Broxton and Wirral Hundreds of Cheshire, for example), neighbours and friends might not have been sufficiently near at hand to provide either assistance or witnesses.[213] In such an environment, resistance to distraints made at the household depended predominantly upon whomever was present and inclined to help, which would most likely be people who lived or worked there. In contrast, constables apprehended individuals wherever they happened to be, which was not necessarily at home. Rescues of persons occurred in or outside alehouses, inns and friends' houses, in fields where people worked alongside or close to others, as well as at the household of the individual taken into

---

[212] Wrightson and Levine, *Poverty and Piety*, 102, 188, 194–5, 194 n. 24.
[213] The exceptions are Malpas in Broxton Hundred, near Cheshire's border with Flintshire and Shropshire, and Neston in Wirral Hundred, which could even boast a Friday market. In general, population density in Cheshire remained low even in the 1660s after considerable demographic growth. Other north western and northern counties shared these characteristics. Phillips and Smith, *Lancashire and Cheshire*, 5; Howard Hodson, *Cheshire, 1660–1780: Restoration to Industrial Revolution* (Chester, 1978), 93–4.

custody. This is one reason why household and family, although still highly significant, are less pronounced in rescues of persons from legal custody. In some third of cases, neighbours and personal friends alone seem to have thwarted the endeavours of arresting officers. Although household members and relatives participated in two-thirds of cases, as opposed to three-quarters of the rescues of goods and livestock, the majority of rescuers of persons have no obvious consanguinity, affinity or household relation to the arrested person. The greater likelihood of arrests and therefore of associated rescues being undertaken outside the immediate vicinity of the household perhaps goes some way to explaining why larger groups were sometimes involved than in the rescues of goods.[214]

Contextualising rescues of goods as household concerns also challenges conventional assumptions about the relative involvement of males and females in unlawful activities. Some historians have accepted at face value stereotypical views that early modern men displayed 'a higher degree of initiative, autonomy, and self-assertion' than women, who acted in a 'more dependent and passive manner' and normally relied on men, especially their husbands, to settle their quarrels for them. These differences are explained by the supposed internalisation of prescriptive gender roles.[215] However, conceptualising gendered behaviour in simple, dichotomous terms of independent/dependent, active/passive, violent/non-violent effects a somewhat crude notion of 'the sexual division of criminality', in which modern categories of 'men' and 'women' are implicitly imposed upon early modern subjects.[216] There is no denying that religious, political, medical, philosophical, legal and a host of other early modern discourses harped on the category 'woman'.[217] Yet in practical matters contemporaries rarely considered the rights or responsibilities of 'women' as a general category opposed to 'men'. In discussions of women's property rights, for example, the relevant division 'was not between women and men but between married women and other adults (single women, single men, married men)'. Hence *The Lawes Resolution of Womens Rights* was organized around separate categories of 'maids,

---

[214] For example, CRO, QJF 53/1/26 (1624), ten male defendants; PRO, CHES 21/3 fo. 148v (1626), twelve defendants, seven male, five female; CRO: QJF 57/2/28, QJB 2/5 fo. 114r (1628), nine defendants (of whom only four men were indicted). The wide variety of issues from which an arrest might ensue was also relevant.

[215] Wiener, 'Sex roles and crime', 45, 46–9, at 49; Mendelson and Crawford, *Women in Early Modern England*, 44.

[216] Sharpe, *Crime*, 154.

[217] For example, Fletcher, *Gender, Sex and Subordination*, Parts 1 and 3; Ian McLean, *The Renaissance Notion of Woman: A Study in the Fortunes of Scholasticism and Medical Science in European Intellectual Life* (Cambridge, 1980); Mendelson and Crawford, *Women in Early Modern England*, ch. 1; M.R. Sommerville, *Sex and Subjection: Attitudes to Women in Early-Modern Society* (London, 1995); Linda Woodbridge, *Women and the English Renaissance: Literature and the Nature of Womankind, 1540–1620* (Urbana, Illinois, 1984).

wives, and widows'.[218] Nor were the distinctions between married and other women always associated with the restrictions of coverture. Distinctive dress and church seating arrangements (which placed wives in the front pews, with maids and then widows behind them) were marks of the elevated status afforded to wives, as mistresses of households, over other women.[219] Much popular practice and literary prescription attests to the investment in wives of special responsibilities for household and neighbourhood order. Interpreting the dynamic of rescue in the light of such responsibilities challenges the conventional and stereotypical view of gendered behaviour.

In absolute terms, men outnumbered women by two to one in rescues of goods and livestock. As a third of those prosecuted, women nevertheless constituted a significant minority, and female involvement was proportionately greater than in many other offences.[220] In the rescue of persons, for instance, men predominated by almost four to one; only a fifth of defendants being female. Counting individuals is not always the best means of revealing the dynamics of a given situation, however. Because rescues were predominantly carried out in small groups, a simple aggregate obscures the fact that rescuers usually acted collectively and that women and men acted together. The effect is severely to underestimate the scale of female participation. An analysis of combinations in which people undertook rescues reveals that women were a significant presence in rescues: they were involved in over three-quarters of all rescues of goods and half of rescues of people. Even the lower of these figures is extremely high in the light of an historiography which insists upon women's negligible participation in disorders other than archetypal 'feminine' offences.[221]

The great majority of women who rescued during or after distraint were married, and were usually the mistresses of the households in question.[222] Mistresses, like masters, were expected to use marital property of course for the benefit of the household. They had a duty to protect their households from material and social dangers, to safeguard household resources from harm, decay and loss. A good housewife 'conserved goods for the family by keeping them within the boundaries of the home'.[223] These wifely obligations were understood in palpable and symbolic terms. At a mundane level,

---

[218] Weil, *Political Passions*, 4; T.E., *Lawes Resolutions*, 6.
[219] Mendelson and Crawford, *Women in Early Modern England*, 131. Amussen, *Ordered Society*, 140–4. Underdown, *Fire From Heaven*, 39.
[220] Of 113 individuals prosecuted for rescuing household goods and livestock, 38 (33.6 per cent) were female and 75 (66.4 per cent) were male.
[221] Sharpe, *Crime*, 154–5; Wiener, 'Sex roles and crime'; Beattie, 'Criminality of women'. The nature and degree of female involvement in violence and disorder is discussed in chapter three.
[222] Seven out of every ten women named on indictments were married.
[223] Purkiss, *Witch in History*, 98.

household goods and livestock evidently mattered to both wives and husbands of middling and lower status. In the light of much historical writing that stresses married women's lack of any proprietary capacity, however, it might be worth noting that the early modern wives prosecuted for rescue appear to have assumed some possessive relationship to household chattels regardless of who actually 'owned' them. Evidence from rescues strongly suggests that ordinary people mostly operated on the basis that, to all intents and purposes, marital property (whether rents, profits, livestock, household goods or other) was understood to be just that – *marital* property – held 'in common' for the benefit and use of both spouses. As Oxford's Regius Professor of Civil Law noted in 1614, the 'community of property' established by husband and wife at marriage effectively 'made her mistress of her husband's goods'. To all intents and purposes, a married couple were 'common owners'.[224] Nor is the high profile of wives in rescues of goods unlikely to be due merely to wifely obedience at the time of the action. Both household ideology and circumstance required wives to maintain the integrity of their households in the absence of their husbands when necessary. While married couples regularly rescued their goods together, a full third of wives carried out rescues without their husbands being present, often in the company of household members or other women.[225]

The connection between married women's defence or assertion of household authority and interests and their role in rescues of goods is further emphasised when compared with the dynamics of rescues of persons. Here, while remaining highly visible, married women were less prominent overall than spinsters.[226] When constables attempted to arrest people at home, however, mistresses along with husbands, family or friends were frequently at the forefront of resistance. Thus, as soon as a constable apprehended John Brown for fathering a bastard, Brown's widowed mother Anne Knevis, with the help of two married female neighbours and a young girl, 'did forcibly set upon me and did beat and abuse me and rescued John Brown out of my hands'.[227] Two men who were sent to attach Alexander Elcock reported that three unmarried women 'violently came upon us, ... rescued the prisoner, and by force took him from us, saying that they neither cared for [n]or regarded either warrant or Justice, bidding me go and be hanged'.[228] The relative involvement of married and unmarried women appears to a

---

[224] Alberico Gentili, *Disputationum de nuptiis libri septem* (Hanoviae, 1614), 184; Sommerville, *Sex and Subjection*, 104, 105.
[225] Two-thirds of wives prosecuted for rescuing goods were joined by their husbands.
[226] Of women who rescued persons, 52.2 per cent were spinsters, 39.1 per cent were wives, and 8.7 per cent were widows. Of women who rescued goods, 73.5 per cent were wives and 26.5 per cent were spinsters.
[227] CRO, QJF 95/3/96, /74–/76 (1667).   [228] CRO, QJF 77/2/43 (1649).

considerable extent to have been related to the environment in which rescues occurred. The argument is not that wives were homebodies; far from it. Rather, there was a greater likelihood of mistresses of households being present when warrants were served in the household than there was that they would be in precisely the same place as household members who were arrested elsewhere.

The comparison of rescues of goods and those of persons challenges historical accounts which make general, overarching statements about the relative propensity of women and men to act assertively and with violence. Certain of women's actions, even those apparently characterised by aggression, should be understood not in terms of spousal dependence on the part of wives, but by the positive status which ordinary women, as the mistresses of economically and morally reliable households, could claim and act upon. Their responsibilities were routinely expressed in ways which suggest that 'initiative, autonomy, and self-assertion' were not limited to men. Initiative and self-assertion were displayed by women and men, while in the context of the household, neither wives nor husbands were truly autonomous in the modern meaning of the term. This was no mere rhetorical trick. The cultural significance of rescue was inextricably bound up with the exigencies of material life.

The preceding discussion of forcible rescue has demonstrated a series of general points. First, positive attempts to avoid negative material and social consequences for one's household could take the form of violent, obstructive or otherwise disorderly behaviour. Secondly, such behaviour was not presumed to arise solely from moral dissolution and the breakdown of authority; in certain circumstances it was interpreted by elite and ordinary people within a discourse of the good household as an effort to maintain the economic and social and, therefore, the moral integrity of the household. Thirdly, participation in disorderly incidents over household concerns reflects the structure of the households in question. For the most part, these were of middling status, ranging from yeomen's, artisans' and tradesmen's households with moderate or small property to those of poorer husbandmen.[229] Fourthly, people seem generally to have been ready to assist distressed kin, neighbours and friends. Fifthly, the allocation of legal and social responsibility within households meant that mistresses as well as masters took leading roles in incidents where household resources were threatened. Finally, the behaviour of women and men was context-related rather than being primarily the product of biology or the internalisation of immutable social conditioning (the implications of which smack of determinism too). Legal and social outcomes were not simply 'determined' by a ranked number of 'factors'; they were produced

---

[229] This applies to most sorts of criminal and civil litigation.

in particular circumstances by the interplay of various influences, including, but not confined to, household, gender, status, class, law and location. Each of these points is to a greater or lesser extent applicable to the divers ranges of incidents that were brought before the courts in early modern England.

Agency in cases of forcible rescue is a matter of consciously defending the position of an individual household within a wider system of credit that is largely agreed upon by the poor, middling sort and the rich. Action was conceived in the name of the household not individuals. It involved much initiative by women alone, together with other women, and alongside men. In distraint, law is used to regulate communal norms, not *vice versa*. People were not protesting against the system but their own personal contested place within that system. Hence, despite blatant conflicts with law enforcement officers, forcible rescues cannot be seen to undermine the broader social structure. Nevertheless, even reproduction of the system involves much negotiation of one's position, contest with others and much knowledge on the part of both women and men. Neither men nor women were passive.

POPULAR RESISTANCE

While acknowledging that 'men at all levels of society felt entitled to assert their own notions of how the law represented the common good', Anthony Fletcher and John Stevenson have asserted that the law was 'backed by norms of behaviour which men at all levels of society held to tenaciously'.[230] However, if the law was not merely the tool of central or local authority, neither was it merely a set of concepts that belonged equally to 'the people'. An emphasis upon shared assumptions and norms exaggerates the homogeneity of plebeian understandings of the law. Notions of law and justice were informed by a conceptual and linguistic range which could be adopted by individuals – sometimes by those who were effectively undermining those same norms which notions of law might be expected to uphold. For this reason, order and disorder must not be seen merely as conflicting facets of the participatory nature of popular assumptions about the law. Rather, order and disorder comprised one multifaceted composite. Context determined the side of the line upon which an individual incident might fall. Nowhere is this more apparent than in the manifestation of popular resistance to law and legal officials. While some people eschewed direct action because 'I honour [your office] more than your person', others were not so inhibited, as we have seen in our discussion of rescue.[231]

Notions of justice might sometimes be in stark opposition to notions of the law and those who administered it. Joan Okes, being served with a

---

[230] Fletcher and Stevenson, 'Introduction', 15–16.   [231] CRO, QJF 81/2/205 (1653).

warrant of the peace in 1663, claimed that she was 'bound from law and could have no justice'. If she had gone to London as she had intended two or three weeks beforehand, she asserted, she 'would have displaced all the Justices in Cheshire and after them the judge'.[232] When Mary Colley and her husband were reported for keeping a disorderly alehouse, Mary said that she 'cared not for all the gentlemen in Audlem parish nor all the Justices in the county for she would have justice'.[233] In such instances, justice is portrayed as something beyond the law. Sometimes the conflict between law and justice was based in a perceived miscarriage of justice, which implied that the mechanisms of the law did not provide it. There was, for instance, much alehouse talk about an assize case between two gentlemen, Robert Duckenfield and John Warren: it was said that Job Charlton 'had not done justice in the said cause', having been bribed by Duckenfield.[234] In cases like these, plebeian respect for the legal process was thin. The aftermath of civil war stretched many people's regard for due process and officialdom still further. William Leftwich, sequestration agent for Northwich Hundred who administered the decisions of the Sequestration Committee and who was responsible for the collection of rents and the sale of sequestered estates and so forth, was assaulted and vilified by those whose estates were sequestered with 'railing accusations' that he was 'a cheating man'.[235] Resistance here (and acted out in many cases of forcible entry and disseisin of sequestered land) amounted to a critique of the dominant political order.

Some people openly flouted their exception from the law. William Barton apparently 'gave it out that there had been many had sworn... warrants [of the peace and good behaviour] against him yet they could never get him bound'.[236] Others, among the poorest sorts, had little to lose if they defaulted on a recognisance and behaved accordingly. Hence one Cheshire man feared that his adversary was 'the rather emboldened' to break the peace because he and his sureties were 'all men of very weak estate, and have not wherewithal to satisfy His Majesty of any forfeiture'.[237] People regularly declared that they 'cared not a fart' for Justices of the peace or other legal officers, that they 'would wipe [their] breech' with warrants, and that they would continue in their offending behaviour 'let the Justices do what they could'.[238] One fellow refused to appear before Thomas Tanat, JP, insisting

[232] CRO, QJF 91/276 (1663).   [233] CRO, QJF 91/4/75 (1664).
[234] CRO, QJF 97/3/73–4 (1669). See also QJF 85/3/15 (1667).
[235] CRO, QJF 83/3/72 (1655). Morrill, *Cheshire*, 87.
[236] CRO, QJF 81/2/188 (1653). See also QJF 91/2//98 (1663); QJF 93/2/56 (1665); QJF 93/4/66 (1666).
[237] Cited in Hindle, *State and Social Change*, 109.
[238] For example, CRO, QJF 79/4/28 (1652); QJF 81/2/268 (1653); QJF 83/1/102 (1655); QJF 83/2/120 (1655); QJF 83/3/46 (1655); QJF 85/1/44 (1657); QJF 85/1/65 (1657); QJF 91/1/88 (1663).

that he would only 'go before somebody that had wit', and referring to him as 'Justice Turd, a just bald ass'.[239] Tanat might have felt keenly this denial of his authority, for he was one of the post-war Justices of yeoman stock, who had previously served as a head constable, far below the calling of a Justice. He rose to the heights of the magistracy in reward for his wartime efficiency in minor public office.[240] Other people found ways to circumvent official interference in their lives. In the 1650s, three suppressed alehouse-keepers got around legal proscription by selling 'strong water' and aqua vitae, which were not legally regulated, for 4*d.* and 3*d.* a gill respectively, and giving a free quart of ale with every gill sold! Doll Wright had been doing this for at least three years before magistrates became aware of it.[241] While defiance of local Justices demonstrates that deference was not an inevitable part of social relations, it does not necessarily suggest a wholesale rejection of law. Some 'resistance' was merely a personal refusal to conform. In a society so theoretically determined by hierarchy, however, even personal acts of defiance had political resonances, even if inadvertently.

Law was not something to be blindly obeyed. It could also be a source of conflict between households. Out of such conflict could emerge a form of communal cohesion against commonly perceived enemies. The tenants on some lands that were in the jointure of Mistress Cotton, the widow of a lesser gentleman, were 'greatly vexed and troubled' by reason of a quarter sessions order 'whereby the churchwardens and overseers of the poor... have authority to distrain their cattle for the relief of the said Mistress Cotton's children'. As they had given security for payment of their rent, they argued that they were now 'double charged'.[242] Although their resistance was manifest through legal forms, their case was underpinned by notions of 'right' and 'wrong' which did not correspond to the order of the court. These men and women combined to defy the court order and their landlady. The tension between lawful and unlawful behaviour was never likely to be resolved easily, yet communal action was an important step in appropriating

---

[239] CRO, QJF 87/1/60, /56 (1659). See also QJF 95/2/119 (1667).
[240] Morrill, *Cheshire*, 224.
[241] CRO, QJF 83/4/62, /63 (1656). Forty-four of Doll [Dorothy] Wright's neighbours in Tattenhall, including twenty-three who could sign their names, certified at the Easter Sessions 1647 that she, an ancient ale-seller, lived in good credit and estimation, always kept good order in her house, 'and is undoubtedly the fittest of and most sufficient in the town for that profession', having all necessaries for horses and men according to the statute: QJF 75/1/83, /84 (1647). In January 1648, however, Doll was fined 12*d.* for absenting herself from church, and had her alehouse licence revoked with the backing of John Bruen, a Puritan JP. If she continued selling, she was to be incarcerated in the county gaol until she paid a fine of twenty-six shillings: QJB 1/6 fo. 152v, QJF 75/4/33 (1648).
[242] CRO, QJF 55/1/89, /90; QJF 55/2/132, /145, /56, QJB 1/5 fo. 162r (1626). For another case, see QJF 55/2/108, 125, /140, QJB 1/5 fos. 122r, 149r (1626).

an authoritative voice. In 1647, the 'poorer inhabitants of Over Tabley' complained to the county bench that 'the quartering of horse and foot is not only troublesome in general, but causeth hatred and malice amongst us, the rich oppressing the poor by a new-found assessment of fourteen mizes'. Their grievance was that by this new method of assessment 'rich men endeavour to ruin us, to gain by our poverty bargains to our overthrow, our wives' and children's'. The poor inhabitants thus wished to return to the old means of assessment whereby 'those that have it yield quarter, those that cannot, be spared'.[243] Here, an older version of lawfulness was pitted against innovation in the name of equity.

Civil war provided people with a new language of sectarian abuse, which legitimated acts of resistance to authority. When minor gentleman Richard Eaton refused to pay arrears to be collected on the instruction of the Deputy Lieutenants and JPs in 1645, he called the head constable 'a stinking Cavalier, and so he would prove me, and nothing (for aught he knew) he owed me, or aught would pay me'. When the head constable sent two soldiers to be quartered at Eaton's house, Eaton and his manservant 'did beat the soldiers out of his house', saying that if the soldiers 'came from such a stinking, roguish Cavalier as I was, he would quarter them with a vengeance so as they should not alike of'.[244] Conversely, in 1647, a man who was illegally cutting down trees in the Crown's Forest of Delamere 'jeered' at the Keeper who described himself as 'the King's servant', and 'in a warring fashion' called him 'a rebel', and said that 'he hoped before Midsummer Day next there would be a course taken with all such Rebel rogues as he [the Forest Keeper] was'.[245] People added to their repertoire of discrediting phrases that people 'hath formerly been in the King's army', 'a notorious delinquent in the late wars', 'a malignant spirit, and no way affected to the cause or beloved in the country'.[246] In 1651, Robert Newton allegedly drank a health to Prince Charles, and wished that 'all those soldiers which were hired to go to Worcester in the Parliament's service might not one of them return back again'.[247] In 1653, William Ridgeway was termed 'a grand enemy to the Parliament's forces and to the peace and government of this Commonwealth', who 'said he was a Cavalier and he would be a Cavalier as long as he could blow'.[248] In the late 1650s, people were still being discredited as 'a papist and one that hath been in arms against the Parliament', and 'an inveterate enemy against the State'.[249] In some cases, these terms and phrases were used to undermine

---

[243] CRO, QJF 75/1/24 (1647).   [244] CRO, QJF 73/3/104 (1645).
[245] CRO, QJF 75/4/87, QJB 1/6 fo. 157v (1648).
[246] CRO, QJF 74/1/62 (1646); QJF 77/2/59 (1649); QJF 74/1/45 (1646).
[247] CRO, QJF 79/3/41 (1651). See also QJF 79/1/61, /63 (1651).
[248] CRO, QJF 81/2/206 (1653).   [249] CRO, QJF 85/2/149 (1657); QJF 87/1/120 (1659).

adversaries, in others they served to show that speakers had slandered the victim. These terms were not always used merely strategically. They could reflect real political differences. Dorothy Eaton *alias* Welsh was examined by Chester's Mayor in 1647 upon the complaint of a New Model Army soldier, to whom she had threatened to 'pick me down the stairs and break my neck' after he had contradicted her loaded remark that plague followed 'the Roundheads...whithersoever they went'. The warrant for Dorothy's arrest described her as 'a woman of very evil conversation' who 'hath used cursing and very ill language against such as are well affected to the Parliament and such as have served them well in the public service'.[250]

Civil war created circumstances in which defiance of law took on new meanings. In 1643, the head constables of Wirral Hundred informed magistrates that they were unable to collect moneys towards the repair of Warrington Bridge because 'the whole country within our several divisions refuse payment and return this answer to say, "It is no time now to repair bridges."'[251] In 1647, churchwardens reported that in Tarvin, 'diverse of the inhabitants...by reason of these distracted times, conceiving that the consistory court being now out of use, there is no law to enforce them to pay their lays assessed on their livings' for the purpose of repairing the church.[252] This was not an isolated incident: there were so many requests that the whole county should be charged with repairing parish churches 'ruined and decayed by soldiers and others in the time of the wars' that the bench made a general order to affirm that the costs were to continue to be born by parishes.[253] Others referred to the civil war years as 'these lawless times'.[254] The court files and order books attest to the degree of resentment against the 'insufferable imposures' and 'extraordinary sufferings' caused by the costs of war incurred in increased taxation, giving troops free quarter, plunder and sequestration, as well as the destruction caused by the fighting.[255] The war

---

[250] CCRO, MF69/4/265–266 (1647).   [251] CRO, QJF 71/4/15 (1643).
[252] CRO, QJB 1/6 fo. 155v, QJF 75/4/64 (1648).
[253] CRO, QJB 1/6 fos. 160r–160v, QJF 75/4/60 (1648).   [254] CRO, QJF 74/1/74 (1646).
[255] For example, CRO, QJB 1/6 fo. 93r (1645); QJF 75/4/103 (1648); QJF 75/4/83 (1648); QJF 76/1/41 (1648); QJF 77/2/58, /70 (1649); QJF 79/2/135 (1651); QJF 79/4/105 (1652). For printed complaints of plunder, see, for example, G.H., *An Answer to a Scandalous Lying Pamphlet, Intituled Prince Rupert his Declaration* (London, 1642), 4, 5; *Speciall and True Passages Worth Observation, From Severall Places of this Kingdome, September 23, and 24* (London, 1642); *Prince Ruperts Burning Love to England: Discovered in Birminghams Flames. Or A More Exact and True Narration of Birmingham's Calamities, under the Barbarous and Inhumane Cruelties of P. Ruperts Forces* (London, 1643); *Severall Letters of Complaint from the Northern Parts of this Kingdom. Setting forth the Barbarous Cruelty and Inhumanity of the Scotch Army, in Destroying Whole Families, and Towns, and Carrying Away All Manner of Portable Goods, and Driving Away All Sorts of Cattle* (London, 1650).

had other financial repercussions. In Nantwich, 'by reason of the late wars and during the siege and garrison there, diverse strangers and soldiers have married wives there, and begotten children, and have since left that town or been slain in the wars and have left their wives and children to the charge of the parish'.[256]

Poor people expressed the belief that they were being cheated by their more affluent neighbours into carrying more than their fair share of the financial burden of the war. Their grievances were articulated in the language of oppression to which the county bench was sensitive. The poorer inhabitants of Over Tabley complained in 1647 about 'the rich oppressing the poorer... rich men endeavour to ruin us, to gain by our poverty'.[257] Parishioners in Bowden objected to the 'grievous oppression of the poorer sorts who carry the weight of the burden' for maimed soldiers and war widows 'by reason of the inequality of the taxation', which unlike other lays were assessed without respect to 'the measure of quality of man's estates'. Hence, on the basis of real property, those worth ten pounds *per annum* paid the same amount as those worth eighty pounds *per annum*, and personal estates were disregarded, 'which is against the common order of equity, charity, and justice'.[258] Poor residents of Marton claimed that 'we are much oppressed' and 'wronged' by the assessors of the town, 'who have no pity nor compassion, and 'who set themselves free by their personal estate and do overrate us' that they will 'bring us to beggary'.[259] Magistrates made orders against those who exhibited 'unequal and dishonest dealing', and referred arguments to local JPs 'who are desired to compose these differences'.[260] This language spread to other concerns. For instance, in 1646, eighty-year-old Thomas Wilcock successfully complained to magistrates about George Venables's refusal to contribute rateably to the cost of a constable, 'he being a rich man and oppressing me'.[261] Here we have a much more radical notion of social relations, which implies that the poor as a category have rights, even though they are asserted through an appeal to the goodwill of the rich. (Indeed, civil war created such a radical atmosphere that Justices found themselves in the ironic position of trying to remove several poor people – six women, four men and six children – who in the mid-1640s squatted in the new House of Correction at Middlewich; they stayed for three years despite the Justices' best efforts.)[262]

[256] CRO, QJF 1/6 fos. 166v–167r (1648).   [257] CRO, QJF 75/1/24 (1647).
[258] CRO, QJF 77/3/15 (1649). See also QJF 79/1/127 (1651).
[259] CRO, QJF 75/4/51 (1648).
[260] CRO, QJF 73/3/105, QJB 1/6 fo. 93r (1645); QJB 1/6 fo. 138v (1647); QJF 75/1/24 (1647).
[261] CRO, QJF 74/6/66 (1646).
[262] CRO, QJF 74/2/70, QJB 1/6 fo. 112v (1646); QJF 75/1/40, QJB 1/6 fo. 133v (1647).

A similar example of this may be found in opposition to the piecemeal extinction of common rights by the landed elite.[263] Cheshire witnessed no enclosure riots on the scale of the Midland Riots of 1607, which involved thousands of participants, but people did band together in sufficiently large numbers to make an impact. For instance, in 1646 some eighty men dug up the ditches surrounding Thomas Littlemore's enclosed land, commonly called, suggestively, 'Littlemore's new enclosure'.[264] However, most disputes over enclosures were acted out on a much smaller scale and protagonists were fined accordingly.[265] In February 1657, for example, three men were separately charged with pulling down the fences of Peter Venables, Baron of Kinderton's enclosure in Hunsterson, called 'the intake'. They drove Venables's cattle out towards the common pound, and put their own animals in to pasture.[266] Small-scale protests like these were not less politically significant than large-scale rioting. They were assertions of the rights of the people over those of the landed elite. These rights were stated overtly. Sixteen men were prosecuted for riotous assemblies and forcible entries after they pulled down 'some part of the new enclosures' upon the waste and commons of Dunham Massey. They petitioned the bench, explaining that they had done so because they were 'unwilling to depart with that right which had anciently and time out of mind belonged unto their tenements', and that when the enclosures 'were laid open again, it was done without any opposition, quarrel, or strife, and without any breach of the peace as we conceive, and no riotous offence by us committed, having good right to our common and constant possession of it'. As they were too poor to traverse the indictments, they requested that the bench mitigate their fines 'with such leniency as your worships shall think fit'. The bench evidently felt that they had a case to be answered, for the fines were set at a mere sixpence apiece.[267] Resistance to enclosures was thus presented as an act within the bounds of 'right' and a form of lawfulness even at the same time as it was differently proscribed by law. Action against enclosure was undertaken in the name of custom, tradition and myth as well as law. In breaking down enclosing walls and putting animals to graze on the land from which they had been excluded, people did more than physically reoccupy contested space; 'they were also symbolically reasserting communal control over space and

---

[263] Steve Hindle, 'Persuasion and protest in the Caddington Common enclosure dispute', *P&P* 158 (1998), 37–78; Manning, *Village Revolts*; Buchanan Sharp, *In Contempt of All Authority: Rural Artisans and Riot in the West of England, 1586–1660* (Berkeley, 1980); Andy Wood, *Riot, Rebellion and Popular Politics in Early Modern England* (London, 2002).
[264] CRO, QJF 74/1/2 (1646).
[265] For example, CRO, QJB 1/6 fo. 123v (1646); QJF 74/4/68 (1647).
[266] CRO, QJF 85/1/6, /7, /8 (1657).   [267] CRO, QJF 79/2/110 (1651).

resources'.[268] Although a detailed discussion of collective protest is beyond the scope of this study, it is notable that protests about enclosures, although remaining focused on individual assaults on the rights of particular commoners, contested economic relations overtly in a way that gender relations never were.[269]

[268] Wood, *Riot, Rebellion and Popular Politics*, 103.
[269] See references to riot and crowd disorder, enclosure riots in Wood, *Riot, Rebellion and Popular Politics*.

7

Conclusion

In the previous chapters, I have attempted to illuminate ways in which practices and discourses were interrelated, each informing the other. Hence, ideas are as important to understanding prosecutions, verdicts and sentences as are behaviours deduced from statistics. In the process, I have offered a critique of studies of crime in which female criminality is considered to be a mere shadow of 'real' male criminality. I have demonstrated that it is not useful to approach female criminality by focusing on the lenience with which women were treated relative to men. Indeed, the idea that women were treated leniently within the criminal justice process has been found wanting.

In chapters two and three, we saw that the formal record and terminology of violence does not take us far in assessing what was peculiarly masculine (or feminine) about violent acts. Indeed, there seems to have been little difference in the actual methods of fighting by men and by women. However, conceptions of the gravity of violence were always dependent upon context, on the relative positions within the social order of the parties concerned. Attending to the discourses with which early modern people expressed violent and disorderly behaviour illuminated the social meanings of violence and the different levels of ease with which male violence was articulated by men and by women. We discovered that a powerful discourse of the 'man of honour' provided a schema in which culpability for violence between men could be evaluated. The hierarchical structure of class relations likewise provided a schema for ascribing meaning to violent acts, in which the violence of the upper sorts could be justified as responses to unreasonable affronts by men of the lower orders. Similarly, elders drew on age hierarchy in legitimately 'correcting' the abuses of youths. But we also saw that these structures were contested. Men of all classes used these discourses to assert their own authority over those who were nominally higher than them in rank. Likewise, the discourse of civility was used to bolster but also to undermine claims of violence. Discourses of restraint were not the preserve of the godly elite but were used and manipulated by men of all sorts to legitimate their actions and undermine those of their adversaries. Moreover, the discourse of restraint incorporated notions of violent self-defence and violent retaliation to extreme provocation. The categories imposed by different discourses and practices were ambiguous.

While male victims of men had various narratives available upon which to draw regardless of their social status, women had to negotiate differently ideas about violence. Women could not ascribe to themselves the positive connotations of violence that were available to men, because female honour resided elsewhere. They primarily emphasised discourses of feminine vulnerability, and weakness, yet this problematised their accounts of physical self-defence. Often, women stressed the violation of household and other boundaries to assert the wrongs they suffered at male hands. Pregnancy, associated again with female vulnerability, provided a discursive opportunity for women to present assailants in vile terms, while exculpating the 'mother' from wrong doing. Sexual assaults were even more problematic because the language of sexual activity itself implicated women by suggesting consent and submission even where they were absent. As a narrative of violence, sexual assault was articulated in similar conventions to that of male *non*-sexual assaults. Women stressed that they were rescued by others rather than escaping through their own agency. They tended to focus on their own resistance only when they were ultimately overcome by male force.

In chapter three, it was argued that although the spectre of the violent female generally had negative associations, men found it difficult to assert that women had physically harmed them without compromising their own claims of manhood. Men stressed instead women's other forms of disorderliness, or women's assaults upon men's children, goods, livestock or household buildings. They also denied women physical power by attributing them with deadly intent without the wherewithal to carry out their physical threats. Nonetheless, positive discourses of feminine force did exist, such as the notion of the virtuous warrior woman who sacrificed herself to fight against oppressive or unjust violence. Women's own violence was justified by drawing on such a model, which worked in tandem with positive images of female vulnerability and passivity because self-sacrifice had the greatest rhetorical force when it ended with figurative or literal death. This notion of the warrior woman was wedded to that of woman's role to preserve and save the integrity of her household. Violence between women was articulated in similar ways to women's assaults on men. Violent women were discredited by other women in a conventional manner, especially by paying particular attention to their verbal disruptiveness regardless of the presence of actual physical force. The category of 'the scold' was also reviewed. Despite an increasing tendency by contemporaries (and historians) to associate 'scolding' with women, the lines drawn around female and male behaviour were blurred, for men were frequently prosecuted for the same kinds of verbal disorders.

In the fourth chapter, homicide law was shown to have been constructed in a way that meant that women and men could not receive like treatment before the courts. Men convicted of murder – killings motivated by greed, hatred, betrayal or brutality – were generally sentenced to hang. But men's homicide was not usually classified as murder but as manslaughter, which was imagined in accordance with a particularly masculine form of ritualised fighting. Men's right to assert their honour and manhood over others was enshrined in homicide law. Most men convicted on homicide charges were thus eligible for benefit of clergy and were sentenced to be branded and released. The deaths of women and children did not fit neatly into the category of manslaughter, which was based on the notion of fair fights between equals. We found instead that women and children were disproportionately victims in cases defined as misfortune, a form of excusable homicide. Homicide law thus worked to the advantage of men as it was constructed in ways that usually mitigated the seriousness of their crime. Not all men were equally advantaged, though. Notions of order, class and manhood intersected to give some men advantages over others.

Women's killings were a different matter entirely. Manslaughter, based on male codes, was not an appropriate schema in which to position women's killings. Because women's homicides did not meet the masculine characteristics required for mitigation, their crimes were nearly always categorised as wilful murders. In addition, the circumstances in which women might defend themselves from violent husbands did not match the legal criteria for a plea of self-defence. Nor was abuse over the course of an unhappy marriage recognised in law as feasible provocation. Discourses of poisoning also emphasised women's accountability. In contrast to most men who were branded for homicide, therefore, convicted females invariably hanged. Neither was excusable homicide, such as death by misfortune, a useful category for women's lethal violence. The positive discourses of feminine violence, such as the virtuous warrior woman, did not apply to the majority of women's victims, who were drawn from within their domestic circle. Women's homicide was institutionalised in ways that made it seem more culpable than men's. In practice, a body of law constructed with male behaviours in mind worked to women's disadvantage.

The one exception – paradoxically, given its reputation among historians of crime – was women's neonatal infanticide prosecuted under the 1624 Infanticide Act. The discourse of shameless murdering mothers that was embodied in the Act itself was not the only infanticide discourse available in early modern culture. Others existed that were more sympathetic to women's plights. Seventeenth-century prosecutions and convictions for infanticide were not as numerous as some historians have suggested. Nor in practice was the law applied in a draconian manner. On the contrary, infanticide had a high acquittal rate. Only if there was manifest evidence of foul play, such as knife wounds on the baby's body, were women likely to be hanged. By making infanticide a special case, it seems that jurors were able to apply 'normal' standards of proof. Despite the wording of the Act, women were rarely convicted on grounds of concealment of the birth and death alone. Those who were convicted on those grounds in fact had a good chance of being pardoned. Indeed, infanticide was the only female homicide for which women regularly received pardons.

Theft and related offences was the subject of chapter five. Here, I challenged a historiography that positioned women's thefts as numerically and hence culturally insignificant. Such a stance was shown to have been underpinned by familiar assumptions about women's actions being petty, and lacking courage and initiative. A common view is that because women's thieving was not conceived to be a problem, women were treated leniently by the courts. Such assumptions are not substantiated by evidence. Proportionately, women thieves were more likely than men to carry out burglaries and house-breakings, for instance. They did not routinely steal items of lower monetary value than men. Neither does what women stole fit the category of petty as opposed to serious crime. Nor were women dependent upon men for their criminal activity. Men and women were each far more likely to operate alone or with partners of their own sex than they were with each other. Female and male participation in theft and related activities was contextualised within the histories of particular criminal behaviours. Hence, women's roles in receiving stolen goods, and stealing and reselling or pawning clothes, linens and household goods, was contextualised in terms of women's own economic activities and interactions. Women's lawful networks of exchange were seen to have served unlawful purposes also. Similarly, the world of horse-stealing was populated by men largely because the public world of horse-dealing was a male preserve. The same applies to the theft of large and small livestock. Occasions for women and men to steal arose frequently from gendered activities and knowledge. Gendered patterns of theft are made sense of in terms of context rather than by ascribing labels such as courage to men and pettiness to women.

As far as conviction rates for theft go, the rates for men were only marginally higher than those for women. Moreover, it is difficult to interpret these figures, for women and men were not equally represented in the types of criminal offences aggregated. Men figured as horse-thieves and robbers, for example, which were non-clergiable crimes and so had higher execution rates. When we compared like offences with like, the gender discrepancy was even less pronounced. For grand larceny, for instance, juries reduced the charges against women more often than they did those against men, probably because women were ineligible for full benefit of clergy. However, the leniency argument is shown to be flawed in that women were disproportionately indicted and convicted by grand and trial juries. Once convicted, women were more likely than men to be hanged. It was also shown that various other factors impacted on sentencing: thefts for profit were treated more severely, as were thefts of items of great value; youth was in contrast a mitigating circumstance. But examining individual sittings of the courts problematised explanations for why people received differential treatment. In a comparison of the benefits of clergy and belly, it was found that whereas benefit of clergy was administered routinely, benefit of belly was rarely granted, and when it was there was no guarantee that a pardon would follow the reprieve. Moreover, when branding was introduced as a female punishment in 1623, the qualification for women was more severe than for men. Men could be branded for thefts of goods up to the value of forty shillings, whereas women were eligible only when the stolen items were worth fewer than ten shillings. In practice, the benefits of clergy and belly were incommensurable.

Chapter six explored issues of authority, agency and law. Members of the county elite used the law to affirm their power. They did this through enforcing laws against others and also through a system of patronage that was used to soften the full force of law on their tenants and poorer neighbours. However, the fact that social order had to be upheld by legal processes suggests the existence of dissident voices. The social deference that the elite wanted so badly to be displayed was not always forthcoming, and when it was, it might be a mere façade. Ordinary people used the law for their own ends too. Litigation itself is evidence of this of course. Yet even poor people drew on legal processes by petitioning Justices of the peace, which they did for a variety of purposes. Popular knowledge of and use of the law was also evident in people's adaptation to new legislation or the concerns of the county bench at particular moments. This does not mean that the middling and lower orders had internalised the law's official message. Law provided a resource as well as a set of rules. People drew on notions of lawfulness to sanction *un*lawful behaviour. However, in doing so, while critiquing the actions of particular individuals, including those of the upper sorts, they tended to reinforce the social system rather than undermine it. At the same time, however, the implications of any challenge to social hierarchies were potentially far-reaching.

The use that bastard bearing women made of the law is a case in point. Poor, single mothers were perhaps among the least likely candidates for evoking a legal framework that privileged the economically and socially viable household. Poor bastard bearers were by definition neither economically nor socially reliable; their unmarried status meant that they were excluded from the positive connotations that were invested in motherhood by the category of the household; their circumstances in fact undermined the orderly household. Moreover, laws against bastardy aimed to control and punish the disorderly sexual behaviour of poor single women in particular. Yet, by various means, the mothers of bastards presented themselves before the courts as lawful, honest and morally superior to the men who had impregnated them. Side-stepping feminine liability by a parent or guardian complaining about the putative father on the woman's behalf was merely one means of doing so. Women themselves frequently and successfully made their own cases. Often they invoked notions of equity. They also frequently inverted the common stereotypes of bastard bearers. Men were portrayed as dishonest scoundrels who had broken promises and sometimes contracts of marriage. The language of credit was similarly appropriated. Women aligned themselves with law and the legal process to access characteristics of lawful honesty. The legal process offered women as well as men a language and set of concepts that could be used to invest their stories with authority. In doing so, the marital household was evoked as a positive force for women, while at the same time, conventional ideas about women being to blame for bastardy were compromised.

Poor cottagers were similarly disadvantaged before the law, but likewise used a variety of means to present themselves as worthy of lawful favour from the bench. They drew on the consent and goodwill of their community, a strategy that became more important as the seventeenth century progressed. They invested their claims with authority by drawing on the patronage of local elites. While such petitions endorsed a paternalistic social system, others suggested that the poor were *entitled* to assistance according to natural law. Petitioners also invoked a sense of entitlement in their claims that they deserved licences to build cottages because they had been mistreated by an evil landlord. We saw that law concerning cottages was challenged, but also that even poor cottagers might have greater purchase on the law than their better-off neighbours. Anti-cottage petitions deployed the same notions of consensus to tell different stories of poor people's lack of entitlement. Whereas some men were able to use the language of skill to lend weight to their claims, women could not, for there was no comparable discourse of feminine contribution to the community. Overall, while the poor's use of law endorsed conventional hierarchies, it also contained some notion that the poor possess collective rights that challenge that same vision of social order.

Social hierarchies and the role of law in upholding the *status quo* was also undermined by those who resisted legal officials or claimed that they were excluded from justice. Resistance to lawful authority was frequently portrayed as right and just, and not unlawful at all. In forcible rescues, we found people using dominant ideas in various ways, especially notions of the economically and socially reliable, orderly household. In resisting distraint, people protested not against the system *per se*, but against the position within that system that the legal process had allocated to them. Forcible rescue was less subversive of the social order than some of the other categories of behaviour that we studied, despite direct physical and verbal resistance aimed at legal officers.

Throughout the book, issues were raised about the centrality of the early modern household to understandings and practices of criminal behaviour. That household ideology was ubiquitous in early modern culture is something of a truism in historical writing. If abstracted from their context, 'dominant' ideas about the household and household governance might pass for a coherent ideology. But in practice, household ideology always intersected with other categories such as gender, status, age, religion and law, in manifold ways, some of which contested the supposedly normative view. It was the household, rather than the individual or class, that provided a context for much male violence and which structured narratives of masculine force. Protecting the household entered masculine and feminine discourses of violence, as both masters and mistresses were expected to do all they could to preserve the integrity of their households in both material and symbolic terms. The household also provided various positive narratives for women who suffered violence at male hands. Women stressed the ways that household boundaries as well as personal ones were violated by men who assaulted them, thereby magnifying the implications of male disorder. In assertions of domestic violence, too, women drew on a discourse of the economically and socially reliable household to portray the ill behaviour of their husbands while asserting their own worth. The household was similarly important to structuring the practices and discourses of feminine violence. Household obligations and responsibilities were shown to be important in defining disputes. Married women in particular had a major role in non-lethal disputes, which was far greater than their demographic profile would suggest. Coverture cannot therefore be taken at face value. The image of the virtuous warrior woman informed the positive role of women in saving and preserving the material and symbolic wealth of their households. The force of women's tales of other women's violence towards them rested with the household, too. The household invested women's fights with the notion of competition. We saw this too in the organisation of resistance to distraint, where married women also predominated. Even scolding was seen to have a household context. The activities of the scold could be seen in a positive light of female strength and protecting household concerns, especially given that one in three wives accused of scolding were prosecuted alongside their husbands.

The household was further implicated in patterns of theft. Criminal associations frequently revolved around households, especially partnerships between husbands and wives. This was so even in crimes such as highway robbery, which have been considered to be the preserve of men alone. The chapter on theft warns also against accepting at face value the category of the *feme covert*. Of course, some women did benefit from coverture. Assertions of coverture were made in sometimes successful attempts to lessen wives' responsibility for their involvement in crime. Yet husbands were far from automatically answerable for their wives' actions. Many married women were held to account for their own behaviour, both when they had been in partnership with their husbands and when they had acted independently. For theft, married women had lower conviction rates than spinsters. But I suggested that this might have been due to the acknowledgement of the responsibilities of mistresses of households rather than the assumption that wives were not responsible for their actions.

The role of the household in organising participation in criminal behaviour has implications for quantification. While married women were over-represented in most sorts of criminal activity, they are nonetheless likely also to be over-represented in the 'dark figure' of unreported crime. There are many, many cases of men alone being prosecuted despite the alleged involvement of women in unlawful acts. There is more than one possible reason for this. There is the matter of cost: it was more expensive to have several persons bound over by recognisance, for example, than just the male head who was supposed to order all those in his household. But men were often attached as the public representatives of their households, not as individuals in the sense of the mythical, rational, autonomous individual. There are, moreover, further reasons for women being under-represented in the official records. For instance, women's assaults on men are likely to have been under-reported if discourses of gender and violence problematised men's complaints about being beaten by women. Similarly, if women did steal things of lower values than men, and if 'petty' thefts were usually dealt with informally, then one would expect women's thefts to be disproportionately represented among unreported crimes. There is no reason to suppose that women's hidden criminal activity was sufficient to wipe out the gender gap in offenders, but it is worth noting that women's involvement in crime was probably far higher than official figures suggest.

I also considered the implications of civil war at various points. The circumstances of war meant that new opportunities opened for particular types of theft, for instance, and not just because the courts themselves for a considerable time did not convene for normal business. Competing notions of order in circulation during the wars and in the Republic and Restoration periods created an expanded repertoire of concepts upon which resistance to authority could be articulated. Defiance of authority took on new meanings. During the wars, the language of class oppression became intensified, and so did the articulation of the notion that the poor had rights, which challenged conventional notions of order. Claims of entitlement expanded in the civil war period, to incorporate the notion of reward for those who had incurred losses in the state's service. This new sense of entitlement informed poor cottagers' petitions to the bench for licences to build cottages on wastes and commons. War also provided people with a new language of sectarian abuse, which was used strategically but could also reflect real political differences between the parties concerned.

The pervasiveness of the household–state analogy meant that notions of acceptable and unacceptable violence and protest within the household were affected by the political environment. This had profound implications for framing domestic disputes. The Parliamentary reconceptualisation of the right of the husband (King) to use force to order an insubordinate wife (people) itself changed as the civil wars progressed. After the first civil war, women portrayed to the Parliamentarian bench their husbands' abuse of them as 'unnatural'. The notion of unnaturalness was expanded to include other members of the household. Following the execution of Charles I in 1649, however, rhetoric shifted again in emphasis, this time as the removal of the King/husband became associated in Royalist propaganda with tyranny and treason. As both Parliamentary and Royalist discourse thus each levelled accusations of tyranny against the other, the language of tyranny became more problematic as a resource. Tyranny was no longer a reliable discourse for women's claims of resistance to authority even when excessive force was present. The idea that tyrannous husbands had acted unnaturally and thereby forfeited their right to rule ceased to be used to bolster claims of domestic violence. In the 1650s, the national government and the Cheshire bench aligned themselves with the traditional concept of hierarchical order. Once again, the emphasis was on the righteousness of the correction of disorderly subordinates. Sensitive to these changes in political rhetoric, female supplicants to the bench now presented themselves as the true preservers of order within a household that their husbands were undermining. In the Restoration period, we saw another shift. The official focus sidestepped issues of naturality, and stressed violence *per se* as a negative force. The restoration of the monarch reinvested with power a narrative of tyranny, which was concurrent with a renewed emphasis upon the passive suffering of women. This made it more difficult once again for abused wives to tell their own stories of domestic abuse.

Women's violence, like men's, was politicised as a result of civil war. During the civil wars, wives were expected to maintain their households against the military enemy, an extension of women's defensive role that must have made easier articulations of resisting male assaults in that it blurred the lines between defence and active violence. During the war, the notion of the dangerous adversary outside the home was also extended to include women. But we must not make too much of all this. Both positive and negative images of feminine violence were assimilated into conventional narratives more than they were used to undermine them. In any case, the impact of war was temporary. With the accession to the throne of Charles II in 1660, women's violence was no longer discussed so overtly. Restoration gender codes which emphasised female passivity also made it more difficult for women to construct stories of their own legitimate violence, even when this violence was undertaken to conserve household resources.

My method of analysis has been to weave together the quantitative and the qualitative in order to illuminate the ways that notions of gender and order intersected and impacted on practice as well as discourse. Gender as a concept always intersects with others. It would have been possible to use the same method to examine other categories, such as religion, say, or to have done more with the concept of class. Others might pursue such lines of enquiry further. Similarly, there inevitably remain aspects of gender and crime that have not been much considered in the book. Adultery and witchcraft, for example, arise incidentally in discussion but are not analysed in their own terms. One book cannot give a comprehensive account of all potential avenues of enquiry. What I have done, however, is demonstrate that a series of assumptions about gender and crime have structured the selection, organisation and interpretation of historical evidence in such a way as to produce self-validating results in the historiography. A fuller understanding of gender has been shown to have implications for the study of crime *per se*. In addition, modern scholarship sometimes gives the impression that early modern women either accepted without question dominant, patriarchal values, or consciously rejected and resisted them. The positions available to women are thus dichotomous: conservative or radical, internalised or politicised.[1] I hope that in the course of this book, I have demonstrated that things were rarely as neat in real life and that early modern women, and indeed men, took up a range of subject positions. In so doing, I hope to have provided a sense, albeit partial, of the rich textures of early modern social life.

---

[1] For example, Kate Aughterson ed., *Renaissance Woman: A Sourcebook. Constructions of Femininity in England* (London, 1995), 3–4, 6; Stevie Davies, *Unbridled Spirits: Women of the Revolution, 1640–1660* (London, 1998). Even careful scholarship can hint at it: Mendelson and Crawford, *Women in Early Modern England*, 44, 71–3.

BIBLIOGRAPHY

MANUSCRIPT SOURCES
BRITISH LIBRARY, LONDON

Additional 36,913	Aston Papers
Harley 2016	Randle Holme Collections Relating to Chester

CHESTER CITY RECORD OFFICE, CHESTER

Eaton Hall Grosvenor Manuscripts	Box 1/2
MB/32	Mayors' Books, 1626–1627
MF/69–/86	Mayors' Files, 1646–1678
QCI/10–/12	Coroners' Inquisitions, 1613–1673
QSE/5–/14	Examinations and Depositions
QSF/40–/79	Quarter Sessions and Crownmote Files, 1590–1672

CHESTER DIOCESAN RECORD OFFICE, CHESTER

EDC 5	Consistory Court Cause Papers, 1590–1641, 1660–1669

CHESHIRE RECORD OFFICE, CHESTER

DAR/D/, /J, /I, /H	Arderne of Alvanley and Harden Collection
DCH/X	Cholmondley of Cholmondley Collection: Private Correspondence
DCH/Y/1/1	Nantwich Manor Court Book, 1636–1688
DCH/Y/2	Nantwich Manor Court Files, 1646–1669
DDX/2	The Rights and Jurisdiction of the County Palatine of Chester
DDX/196	Examinations touching the death of Roger Crockett
DDX/210	Wilbraham Family Diary
DLT/unlisted/16-/19	Leicester-Warren of Tabley Collection
QJB 2/3–/7, 3/1	Quarter Sessions Books, 1589–1670
QJF 19–103	Quarter Sessions Files, 1589–1676

PUBLIC RECORD OFFICE, LONDON

CHES 21/1–/5 — Palatinate of Chester Crown Books, 1591–1687
CHES 24/102–/136 — Palatinate of Chester Gaol Files, 1591–1680
CHES 38/41 — Palatinate of Chester Miscellanea: Examinations, 1625–1687
CHES 38/48 — Whitby Papers
SO 3 — Signet Office Docquet Books, 1616–1666
STAC 7 — Star Chamber, Elizabeth I, addenda
STAC 8 — Star Chamber, James I

PRIMARY PRINTED SOURCES

A., I., *The Good Woman's Champion, or, A Defence for the Weaker Vessell* (London, 1650).
Adams, Jonas, *The Order of Keeping a Courte Leete and Courte Baron: With the Charges Appertayning to the same: Truely and Playnly Deliuered in the English Tongue* (London, 1599).
Adams, Thomas, *The Soldiers Honour* (London, 1617).
Allestree, Richard, *The Whole Duty of Man, Laid Down in a Plain and Familiar Way for the Use of All, But Especially the Meanest Reader* (1659; London, 1678).
Anne Wallen's Lamentation (London, 1616).
The Araignment and Burning of Margaret Ferne-seede for the Murther of her Late Husband Anthony Ferne-seede (London, 1608).
Aretino, Pietro, *The Fifth and Last Part of the Wandering Whore...* (s.n., 1661).
Armstrong, Archie, *A Banquet of Jests* (London, 1640).
The Arraignment and Acquittal of Sir Edward Mosely, Baronet, Indicted at the King's Bench Bar for a Rape, Upon the Body of Mistress Anne Swinnerton, January 28 1647 (London, 1648).
B., Ste., *Counsel to the Husband: To the Wife Instruction* (London, 1608).
Babington, Zachary, *Advice to Grand Jurors in Cases of Blood* (1676; London, 1680).
Bacon, Francis, *Charge Touching Duels*, reprinted in James Spedding ed., *The Letters and Life of Francis Bacon* (London, 1868–90).
Beard, Thomas, *The Theatre of Gods Judgements* (London, 1631).
Becon, Thomas, *An Inuectyue Agenst the Moste Wicked [and] Detestable Vice of Swearing, Newly Co[m]piled by Theodore Basille* (London, 1543).
Bicknoll, Edmond, *A Swoord Agaynst Swearyng* (London, 1579).
Blackstone, William, *Commentaries on the Laws of England*, 3rd edn (Oxford, 1768–9), 4 vols.
Blount, Thomas, *Nomo-Lexikon: A Law Dictionary* (London, 1670).
Blount, Thomas, *Glossographia, or, A Dictionary Interpreting All Such Hard Words Of Whatsoever Language Now Used In Our Refined English Tongue* (London, 1656).
A Briefe Discourse Of Two Most Cruell and Bloudie Murthers... (London, 1583).
Brinsley, John, *A Looking-Glass for Good Women, Held Forth By Way of Counsell and Advice to Such of That Sex and Quality, As In The Simplicity of Their Hearts, Are Led Away to the Imbracing or Looking Towards Any of the*

Dangerous Errors of the Times, Specially that of the Separation (London, 1645).

Bulwer, John, *Anthropometamorphosis: Man Transform'd, or, the Artificiall Changling Historically Presented, in the Mad and Cruell Gallantry, Foolish Bravery, Ridiculous Beauty, Filthy Finenesse, and Loathsome Loveliness of most Nations, Fashioning and Altering their Bodies from the Mould intended by Nature* (London, 1653).

Bulwer, John, *Chirologia: Or the Natural Language of the Hand... whereunto is added Chiromania: or, the Art of Manuall Rhetoricke* (London, 1644).

C., W., *A Schoole of Nurture for Children, or the Duty of Children in Honouring their Parents* (London, 1656).

Calendar of Assize Records: Kent Indictments. Charles I, ed. J.S. Cockburn (London, 1995).

Calendar of Assize Records: Kent Indictments. Charles II, 1660–1675, ed. J.S. Cockburn (London, 1995).

Calendar of Assize Records: Kent Indictments. 1649–1659, ed. J.S. Cockburn (London, 1989).

Calendar of Assize Records: Kent Indictments. James I, ed. J.S. Cockburn (London, 1980).

Calendar of Assize Records: Kent Indictments. Elizabeth I, ed. J.S. Cockburn (London, 1979).

The Catterpillers of this Nation Anatomized, In a Brief Yet Notable Discovery of House-breakers, Pick-pockets... A New Discovery of the Highway Thieves (London, 1659).

Cawdrey, Daniel, *Family Reformation Promoted* (London, 1656).

A Challenge from Richard Gravener, Gentleman and Soldier, Scholar... (London, 1629).

The Character of a Town-Gallant (1675; London, 1680).

Cheshire's Success Since their Pious and Truly Valient Colonel Sir William Brereton Came to their Rescue (London, 1643).

The Chester Mystery Cycle: Volume I, Text, eds. R.M. Lumiansky and David Mills (London, 1974).

Clavell, John, *A Recantation of an Ill Led Life: Or, A Discoverie of the High-Way Law* (London, 1628).

Cobbet, Thomas, *A Fruitful and Useful Discourse Touching the Honour Due from Children* (London, 1656).

Codrington, Robert, *The Second Part of Youths Behaviour: Or, Decency in Conversation Among Women* (London, 2nd edn, 1672).

Coke, Edward, *The Third Part of the Institutes of the Laws of England: concerning High Treason and other Pleas of the Crown* (London, 1644).

The Complete Justice: A Compendium of the Particulars Incident to Justices of the Peace, Either In Sessions or Out of Sessions (London, 1637).

Complete Selection of State Trials, Vol. II, ed. T.B. Howell (London, 1816).

The Confession and Execution of the Eight Prisoners Suffering at Tyburn on Wednesday the 30th of August 1676 (London, 1676).

The Confession and Execution of the Prisoners at Tyburn on Wednesday the 11th of this Instant June 1679 (London, 1679).

The Confession and Execution of the Seven Prisoners Suffering at Tyburn on Fryday the 4th of May 1677 (London, 1677).

A Copy of the King's Majesties Letters Pattents for the Rating and Assessing the Prices of Horsemeat for Innes and Hostelries thorowout the Kingdome (London, 1619).
The Court of Good Counsell. Wherein is Set Down the True Rules How a Man Should Choose a Good Wife from a Bad (London, 1607).
Coverdale, Miles, *A Christe[n] Exhortacion Unto Customable Swearers* (London, 1552).
D., W., 'Diverse prette inventions in English verse', in Giovanni Della Casa, *A Short Discourse of the Life of Servingmen* (London, 1578).
Dalton, Michael, *The Countrey Justice: Containing the Practice of the Justices of the Peace out of their Sessions* (London, 1619).
Davies, John, *The Scourge of Folly* (London, 1611).
De Grey, Thomas, *The Compleat Horse-man and Expert Ferrier* (London, 1651).
A Declaration Sent from Several Officers of His Majesty's Army (London, 1642).
Deeds against Nature and Monsters by Kinde (London, 1616).
Della Casa, Giovanni, *A Short Discourse of the Life of Servingmen* (London, 1578).
The Devils Cabinet Broke Open: Or, A New Discovery of Highway Thieves (London, 1657).
Digges, Dudley, *The Unlawfulnesse of Subjects Taking Up Armes Against their Soveraigne in What Case Soever* (Oxford, 1643).
Digges, Dudley, *An Answer to a Printed Book Intituled Observations upon some of His Majesties Late Answers and Expresses* (Oxford, 1642).
A Discourse of Two Cruell Murders... An Other Most Cruell and Bloody Murder (London, 1577).
Dod, John, and Cleaver, Robert, *A Godly Forme of Household Government for the Ordering of Private Families According to the Direction of God's Word*, 2nd edn (London, 1630).
Downame, John, *Spiritual Physicke to Cure the Diseases of the Soule, Arising from Superfluitie of Choller, Prescribed out of God's Word* (London, 1616).
Dugdale, Gilbert, *A True Discourse of the Practices of Elizabeth Caldwell... In the County of Chester...* (London, 1604).
E., T., *The Lawes Resolutions of Womens Rights: Or, the Laws Provision for Woemen* (London, 1632).
Evelyn, John, *A Character of England*, reprinted in T. Park ed., *Harleian Miscellany* 10 (1808–13), 189–98.
An Exact Narrative of the Bloody Murder and Robbery Committed by Stephen Eaton, Sarah Swift, et al.... (London, 1669).
The Female Warrior (London, 1681).
Filmer, Robert, 'In praise of the virtuous wife', in Margaret Ezell, *The Patriarch's Wife* (Chapel Hill and London, 1987), 169–90.
Fitzherbert, Anthony, *The Booke of Husbandrye*, 2nd edn (London, 1562).
Forster, Thomas, *The Layman's Lawyer, Reviewed and Enlarged. Being a Second Part of the Practice of the Law Relating to Offences Committed Against the Publique Peace* (London, 1656).
G., A., *Briefe Discourse of the Late Murther of Master George Saunders* (London, 1573).
Gardiner, Ralph, *Englands Grievance Discovered, in Relation to the Coal-Trade with the Map of the River of Tine, and Situation of the Town and Corporation of Newcastle* (London, 1655).

Gaule, John, *Select Cases of Conscience Touching Witches and Witchcraft* (London, 1645).
Gearing, William, *A Bridle for the Tongue: Or, A Treatise of Ten Sins of the Tongue* (London, 1663).
Gentili, Alberico, *Disputationum de nuptiis libri septem* (Hanoviae, 1614).
Gibson, Abraham, *The Lands Mourning, For Vaine Swearing: Or The Downe-fall of Oathes* (London, 1613).
Gibson, Anthony, *A Woman's Worth Defended Against All Men in the World* (London, 1599).
Gods Justice Against Murther, or The Bloudy Apprentice Executed (London, 1668).
Goodcole, Henry, *The Adulteresses Funerall Day in Flaming, Scorching and Consuming Fire* (London, 1635).
Gouge, William, *Of Domesticall Duties: Eight Treatises*, 3rd edn (London, 1634).
The Great Advocate and Oratour for Women, Or, the Arraignment, Tryall and Conviction of all Such Wicked Husbands (or Monsters) who Hold it Lawfull to Beat their Wives, or to Demeane themselves Severely and Tyrannically towards them (n.s., 1682).
A Great Robbery in the North, neer Swanton in Yorkshire; Shewing how one Mr. Tailour was Robbed by a Company of Cavaliers (London, 1642).
The Great Robbery in the West: Or, The Innkeeper Turn'd Highway-man (London, 1678).
Griffith, Matthew, *Bethel: Or, a Forme for Families* (London, 1633).
H., G., *An Answer to a Scandalous Lying Pamphlet, Intituled Prince Rupert his Declaration* (London, 1642).
H., I., *A Strange Wonder in a Woman* (London, 1642).
H., W., *An Apologie for Women or an Opposition to Mr Dr G. his Assertion who Held in the Act at Oxforde anno 1608 that it Was Lawfull for Husbands to Beate their Wives* (London, 1609).
Hale, Matthew, *Historia Placitorum Coronae: The History of the Pleas of the Crown* (London, 1800), 2 vols.
Hale, Matthew, *History of the Pleas of the Crown* (London, 1736).
Hale, Matthew, *Pleas of the Crown: Or, A Brief but Full Account of Whatsoever can be Found Relating to that Subject* (London, 1678).
Hale, Matthew, *Pleas of the Crown: Or, A Methodical Summary* (London, 1678).
Hall, Thomas, *Comarum Akosmia: The Loathsomeness of Long Haire* (London, 1653).
Harman, Thomas, *A Caveat for Commen Cursetors Vulgarely called Vagabones* (London, 1567).
Hawes, Stephen, *The Conversyon of Swerers* (London, 1509).
Heale, William, *An Apologie for Women: Or an Opposition to Mr Dr G. His Assertion that Men Should Beat their Wives* (London, 1608).
Hell Open'd, or the Infernal Sin of Murther Punished. Being a True Relation of the Poysoning of a Whole Family in Plymouth, whereof Two Died in a Short Time... (London, 1676).
Heywood, Thomas, *The Exemplary Lives and Memorable Acts of Nine of the Most Worthy Women in the World* (London, 1640).
Heywood, Thomas, *Gynaikeion: Or, Nine Books of Various History Concerning Women* (London, 1624).
The Highway Mans Advice to his Brethren (London, n.d.).

Higson, William, *Institutions, Or Advice to his Grandson* (London, 1658; reprinted as *The Institution of a Gentleman*, 1660).
Holinshed, Raphael, et al., *The Third Volume of Chronicles... Newly Recognised, Augmented and Continued* (London, 1587).
The Honour of an Apprentice of London, Wherein is Declared his Matchless Manhood... (London, 1664).
The Humble Petition of Divers Wel-Affected Women (London, 1649).
Hutchinson, Lucy, *Memoirs of the Life of Colonel Hutchinson* (London, 1968).
I., S., *Here Begynneth the Proprytees and Medycynes for Hors* (London, 1502).
The Institucion of a Gentleman (1555; London, 1568), sig. Av.
Instructions to be Observed by the Several Justices of Peace in the Several Counties within this Commonwealth, for the Better Prevention of Robberies, Burglaries, and Other Outrages (London, 1649).
Isack, J., *A Famous Victory Obtained by Sir William Brereton, Sir Thomas Fairfax. Sir William Fairfax. In a Pitcht Battle against the Lord Byron, (Chief Commander of the Kings Forces) at the Raising of the Siedge of Namptwitch* (London, 1644).
Jermin, Michael, *The Fathers Institution of his Childe* (London, 1658).
Jessey, Henry, *A Catechism for Babes or Little Ones* (London, 1652).
Jewel, Edward, *A Brief Discourse of the Stomach and Parts Subservient Unto It* (London, 1678).
Kent at Law, 1602. Vol. I, The County Jurisdiction: Assizes and Sessions of the Peace, ed. Louis A. Knafla (London, 1994).
King's Vale Royal (London, 1656).
Knox, John, *The First Blast of the Trumpet Against the Monstruous Regiment of Women* (Geneva, 1558).
Lambarde, William, *Eirenarcha, or the Office of Justices of Peace* (London, 1581).
Langbaine, Gerard, *The Hunter: A Discourse of Horsemanship Directing the Right Way to Breed, Keep, and Train a Horse, for Ordinary Hunting* (London, 1685).
The Lawyers Clarke Trappand by the Crafy Whore of Canterbury, or A True Relation of the Whole Life of Mary Manders (London, 1663).
A Leicestershire Frolick; or, the Valiant Cook-Maid. Being a Merry Composed Jest (London, 1680).
Lenton, Francis, *The Young Gallants Whirligigg: Or Youths Reakes* (London, 1629).
The Life of Deval. Shewing How He Came to be a Highway-Man; and How He Committed Several Robberies Afterwards (London, 1669).
The Life of Long Meg of Westminster (London, 1635).
The Life and Pranks of Long Meg (London, 1582).
Loe, William, *The Incomparable Jewell* (London, 1634).
Lyly, John, *Euphues and his England* (London, 1580).
Magnalia Die. A Relation of Some of the Many Remarkable Passages in Cheshire Before the Siege of Namptwich, During the Continuance of It: And at the Raising of It (London, 1644).
Maltbey, Nicholas, *Remedies for Diseases in Horses Approved and Allowed by Divers Very Auncient Learned Mareschals* (London, 1588).
The Maner of Kepynge a Courte Baron and a Lete (London, 1536).
Marconville, Jean de, *A Treatise of the Good and Evell Tounge* (London, 1592).
Marconville, John of, *A Treatise on the Good and Evill Tongue* (London, 1590).

Markham, Gervase, *A Way to Get Wealth, by Approved Rules of Practice in Good Husbandry and Huswifrie* (London, 1631).
Markham, Gervase, *How to Chuse, Ride, Trayne, and Dyet, both Hunting-horses and Running Horses* (London, 1606).
Mason, J., *The History of the Young Converted Gallant* (London, 1675).
Massinger, Philip, and Fletcher, John, *The Elder Brother: A Comedy* (1637).
Mercurius Rusticus, Or, The Countries Complaint of the Murthers, Robberies, Plundrings, and Other Outrages Committed by the Rebells on His Majesties Faithfull Subjects (London, 1643).
Middleton, Thomas, and Dekker, Thomas, *The Roaring Girl, Or Moll Cut-Purse* (London, 1611).
Milton, John, *The Doctrine and Discipline of Divorce* (London, 1643).
More, Thomas, *Utopia*, trans. Ralph Robinson (1551; London, 1597).
Morgan, Nicholas, *The Horse-mans Honour, or, the Beautie of Horsemanship* (London, 1620).
Murder upon Murder (London, 1635).
A Narrative of the Proceedings at the Sessions in the Old-Baily, June the 1st 1677 (London, 1677).
A Narrative of the Life, Apprehension, Imprisonment and Condemnation of Richard Dudly the Great Robber (London, 1669).
A Narrative of the Sessions, Or, An Account of the Notorious High-way-men and Others, Lately Tryed and Condemned at the Old-Bayly (London, 1673).
A Narrative of the Proceedings at the Sessions, Held in Justice-Hall at the Old-Baly. Shewing the Several Crimes of the Mallefactors (London, 1676).
A New Ballad of Three Merry Butchers and Ten High-way Men (London, n.d.).
No Jest Like a True Jest, Being a Compendious Record of the Merry Life and Mad Exploits of Captain James Hind, the Great Robber of England (London, 1657).
Norris, James, *The Accomplished Lady or Deserving Gentlewoman* (London, 1683).
The Notorious Robber's Lamentation or, Whitney's Sorrowful Ditty (London, n.d.).
Old English Ballads 1553–1625, ed. Hyder E. Rollins (Cambridge, 1920).
P., M., *Hold Your Hands, Honest Men* (London, 1634), reprinted in *Roxburghe Ballads*, Vol. III, 242–8.
P., M., *Keep a Good Tongue in Your Head* (London, 1634), reprinted in *Roxburghe Ballads*, Vol. III, 236–42.
Palsgrave, John, *Lesclarcissement de la Langue Francoyse Compose par Maistre Johan Palsgraue Angloyse Natyf de Londres, et Gradue de Paris* (London, 1530).
Partridge, John, *The Widowes Treasure* (London, 1588).
Peacham, Henry, *The Compleat Gentleman* (London, 1622).
The Penitent Robber, or The Woeful Lamentation of Captain James Whitney (London, n.d.).
A Pepysian Garland, ed. Hyder E. Rollins (Cambridge, Mass., 1971).
A Perfect Narrative of the Robbery and Murder Committed near Dame Annis So Cleer (London, 1669).
Philipps, Fabian, *King Charles the First, No Man of Blood: But a Martyr for his People* (London, 1649).

A Physical Discourse Touching the Nature and Effects of the Courageous Passions (London, 1658).
Pickering, Thomas, *Christian Oeconomie: Or, A Short Survey of the Right Manner of Erecting and Ordering a Familie* (London, 1609).
A Pittilesse Mother (London, 1616).
Porter, Henry, *The Pleasant History of the Two Angry Women of Abington* (London, 1599).
Primrose, Lady Diana, *A Chaine of Pearle. Or, A Memoriall of the Peerles Graces, and Heroick Vertues of Queene Elizabeth, of Glorious Memory* (London, 1630).
Prince Ruperts Burning Love to England: Discovered in Birminghams Flames. Or A More Exact and True Narration of Birmingham's Calamities, Under the Barbarous and Inhumane Cruelties of P. Ruperts Forces (London, 1643).
The Proceedings at the Assizes in Southwark, for the County of Surrey begun on Thursday the 21th of March, and not ended till Tuesday the 26 of the same month (London, 1678).
A Proclamation for the Apprehension of Certain Notorious Robbers (London, 1668).
A Proclamation for the Better Discovery and Prevention of Burglaries, Robberies, and Other Frauds and Abuses... (London, 1630).
A Proclamation for the Better Government of His Majesties Army, and for the Preventing the Plundring, Spoyling, and Robbing of His Majesties Subjects, under any Pretense Whatsoever, upon Pain of the Punishments Herein Declared (London, 1642).
A Proclamation Commanding the Due Observation of the Desires of the Commissioners for the Contribution of the County of Oxford, and for Punishing all Stragling Souldiers and Others, Robbing, and Plundering the Country (London, 1644).
A Proclamation for Discovery of Robberies and Burglaries, and for a Reward to the Discoverers (London, 1661).
Pulton, Ferdinando, *De Pace Regis et Regni, viz., A Treatise Declaring which be the Great and Generall Offences of the Realme, and the Chiefe Impediments of the Peace of the King and Kingdome* (London, 1609).
Puritanism and Liberty Being the Army Debates (1647–49): From the Clarke Manuscripts, ed. A.S.P. Woodhouse (1938; London, 1992).
R., R., *The House-Holders Helpe, for Domesticall Discipline: Or a Familiar Conference of Household Instruction and Correction, Fit for the Godly Government of Christian Families* (London, 1615).
Relation of the Most Remarkable Proceedings at the Late Assizes at Northampton (London, 1674).
Romei, [H]annibale *The Courtier's Academie* (London, 1597).
Rösslin, Eucharius, *The Rose Garden for Pregnant Women and Midwives, Newly Englished*, trans. Wendy Arons (Jefferson, North Carolina, and London, 1994).
The Roxburghe Ballads, 9 vols., ed. William Chappel (London, 1869)
A Royal Proclamation for Suppressing Insolent Abuses Committed by Base People Against Persons of Quality... (London, 1621).
S., G., *A True Relation of the Sad Passages, Between the Two Armies in the West* (London, 1644).
Scot, Reginald, *The Discoverie of Witchcraft* (London, 1584).

Seasonable Advice From the Ancient Separation to All, Especially to the Professors of this Backsliding Age (s.n., 1650).
Seller, John, *A Booke of the Punishments of the Common Laws of England* (London, 1678).
Severall Letters of Complaint from the Northern Parts of this Kingdom. Setting Forth the Barbarous Cruelty and Inhumanity of the Scotch Army, in Destroying Whole Families, and Towns, and Carrying Away All Manner of Portable Goods, and Driving Away All Sorts of Cattle (London, 1650).
Smith, Henry, *A Preparative to Marriage* (London, 1591).
Sowernam, Ester, *Ester Hath Hang'd Haman: or, an Answer to a Lewd Pamphlet entituled* The Arraignment of Women (London, 1617).
Speciall and True Passages Worth Observation, From Severall Places of this Kingdome, September 23, and 24 . . . IV. From Yorkshire, that the Cavaliers, and Malignant Party of That County, Doe Still Persist in Robbing and Spoiling the Kings Subjects, & c. . . . (London, 1642).
Spelman, John, *The Reports of Sir John Spelman*, 2 vols., ed. J.H. Baker (London, 1977).
A Spirit Moving in the Women-Preachers (London, 1646).
Strong, James, *Joanereidos: Or, Feminine Valour; Eminently Discovered in Western Women at the Siege of Lyme* (London, 1645; 1674).
Sundrye Strange and Inhumaine Murthers Lately Committed (London, 1591).
Swetnam, Joseph, *The Araignment of Lewd, Idle, Froward and Unconstant Women* (London, 1615).
Swift, Jonathan, *The Tale of a Tub* (1709; London, 1975).
T., D., *Asylum Veneris, or A Sanctuary for Ladies* (London, 1616).
T., N., *The Resolver Continued, or Satisfaction to Some Scruples about Putting the Late King to Death* (London, 1649).
Taylor, John, *A Juniper Lecture* (London, 1652).
Taylor, John, *Christian Admonitions Against the Two Fearefull Sinnes of Cursing and Swearing Most Fit To Be Set Up In Every House* (London, 1630).
Thomas, Thomas, *Thomae Thomasii Dictionarium* (London, 1587).
A True and Impartiall Account of the Arraignment, Tryal, Examination, Confession and Condemnation of Col. James Turner (London, 1663).
A True Narrative of the Proceedings at the Hertfordshire Assizes, this Instant July 1676 (London, 1676).
A True Narrative of the Proceedings at the Sessions-House in the Old-Bayley, April 11, 12, & 13, 1678 (London, 1678).
A True Narrative of the Proceedings at the Sessions-House in the Old-Baily: Begun the 28 and Continued till the 31 of August 1678 (London, 1678).
A True Narrative of the Proceedings at the Sessions-House in the Old-Bayly, October 10, 11 and 12 (London, 1677).
A True Narrative of the Proceedings at the Sessions-House in the Old-Bayly, at a Sessions of Peace There Held; Which Began on Wednesday the 23rd of this Instant August, and Ended on Fryday the 25th 1676 (London, 1676).
The True Narrative of the Proceedings at the Sessions-House in the Old-Bayly which Began on Wednesday the 8th of this Instant December 1680 (London, 1680).
The True Narrative of the Proceedings at the Sessions-House in the Old-Bayly which Began on Thursday the 15th of this Instant January 1679 (London, 1680).

The True Narrative of the Proceedings at the Sessions-House in the Old-Bayly which Began on Wednesday the 26th of this Instant May 1680 (London, 1680).
True Narrative of the Proceedings at the Sessions-House in the Old-Bayley, April 11, 12 and 13, 1678.
A True Relation of a Great Robbery Committed near Andiver in Hampshire (London, 1648).
Twelve Ingenious Characters: Or, Pleasant Descriptions of the Properties of Sundry Persons and Things (London, 1686).
The Two Books of Homilies Appointed to be Read in Churches (Oxford, 1859).
Underwood, Robert, *A New Anatomy: Wherein the Body is Very Fitly and Aptly Compared to a Household* (London, 1605).
The Valiant Commander with his Resolute Lady (s.n., 1685).
Vauts, Moses, *The Husband's Authority Unvail'd* (London, 1650).
Vernon, John, *The Young Horse-man, or, The Honest Plain-dealing Cavalier* (London, 1644).
Vicars, John, *Gods Arke Overtopping the Worlds Waves, or the Third Part of the Parliamentary Chronicle* (London, 1645).
W., J., *Youths Safety: Or, Advice to the Younger Sort of Either Sex* (London, 1698).
Walker, Nathaniel, *The Refin'd Courtier* (London, 1663).
A Warning for Bad Wives, or the Manner of the Burning of Sarah Elston (London, 1678).
A Warning for House-keepers or A Discovery of All Sorts of Thieves and Robbers (London, 1674).
Whately, William, *A Bride-bush. Or, A Direction for Married Persons* (London, 1623).
Whipping Tom Brought to Light and Exposed to View (London, 1681).
Whitelocke, James, *Liber Famelicus of Sir James Whitelocke*, ed. John Bruce (Manchester, 1858).
Wilson, Thomas, *The State of England, 1600, by Sir Thomas Wilson*, ed. F.J. Fisher, Camden Soc., 3rd ser. (1936), 16–25.
Wing, John, *The Crowne Conjugall, or the Spouse Royal: A Discoverie of the True Honour and Happiness of Christian Matrimoniel* (London, 1632).
Wither, George, *Abuses Stript and Whipt: Or, Satirical Essayes* (London, 1613).
The Witty Rogue Arraigned, Condemned and Executed (London, 1656).
Wotton, Sir Henry, *A Courtlie Controversie of Cupids Cautels* (London, 1578).

BOOKS AND ARTICLES

Achinstein, Sharon, 'Women on top in the pamphlet literature of the English revolution', *Women's Studies* 24, 1–2 (1994), 131–3.
Amussen, Susan Dwyer, 'Punishment, discipline and power: the social meanings of violence in early modern England', *Journal of British Studies* 34, 1 (1995), 1–34.
Amussen, Susan Dwyer, '"The part of a Christian man": the cultural politics of manhood in early modern England', in Susan D. Amussen and Mark A. Kishlansky eds., *Political Culture and Cultural Politics in Early Modern England* (Manchester, 1995), 213–33.
Amussen, Susan Dwyer, '"Being stirred to much unquietness": violence and domestic violence in early modern England', *Journal of Women's History* 6, 2 (1994), 70–89.

Amussen, Susan Dwyer, *An Ordered Society: Gender and Class in Early Modern England* (Oxford, 1988).
Amussen, Susan Dwyer, 'Gender, family and the social order, 1560–1725', in Anthony Fletcher and John Stevenson eds., *Order and Disorder in Early Modern England* (Cambridge, 1985), 196–218.
Anderson, Perry, *Arguments Within English Marxism* (London, 1980).
Andrew, Donna, 'The code of honour and its critics: the opposition to duelling in England, 1700–1850', *Social History* 5 (1980), 409–34.
Archer, J., and Lloyd, B., *Sex and Gender* (Cambridge, 1985).
Arnold, John H., 'The historian as inquisitor: the ethics of interrogating subaltern voices', *Rethinking History* 2, 3 (1998), 379–86.
Aughterson, Kate, ed., *Renaissance Woman: A Sourcebook. Constructions of Femininity in England* (London, 1995).
Aylmer, G.E., 'The meaning and definition of "property" in seventeenth-century England', *P&P* 86 (1980), 87–97.
Bailey, V., 'Bibliographical essay: crime, criminal justice and authority in England', *Bulletin for the Society for the Study of Labour History* 40 (1980), 36–46.
Baker, J.H., *An Introduction to English Legal History*, 3rd edn (London, 1990).
Baker, J.H., ed., *Legal Records and the Historian* (London, 1978).
Baldwin, F.E., *Sumptuary Legislation and Personal Regulation in England* (Baltimore, 1926).
Balzaretti, Ross, '"These are things that men do, not women": the social regulation of female violence in Langobard Italy', in Guy Halsall ed., *Violence and Society in the Early Medieval West* (Woodbridge, 1998), 175–92.
Barash, Carol, *English Women's Poetry, 1649–1714: Politics, Community and Linguistic Authority* (Oxford, 1996).
Barraclough, G., 'The Earldom and County Palatine of Chester', *Transactions of the Historic Society of Lancashire and Cheshire* 103 (1951).
Bashar, Nazife, 'Rape in England between 1550 and 1700', in London Feminist History Group ed., *The Sexual Dynamics of History* (London, 1983), 28–42.
Beattie, J.M., *Policing and Punishment in London, 1660–1750: Urban Crime and the Limits of Terror* (Oxford, 2001).
Beattie, J.M., 'The royal pardon and criminal procedure', *Historical Papers* (1987), 9–22.
Beattie, J.M., *Crime and the Courts in England, 1660–1800* (Oxford, 1986).
Beattie, J.M., 'The criminality of women in eighteenth-century England', *Journal of Social History* 8 (1974–5), 80–116.
Beattie, J.M., 'The pattern of crime in England, 1660–1800', *P&P* 62 (1974), 47–95.
Beck, J., *Tudor Cheshire* (Chester, 1969).
Beier, A.L., *Masterless Men: The Vagrancy Problem in England, 1560–1640* (London, 1985).
Bellamy, J.G., *The Criminal Trial in Later Medieval England* (Stroud, 1998).
Bellamy, J.G., *Crime and Public Order in the Later Middle Ages* (London, 1973).
Bellany, Alastair, '"Raylinge rymes and vaunting verse": libellous politics in early Stuart England, 1603–1628', in Kevin Sharpe and Peter Lake eds., *Culture and Politics in Early Stuart England* (Basingstoke, 1994), 285–310.
Ben-Amos, Ilana, *Adolescence and Youth in Early Modern England* (London, 1994).
Ben-Amos, Ilana, 'Women apprentices in the trades and crafts of early modern Bristol', *Continuity and Change* 6 (1991), 227–52.

Bennett, J.M., 'Feminism and history', *Gender and History* 1 (1989), 251–72.
Bennett, L.W., and Feldman, M.S., *Reconstructing Reality in the Courtroom* (London, 1981).
Boose, Lynda E., 'The priest, the slanderer, the historian and the feminist', *English Literary Renaissance* 25, 3 (1995), 320–40.
Boose, Lynda E., 'Scolding brides and bridling scolds: taming the woman's unruly member', *Shakespeare Quarterly* 42, 2 (1991), 184–5.
Bowden, Peter, 'Agricultural prices, farm profits, and rents', in Joan Thirsk ed., *The Agrarian History of England and Wales. Vol. IV. 1500–1640* (Cambridge, 1967), 593–695.
Brennan, Thomas, *Public Drinking and Popular Culture in Eighteenth-Century Paris* (Princeton, 1988).
Brewer, John, and Styles, John, 'Introduction' to John Brewer and John Styles eds., *An Ungovernable People: The English and their Law in the Seventeenth and Eighteenth Centuries* (London, 1980), 1–20.
Bridenbaugh, Carl, *Vexed and Troubled Englishmen, 1590–1642* (Oxford, 1968).
Brooks, Christopher, 'A law-abiding and litigious society', in John Morrill ed., *The Oxford Illustrated History of Tudor and Stuart Britain* (Oxford, 1996).
Brown, Joanne Carlson, and Parker, Rebecca, 'For God so loved the world?', in Carol J. Adams and Marie M. Fortune eds., *Violence Against Women and Children: A Christian Theological Sourcebook* (New York, 1995).
Brown, Keith M., 'Gentlemen and thugs in seventeenth-century Britain', *History Today* 40 (October, 1990), 27–32.
Browne, Angela, and Williams, Kirk R., 'Exploring the effect of resource availability and the likelihood of female-perpetrated homicides', *Law and Society Review* 23, 1 (1989), 76–94.
Brushfield, T.N., 'On obsolete punishments, with particular reference to those of Cheshire', Part I 'The branks or scold's bridle', *Journal of the Architectural, Archaeological, and Historic Society for the County, City and Neighbourhood of Chester*, 2 (1864), 41–7.
Bryson, Anna, *From Courtesy to Civility: Changing Codes of Conduct in Early Modern England* (Oxford, 1998).
Burckhardt, Jacob, *The Civilisation of the Renaissance in Italy*, 2 vols., trans. S.G.C. Middlemois (New York, 1958), Vol. II.
Burford, E.J., and Shuhman, Sandra, *Of Bridles and Burnings: The Punishment of Women* (London, 1992).
Burgess, Glenn, 'The impact on political thought: rhetorics for troubled times', in John Morrill ed., *The Impact of the English Civil War* (London, 1991), 67–83.
Campbell, Ruth, 'Sentence of death by burning for women', *Journal of Legal History* 5 (1984), 44–59.
Capp, Bernard, 'Women and the everyday in early modern Europe', *Historical Journal* 44, 1 (2001), 291–6.
Capp, Bernard, 'The double standard revisited: plebeian women and male sexual reputation in early modern England', *P&P* 162 (1999), 70–100.
Capp, Bernard, 'Separate domains? Women and authority in early modern England', in Paul Griffiths, Adam Fox and Steve Hindle eds., *The Experience of Authority in Early Modern England* (Basingstoke, 1996).
Capp, Bernard, 'Popular literature', in Barry Reay ed., *Popular Culture in Seventeenth-Century England* (London, 1985), 198–243.
Carlton, Charles, *Going to the Wars: The Experience of the British Civil Wars, 1638–1651* (London, 1992).

Catty, Jocelyn, *Writing Rape, Writing Women in Early Modern England* (Basingstoke, 1999).
Cheyney, Edward P., 'The Court of Star Chamber', *American Historical Review* 18, 4 (1913), 727–50.
Cholakian, Patricia Frances, *Rape and Writing in the* Heptaméron *of Marguerite de Navarre* (Carbondale, 1991).
Clarke, Alice, *The Working Life of Women in the Seventeenth Century* (1919; London, 1982).
Clarke, Peter, *The English Alehouse: A Social History, 1200–1830* (London, 1983).
Clayton, Dorothy J., *The Administration of the County Palatine of Chester, 1442–1485* (Manchester, 1990).
Cockburn, J.S., 'Patterns of violence in English society: homicide in Kent, 1560–1985', *P&P* 130 (1991), 70–106.
Cockburn, J.S., 'Twelve silly men? The trial jury at assizes, 1560–1670', in J.S. Cockburn and Thomas A. Green eds., *Twelve Good Men and True: The Criminal Trial Jury in England, 1200–1800* (Oxford, 1988), 158–81.
Cockburn, J.S., *Calendar of Assize Records: Home Circuit Indictments: Elizabeth I and James I. Introduction* (London, 1985).
Cockburn, J.S., 'Trial by the book? Fact and theory in the criminal process, 1558–1625', in J.H. Baker ed., *Legal Records and the Historian* (London, 1978), 60–79.
Cockburn, J.S., 'The nature and incidence of crime in England, 1559–1625: a preliminary survey', in J.S. Cockburn ed., *Crime in England, 1500–1800* (London, 1977), 60–79.
Cockburn, J.S., 'Early modern assize records as historical evidence', *Journal of the Society of Archivists* 5 (1975), 215–31.
Cockburn, J.S., *A History of the English Assizes, 1558–1714* (Cambridge, 1972).
Corry, John, *The History of Macclesfield* (London, 1817).
Courtwright, David T., *Violent Land: Single Men and Social Disorder from the Frontier to the Inner City* (London, 1996).
Coward, Barry, 'The Lieutenancy of Lancashire and Cheshire in the sixteenth and seventeenth centuries', *Transactions of the Historic Society of Lancashire and Cheshire* 119 (1969), 39–64.
Crawford, Patricia, 'Public duty, conscience and women in early modern England', in J.S. Morrill, P. Slack and D. Woolf eds., *Public Duty, Private Conscience in Seventeenth-Century England: Essays Presented to G.E. Aylmer* (Oxford, 1993), 57–76.
Crawford, Patricia, 'The challenges to patriarchalism', in J.S. Morrill ed., *Revolution and Restoration* (London, 1992), 112–28.
Crawford, Patricia, 'Historians, women and the civil war sects', *Parergon* new ser., 6 (1988), 19–32.
Csikszentmihalyi, Mihaly, and Rochberg-Halton, Eugene, *The Meaning of Things: Domestic Symbols and the Self* (Cambridge, 1981).
Curtis, T.C., 'Quarter sessions appearances and their background: a seventeenth-century regional study' in J.S. Cockburn ed., *Crime in England, 1500–1800* (London, 1977), 135–54.
Daly, Martin, and Wilson, Margo, *Homicide* (New York, 1988).
Davie, Neil, 'Chalk and cheese: "fielden" and "forest" communities in early modern England', *Journal of Historical Sociology* 4 (1991), 1–31.

Davies, Stevie, *Unbridled Spirits: Women of the Revolution, 1640–1660* (London, 1998).
Davis, Natalie Zemon, *Fiction in the Archives: Pardon Tales and their Tellers in Sixteenth-Century France* (Oxford, 1988).
Davis, Robert C., *The War of the Fists: Popular Culture and Public Violence in Late Renaissance Venice* (Oxford, 1994).
Dean, David, *Law-making and Society in Late Elizabethan England: The Parliament of England, 1584–1601* (Cambridge, 1996).
Dolan, Frances E., *Dangerous Familiars: Representations of Domestic Crime in England, 1550–1700* (London, 1994).
Donagan, Barbara, 'Atrocity, war crime and treason in the English civil war', *American Historical Review* 99, 4 (1994), 1137–66.
Dore, R.N., *Cheshire* (London, 1977).
Duden, Barbara, *Disembodying Women: Perspectives on Pregnancy and the Unborn*, trans. Lee Hoinacki (Cambridge, Mass., 1993).
Dugaw, Diane, *Warrior Women and Popular Balladry, 1650–1850* (Cambridge, 1989).
Dunn, F.I., *The Ancient Parishes, Townships and Chapelries of Cheshire* (Chester, 1987).
Durston, Christopher, *The Family in the English Revolution* (London, 1989).
Earle, Peter, *The Making of the English Middle Class: Business, Society and Family Life in London, 1660–1730* (London, 1989).
Edwards, Peter, *The Horse Trade of Tudor and Stuart England* (Cambridge, 1988).
Edwards, Peter, 'The horse trade of the Midlands in the seventeenth century', *Agricultural History Review* 27, 2 (1979), 90–100.
Edwards, Susan S.M., *Sex and Gender in the Legal Process* (London, 1996).
Edwards, Valerie C., 'The case of the married spinster: an alternative explanation, *American Journal of Legal History* 21 (1977), 260–5.
Emmison, F.G., *Elizabethan Life: Disorder* (Chelmsford, 1970).
Erickson, Amy Louise, *Women and Property in Early Modern England* (London, 1993).
Erickson, Amy Louise, 'Common law versus common practice: the use of marriage settlements in early modern England', *Economic History Review* 2nd ser., 43 (1990), 21–39.
Ferguson, Arthur B., *The Chivalric Tradition in Renaissance England* (Cranbury, N.J., 1986).
Ferraro, Joanne M., 'The power to decide: battered wives in early modern Venice', *Renaissance Quarterly* 48, 3 (1995), 492–512.
Finch, Andrew, 'Women and violence in the later middle ages: the evidence of the Officiality of Cerisy', *Continuity and Change* 7 (1991), 22–45.
Fletcher, Anthony, *Gender, Sex and Subordination in England, 1500–1800* (London and New Haven, 1995).
Fletcher, Anthony, 'Honour, reputation and local officeholding in Elizabethan and Stuart England', in Anthony Fletcher and John Stevenson eds., *Order and Disorder in Early Modern England* (Cambridge, 1985), 92–115.
Fletcher, Anthony, *The Outbreak of the English Civil War* (London, 1981).
Fletcher, Anthony, and Stevenson, John, 'Introduction' to Anthony Fletcher and John Stevenson eds., *Order and Disorder in Early Modern England* (Cambridge, 1985), 1–40.
Foucault, Michel, *Discipline and Punish: The Birth of the Prison*, trans. Alan Sheridan (London, 1977).

Fox, Adam, 'Ballads, libels and popular ridicule in Jacobean England', *P&P* 145 (1994), 47–83.
Foyster, Elizabeth A., *Manhood in Early Modern England: Honour, Sex and Marriage* (London, 1999).
Fraser, Antonia, *The Weaker Vessel: Women's Lot in Seventeenth-Century England* (London, 1984).
Gabel, Leonora C., *Benefit of Clergy in England in the Later Middle Ages* (New York, 1969).
Gaskill, Malcolm, *Crime and Mentalities in Early Modern England* (Cambridge, 2000).
Gatrell, V.A.C., *The Hanging Tree: Execution and the English People, 1770–1868* (Oxford, 1994).
Gentles, Ian, *The New Model Army in England, Ireland and Scotland, 1645–1653* (Oxford, 1992).
Giddens, Anthony, *Social Theory and Modern Sociology* (Oxford, 1987).
Gillespie, Cynthia K., *Justifiable Homicide: Battered Women, Self-defence and the Law* (Columbus, 1989).
Gillespie, R., 'Women and crime in seventeenth-century Ireland', in Margaret MacCurtain and Mary O' Dowd eds., *Women in Early Modern Ireland* (Dublin, 1991), 43–52.
Ginsburg, Madeline, 'Rags to riches: The second hand clothes trade, 1700–1978', *Costume* 14 (1980), 121–35.
Given, James B., *Society and Homicide in Thirteenth-Century England* (Stanford, 1977).
Gleason, J.H., *The Justices of the Peace in England, 1558–1640: A Later Eirenarcha* (Oxford, 1969).
Gowing, Laura, 'Secret births and infanticide in seventeenth-century England', *P&P* 156 (1997), 87–115.
Gowing, Laura, *Domestic Dangers: Women, Words and Sex in Early Modern London* (Oxford, 1996).
Gowing, Laura, 'Language, power and the law: Women's slander litigation in early modern London', in Jenny Kermode and Garthine Walker eds., *Women, Crime and the Courts in Early Modern England* (London, 1994), 26–47.
Green, Thomas A., *Verdict According to Conscience: Perspectives on the English Criminal Trial Jury, 1200–1800* (London, 1985).
Green, Thomas A., 'Societal concepts of criminal liability for homicide in medieval England', *Speculum* 47 (1972), 669–94.
Griffiths, Paul, *Youth and Authority: Formative Experiences in England, 1560–1640* (Oxford, 1996).
Hackett, Helen, *Virgin Mother, Maiden Queen: Elizabeth I and the Cult of the Virgin Mary* (Basingstoke, 1995).
Haigh, Christopher, 'Slander and the church courts in the sixteenth century', *Transactions of the Historic Society of Lancashire and Cheshire* 78 (1975), 1–13.
Hall, James, *A History of the Town and Parish of Nantwich* (Manchester, 1972).
Hanawalt, Barbara A., *Crime and Conflict in English Communities, 1300–1348* (Cambridge, Mass., 1979).
Hanawalt, Barbara A., 'The female felon in fourteenth-century England', *Viator* 5 (1974), 253–68.

Harding, Alan, *A Social History of English Law* (London, 1966).
Hardwick, Julie, *The Practice of Patriarchy: Gender and the Politics of Household Authority in Early Modern France* (University Park, Penn., 1998).
Harrison, Simon, Kennet, Annette M., Shepherd, Elizabeth J., and Willshaw, Eileen M., *Tudor Chester: A Study of Chester in the Reigns of the Tudor Monarchs, 1485–1603* (Chester, 1986).
Harrison, Simon, Kennet, Annette M., Shepherd, Elizabeth J., and Willshaw, Eileen M., *Loyal Chester: A Brief History of Chester in the Civil War Period* (Chester, 1984).
Harte, Negley B., 'State control of dress and social change in pre-industrial England', in D.C. Coleman and A.H. John eds., *Trade, Government and Economy in Pre-Industrial England. Essays Presented to F.J. Fisher* (London, 1976), 132–65.
Harvey, A.D., 'Research note: burning women at the stake in eighteenth-century England', *Criminal Justice History* 11, (1990), 193–5.
Haste, Helen, *The Sexual Metaphor* (London, 1993).
Hay, Douglas, 'War, dearth and theft in the eighteenth century: the record of the English courts', *P&P* 95 (1982), 117–59.
Hay, Douglas, 'Property, authority and the criminal law', in Douglas Hay et al. eds., *Albion's Fatal Tree: Crime and Society in Eighteenth-Century England* (London, 1975), 17–64.
Head, Robert, *Congleton Past and Present: A History of this Old Cheshire Town* (Congleton, 1887).
Heidensohn, Frances, *Women and Crime* (1985; London, 1990).
Henderson, Katherine Usher, and McManus, Barbara F., eds., *Half Humankind: Contexts and Texts of the Controversy about Women in England, 1540–1640* Urbana and Chicago, 1985).
Herrup, Cynthia B., *A House in Gross Disorder: Sex, Law and The Second Earl of Castlehaven* (Oxford, 1999).
Herrup, Cynthia B., *The Common Peace: Participation and the Criminal Law in Seventeenth-Century England* (Cambridge, 1987).
Herrup, Cynthia B., 'Law and morality in seventeenth-century England', *P&P* 106 (1985), 102–22.
Hester, Marianne, Kelly, Liz, and Radford, Jill, *Women, Violence and Male Power* (Buckingham, 1996).
Higgins, G.P., 'The government of early Stuart Cheshire', *Northern History* 12 (1976), 32–52.
Higgins, P., 'The reactions of women, with special reference to women petitioners', in Brian Manning ed., *Politics, Religion and the English Civil War* (Manchester, 1973), 177–222.
Hill, Christopher, *The World Turned Upside Down: Radical Ideas During the English Revolution* (London, 1972).
Hindle, Steve, *The State and Social Change, c.1550–1640* (London, 2000).
Hindle, Steve, 'Persuasion and protest in the Caddington Common enclosure dispute', *P&P* 158 (1998), 37–78.
Hindle, Steve, 'The shaming of Margaret Knowsley: gossip, gender and the experience of authority in early modern England', *Continuity and Change* 9, 3 (1994), 391–419.
Hodson, Howard, *Cheshire, 1660–1780: Restoration to Industrial Revolution* (Chester, 1978).

Hoffer, P.C., and Hull, N.E., *Murdering Mothers: Infanticide in England and New England, 1558–1803* (New York, 1981).
Hogrefe, P., 'The legal rights of Tudor women and their circumvention by men and women', *Sixteenth Century Journal* 3 (1972), 97–105.
Holdsworth, William, *A History of English Law*, 16 vols., 5th edn (London, 1966), Vol. III.
Holmes, Clive, 'Women: witnesses and witches', *P&P* 140 (1993), 45–78.
Holmes, Clive, 'Drainers and fenmen: the problem of popular political consciousness in the seventeenth century', in Anthony Fletcher and John Stevenson eds., *Order and Disorder in Early Modern England* (Cambridge, 1985), 166–95.
Holmes, Clive, 'Popular culture? Witches, magistrates and divines in early modern England', in S.L. Kaplan ed., *Understanding Popular Culture: Europe from the Middle Ages to the Nineteenth Century* (Berlin, New York and Amsterdam, 1984), 85–111.
Holmes, Clive, 'The county community in Stuart historiography', *Journal of British Studies* 19 (1980), 53–74.
Horder, Jeremy, *Provocation and Responsibility* (Oxford, 1992).
Houlbrooke, Ralph A., *Church Courts and the People during the English Reformation, 1520–1570* (Oxford, 1979).
Hudson, Geoffrey L., 'Negotiating for blood money: war widows and the courts in seventeenth-century England', in Jenny Kermode and Garthine Walker eds., *Women, Crime and the Courts in Early Modern England* (London, 1994), 146–69.
Hufton, Olwen, 'Women and violence in early modern Europe', in Fia Dieteren and Els Kloek eds., *Writing Women into History* (Amsterdam, 1991), 75–95.
Hughes, Ann, 'Local history and the origins of the civil war', in Richard Cust and Ann Hughes eds., *Conflict in Early Stuart England: Studies in Religion and Politics, 1603–1642* (London, 1989), 224–53.
Hughes, Ann, *Politics, Society and Civil War in Warwickshire, 1620–1660* (Cambridge, 1987).
Hughes, Ann, 'Warwickshire on the eve of the civil war: a "county community"?', *Midland History* 7 (1982), 42–72.
Hughes, Geoffrey, *Swearing: A Social History of Foul Language, Oaths and Profanity in English* (Oxford, 1991).
Hunnisett, R.F., 'The importance of eighteenth-century coroners' bills', in E.W. Ives and A.H. Manchester eds., *Law, Litigants and the Legal Profession* (London, 1983), 126–39.
Hunt, Margaret, 'Wife-beating, domesticity and women's independence in eighteenth-century London', *Gender and History* 4, 1 (1992), 10–33.
Ingham, Alfred, *Cheshire: Its Traditions and History* (Edinburgh, 1920).
Ingram, Martin, 'Law, litigants and the construction of "honour": slander suits in early modern England', in Peter Coss ed., *The Moral World of the Law* (Cambridge, 2000), 134–60.
Ingram, Martin, '"Scolding women cucked or washed": a crisis in gender relations in early modern England?', in Jenny Kermode and Garthine Walker eds., *Women, Crime and the Courts in Early Modern England* (London, 1994), 48–80.
Ingram, Martin, *Church Courts, Sex and Marriage in England, 1570–1640* (Cambridge, 1987).

Ingram, Martin, 'Ridings, rough music and mocking rhymes in early modern England', in Barry Reay ed., *Popular Culture in Seventeenth-Century England* (London, 1985), 166–97.
Ingram, Martin, 'Communities and courts: law and disorder in early seventeenth-century Wiltshire', in J. S. Cockburn ed., *Crime in England, 1500–1800* (London, 1977), 110–34.
Innes, Joanna, and Styles, John, 'The crime wave: recent writing on crime and criminal justice in eighteenth-century England', *Journal of British Studies* 25 (1986), 380–435.
Jackson, Mark, *New-Born Child Murder: Women, Illegitimacy and the Courts in Eighteenth-Century England* (Manchester, 1996).
James, Mervyn, *English Politics and the Concept of Honour, 1485–1642* (Cambridge, 1978).
Jenkins, Keith, ed., *The Postmodern History Reader* (London, 1997).
Jones, Ann Rosalind, and Stallybrass, Peter, *Renaissance Clothing and the Materials of Memory* (Cambridge, 2000).
Kaye, J.M., 'The early history of murder and manslaughter', *Law Quarterly Review* 83 (1967), 365–95, 569–601.
Kennedy, Helena, *Eve was Framed: Women and British Justice* (London, 1993).
Kennett, Annette, *Archives and Records of the City of Chester* (Chester, 1985).
Kent, Joan, 'The English village constable, 1580–1642', *Journal of British Studies* 20 (1981), 26–49.
Kent, Joan, 'Attitudes of Members of the House of Commons to the regulation of "personal conduct" in late Elizabethan and early Stuart England', *Bulletin of the Institute of Historical Research* 46 (1973), 41–71.
Kent, Susan Kingsley, *Gender and Power in Britain, 1660–1990* (London, 1999).
Kiernan, V.G., *The Duel in European History: Honour and the Reign of Aristocracy* (Oxford, 1986).
King, P.J.R., 'Decision makers and decision making', *Historical Journal* 27 (1984), 25–58.
King, Peter, *Crime, Justice, and Discretion in England, 1740–1820* (Oxford, 2000).
King, W.J., 'Untapped resources for social historians: court leet records', *Journal of Social History* 15 (1981–2), 699–704.
King, W.J., 'Leet jurors and the search for law and order in seventeenth-century England: "galling persecution" or reasonable justice?', *Histoire Sociale: Social History* 13 (1980), 305–23.
Kloek, Els, 'Criminality and gender in Leiden's *confessieboeken*, 1678–1794', *Criminal Justice History* 11 (1990), 1–29.
Knafla, Louis A., '"Sin of all sorts swarmeth": criminal litigation in an English county in the early seventeenth century', in E.W. Ives and A.H. Manchester eds., *Law, Litigants and the Legal Profession* (London, 1983), 50–67.
Knight, Stephen, *Robin Hood: A Complete Study of the English Outlaw* (Oxford, 1994).
Kreps, Barbara, 'The paradox of women: the legal position of early modern wives and Thomas Dekker's *The Honest Whore*', *ELH* 69 (2002), 83–102.
Lake, Jeremy, *The Great Fire of Nantwich* (Nantwich, 1983).
Lake, Peter, 'Deeds against nature: cheap print, Protestantism and murder in early seventeenth-century England', in Kevin Sharpe and Peter Lake eds., *Culture and Politics in Early Stuart England* (London, 1994), 257–84.
Langbein, John H., '*Albion*'s fatal flaws', *P&P* 98 (1983), 96–120.

Langbein, John H., *Prosecuting Crime in the Renaissance: England, Germany, France* (Cambridge, Mass., 1974).
Laslett, Peter, *The World We Have Lost – Further Explored* (1983; London, 1988).
Laslett, Peter, *Family Life and Illicit Love in Earlier Generations* (Cambridge, 1977).
Laslett, Peter, 'Mean household size in England since the sixteenth century', in Peter Laslett and Richard Wall eds., *Household and Family in Past Times* (Cambridge, 1972), 125–58.
Laslett, Peter, Oosterveen, Karla, and Smith, Richard M., eds., *Bastardy and its Comparative History* (London, 1980).
Laurence, Anne, *Women in England, 1500–1760: A Social History* (London, 1994).
Laurence, Anne, 'Women's work and the English civil war', *History Today* 42 (1992), 20–5.
Laver, James, *Modesty in Dress* (Boston, 1969).
Lawson, P.G., 'Lawless juries? The composition and behaviour of Hertfordshire juries, 1573–1624', in J.S. Cockburn and Thomas A. Green eds., *Twelve Good Men and True: The Criminal Trial Jury in England, 1200–1800* (Princeton, 1988), 117–57.
Lemire, Beverly, *Dress, Culture and Commerce: The English Clothing Trade Before the Factory, 1660–1800* (London, 1997).
Lemire, Beverly, 'Peddling fashion: salesmen, pawnbrokers, taylors, thieves and the second-hand clothes trade in England, c.1700–1800', *Textile History* 22, 1 (1991), 67–82.
Lemire, Beverly, 'Consumerism in pre-industrial and early industrial England: the trade in second-hand clothes', *Journal of British Studies* 27 (1988), 1–24.
Levi, Giovanni, 'On microhistory', in Peter Burke ed., *New Perspectives on Historical Writing* (Oxford, 1991), 93–113.
Levin, Carole, *The Heart and Stomach of a King: Elizabeth I and the Politics of Sex and Power* (Philadelphia, 1994).
Liddle, A. Mark, 'State, masculinities and law: some comments on gender and English state-formation', *British Journal of Criminology* 36, 3 (1996), 361–81.
Lindley, Keith, *Fenland Riots and the English Revolution* (London, 1982).
Linebaugh, Peter, *The London Hanged: Crime and Civil Society in the Eighteenth Century* (London, 1991).
Lis, Catharina, and Soly, Hugo, *Disordered Lives: Eighteenth-Century Families and their Unruly Relatives*, trans. Alexander Brown (Oxford, 1996).
MacDonald, Michael, *Sleepless Souls: Suicide in Early Modern England* (Oxford, 1990).
Macfarlane, Alan, *The Justice and the Mare's Ale: Law and Disorder in Seventeenth-Century England* (Cambridge, 1981).
MacKay, Lynn, 'Why they stole: women in the Old Bailey, 1779–1789', *Journal of Social History* 32, 3 (1999), 623–39.
MacKinnon, Catharine A., *Towards a Feminist Theory of the State* (London, 1989).
Maddern, Phillipa C., *Violence and the Social Order: East Anglia, 1422–1442* (Oxford, 1992).
Malcolmson, R.W., 'Infanticide in the eighteenth century', in J.S. Cockburn ed., *Crime in England, 1500–1800* (London, 1977), 187–209.
Malmgreen, Gail, *Silk Town: Industry and Culture in Macclesfield, 1750–1835* (Hull, 1985).

Maltby, Judith, *Prayer Book and People in Elizabethan and Early Stuart England* (Cambridge, 1998).
Manning, Brian, *The English People and the English Revolution, 1640–1649* (London, 1976).
Manning, Roger B., *Village Revolts: Social Protest and Popular Disturbance in England, 1509–1640* (Oxford, 1988).
May, Allyson N., '"She at first denied it": infanticide trials at the Old Bailey', in Valerie Frith ed., *Women and History: Voices of Early Modern England* (Toronto, 1995), 19–50.
McArthur, E.A., 'Women petitioners and the Long Parliament', *English Historical Review* 24 (1909), 698–709.
McColgan, Aileen, *The Case for Taking the Date Out of Rape* (London, 1996).
McGowen, Randall, 'The body and punishment in eighteenth-century England', *Journal of Modern History* 59, 4 (1987), 651–79.
McIntosh, Marjorie Keniston, 'The diversity of social capital in English communities, 1300–1640 (with a glance at modern Nigeria)', *Journal of Interdisciplinary History* 29, 3 (1999), 459–90.
McIntosh, Marjorie Keniston, *Controlling Misbehavior in England, 1370–1600* (Cambridge, 1998).
McLaren, Angus, *Reproductive Rituals: The Perception of Fertility in England from the Sixteenth Century to the Nineteenth Century* (London, 1984).
McLean, Ian, *The Renaissance Notion of Woman: A Study in the Fortunes of Scholasticism and Medical Science in European Intellectual Life* (Cambridge, 1980).
McLynn, Frank, *Crime and Punishment in Eighteenth-Century England* (Oxford, 1989).
McMullan, J.L., 'Crime, law and order in early modern England', *British Journal of Criminology* 27 (1987), 252–74.
McMullan, J.L., *The Canting Crew: London's Criminal Underworld, 1550–1700* (Baltimore, 1984).
Mendelson, Sara, and Crawford, Patricia, *Women in Early Modern England, 1550–1720* (Oxford, 1998).
Mercer, Sarah, 'Crime in late-seventeenth-century Yorkshire: an exception to a national pattern?', *Northern History* 27 (1991), 106–19.
Morgan, Gwenda, and Rushton, Peter, *Rogues, Thieves and the Rule of Law: The Problem of Law Enforcement in North-East England, 1718–1800* (London, 1998).
Morrill, J.S., 'The ecology of allegiance in the English Revolution', *Journal of British Studies* 26 (1987), 451–67.
Morrill, John, 'The religious context of the English civil war', *TRHS*, 5th ser., 34 (1984), 155–78.
Morrill, J.S., *The Cheshire Grand Jury, 1625–1659* (Leicester, 1976).
Morrill, J.S., *Cheshire, 1630–1660: County Government and Society during the English Revolution* (Oxford, 1974).
Muldrew, Craig, *The Economy of Obligation: The Culture of Credit and Social Relations in Early Modern England* (Basingstoke, 1998).
Nash, Jerry C., 'Renaissance misogyny, biblical feminism, and Helisènne de Crenne's *Epistres Familières et Invectives*', *Renaissance Quarterly* 50, 2 (1997), 379–410.

Nussbaum, Felicity A., *The Brink of All We Hate: English Satires on Women, 1660–1750* (Lexington, 1984).
Oldham, James C., 'On pleading the belly: a history of the jury of matrons', *Criminal Justice History* 6 (1985), 1–64.
Orlin, Lena Cowen, 'Women on the threshold', *Shakespeare Studies* 25 (1997), 50–9.
Pateman, Carole, *The Disorder of Women* (Oxford, 1989).
Pateman, Carole, *The Sexual Contract* (Stanford, 1988).
Pelling, Margaret, 'Old age, poverty and disability in early modern Norwich', in Margaret Pelling and Richard M. Smith eds., *Life, Death and the Elderly: Historical Perspectives* (London, 1991), 74–101.
Perry, Mary Elizabeth, *Gender and Disorder in Early Modern Seville* (Princeton, 1990).
Phillips, C.B., and Smith, J.H., *Lancashire and Cheshire from AD 1540* (London, 1994).
Plowden, Alison, *Women All On Fire: The Women of the English Civil War* (Stroud, 1998).
Pollock, Linda A., 'Rethinking patriarchy and the family in seventeenth-century England', *Journal of Family History* 23, 1 (1998), 3–27.
Porter, Roy, 'F for felon', *The London Review of Books* 24, 7 (2002), 23–4.
Prest, Wilfred, 'Law and women's rights in early modern England', *The Seventeenth Century* 6 (1991), 169–87.
Prest, Wilfred, 'Judicial corruption in early modern England', *P&P* 133 (1988), 67–95.
Purkiss, Diane, *The Witch in History: Early Modern and Twentieth-Century Representations* (London, 1996).
Purkiss, Diane, 'Material girls: the seventeenth-century woman debate', in Clare Brant and Diane Purkiss eds., *Women, Texts and Histories, 1575–1760* (London, 1992), 69–101.
Quintrell, B.W., 'The making of Charles I's Books of Orders', *English Historical Review* 95 (1980), 553–72.
Reeve, A., 'The meaning and definition of "property" in seventeenth-century England', *P&P* 89 (1980), 139–42.
Roberts, Michael, 'Women and work in sixteenth-century English towns', in Penelope J. Corfield and Derek Keene eds., *Work in Towns, 850–1850* (Leicester, 1990), 86–102.
Roberts, Stephen K., *Recovery and Restoration in an English County: Devon Local Administration, 1646–1670* (Exeter, 1985).
Roper, Lyndal, *Oedipus and the Devil: Witchcraft, Sexuality and Religion in Early Modern Europe* (London, 1994).
Roper, Lyndal, *The Holy Household: Women and Morals in Reformation Augsburg* (Oxford, 1989).
Rose, Lionel, *The Massacre of the Innocents: Infanticide in Britain, 1800–1939* (London, 1986).
Royal Commission on Historical Manuscripts. Sixth Report (London, 1877).
Rublack, Ulinka, *The Crimes of Women in Early Modern Germany* (Oxford, 1999).
Rublack, Ulinka, 'Pregnancy, childbirth and the female body in early modern Germany', *P&P* 150 (1996), 84–110.
Ryan, Denise, 'Womanly weaponry: language and power in the Chester *Slaughter of the Innocents*', *Studies in Philology* 98, 1 (2001), 76–92.

Sabean, David Warren, *Property, Production, and Family in Neckarhausen, 1700–1870* (Cambridge, 1990).
Samaha, Joel, 'Hanging for felony: the rule of law in Elizabethan Colchester', *Historical Journal* 21 (1978), 763–82.
Samaha, Joel, 'Gleanings from local criminal court records: sedition among the "inarticulate" in Elizabethan Essex', *Journal of Social History* 8 (1975), 61–79.
Samaha, Joel, *Law and Order in Historical Perspective: The Case of Elizabethan Essex* (New York, 1974).
Schleiner, Winfried, '"*Divina virago*": Queen Elizabeth as an Amazon', *Studies in Philology* 75 (1978), 163–80.
Schochet, Gordon J., *Patriarchalism in Political Thought: The Authoritarian Family and Political Speculation and Attitudes Especially in Seventeenth-Century England* (Oxford, 1975).
Schwoerer, Lois G., 'Propaganda in the Revolution of 1688–89', *American Historical Review* 82, 4 (1977), 843–74.
Scott, Joan Wallach, 'Gender: a useful category of historical analysis', *American Historical Review* 91 (1986), 1053–75.
Scott, James C., *Domination and the Arts of Resistance* (London, 1990).
Segrave, Kerry, *Women Serial and Mass Murderers: A Worldwide Reference, 1580 through 1990* (London, 1992).
Shapiro, Barbara J., *A Culture of Fact: England, 1550–1720* (London, 2000).
Shapiro, Barbara J., *Beyond Reasonable Doubt and Probable Cause: Historical Perspectives on the Anglo-American Law of Evidence* (London, 1991).
Shapiro, Barbara J., *Probability and Certainty in Seventeenth-Century England: The Relationship between Religion, Natural Science, Law, History and Literature* (Princeton, 1983).
Sharp, Buchanan, *In Contempt of All Authority: Rural Artisans and Riot in the West of England, 1586–1660* (Berkeley, 1980).
Sharpe, J.A., *Crime in Early Modern England*, 2nd edn (London, 1999).
Sharpe, J.A., *Judicial Punishment in England* (London, 1990).
Sharpe, J.A., *Early Modern England: A Social History, 1550–1760* (London, 1987).
Sharpe, J.A., 'The history of violence in England: some observations', *P&P* 103 (1985), 206–24.
Sharpe, J.A., '"Last dying speeches": religion, ideology and public execution in seventeenth-century England', *P&P* 107 (1985), 147–65.
Sharpe, J.A., *Crime in Seventeenth-Century England: A County Study* (Cambridge, 1983).
Sharpe, J.A., '"Such disagreements betwyx neighbours": litigation and human relations in early modern England', in John Bossy ed., *Disputes and Settlements: Law and Human Relations in the West* (Cambridge, 1983), 167–87.
Sharpe, J.A., 'Domestic homicide in early modern England', *Historical Journal* 24 (1981), 29–48.
Sharpe, James, 'The people and the law', in Barry Reay ed., *Popular Culture in Seventeenth-Century England* (London, 1985), 244–70.
Shepherd, Simon, *Amazons and Warrior Women: Varieties of Feminism in Seventeenth-Century English Drama* (Brighton, 1981).
Shoemaker, Robert B., 'Reforming male manners: public insult and the decline of violence in London, 1660–1740', in Tim Hitchcock and Michèle Cohen eds., *English Masculinities, 1660–1800* (London, 1999), 133–50.

Shoemaker, Robert B., *Gender in English Society, 1650–1850* (London, 1998).
Shoemaker, Robert B., *Prosecution and Punishment: Petty Crime and the Law in London and Rural Middlesex, c. 1660–1725* (Cambridge, 1991).
Simpson, Antony E., 'Vulnerability and the age of female consent: legal innovation and its effect on prosecutions for rape in eighteenth-century London', in G.S. Rousseau and Roy Porter eds., *Sexual Underworlds of the Enlightenment* (Manchester, 1987), 181–205.
Skerpan, Elizabeth, *The Rhetoric of Politics in the English Revolution, 1642–1660* (London, 1992).
Slack, Paul, 'Dearth and social policy in early modern England', *Social History of Medicine* 1 (1992), 1–17.
Slack, Paul, *Poverty and Policy in Tudor and Stuart England* (London, 1988).
Smith, Carrie, 'Medieval coroners' rolls: legal fiction or historical fact', in Diana E. S. Dunn ed., *Courts, Counties and the Capital in the Later Middle Ages* (Stroud and New York, 1996), 93–116.
Sommerville, M.R., *Sex and Subjection: Attitudes to Women in Early-Modern Society* (London, 1995).
Spargo, John Webster, *Judicial Folklore in England, Illustrated by the Cucking Stool* (Durham, North Carolina, 1944).
Spierenburg, Pieter, 'How violent were women? Court cases in Amsterdam, 1650–1810', *Crime, Histoire et Sociétés/Crime, History and Societies* 1, 1 (1997), 9–28.
Spierenburg, Pieter, *The Prison Experience: Disciplinary Institutions and their Inmates in Early Modern Europe* (New Brunswick, 1991).
Spraggs, Gillian, *Outlaws and Highwaymen: The Cult of the Robber from the Middle Ages to the Nineteenth Century* (London, 2001).
Sproxton, Judy, *Violence and Religion: Attitudes towards Militancy in the French Civil Wars and the English Revolution* (London, 1995).
Spufford, Margaret, *The Great Reclothing of Rural England: Petty Chapmen and their Wares in the Seventeenth Century* (London, 1984).
Spurr, John, *English Puritanism, 1603–1669* (Basingstoke and London, 1998).
Stanko, Elizabeth A., 'Challenging the problem of men's individual violence', in Tim Newburn and Elizabeth A. Stanko eds., *Just Boys Doing Business? Men, Masculinities and Crime* (London, 1994), 32–45.
Staves, Susan, *Married Women's Separate Property in England, 1660–1833* (Cambridge, Mass., 1990).
Stone, Lawrence, *The Past and the Present Revisited* (London and New York, 1987).
Stone, Lawrence, 'A rejoinder', *P&P* 108 (1985), 206–24
Stone, Lawrence, 'Interpersonal violence in English society, 1300–1980', *P&P* 101 (1983), 22–33.
Stone, Lawrence, *The Crisis of the Aristocracy, 1558–1641*, abridged edn (Oxford, 1967).
Stretton, Tim, *Women Waging War in Elizabethan England* (Cambridge, 1998).
Sylvester, Dorothy, *A History of Cheshire*, 2nd edn (London 1980).
Sylvester, Dorothy, 'Parish and township in Cheshire and north-east Wales', *Journal of the Chester Archaeological Society* 54 (1967), 23–35.
Sylvester, Dorothy, 'The manor and the Cheshire landscape', *Transactions of the Historic Society of Lancashire and Cheshire*, 70 (1960).
Tawney, R.H., *The Agrarian Problem in the Sixteenth Century* (London, 1912).

Taylor, W.M., *A History of the Stockport Court Leet* (Stockport, 1971).
Thirsk, Joan, *England's Agricultural Regions and Agrarian History, 1500–1750* (London, 1987).
Thirsk, Joan, *The Rural Economy of England: Collected Essays* (London, 1984).
Thirsk, Joan, *The Agrarian History of England and Wales. Vol. V. Part 1: 1640–1750. Regional Farming Systems* (Cambridge, 1984).
Thirsk, Joan, *Horses in Early Modern England: For Service, For Pleasure, For Power* (Reading, 1977).
Thomas, Keith, *Man and the Natural World: Changing Attitudes in England, 1500–1800* (London, 1983).
Thomas, Keith, 'Age and authority in early modern England', *Proceedings of the British Academy* 62 (1976), 205–48.
Thomas, Keith, 'The double standard', *Journal of the History of Ideas* 20 (1959), 195–216.
Thompson, C.J.S., *Poisons and Poisoners* (London, 1993).
Thompson, E.P., *Customs in Common* (London, 1991).
Thompson, E.P., 'The grid of inheritance: a comment', in J. Goody, J. Thirsk and E.P. Thompson eds., *Family and Inheritance: Rural Society in Western Europe, 1200–1800* (Cambridge, 1976), 328–60.
Thompson, E.P., *Whigs and Hunters: The Origins of the Black Act* (London, 1975).
Thornton, Tim, 'The integration of Cheshire into the Tudor nation state in the early sixteenth century', *Northern History* 29 (1993), 40–63.
Thurston, Richard, and Beynon, John, 'Men's own stories, lives and violence: research as practice', in R. Emerson Dobash, Russell P. Dobash and Lesley Noaks eds., *Gender and Crime* (Cardiff, 1995), 191–201.
Toliver, Harold, 'Herrick's Book of Realms and Monuments', *ELH* 49, 2 (1982), 429–48.
Underdown, David, *A Freeborn People: Politics and the Nation in Seventeenth-Century England* (Oxford, 1996).
Underdown, David, *Fire from Heaven: Life in an English Town in Seventeenth-Century England* (London, 1993).
Underdown, David, 'The taming of the scold: the enforcement of patriarchal authority in early modern England', in Anthony Fletcher and John Stevenson eds., *Order and Disorder in Early Modern England* (Cambridge, 1986), 116–36.
Underdown, David, *Revel, Riot and Rebellion: Popular Politics and Culture in England, 1603–1660* (Oxford, 1985).
Vickery, Amanda, 'Women and the world of goods: a Lancashire consumer and her possessions, 1751–81', in John Brewer and Roy Porter eds., *Consumption and the World of Goods* (London, 1991), 274–801.
Victoria History of the Counties of England. Cheshire. 3 vols. (London, 1979–87).
Walker, Garthine, 'Just stories: telling tales of infant death in early modern England', in Margaret Mikesell and Adele Seefe eds., *Attending to Early Modern Women: Culture and Change* (London, 2003).
Walker, Garthine, '"Strange kind of stealing": abduction in early modern Wales', in Michael Roberts and Simone Clarke eds., *Women and Gender in Early Modern Wales* (Cardiff, 2000), 50–74.
Walker, Garthine, 'Widernatürliche Mütter? Die Tötung neugeborener Kinder und das englische Gesetz im siebzehnten Jahrhundert', *Querelles: Jahrbuch für Frauenforschung* 5 (2000), 255–63.

Walker, Garthine, 'Rereading rape and sexual violence in early modern England', *Gender and History* 10, 1 (1998), 1–25.
Walker, Garthine, '"Demons in female form": representations of women and gender in murder pamphlets of the late sixteenth and early seventeenth centuries', in William Zunder and Suzanne Trill eds., *Writing and the English Renaissance* (London, 1996), 123–39.
Walker, Garthine, 'Expanding the boundaries of female honour in early modern England', *TRHS* 6th ser., 6 (1996), 235–45.
Walker, Garthine, 'Women, theft and the world of stolen goods', in Jenny Kermode and Garthine Walker eds., *Women, Crime and the Courts in Early Modern England* (London, 1994), 81–105.
Walker, Garthine, and Kermode, Jenny, 'Introduction' to Jenny Kermode and Garthine Walker eds., *Women, Crime and the Courts in Early Modern England* (London, 1994), 1–25.
Weatherill, Lorna, 'Consumer behaviour, textiles and dress in the late seventeenth and early eighteenth centuries', *Textile History* 22 (1991), 297–310.
Weil, Rachel, *Political Passions: Gender, the Family and Political Argument in England, 1680–1714* (Manchester, 1999).
Wiener, Carol Z., 'Is a spinster an unmarried woman?', *American Journal of Legal History*, 20 (1976), 27–31.
Wiener, Carol Z., 'Sex roles and crime in late Elizabethan Hertfordshire', *Journal of Social History* 8 (1974–5), 38–60.
Wiggins, Martin, *Journeymen in Murder: The Assassin in English Renaissance Drama* (Oxford, 1991).
Wiltenburg, Joy, *Disorderly Women and Female Power in the Street Literature of Early Modern England and Germany* (London, 1992).
Wood, Andy, *Riot, Rebellion and Popular Politics in Early Modern England* (London, 2002).
Wood, Andy, *The Politics of Social Conflict: the Peak Country 1520–1770* (Cambridge, 1999).
Wood, Andy, 'Beyond post-revisionism? The civil war allegiances of the miners of the Derbyshire "peak country"', *Historical Journal* 40, 1 (1997), 23–40.
Wood, Andy, 'Custom, identity and resistance: English free miners and their law, c. 1500–1800', in Paul Griffiths, Adam Fox and Steve Hindle eds., *The Experience of Authority in Early Modern England* (Basingstoke, 1996), 249–85.
Woodbridge, Linda, *Women and the English Renaissance: Literature and the Nature of Womankind, 1540–1620* (Urbana, Ill., 1984).
Wrightson, Keith, 'The politics of the parish in early modern England', in Paul Griffiths, Adam Fox and Steve Hindle eds., *The Experience of Authority in Early Modern England* (Basingstoke, 1996), 10–46.
Wrightson, Keith, *English Society, 1580–1680* (London, 1982).
Wrightson, Keith, 'Infanticide in European history', *Criminal Justice History*, 3 (1982), 6–7.
Wrightson, Keith, 'Two concepts of order: justices, constables and jurymen in seventeenth-century England', in John Brewer and John Styles eds., *An Ungovernable People: The English and their Law in the Seventeenth and Eighteenth Centuries* (London, 1980), 21–46.

Wrightson, Keith, and Levine, David, *Poverty and Piety in an English Village: Terling, 1525–1700*, 2nd edn (1979; Oxford, 1995).

UNPUBLISHED DISSERTATIONS

Cioni, Maria, 'Women and law in Elizabethan England, with particular reference to the Court of Chancery', Ph.D. thesis, University of Cambridge (1975).

Curtis, T.C., 'Some aspects of the history of crime in seventeenth-century England, with special reference to Cheshire and Middlesex', Ph.D. thesis, University of Manchester (1973).

Glanz, L.M., 'The legal position of English women under the early Stuart kings and the Interregnum, 1603–1660', Ph.D. dissertation, Loyola University of Chicago (1973).

Higgins, G.P., 'County government and society in Cheshire, c. 1590–1640', M.A. thesis, University of Liverpool (1973).

Hindle, Steve, 'Aspects of the relationship of the state and local society in early modern England, with special reference to Cheshire c. 1590–1630', Ph.D. thesis, University of Cambridge (1993).

Kerby, G.A., 'Inequality in a pre-industrial society: a study of wealth, office and taxation in Tudor and Stuart England, with particular reference to Cheshire', Ph.D. thesis, University of Cambridge (1983).

Rabin, Dana Y., '"Of persons capable of committing crimes": law and responsibility in England 1660–1800', Ph.D. dissertation, University of Michigan (1996).

Todd, Sarah Annice, 'The representation of aggression in the seventeenth-century English broadside ballad', Ph.D. thesis, University of Wales, Aberystwyth (1998).

Walker, Garthine, 'Crime, gender and social order in early modern Cheshire', Ph.D. thesis, University of Liverpool (1994).

INDEX

Abortion 61
Accidental death 116, 130, 132–4, 142–3, 157–8, 272
Acton near Nantwich 108
Adlington 226
Adultery 66, 100, 143
Agden 242
Agency 8, 32, 33, 48, 75, 84, 111, 212–13, 226, 248, 262, 271, 274
Alehouses 47, 219–21, 226, 264
Altrincham 18, 108
Amazons 86, 94, 96
　see also warrior-women
Amussen, Susan 44, 101
Apprentices 36–7, 47, 49
Assault
　indictments, nature of 24, 25–6, 27–9, 31
　narratives, nature of 7, 26–7, 29–33, 97
　recognisances, nature of 24–5
　see also domestic violence; violence
Astbury 219, 240
Authority 11, 40, 63, 67, 68–9, 71, 87, 89, 92, 95, 101, 111, 210–69, 274, 275
　men's 11, 40–4, 49, 64, 92, 140
　women's 30, 52, 53, 62, 66, 77, 88, 90, 91, 98, 111, 112, 236, 255, 261, 274
　see also correction; domestic violence; household

Babington, Zachary 140, 148
Bacon, Sir Francis 114, 132
Bakhtin, M.M. 7
Ballads 47, 65, 71–3, 74, 82, 87, 110, 117, 142, 148, 190, 253
Barratry 31, 100, 104–6, 107–8
Bastardy 62, 96, 148, 150, 226, 227–37, 260, 274–5
Beard, Thomas 158
Beattie, J.M. 2, 136, 140, 141, 142, 171
Benefit of belly 62, 113, 184, 197–201, 208, 274

Benefit of clergy 113, 116, 121, 123, 137–8, 178, 181, 184, 186, 188, 197–201, 208, 272, 274
　partially extended to women 111, 182–3, 200–1, 274
Blackden 243
Blackstone, Sir William 139, 185
Body, the 42–3, 91–2, 120
　female 53, 54, 61–2
　male 34, 64, 82, 85, 192
　see also hair; household, representing the body
Bollin Fee 19
Booth, Sir George 15, 42, 213
Bowden 267
Bradshaw, John 14, 70
Branding, see benefit of clergy
Branks 108
　see also scolding
Brereton, Sir William 15, 43, 132, 215
Bridgeman, Sir John 147, 155
Bridgeman, Sir Orlando 125, 126, 127
Broxton hundred 16, 257
Bryson, Anna 46
Buckinghamshire 190
Bucklow hundred 16, 215
Bulwer, John 27
Burgess, Glen 48
Burglary 54, 159, 160–7, 171–2, 176, 177, 181–5, 187, 195, 208, 273
Burton 196

Carrington 108
Castration 92–3
Charles I 15, 68–9, 70
Charlton, Sir Job 126, 263
Chelford 246
Cheshire 13–22
　as a 'dark corner of the land' 13–15
　economy 18–22
　Palatinate status 13–14

306

Index

Chester 14, 15, 16, 17, 19, 20, 93, 98, 108, 174
   population 18
Children 12, 27, 49, 64, 66–7, 71, 88, 90, 124, 134, 135, 140, 237, 256, 272
Church Hulme 242
Civil wars 15, 42, 43, 48, 77, 218–19, 224, 238, 242
   changing ideas and practices 67, 93–5, 98–9, 174, 196–7, 215, 239, 240–1, 244, 263, 265–7, 277–9
Civility 41, 42, 46, 270
Class 2–3, 24, 32, 36, 40, 41–2, 44, 46, 54, 115, 125–30, 131, 192, 193–4, 195, 211, 213, 214–17, 221, 225, 226, 265, 267–9, 270–1, 272, 274, 275, 278
Clothing 42–3, 54, 58, 82, 90, 98–9, 140, 162, 163–5, 169–75, 191–2, 214, 215, 235, 273
Cockburn, J.S. 131
Coke, Sir Edward 144
Congleton 16, 18, 19, 21, 108, 110, 171, 213
   population 18
Correction 27, 32, 49, 63, 64–5, 87, 98, 111, 122, 140
   see also domestic violence
Cottagers 237–49, 275, 278
'County study' 13
Courts
   chancery 230
   common pleas 155
   consistory 17, 65, 107, 232, 266
   county 250–1, 253
   manorial 16, 25, 30, 103, 104, 106, 109, 215, 216, 250–1, 255
   Palatinate of Chester exchequer 14, 129
   Palatinate of Chester great sessions 14, 15–16
   quarter sessions 16, 17
   Queen's/King's bench 17, 25
   requests 230
   sheriff's court 250
   Star Chamber 17, 25, 92, 129, 132
Coverture 12, 76, 147, 201–5, 206, 209, 277
Credit 10, 31, 66, 89, 106, 129, 206, 233–5, 237, 252–3, 257, 275
   see also reputation
'Crisis in gender relations' 8, 101
Cutpursing, *see* pocketpicking

Dalton, Michael 116, 144, 184
Daresbury 228
Davis, Natalie Zemon 97
Dearth 21, 220, 254

Debt 10, 30, 31, 79, 216, 250, 251, 252–3, 256
Defamation 36
Delamere forest 18, 194, 265
Derbyshire 167, 221
Derrida, Jacques 7
Disseisin 77
Distraint 30, 89, 95, 206, 224, 249, 250–5, 264, 276
Domestic violence 63–74, 118–24, 145–8, 272, 278
   see also correction
Drowning 133
Duelling 37, 42, 46, 47, 114, 131–2
Dugdale, Gilbert 117
Dunham Massey 268

Eddisbury hundred 16
Elizabeth I 87–8, 129
Enclosure 226, 242, 268–9
Equity 216, 218, 229–30, 241, 243, 265, 267, 275
Essex 151

Fathers 12
Feme covert, see coverture; wives
Feme sole, see servants; single women; widows
'Feminine' crimes 4, 163
Fletcher, Anthony 262
Forcible entry, *see* disseisin
Forcible rescue 30, 76–7, 89–90, 95–6, 249–62, 275–6
Foucault, Michel 6–7, 8
Frodsham 19

Gatrell, V.A.C. 118
Gender as an analytic category 3, 8–9, 12, 279
Giddens, Anthony 212
Gouge, William 109
Great Budworth 16
Green, Thomas A. 147, 198
Grosvenor, Sir Richard 117, 207, 210, 217

Hair 42–3, 90–1
   see also the body; clothing
Hale 220
Hale, Sir Matthew 55, 156
Halton 19
Hanawalt, Barbara A. 171
Harman, Thomas 90
Hay, Douglas 2
Heale, William 73

Heresy 139
Herrup, Cynthia 119, 186, 198, 207–8
Hertfordshire 11
Heteroglossia 7
Highway robbery 82–3, 118, 159, 176, 190–4
Homicide 38, 39, 113–58
  legal categories of 114–16
  see also accidental death; infanticide; manslaughter; murder; self-defence, killing in
Honour
  feminine 33–7, 157, 230–3, 271
  household 33–7, 44
  masculine 33–9, 43, 44, 49, 97, 124, 127–8, 132, 157, 230–3, 270, 272
Horse-theft 41, 159, 160, 162, 167–9, 177, 185, 187, 195–7, 202, 208, 273
Housebreaking 159, 160–7, 171–2, 176, 181–5, 187, 208, 273
Household 9–13, 52, 61, 62, 65, 89–90, 135, 213, 217–18, 223, 250, 274, 276
  boundaries 35, 52, 53, 59, 271, 276
  ideology 9, 10–11, 67, 68, 87, 88, 101, 276
  implicated in criminal activity 5, 11, 12–13, 35–7, 80, 88, 98, 166–7, 168–9, 170, 175–6, 206, 208, 249, 254, 255–9, 261–2, 276, 277
  representing the body 34, 35, 44, 52, 53, 59, 82
  violation of security 32, 34–5, 53–4, 135–8, 181–2, 276
  women's authority 30, 53, 66, 88, 90, 98, 111, 112, 236, 255, 271, 276
  see also correction; honour
Hudson, Geoffrey L. 240
Hunsterson 268
Hunt, Margaret 67
Husbands 11, 12, 34, 35, 63–74, 111, 175–6, 201–5, 274

Infanticide 4, 8, 36, 148–58, 272–3
  committed by men 153, 154–5
Infanticide Act (1624) 148, 150, 151, 152, 153, 155, 158, 272–3
Ingram, Martin 103
Innes, Joanne 1
Insanity 133, 155–6

Jackson, Mark 148, 149
James I 15
Jeffreys, Sir George 153
Jurors 102, 126, 147, 178, 207–8

Justice 115, 116, 118, 120, 127, 129, 130, 210, 216, 217, 218, 229, 240, 262, 267, 274, 275
Justices of the peace 214–17
  in Cheshire 41, 45, 69–70, 210, 215, 219–20
  in Chester 17

Kent 18, 25, 172
King, Gregory 9
King, Peter 2
Knafla, L.A. 18
Knutsford 16, 18, 108
  heath 18

Lancashire 20, 184, 205
Larceny 159, 160, 161–7, 172, 177–81, 195, 208, 273
Levellers, the 9, 93–4, 101, 217
Lincolnshire 16
Linebaugh, Peter 2
'Long Meg of Westminster' 87
Lyme 99
Lymm 246

Macclesfield 16, 18, 19, 20, 84, 108
  forest 18
  hundred 16
  population 18
Malpas 19, 257
Manhood 33–48, 49, 66, 80, 82–5, 97, 98, 124–5, 127–8, 141, 157, 168–9, 191–2, 272
Manslaughter 38, 39, 115, 121–30, 133, 134, 136–8, 157–8, 272
Marton 267
Masculinity 4, 27
  see also manhood
Matthew, Henry 148
Mayhem 27, 28
McIntosh, Marjorie 103
McLynn, Frank 201
Mercer, Sarah 18
Middlewich 15, 16, 18, 19, 197, 267
Milton, John 68
Miscarriage 30, 31, 60
  see also pregnancy
Mobberley 234
Mocking rhymes 91, 100
More, Thomas 192
Motherhood 61, 69, 88, 90
  see also infanticide; pregnancy
Mottram-in-Longdendale 21
Muldrew, Craig 10
Multivocality 7–8, 211, 216

Index

Murder 39, 115, 116–21, 122, 126–7, 157–8, 272
Mutilation 31, 91–2, 94, 100

Nantwich 14, 15, 16, 18, 19, 79, 93, 94, 106, 119, 123, 125, 173, 174, 220, 267
  population 18
Nantwich hundred 16
Neston 20, 257
New-born child murder, *see* infanticide
Newcastle-upon-Tyne 109
Norfolk 151
Northwich 16, 18, 19
Northwich hundred 16, 263

Over 30
Over Tabley 265, 267
Over Whitley 245

Pardons 116, 119, 121, 126, 131, 136, 152, 155–6, 179, 185, 195, 198, 199, 200, 205, 273
Parliamentarians 42, 43, 48, 68, 70, 94, 241, 265–6, 278
Parricide 138
Patriarchy 9, 12, 49, 63–4, 66, 67, 75, 85, 86, 87, 206
Patronage 116, 125–8, 129–30, 215–16, 221, 224, 239, 244, 274
Pawning 165, 166, 167, 174, 273
Petitions 222, 237
Petty treason 64, 70, 113, 138–48, 150, 156
Pocketpicking 159, 160–1, 185–90, 201, 208
Poisoning 85, 118, 141, 143, 186, 272
Porter, Roy 2
Poststructuralism 3, 6
Pownall Fee 19
Poynton 20
Pregnancy 60–3, 121, 243, 271
  see also benefit of belly; miscarriage
Prestbury 16
Puddington 196
Pulton, Ferdinando 123
Puritans 41, 46, 219

Quakers 225
Qualitative approach 5
Quantification 1, 4–5, 12, 18, 24–5, 75, 177, 277

Rage 41, 46, 73, 85, 96, 141
Rainow near Bollington 19
Rape 55–60, 62, 70, 174
Receiving stolen goods 165–7, 168–74, 204, 214, 273

Recognisances for the peace or good behaviour 4, 24–5, 63, 99, 107–8, 215, 263
Recusancy 106
Regicide 70, 218–19
Reputation 10, 31, 32, 45, 54, 55, 62, 91, 128, 206, 233, 235, 245, 252–3
  see also credit
Rescue, *see* forcible rescue
Riot 214
Robbery 59–60, 160, 177, 187, 208, 273
  see also highway robbery
Roberts, Michael 167
'Robin Hood' 192
Rowton Moor 15
Royalists 42, 43, 48, 67, 70, 94, 174, 219, 241, 265–6, 278
Rudheath 18

Sailors 173
Sandbach 18, 19
Saussure, Ferdinand de 7
Scolding 4, 31, 65, 81, 82, 100–11, 271, 276
  scold's bridles, *see* branks
Scot, Reginald 144
Scotland 93
Scott, Joan Wallach 8
Second-hand market 163, 165–6
Seldon, Sir John 132
Self-defence
  female 49, 56–8, 60, 141–3, 271, 272
  killing in 116, 130–2, 133, 141–3, 157–8
  male 45, 46, 49, 116, 130–2, 133
Sequestration 241, 263, 266
Servants 9, 34, 36–7, 49, 64, 77, 138, 256
  maidservants 82–3, 89, 101, 163, 164, 166, 167, 172, 174–5, 179, 185, 217, 222
  manservants 44, 84, 175, 217
Settlement Act (1662) 237, 238
Sex 50–5, 66, 100, 109, 227–8
  see also adultery; bastardy; rape
Sexual insult 53, 54, 97, 231
Shakerley, Sir Geoffrey 194
Sharpe, J.A. 1
Shrewishness, *see* scolding
Shropshire 179
Single women 20, 62, 77, 98, 111, 148, 163, 205–6, 227–35, 254–5, 258, 260–1
  see also servants, maidservants
Slack, Paul 226
Slander 99, 100, 103, 106, 107
Social history 1
Soldiers 37, 48, 92, 94, 173–4, 196–7, 240–1

Speech 7–8, 23, 32–3, 40, 55, 81, 84, 95, 97, 99–111, 213, 214–15, 218, 225
Spierenburg, Pieter 6
Stabbing Statute (1604) 38–9, 115, 122, 125
Staffordshire 16, 129, 167, 188
Stevenson, John 262
Stockport 18, 20, 108, 173, 214
  population 18
Styles, John 1
Subjectivity 8, 32, 62, 279
Suicide 89, 144
Surrey 135, 141, 142, 157, 186
Sussex 151, 186
Sutton near Macclesfield 19
Swearing 223–4, 226

Tarporley 43, 133
Tarvin 19, 266
Tattenhall 264
Taxation 9, 14, 20, 21, 249, 256, 266, 267
Theft, *see* burglary, highway robbery, horse-theft, housebreaking, larceny, pocketpicking, robbery
Thompson, E.P. 2, 212
Townshend, Sir Henry 15
Treason 70, 93, 106, 131, 143, 218
  see also petty treason
Treason Act (1649) 218
Trespass 105, 108
Truth 25, 114, 210

Underdown, David 101, 110
Uxoricide 118, 121–4, 135–8, 140, 145, 146

Vauts, Moses 100, 111
Violence 7, 8, 11, 23–74
  female 75–112, 135–58, 271–2
  male 23–74, 116–35, 270–1
  relationship between non-lethal and lethal 39
  relationship between verbal and physical 23, 81, 97, 99, 107
  'righteous' 32, 38, 48, 49, 125, 132, 134

terminology 27, 77–8, 114–16
see also accidental death; assault; correction; domestic violence; homicide; infanticide; manslaughter; murder; petty treason; self-defence

Wages 21, 195
Wales 20
Warrington 194
Warrior-women 86–8, 93, 96, 112, 156, 271, 272, 276
Weapons 27–9, 38, 78–9, 100, 122, 141, 145
Weaverham 256
Whateley, William 64
Whitelocke, Bulstrode 101
Whitelocke, Sir James 15, 123
Widows 52, 53–4, 62, 77, 111, 143, 221, 238, 240, 242, 247, 254–5, 258
Williamson, Sir Joseph 194
Wilmslow 19, 20, 48
Wing, John 64, 138
Wirral 18
Wirral hundred 16, 257, 266
Witchcraft 4, 36, 85, 98, 101, 144, 150, 186
  as insult 97
Witnesses 128
Wives 52, 53, 62, 63–6, 71–3, 74, 76–7, 88, 98, 101, 111, 138, 163–4, 175–6, 201–6, 209, 235–6, 254–5, 258, 259–61
  see also household, women's authority
Women
  as property 12, 140
  in the salt industry 19–20
  Irish women 94, 99
  Scottish women 93
  Welsh women 92, 94
  see also Amazons; coverture; household, women's authority; motherhood; single women; warrior-women; widows; wives
Wood, Andy 2
Woodchurch 244
Wrightson, Keith 211, 226
Wybunbury 125

Yorkshire 20
Youth 40, 43, 46–7, 90, 184–5, 189, 220
  see also apprentices; servants

Titles in the series

*The Common Peace: Participation and the Criminal Law in Seventeenth-Century England**
CYNTHIA B. HERRUP

*Politics, Society and Civil War in Warwickshire, 1620–1660**
ANN HUGHES

*London Crowds in the Reign of Charles II: Propaganda and Politics from the Restoration to the Exclusion Crisis**
TIM HARRIS

*Criticism and Compliment: The Politics of Literature in the England of Charles I**
KEVIN SHARPE

*Central Government and the Localities: Hampshire, 1649–1689**
ANDREW COLEBY

*John Skelton and the Politics of the 1520s**
GREG WALKER

Algernon Sidney and the English Republic, 1623–1677
JONATHAN SCOTT

*Thomas Starkey and the Commonweal: Humanist Politics and Religion in the Reign of Henry VIII**
THOMAS F. MAYER

*The Blind Devotion of the People: Popular Religion and the English Reformation**
ROBERT WHITING

*The Cavalier Parliament and the Reconstruction of the Old Regime, 1661–1667**
PAUL SEAWARD

*The Blessed Revolution: English Politics and the Coming of War, 1621–1624**
THOMAS COGSWELL

*Charles I and the Road to Personal Rule**
L. J. REEVE

*George Lawson's 'Politica' and the English Revolution**
CONAL CONDREN

Puritans and Roundheads: The Harleys of Brampton Bryan and the Outbreak of the Civil War
JACQUELINE EALES

*An Uncounselled King: Charles I and the Scottish Troubles, 1637–1641**
PETER DONALD

*Cheap Print and Popular Piety, 1550–1640**
TESSA WATT

*The Pursuit of Stability: Social Relations in Elizabethan London**
IAN W. ARCHER

Prosecution and Punishment: Petty Crime and the Law in London and Rural Middlesex, c. 1660–1725
ROBERT B. SHOEMAKER

Algernon Sidney and the Restoration Crisis, 1677–1683*
JONATHAN SCOTT

Exile and Kingdom: History and Apocalpyse in the Puritan Migration to America*
AVIHU ZAKAI

The Pillars of Priestcraft Shaken: The Church of England and its Enemies, 1660–1730
J. A. I. CHAMPION

Steward, Lords and People: The Estate Steward and his World in Later Stuart England
D. R. HAINSWORTH

Civil War and Restoration in the Three Stuart Kingdoms: The Career of Randal MacDonnell, Marquis of Antrim, 1609–1683
JANE H. OHLMEYER

The Family of Love in English Society, 1550–1630
CHRISTOPHER W. MARSH

The Bishops' Wars: Charles I's Campaign against Scotland, 1638–1640*
MARK FISSELL

John Locke: Resistance, Religion and Responsibility*
JOHN MARSHALL

Constitutional Royalism and the Search for Settlement, c. 1640–1649*
DAVID L. SMITH

Intelligence and Espionage in the Reign of Charles II, 1660–1685*
ALAN MARSHALL

The Chief Governors: The Rise and Fall of Reform Government in Tudor Ireland, 1536–1588*
CIARAN BRADY

Politics and Opinion in Crisis, 1678–1681
MARK KNIGHTS

Catholic and Reformed: The Roman and Protestant Churches in English Protestant Thought, 1604–1640*
ANTHONY MILTON

Sir Matthew Hale, 1609–1676: Law, Religion and Natural Philosophy*
ALAN CROMARTIE

Henry Parker and the English Civil War: The Political Thought of the Public's 'Privado'*
MICHAEL MENDLE

Protestantism and Patriotism: Ideologies and the Making of English Foreign Policy, 1650–1668*
STEVEN C. A. PINCUS

Gender in Mystical and Occult Thought: Behmenism and its Development in England*
B. J. GIBBONS

William III and the Godly Revolution
TONY CLAYDON

Law-Making and Society in Late Elizabethan England: The Parliament of England, 1584–1601*
DAVID DEAN

The House of Lords in the Reign of Charles II*
ANDREW SWATLAND

Conversion, Politics and Religion in England, 1580–1625
MICHAEL C. QUESTIER

Politics, Religion and the British Revolutions: The Mind of Samuel Rutherford*
JOHN COFFEY

King James VI and I and the Reunion of Christendom*
W. B. PATTERSON

The English Reformation and the Laity: Gloucestershire, 1540–1580*
CAROLINE LITZENBERGER

Godly Clergy in Early England: The Caroline Puritan Movement, c. 1620–1643*
TOM WEBSTER

Prayer Book and People in Elizabethan and Early Stuart England*
JUDITH MALTBY

Sermons at Court, 1559–1629: Religion and Politics in Elizabethan and Jacobean Preaching
PETER E. MCCULLOUGH

Dismembering the Body Politic: Partisan Politics in England's Towns, 1650–1730*
PAUL D. HALLIDAY

Women Waging Law in Elizabethan England
TIMOTHY STRETTON

The Early Elizabethan Polity: William Cecil and the British Succession Crisis, 1558–1569*
STEPHEN ALFORD

The Polarisation of Elizabethan Politics: The Political Career of Robert Devereux, 2nd Earl of Essex
PAUL J. HAMMER

The Politics of Social Conflict: The Peak Country, 1520–1770
ANDY WOOD

Crime and Mentalities in Early Modern England*
MALCOLM GASKILL

The Church in an Age of Danger: Parsons and Parishioners, 1660–1740
DONALD A. SPAETH

Reading History in Early Modern England
D. R. WOOLF

The Politics of Court Scandal in Early Modern England: News Culture and the Overbury Affair, 1603–1660
ALASTAIR BELLANY

The Politics of Religion in the Age of Mary, Queen of Scots: The Earl of Argyll and the Struggle for Britain and Ireland
JANE E. A. DAWSON

Treason and the State: Law, Politics and Ideology in the English Civil War
D. ALAN ORR

Preaching during the English Reformation
SUSAN WABUDA

Pamphlets and Pamphleteering in Early Modern Britain
JOAD RAYMOND

*Popular Politics and the English Reformation**
ETHAN H. SHAGAN

Patterns of Piety: Women, Gender and Religion in Late Medieval and Reformation England
CHRISTINE PETERS

Crime, Gender and Social Order in Early Modern England
GARTHINE WALKER

*Also published as a paperback